CRIME, CULPABILITY, AND REMEDY

CRIME, CULPABILITY, AND REMEDY

Edited by

Ellen Frankel Paul, Fred D. Miller Jr,

and Jeffrey Paul

BASIL BLACKWELL

ISBN 0–631–17304–8

First published 1990

Basil Blackwell Ltd
108 Cowley Road, Oxford, OX4 1JF, UK

Basil Blackwell Inc.
3 Cambridge Center,
Cambridge, MA 02142, USA

British Library Cataloguing in Publication Data
Crime, culpability and remedy.
1. Crime & punishment
I. Paul, Ellen Frankel. II. Miller, Fred D. (Fred Dycus), 1944–
III. Paul, Jeffrey
364

ISBN 0-631-17304-8

Library of Congress Cataloguing-in-Publication Data
Crime, culpability, and remedy/edited by Ellen Frankel Paul, Fred D. Miller, Jr., and Jeffrey Paul.
p. cm.
Includes bibliographical references.
ISBN 0-631-17304-8
1. Punishment—Philosophy. 2. Criminal law—Philosophy.
I. Paul, Ellen Frankel. II. Miller, Fred Dycus, 1944–
III. Paul, Jeffrey.
HV8675 C74 1990
364.6-dc20.

Typeset in 10 on 12 pt Ehrhardt
by SB Datagraphics Ltd, Colchester
Printed in Great Britain by Whitstable Litho, Kent.

CONTENTS

INTRODUCTION

Crime, culpability, and punishment pose deep and long-debated philosophical questions. In this volume, twelve philosophers and academic lawyers seek to shed new light on several questions concerning the criminal law. What is the nature of wrongdoing in general? That is, is there an element contained in all instances of wrongdoing which mark them as being wrong? When is it proper to excuse someone for his or her actions? How does one determine the proper form and amount of punishment? What justification is there for the practice of punishment? In what ways ought one to punish or reward people for taking risks? Is it the case that (to paraphrase an ancient maxim of law) we ought to be so wary of punishing one innocent person that we risk not punishing a great number of guilty ones? What features might the Anglo-American tradition of law incorporate from other legal systems? Should there be special rules in law for classes of persons who in the past have been treated unfairly by the legal system or by society – for example, women or victims of crimes?

Jean Hampton's "*Mens Rea*" begins the volume with an investigation and analysis of three reasons often given to explain why certain sorts of actions are considered "wrong": that they are irrational, immoral, or illegal. Hampton argues that each of these presupposes a judgment that the agent in question has acted culpably, and that the source of culpability for the non-negligent commission of any of the three types of wrong is the same: that is, that the wrongdoer has engaged in what Hampton calls the "defiance" of a rational, moral, or legal norm. She maintains that an inquiry to determine whether a wrongdoer has a *mens rea* (that is, a guilty mind) is in fact an inquiry to determine whether such an act of defiance occurred in the mind of the wrongdoer.

Michael Moore, in his essay "Choice, Character, and Excuse," compares two rival theories of excuse, investigating what circumstances ought to make an actor free from liability for some action. He first discusses a theory of excuse according to which we free an actor from liability only when his wrongful act was done either without the capacity to choose not to do the act or without his having a fair opportunity to exercise that capacity. He then discusses a rival theory of excuse which frees someone from liability only when his wrongful act does not manifest a generally bad character. Moore argues that the first theory of excuse is the correct one. Only that theory captures our responsibility for actions "out of character" that, nonetheless, are performed. And only that theory shows why it is unfair to punish bad character when it is unaccompanied by a culpable act.

Peter Arenella, however, thinks Moore has made the wrong choice. In "Character, Choice, and Moral Agency: The Relevance of Character to Our Moral Blaming Judgments," Arenella approaches the issue from a different perspective. He initially examines the attributes a person would have to possess in order to justify treating him as a responsible agent. He then compares Moore's two competing conceptions of moral agency, which he calls the rational choice model and the character-based model. His central thesis is that the rational choice model's minimalist version of a moral agent's necessary attributes – the capacity to reason instrumentally and the ability to comply with governing moral norms for non-moral reasons – does not justify treating the actor as worthy of moral blame or praise. According to the rational choice model, deserved attributions of moral blame do not depend on any assumptions about the nature of the actor's motivations or his ability to control the aspects of his character that motivate his rational choices. That model, therefore, permits blaming actors who lack the capacity to respond appropriately to moral norms as reasons for their choices. Arenella closes his essay by arguing that the character-based conception of a moral agent's necessary attributes contains the only satisfactory explanation of how this capacity for moral responsiveness develops.

Larry Alexander maintains that there are deep and unresolved tensions among three basic principles in the criminal law: the voluntary act principle, the strict liability principle, and the negligence principle. In "Reconsidering the Relationship Among Voluntary Acts, Strict Liability, and Negligence in Criminal Law," Alexander argues that if the voluntary act principle is construed in light of its most promising normative rationale, it is then in direct conflict with the strict liability principle. Alternatively, if the voluntary act principle is brought into alignment with the strict liability principle, the former is rendered virtually empty. He also demonstrates that there are grave problems with non-arbitrarily differentiating between the voluntary act principle and the strict liability principle, and that they therefore seem to collapse into each other. Alexander ultimately concludes that taking the voluntary act principle seriously – taking it to the fullest extent that its rationale suggests – requires us to reject strict liability or negligence as the standards for culpability. However, since the considerations behind these two principles are valid ones, he argues that they should sometimes overrule the application of the voluntary act principle.

In "The Gender Question in Criminal Law," Stephen J. Schulhofer inspects a comparatively new set of principles for criminal law which have emerged from feminist jurisprudence. Both the doctrines and the enforcement of criminal law have recently come under strong and sustained examination and criticism by feminists. Schulhofer identifies several distinct strands in feminist thought and shows how they suggest important areas of gender bias in both the specific rules of criminal liability and in the entire framework of analysis of moral and legal responsibility. He also discusses three foundational principles of the traditional approach to criminal law – its judgmental, demanding, and pacifist principles – and shows how they collide with one or another of the important strands of modern feminism. The last part of Schulhofer's essay suggests ways in which traditional thinking about criminal responsibility needs to be revised in response to feminist insights, with particular emphasis on illustrations drawn from controversial contemporary issues in the law of rape and self-defense by battered women.

Leo Katz analyzes a common affirmative defense to an action of negligence: that the victim of an injury voluntarily assumed a risk, and thus has no right of recovery for any injury that he might sustain. In "The Assumption of Risk Argument," Katz notes that it is hard to see why there are certain circumstances in which we are persuaded by this sort of argument but others in which we are not. Paternalism and duress are typically offered as two reasons why the assumption of risk argument is in some instances considered unacceptable, but Katz provides a number of cases where neither reason is satisfactory. He then provides a number of alternative reasons which seem to be more plausible. They include the indeterminacy of the assumption of risk argument in certain cases, the special problems posed by collective risk assumption, the phenomenon of victimless injuries, the incommensurability of choices under extreme uncertainty, the built-in qualifications of conditional promises, and the immorality of avoiding certain gambles. Finally, he considers the inappropriateness of the assumption of argument in the criminal law.

The law of self-defense is given a comparative treatment by George P. Fletcher, who analyzes the different forms it takes in Western legal thought as against Jewish law. In "Defensive Force as an Act of Rescue," he notes that Jewish law on self-defense departs dramatically from Western assumptions in two ways. First, it stresses that the roots of self-defense contain a command to defend oneself, rather than merely an option to; second, it treats defense of a third party as logically prior to defense of oneself. Fletcher's essay shows how these assumptions radically change the structure of the law of self-defense and strip it of the justification and foundation that it possesses under a legal system informed by Western values.

Gerald Dworkin, in "Equal Respect and the Enforcement of Morality," analyzes Ronald Dworkin's views on the proper role of the state in proscribing by law what the majority takes to be morally wrong activities. Ronald Dworkin's writings on this topic spring primarily from the idea that the state must treat all citizens with equal concern and respect; his conclusion is that the enforcement of morality by the state necessarily implies that its citizens are not being treated equally. The author of this essay argues that the conclusion does not follow from the premise of equal respect, and provides his own theory of the proper role of the state in relation to the enforcement of morality.

The three essays which close the volume treat various problems in the theory of punishment. C. L. Ten's "Positive Retributivism" begins with an analysis of the nature of retributivism, the doctrine which seeks to provide a rationale for punishment without appealing to its deterrent effects. Two such theories are examined. The first theory boils down to the claim that punishment restores the fair balance of benefits and burdens which the criminal's act upsets. However, it is unclear just how the balance could be restored by state punishment, which does nothing to recompense the victims of crime. The second theory regards the penitential reform of offenders as the aim and justification of punishment. However, this theory provides no satisfactory explanation of why incarceration is necessary to induce penitence, nor how this aim will be achieved by such punishment. He concludes by providing a limited defense of an alternative rationale for punishment: general deterrence.

Jeffrie G. Murphy discusses the question of whether a legal system should recognize victims' rights. Crime victims often want to influence the sentencing of those who have harmed them, and their motives for this may seem to others merely hateful and vindictive. It is generally assumed that granting a role to victims so motivated would do serious damage to our system of criminal justice. "Getting Even: The Role of the Victim" suggests that these assumptions are in no way uncontroversial; rather, they need to be argued for, and most arguments that can be given for them turn out to be surprisingly weak. Fairness to crime victims, Murphy argues, demands that the state give careful consideration to the passionate demands of those citizens it has failed to protect from criminal violence.

Finally, Jeffrey Reiman and Ernest van den Haag conclude this volume with a paper which is, in effect, a debate, with one author arguing for and the other arguing against an ancient maxim that is often uncritically accepted. "On the Common Saying that It Is Better that Ten Guilty Persons Escape than that One Innocent Suffer, *Pro* and *Con*" begins with a brief sketch of the history of this maxim. An analysis of the core of the saying – that it is morally worse to punish an innocent person than to acquit a guilty one – is then conducted by both authors. Some ostensibly appealing arguments in favor of it are found by both Reiman and van den Haag to be unworkable. Reiman then presents retributivist, utilitarian, and contractarian arguments for the maxim, and van den Haag attempts to refute them and to depict the saying as inconsistent with penal justice.

As these essays indicate, criminal law is laden with a striking array of moral, psychological, and linguistic problems involving notions of causation, intention, negligence, necessity, duress, complicity, and attempt. By approaching these problems with different methodologies and viewpoints, the contributors to this volume offer many valuable insights into the criminal law, reflecting important recent developments in jurisprudence and the philosophy of law.

CONTRIBUTORS

Jean Hampton is Associate Professor of Philosophy at University of California, Davis, and has taught at UCLA and the University of Pittsburgh. She is the author of *Hobbes and the Social Contract Tradition*, and, with Jeffrie Murphy, *Forgiveness and Mercy* (both published by Cambridge University Press). Her interests range over topics in political philosophy, ethics, and the philosophy of law. The paper in this volume is part of her research on theories of moral culpability, irrationality, and the role of retributive punishment in a liberal state.

Michael S. Moore has recently joined the law faculty of the University of Pennsylvania, where he is Leon Meltzer Professor of Law. He has previously held appointments in the law schools of the University of Southern California, the University of California at Berkeley, Stanford University, and the University of Kansas; he has been both a Fellow and a Senior Fellow in the Law and Humanities Program of Harvard University and a Resident Fellow of the Humanities Research Institute, University of California at Irvine. He is the author of *Law and Psychiatry: Rethinking the Relationship* (Cambridge University Press, 1984) and of numerous articles appearing in legal, philosophical, and psychiatric journals. He is currently working on two books, both to be published by Oxford University Press, one on legal reasoning and the other on a general theory of the substantive criminal law (of which the essay in this volume will be a part).

Peter Arenella is a Professor of Law at the University of California at Los Angeles School of Law. He holds a degree in law from Harvard University and did his undergraduate work at Wesleyan University. He has published widely in the fields of substantive criminal law and constitutional criminal procedure. He is currently working on a book that examines the extent to which we rely on descriptive and normative conceptions of character to help us interpret and defend the moral significance of human action in our blaming theories and practices.

Larry Alexander is a graduate of Williams College and Yale Law School and is currently Professor of Law at the University of San Diego, where he teaches constitutional law and criminal law. He is co-author of *Whom Does the Constitution Command?*, a book on constitutional theory. He has written a number of articles in both legal and philosophical journals on moral theory, legal theory, constitutional law, and criminal law.

Stephen J. Schulhofer is the Frank and Bernice J. Greenberg Professor of Law at the University of Chicago and Director of its Center for Studies in Criminal Justice. He graduated from Princeton University and Harvard Law School before serving as law clerk to U.S. Supreme Court Justice Hugo Black. He practiced law for three years and joined the faculty of the University of Pennsylvania Law School in 1972. He has held his present positions at the University of Chicago since 1986. He has published journal articles on (among other topics) attempts, harm sentencing, plea bargaining and police interrogation. He is the author, with Sanford Kadish, of *Criminal Law and Its Processes.*

Leo Katz is Assistant Professor at the University of Michigan Law School. He is the author of *Bad Acts and Guilty Minds: Conundrums of the Criminal Law.*

George P. Fletcher is Beekman Professor of Law at Columbia University School of Law. His writings including *Rethinking Criminal Law* (Little, Brown, 1978) and *A Crime of Self-Defense: Bernard Goetz and the Law on Trial* (The Free Press, 1988), as well as numerous articles on criminal law and legal philosophy. He is currently working on a book on loyalty.

Gerald Dworkin is Professor of Philosophy at the University of Illinois at Chicago. He is the author of *The Theory and Practice of Autonomy* (Cambridge University Press). He has published articles on paternalism, nuclear deterrence, entrapment, responsibility, and other topics in moral and legal philosophy. He is currently working on issues related to the enforcement of morality by the criminal law.

Chin Liew Ten is a Reader in Philosophy at Monash University, Australia. He is the author of *Mill on Liberty* (Clarendon Press, 1980) and *Crime, Guilt, and Punishment* (Clarendon Press, 1987). His main interests are in legal and political philosophy. He is on the editorial committee of *Utilitas: A Journal of Utilitarian Studies*, which commenced publication in May 1989. He has served as an Honorary Consultant to the Law Reform Commission of Victoria.

Jeffrie G. Murphy is Professor of Law and Philosophy at Arizona State University. His most recent book (co-authored with Jean Hampton) is *Foregiveness and Mercy*, published in 1988 by Cambridge University Press. A revised edition of his *The Philosophy of Law: An Introduction to Jurisprudence* (co-authored with Jules L. Coleman) was published in 1989.

Jeffrey Reiman is Professor of Philosophy and Director of the Master's Program in Philosophy and Social Policy at The American University in Washington, D.C., where he has been on the faculty since 1970. Prior to 1988, he held an appointment in American University's School of Justice. He received his Ph.D. in philosophy from the Pennsylvania State University in 1968. Professor Reiman is the author of *In Defense of Political Philosophy: A Reply to R. P. Wolff's In Defense of Anarchism* (Harper & Row, 1972), *The Rich Get Richer and the Poor Get Prison: Ideology, Class, and Criminal Justice* (Wiley, 1979, 1984; Macmillan, 1990), *Justice and Modern Moral Philosophy* (Yale, 1990), and numerous articles in moral, political, and legal philosophy.

Ernest van den Haag recently retired as John M. Olin Professor of Jurisprudence and Public Policy at Fordham University in New York. He is the author of *Punishing Criminals* and twelve other books. He has published about two hundred essays on diverse subjects.

MENS REA

BY JEAN HAMPTON

The greatest incitement to guilt is the hope of sinning with impunity. Cicero

INTRODUCTION

Accusing, condemning, and avenging are part of our daily life. However, a review of many years of literature attempting to analyze our blaming practices suggests that we do not understand very well what we are doing when we judge people culpable for a wrong they have committed. Of course, everyone agrees that, for example, someone deserves censure and punishment when she is guilty of a wrong, and the law has traditionally looked for a *mens rea*, or "guilty mind," in order to convict someone of a criminal wrongdoing. But philosophers and legal theorists have found it interestingly difficult to say what *mens rea* is. For example, noting the way in which we intuitively think people aren't culpable for a crime if they disobey the law by mistake, or under duress, or while insane, theorists such as H.L.A. Hart[1] have tried to define *mens rea* negatively, as that which an agent has if he is not in what we consider to be an excusing state. But such an approach only circumscribes and does not unravel the central mystery; it also fails to explain why the law recognizes any excusing states as mitigating or absolving one of guilt, much less why all and only the excusing states that are recognized by the law are the right ones. Moreover, the Model Penal Code, which gives a very detailed account of the kinds of mental states which justify criminal conviction,[2] does not tell us (nor was it designed to tell us) why these states of mind (e.g., knowledge, purposiveness, intention, assumption of risk of harm, negligence) are relevant to an assessment of legal guilt.

In this article I want to try to develop a positive account of *mens rea*, or legal culpability, which explains why the mental states detailed in the Model Penal Code are relevant to recognizing it. Because negligence introduces difficulties into the discussion that I cannot properly pursue here, my focus will be on non-negligent culpable acts, although I will have something to say about criminal negligence in the final section of the paper.

The procedure I will follow for analyzing the legally guilty mind is to clarify, first, what non-negligent culpability is more generally. People can be judged to be

[1] See Hart's *Punishment and Responsibility*, ch. 2, "Legal Responsibility and Excuses," pp. 28–53 (Oxford: Clarenden Press, 1968).

[2] The Model Penal Code has been drafted, with commentary, by the American Law Institute and has had considerable influence upon legal reform in the United States during the past 30 years. For a presentation and discussion of the Code's minimum requirements for culpability, see *Criminal Law and its Processes*, ed. Sanford Kadish and Monrad Paulsen (Boston: Little, Brown and Co., 1975; 3rd edition), p. 95.

"at fault" in three different circumstances: when they act illegally, when they act immorally, and when they act irrationally.[3] I want to argue, however, that there is one distinctive kind of "mental act" that underlies all three kinds of culpability, and which is definitive of the (non-negligent) guilty mind. Hence, I will start by giving an analysis of rational and moral culpability, and then use these analyses as models for the explication of legal culpability.

Let me also make clear that I will merely be analyzing the concept of culpability and not justifying it. Proponents of deterrence theory and consequentialist approaches to legal blame should see this paper as robbing them of only one of their arguments against their opponents, namely that the concept of *mens rea* is not intelligible. Even if I succeed in making the notion intelligible in the context of non-negligent culpable acts, there is still plenty of room for attacks against it as the wrong notion for our legal system to rely upon in its conceptualization of the point of criminal sanctions. Nonetheless, I am interested in formulating an intelligible conception of culpability because I am committed to it, and so wish to see a deeper understanding of an idea that is (and should be) central to our legal system and our moral practices generally.

It was common in ancient times to think that there was something about the way human beings are by nature that explains why they are invariably culpable for violations of the norms of morality, reason, and law. This article, one might say, tries to cash out that ancient view by arguing that it is because human beings are prone to a particular mental act definitive of being "at fault" in any of these three ways that they have a "fallen" nature. Nonetheless, I will contend that this natural basis for human culpability does not afford us an excuse for our wrongdoings. The following explication of *mens rea* aims to establish why we are appropriately blamed, punished, and (one hopes) finally forgiven for our culpable acts.

I. Defiance of Reason

An analysis of culpability should start not with a discussion of legal culpability, and not even with a discussion of moral culpability, but with an analysis of what I will call "rational culpability," which is a way of being rationally "at fault."

To be rationally culpable is to be irrational, but not every kind of irrationality counts as culpable irrationality, and not every mistake people make when they reason constitutes being irrational. Consider that a person who makes a mistake about how to achieve his goals fails to act rationally, but he is not for that reason alone criticized as 'irrational'. When Henry Hudson headed up the large river that emptied into the Atlantic by the island of Manhattan thinking that it was the Northwest Passage, he wasn't irrational: he was mistaken. Unlike Henry, those we consider culpably irrational are not in some sense "innocent" in their performance of the mistaken action. We think either that they knew that their action was imprudent but did it anyway or that they ought to have known that it was imprudent. Of the former, we might say they demonstrated "willful irrationality";

[3] This article builds on my initial attempts to understand moral culpability in "The Nature of Immorality," *The Foundations of Moral and Political Philosophy*, ed. Ellen Frankel Paul, *et al.* (Oxford: Basil Blackwell, 1990); also published in *Social Philosophy and Policy*, volume 7, issue 1 (Autumn 1989).

of the latter, we might say they demonstrated "negligent irrationality." Leaving aside negligence here, I will attempt an analysis of willful irrationality in this section. I will argue that the notion of "fault" implicit in the judgment of someone as irrational in this sense involves the attribution of a mental state to this person which is importantly similar to the mental state attributed to those who are judged morally or legally "at fault."

Being willfully irrational is also not the same as another species of irrationality, which I will distinguish with the term 'non-rational'. There are certain mistakes in reasoning that human beings commonly make and which psychologists study – mistakes in the way they process information, in the way they reason logically, and in the way they think about the world.[4] When we make such errors, we are not thinking or behaving rationally, but there is nothing intentional about our mistakes. We are "afflicted" with the disposition to make them (for reasons worthy of psychological study), and they cannot be considered "our fault" unless others consider us negligent in failing to remedy our tendency to make them. In this article I also will not discuss these non-culpable failures of reason, and henceforth when I use the word 'irrational' I will be doing so to refer to those non-negligent failures of rationality which we believe the individual engaged in willfully in order to advance some objective, and not innocent "cognitive slips."

It is not hard to recognize this species of irrationality. "Johnny knows he won't get through college if he doesn't study," says his father, "but, for him, every night is party night. How can he be so irrational?" Johnny's persistence in behavior that we believe he knows will preclude the achievement of a preeminent goal he has is central to our perception of him as "at fault"; it is this knowledge which makes him deserving of our criticism for his behavior. It may be tempting for Johnny's father, who realizes that Johnny is aware that his behavior doesn't make sense given his goals, to explain Johnny's behavior in a way proposed by the American comedian Bill Cosby. Cosby, in order to account for his children's penchant for knowing the better but doing the worse, explains it in two words: brain damage.

The joke highlights the fact that it is difficult to make this kind of behavior intelligible. In order to try to make sense of this difficulty, let me develop and analyze an actual (and I think interesting) example of genuine irrationality. I once knew an 18-year-old who decided he wanted to live the "natural life," raising his own food, living in a house built with his own hands, in a rural area along the coast of Maine. After getting permission to use a piece of his grandmother's land, he attempted to build his house – a kind of log cabin affair – despite the fact that he knew little about building houses. His father, on the other hand, knew a great deal about house-building techniques. Nonetheless, this young man refused to take any advice from his father about how to build the house, and refused all offers of help from him because he wanted to live independently of his parents. The result, predictably enough, was disastrous: what was built was poor and did not stand up to

[4] For examples of discussions of such failures of reasoning, see A. Tversky and D. Kanneman, "The Framing of Decisions and the Rationality of Choice," *Science* (1981), pp. 543–58; and David Pears, *Motivated Irrationality* (Oxford: Clarendon Press, 1984), esp. pp. 45ff.

the winter storms. In the end, the teenager had to seek refuge with his grandmother, and eventually had to go to his father and accept the help he had insisted on refusing before.

We would not, of course, consider this person immoral for what he had done, but we would not be kind in our assessment of him: 'pig-headed', 'stupid', 'imprudent' are the sorts of descriptions we would use – words which indicate a kind of culpability in our minds, but a non-moral one.

We would make this assessment of him because we would believe of him that he "knew better." But what did he really know? If we believe that the boy wasn't insensible and thus paid attention both to the facts of the world around him and all the things that parents, teachers, and friends were telling him, then we have to believe that he knew that he didn't really have enough technical ability to build a log house himself. In particular, we think he knew, first, that he didn't have the technical ability to build a house by himself; second, that the chances of him learning to do this by winter's arrival were very bad; and third, that his father did indeed know how to build one. In virtue of these three beliefs, we can attribute to him at least the following item of knowledge:

a) attempting to build the house alone is not the most effective way, and probably not even a possible way, to achieve his goal, so that his actions are irrational.

His abysmal ignorance must have been obvious even, we think, to himself. We would say of any remarks he might make to the contrary that "he's fooling himself."

So why did he try to build the house if he knew the action was imprudent? Was he simply ignoring the counsels of prudence? To say that he was simply ignoring them would be to say that he was pursuing something else besides the prudent course of action, and that this prudent course of action therefore "lost" fair and square in his calculations about what to do. For example, we might see the son as having to choose between two incommensurable goods, being prudent, and something else – say, being independent, and finally deciding to choose the latter because he concluded somehow that he had a better reason to be independent than to be prudent.

But this isn't an accurate picture of what was going on. In this situation there was not some neat clash of incommensurable goods, with the teenager feeling he had better reason to choose the imprudent option. Granted, the goal that the teenager had was independence; nonetheless, that goal could only be achieved if he accepted his father's help to build the house. So to live an independent life, the boy had to depend upon his father in the short term. And given that the boy was not in any way intellectually deficient, we impute to him the knowledge, supplied by reason, that to achieve independence he had to accept his father's help. Reason's directive to this effect, we think, must have had real force for him. He must have appreciated that going to his father and asking for help was what he *ought* to do, given what was necessary to achieve his ultimate goal. To put it in a different way: given his goal, this person knew that he ought to be rational and do that which would allow him to successfully achieve his goal. So reason had authority for the teenager in this situation. We conclude, then, that the teenager had the following knowledge:

b) The fact that the action he contemplates is irrational gives him not just a reason but the best reason in the circumstances not to do the action; reason's directives are "authoritative" in the situation.

But if he knew not just that his action was irrational but that he had the best possible reason in the circumstances to act rationally, why did he persist in irrational behavior? This is the standard sort of question that trips up those who try to recognize and explain akratic action. If we believe, with Aristotle, that every act we take aims at what we believe to be good, then knowing the better but doing the worse seems to be impossible.

So how do we make the teenager's action intelligible? We take seriously the natural characterization we make of him as rebellious and we make sense of his action as a rebellion. Consider that the boy knew both that building the house without his father's help was irrational, and that he hated the idea of having his father help him. Indeed, the prospects of accepting the help were sufficiently repulsive to him that he could not bear to let it happen. Hence he was faced with a choice: he could conform his actions and desires to the dictates of reason, which would mean temporarily giving up his goal of being independent of his father and accepting his help, *or* he could defy reason's authority and substitute in its place the authority of his desire to build the house by himself. He chose defiance. And, as I shall now argue, anyone whom we consider to be willfully irrational is someone whom we believe to be defiant of reason.

Those who defy reason do not merely rebel against its directives, but attempt to install another authority in its place which will endorse the action they wish to perform. To put it in an Aristotelian way, they are able to do what is worse, despite always taking action to achieve the good, by challenging the authority of that which judges the action worse, and choosing instead to respect as authoritative that which makes the action good. Of course every act we take aims at the good, but when we want to see the worse action as the better one, we can depose our reason which judges it worse and install a new authority that makes it an act that aims at the good.

What is the new authority? Normally, it will be whatever desire motivates the interest in performing the action. However, one might also want to install in the place of reason what one thought was a less authoritative norm – e.g., a moral or legal norm – to which one had allegiance and which directed one to perform an action one's reason told one not to perform. However, many theorists, particularly Kantians, argue that moral norms have more (rather than less) authority than practical reason; in any conflict between them, the right choice would be the choice to obey morality. In view of this, Kantians would believe any rebellion against the directives of reason in the name of morality would be commendable rather than wrong, and thus improperly classified as defiance (you don't defy a legitimate ruler when you support her and not a rival faction after her throne). Indeed, Kantians would expect to see defiance of morality by those who preferred the directives of reason, rather than the reverse. It also seems strange to think that one would have more allegiance to legal norms than to the directives of practical reason, hence making it unlikely that a person would defy the latter in order to install the former.

What is not strange at all, however, is the defiance of the authority of law in order to install the authority of reason, when it directs one to behave in ways that are illegal. (We will discuss this form of defiance in our discussion of legal culpability.) So the normal and natural explanation for why we would behave irrationally and defy the directives of practical reason is that those directives conflict with the satisfaction of a desire which ought not to have sway in this situation, but which we insist should be authoritative. To use an English locution, when we are defiant of reason we "would have it that" we are right to do what our desires dictate, and not what reason dictates.

There are two ways in which such defiance of practical reason can work. One can either defy the normative power of practical reason directly, or one can defy it indirectly by defying the information provided by theoretical reason on which the disliked directives of practical reason are based.

The form of reasoning constitutive of the direct defiance of practical reason is: "I want to do *x* but I know that doing *x* will not allow me to achieve *y* and achieving *y* is my preeminent goal; nonetheless, I will do *x*." Here the reasoner is defying the norm that tells him that he ought to do what will allow him to achieve his preeminent goal. He refuses to bow to the authority of this norm, and, as the American expression goes, "he tries to have his cake and eat it too." Children are wonderfully good at this kind of reasoning. A weary babysitter once told me that his little charge had wanted a hamburger but refused to go with him to the only place where she could get the hamburger, telling him that she wanted to "have the hamburger without getting it." She threw a kind of tantrum in the face of an unacceptable directive of practical reason.

Such childish defiance may persist into adulthood, but it is more common for an adult to try another kind of defiance of reason. Adults normally do not defy the directives issued by practical reason because, I suspect, they have learned that it doesn't work – one simply cannot have one's cake and eat it too. But a different and more sophisticated style of defiance can seem more promising: in this case, one defies any pronouncements about the world made by theoretical reason which indicate that one's desired course of action is an ineffective way to achieve one's goal. Thus one reasons, "I will perform the most effective action that I can to achieve my goal *y*, but I want to perform action *x*, and so I 'would have it that' *x* will allow me to achieve that goal." But (one might say) this kind of reasoning is crazy! The mountain won't come to Mohammed, and reality can't be altered to suit your convenience. How could anyone believe that it could?

But we all do. We all find ourselves not only wanting but demanding that the world go our way, and even expecting that it will because we have demanded it to do so. So if our teenage house-builder chose this method of defiance, he defied the pronouncement of his theoretical reason that attempting to build the house was too unlikely to succeed to be worth the risk. "I don't like to believe that this is true," he said to himself, "therefore it isn't going to be that way. I 'would have it that' I have enough expertise to build the house." This method of defiance involves an indirect way of getting around the authority of practical reason. He is accepting that he ought to do what will allow him to best achieve his preeminent goal. But he is defying the information supplied to him by his theoretical reason about what the best thing to do actually is.

There are various ways we can challenge the pronouncements of our theoretical reason about the world so as to allow us to believe that what we want to do is also what will best achieve our goals. And these various ways are reflected in the different kinds of *rationalizations* we offer to justify our irrational acts. For example, a person can postulate a kind of magical control over the world, so that doing what he wishes will also seem consistent with the commands of practical reason. This strategy amounts to saying: "My reason tells me that the world is *x*, but I don't like its being *x*, because that means I can't perform the action I want and achieve my goal. Therefore, because I want it to change, it *will* change." This characterizes the reasoning of a graduate student who once told me that even when he knows his credit card limit has been reached, he still pulls out the credit card at his favorite record store. "Because," he says, "I want the albums."

Or people can decide to believe that they are permitted to try a forbidden activity because they are exempted from the sorts of problems that normally plague those who engage in it. For example, drug-users often insist that other people get addicted to heroin, but not them. And the teenage house-builder might have insisted that although other people require instruction in the art of house-building, he was talented enough not to need it.

People can even decide to revise the rules of logic to achieve their goals. Consider the logic student who must prove a theorem on a problem set, but finds it difficult to do so if she is limited to the standard rules of inference: it is not unusual for a student in this situation to "change" these rules and "prove" the theorem using her new ones, only to wince when the problem set comes back with a bad grade. And when asked by her logic professor why she came up with this proof when she *knew* the correct rules of inference, such a student generally has nothing to say – except, perhaps, "I was hoping it would work." And, in general, we hate to answer such questions because the answer is so embarrassing: we *did* hope that we could fix the pronouncements of reason to suit our interests, and when we're caught, our hubris is brought painfully to our own attention.

So what we call the rationalizations which frequently attend our irrational actions are, in fact, expressions of our defiance of the dictates of theoretical rationality that seem to make it impossible for us to do what we want and still follow the dictates of practical reason. Those rationalizations can either be articulations of the way we defiantly see the world in conformity with our desires, or they can be ways of *bolstering* that defiance in situations where we have some doubt that we can pull it off. "Not everyone is as good with his hands as I am," our teenage house-builder might say (following a moment of doubt), "so I'm special enough to be able to do something other people can't do."

No matter which of these reason-defying strategies our teenager chose, and no matter how he rationalized what he was doing, the fact of his choosing one of them means we must attribute to him one further (false) belief:

c) the authoritative directives of reason that tell him to do what he prefers not to do can be successfully defied, and the desire dictating the irrational action can be installed as the authority in this situation, so that this desire, and not reason, will rightly direct him as to how he should act.

His irrationality is therefore the result of his choice to respect an authority other than reason.

It is intriguing to me that in all of the discussions of akrasia and self-deception purporting to make sense of knowing the better and doing the worse, this way of rendering the phenomenon intelligible has never been proposed. (Perhaps it has been missed because those who have worked in this area have not spent a great deal of time with small children, and have therefore missed the opportunity to see the faults of humanity undisguised by the veneer of civilization. Or so it seemed to me one day as I marveled at my three-year-old son determinedly setting out to ride his tricycle to San Francisco.) Yet it is clearly a possible explanatory hypothesis: if somebody knows the better and does the worse, doesn't this suggest that *she does so because she believes she can insist that the worse is better*? Thus the smoker aware of the surgeon general's report can quit smoking, or she can insist that this report has nothing to do with her because she simply isn't going to get cancer. (Once, in presenting this account to a philosopher who smoked, I gave him this example, and he told me in dead earnest that he really wasn't going to get cancer.) And the Malibu home owner whose home is threatened every year by the winter tides – and who explains why he doesn't move from his home on the beach by saying "Every year it gets worse, but I just bury my head in the surf"[5] – believes he has a choice between accepting the pronouncements of theoretical reason and performing the prudent action given those pronouncements, or ignoring those pronouncements so as to enjoy himself. Quite clearly he prefers the second option. "But," we say, "this is nuts! People can't make the world behave the way they want it to behave." That's true; that's why these people are irrational. But they, and we, try anyway.

But why aren't these people (i.e., us) genuinely crazy? The reason is that, on this analysis, they are genuinely ignorant of something; they are ignorant of what they can realistically accomplish in the world. But the nature of their ignorance is not the sort of thing that we normally take to be a sign of mental illness. The person who defies reason has a certain conception of who he is and what he needs which makes him treat a stupid strategy as a plausible one. His parents and friends, when they see him act irrationally, might complain "Who does he think he is?" The answer is that he thinks that he is someone special enough to have his desires prevail. The smoker who knows the statistics about cancer and smoking says "the disease won't get *me*." And the Malibu coast-dweller who knows the danger of flooding insists that the world dishes out disaster to other people, not to him. So, to use an old-fashioned word, although none of these people behaves immorally, all of them are guilty of the "sin of pride." This pridefulness is not craziness because their defiance of the pronouncements of reason occurs in situations where there is some probability that their wishes can come true. Akratic people don't jump off

[5] CBS News, March 1983.

cliffs wishing they could fly; they do, however, smoke in situations where they know there is a chance that they won't get cancer, and they go to graduate school in philosophy when they know there is a chance (albeit small) that they will be able to get a job, and they attempt to build houses even when they don't know how to do so because there is a chance that they'll be able to build something good enough before winter comes.

So when the teenager in my example realized that his makeshift house was inadequate for the winter, he learned something. He not only learned what he could plausibly accomplish and what he could not, but he also learned something about himself: his place in the world turned out not to be as high as he thought, and he realized he was a lot more like other people in power and importance than he thought.

And now we see why the defiance account can render deliberate irrationality intelligible: it explains the irrational action as that which is precipitated by a defiant act in which one installed as authoritative something other than reason which endorsed the irrational action, and it also explains that defiance as a function of the agent's ignorance about something fundamental. The agent who defies the authority of practical reason, insisting that the worse is better in a situation where he wants to perform the action his reason calls worse, does so because he does not understand that he simply cannot supplant reason's authority with something more congenial. The logic student, the drug addict, the Malibu homeowner, and the teenage house-builder all mistakenly attribute to themselves a control over reality that they simply do not and cannot have. Such ignorance is striking in the very young, and it is part of the reason we call young people 'immature'. But such immaturity persists into adulthood, albeit in a less obviously false form. Perhaps human self-love is such that we are invariably inclined to see ourselves as more powerful, more special, and more significant than we in fact are. (Perhaps we are, to borrow a phrase from Hobbes, naturally and irredeemably vainglorious.) As we grow we learn, sometimes painfully, just how much and how little we can accomplish, and thus how significant our wishes will be in determining the future course of the world.

A reader might accept that this style of explanation fits some non-negligent forms of irrationality, but not all of them. Such a critic might argue that to say that the irrational person is "defiant" appears to attribute to him a fist-shaking rebelliousness that not every irrational individual has. For example, even if the defiance account explains the proud but self-deceived smoker, does it really explain the smoker who hates the fact that he smokes, does so regretfully, and longs to quit? It does: the word 'defiance' doesn't describe the emotional attitudes of the irrational agent, but rather the kind of mental act that explains how he can know the better and do the worse. The reluctant smoker, no matter how much he claims to hate smoking and to prefer to refrain from it for the rest of his life, picks up the cigarette on this occasion because, right now, smoking this cigarette is what he badly desires and he "would have it that" doing what he desires at this moment is not the worse but the better course of action. "This cigarette won't matter that much to my health, so I might as well enjoy myself," he might say in order to bolster his defiance of the dictates of reason. Or he might say to himself, "I can't live without these things, so I might as well have one now." This way of representing things makes the better course of action impossible at this moment, so that the worse course of action is now permitted, in defiance of the information given him by his theoretical and practical reason. Even the term 'weakness of will' is itself a defiant misrepresentation of the phenomenon of incontinent action: a person who describes his actions in this way is suggesting that he was "too weak" to avoid the action that he claims to acknowledge as worse, thereby representing his action as somehow inevitable when it was not. On the view I am presenting, what he is actually doing is choosing the action he calls worse, even while understanding that it is worse from the standpoint of reason – a standpoint he knows is supposed to be authoritative – because he believes he can defy that authority and substitute in its place the authority of his desires, which direct him to perform the desired action.

There is one other very important way in which defiance can operate to make someone culpably irrational (a way that some might contend constitutes negligence, or at least what has been called "advertent negligence").[6] Suppose I perform action *x* in ignorance of the fact that it will prevent me from achieving my goal. *Prima facie*, such ignorance excuses me; but if that ignorance was something I knew that, at some earlier time, I ought to remedy, then the ignorance does not excuse me because it is itself effected by a culpable act. So if I know that I ought to have my cholesterol level checked, but fail to do so and continue to eat large quantities of beef, cheese, and ice cream, then when I have my first heart attack I cannot say that my ignorance of my high cholesterol level excuses me from charges of irrationality. I knew that I should not remain ignorant, because an extremely important desire of mine, self-preservation, could only be effectively pursued if I obtained certain information. In this example, what could explain the fact that I did not get that information? It is not hard to give a perfectly good explanation; I knew, if I got it, that I might have to give up eating the foods I loved, so therefore I did not do so. In this situation I declared that I "would have it that" these foods posed no risk to my future survival, making it unnecessary for me to procure information that might suggest otherwise. There are many ways in which I could rationalize my defiance, as we discussed previously. The point is, however, that my ignorance in this situation would be culpable precisely because it could be traced to a defiant action: I defied reason (in its theoretical or practical guise) in order to choose to remain ignorant, and for this reason my failure to procure my goals by virtue of that ignorance makes it appropriate to call me 'irrational' rather than merely 'mistaken'.

II. Moral Culpability

Whether one thinks that moral culpability even exists depends upon what one's moral theory says about the authority of moral imperatives. In particular, if one

[6] The distinction is from Glanville Williams, *Criminal Law: The General Part* (London: Stevens and Sons Ltd., 1953), pp. 49–59. For a nice overview of the controversies surrounding the topic of negligence, see the readings on negligence, recklessness, and strict liability in *Freedom and Responsibility*, ed. H. Morris (Stanford: Stanford University Press, 1961).

believes that moral imperatives are hypothetical rather than categorical, then one must consider irrational those people who know that these imperatives offer them the best way to satisfy their desires but who fail to follow them anyway. The term 'immoral' could, at most, designate those irrational agents who violate a species of rationally-dictated imperative – e.g., the imperatives that direct people as to how to achieve peace, or cooperation, or impartial behavior. Philosophers such as David Gauthier and Philippa Foot, who have proposed that moral imperatives may be just a species of rational hypothetical imperatives, are committed to assimilating immorality to irrationality in this way.[7] And the preceding section on the defiance of reason would be, for such philosophers, all that would be necessary to capture the sense in which those who fail to follow these imperatives are culpable.

If the reader agrees with this view, the analysis to follow postulating defiance of a distinctively moral kind of authority will be at best psychologically interesting – an account of what people who postulate this nonexistent authority think they are doing when they behave immorally.

However, philosophers who are committed to the idea that morality has a distinctive authority and who describe moral imperatives as categorical want an explanation of immorality that makes it something other than irrationality. If these theorists are right that moral imperatives bind with an authority that often (and maybe always)[8] supersedes even the authority of reason,[9] then someone who understands that authority should also understand that she should always act from these moral imperatives – even in situations where moral behavior prevents her from satisfying her desires, and is to that extent irrational. So why would she fail to do so?

Despite enormous interest in the authority of morality, moral theorists as a whole have been not only unsuccessful at but also markedly uninterested in explaining immoral action.[10] The founder of our discipline, Socrates, was one of the few who took on the issue explicitly, but his explanation is one of the most unsuccessful. Immoral people, says Socrates, are ignorant of the good, and hence deserving of pity rather than anger, education rather than pain.[11] Yet unlike genuinely ignorant people, the immoral among us do not seem to welcome instruction! Are they really just ignorant? Moreover, it is striking that despite advocating this account of immorality, Socrates was prepared to support

[7] See David Gauthier's *Morals by Agreement* (Oxford: Oxford University Press, 1986), and Philippa Foot's "Morality as a System of Hypothetical Imperatives," in *Virtues and Vices* (Berkeley: University of California Press, 1988).

[8] Kant appears to insist on the total supremacy of morality in his writings, but this idea has been challenged recently. For example, see Susan Wolf, "Moral Saints," *Journal of Philosophy*, vol. 79, no. 8 (August 1982), pp. 419–39.

[9] Note here that the word 'reason' is used in a very narrow sense to refer to a norm of action directed at the individual intent on satisfying his desires. This is the economist's notion of reason, roughly equivalent to prudential calculation. Philosophers such as Kant use the word 'reason' more broadly to cover both prudential and moral calculation. Despite my sympathies with Kant's use of the word, I will retain the narrow use of 'reason' in this paper to mark the distinction between two quite different forms of normative reasoning.

[10] The following historical remarks are taken from a much longer and more detailed account of various theories of culpability in my "The Nature of Immorality." See note 3.

[11] See *Meno*, 77b–78b (in the translation of W. R. M. Lamb, Harvard University Press, 1924, p. 289), and *Protagoras*, 357d–e (in the translation by W. R. M. Lamb, Harvard University Press, 1924, p. 243).

punishment of immoral people; clearly, punishment is an unusual educational technique! The fact that punishment rather than college courses seems to be the appropriate kind of response to those who act immorally suggests that their immoral action is a function of a certain kind of resistance inside them, which the Socratic punishment is somehow supposed to break. Understanding immoral agents simply as ignorant fails to capture or explain this resistance.

Perhaps the most serious problem with Socrates's account, however, is that it does not seem hard to find morally culpable people who not only know but even take delight in the fact that what they are doing is wrong. In fact, isn't this knowledge just what makes us want to blame them? After all, outside of legal contexts, ignorance normally excuses.[12] Consider the foreigner who does not know that his behavior in this culture is rude, or the child who does not realize that her words to a friend are wounding, or the doctor who administers a fatal dose of medication negligently prepared by another doctor who had always been trustworthy before: such people bring about injury through their ignorance, but in view of that ignorance – an ignorance we find reasonable under the circumstances – we do not judge them culpable. If immoral people are assimilated with these kinds of folk, it is no wonder that Socrates thought pity rather than anger was the appropriate emotional response toward them. Socrate's explanation seems to destroy the moral culpability it was meant to explain.

If ignorance excuses then knowledge must convict. But once we attribute knowledge to the culpable agent, it is difficult to know how to explain his immoral action in a way that makes it both intelligible and a genuine instance of *culpable* action. Suppose we say, for example, that the person who acts immorally is genuinely indifferent to the authority of moral imperatives. If she is not making any mistake by ignoring them, then that must mean the imperatives, however wonderful we think them, do not in fact apply to this person. She is outside their scope, and hence does nothing wrong when she does not follow them. Such a person is properly called 'amoral' rather than 'immoral', since we cannot say about her that "she should have done otherwise." We might hate her from a moral point of view, and wish her to be removed from our world, but this way of viewing her makes her into a kind of monster that, although worthy of our hatred and opposition, is no more a justifiable subject of moral *blame* than any other dangerous creature outside the reach of moral imperatives. So, once again, we see that what was supposed to be an explanation of culpable action actually destroys the phenomenon it was supposed to explain.

There is one more popular style of explanation, which I call the Manichean account of immorality. On this view, immoral behavior is a function of a certain "part" of us (Plato would call it the appetite or the spirited part, Freud would call it the id, St. Paul would call it "sin that has its lodging in us")[13] which fights against (and wins against) the part within us (reason, or the superego, or knowledge of

[12] As the saying goes, "*Ignoratia legis non excusat.*" We will be discussing later why ignorance is not a good excuse in legal contexts.

[13] Romans 7:14–20.

God's commands) that is directing the moral action.[14] But how can this view explain a person's culpability for a bad deed when that deed was precipitated by a force about which he could do nothing? On this view, immoral action is not something chosen but something effected by an event – the event of the good part being overpowered by that of the bad part. This loss is presumably something that the good part could do nothing to prevent. Buf if the good part of you is too weak to win some or all battles with the bad part, then the bad action precipitated by the victory of the bad part is not chosen by the good part. And since the good part is supposed to be who you really are, this means the bad action is not chosen by you, and thus it is not something for which you are responsible. If "the devil made you do it" – where the "devil" is understood variously as your id, or your appetites, or your hormones, and "you" are associated with that within you which wanted to do good but couldn't – then "you" are not to blame. You are its victim, and hence not the appropriate recipient of our condemnation. However intelligible this style of explanation for immoral behavior is, it once again destroys the phenomenon to be explained.

After considering the way that these accounts failed to capture our conception of (non-negligent) culpability, I found myself looking for one particular kind of inner event that would be the secret of it. Clearly, there are many kinds of people who do immoral deeds, with all sorts of characters from good to bad to awful. If one undertook the project of "explaining" immorality, one would have to come to grips with the variety of motivations, character traits, and desires that are all part of the reason human beings prefer to act badly rather than morally. But despite this diversity, all people who act immorally, no matter whether they are normally saintly or devilish, have something in common which grounds the judgment that they are "at fault," and thus culpable for a wrongdoing. If it isn't ignorance, or indifference, or weakness in the face of a force for evil, then what could be present in all of them – even in the actions of people whom we think have, by and large, a good character – that makes them the appropriate subjects of blame for the particular immoral action they perform?

To understand what it is, consider the following description of what is supposed to be the first morally culpable act committed by a human being:

> The serpent was more crafty than any wild creature that the Lord God had made. He said to the woman, "Is it true that God has forbidden you to eat from any tree in the garden?" The woman answered the serpent, "We may eat the fruit of any tree in the garden, except for the tree in the middle of the garden: God has forbidden us either to eat or to touch the fruit of that: if we do, we shall die." The serpent said, "Of course you will not die. God knows that as soon as you eat it, your eyes will be opened and you will be like gods knowing both good and evil." When the woman saw that thc fruit of the tree was good to eat, and that it was pleasing to the eye and

[14] This style of explanation is also popular with those who want to understand akratic behavior. See the articles discussing this style of approach in *The Multiple Self*, ed. Jon Elster (Cambridge: Cambridge University Press, 1986).

> tempting to contemplate, she took some and ate it. She also gave her husband some and he ate it. Then the eyes of both of them were opened and they discovered they were naked; so they stitched fig-leaves together and made themselves loin-cloths.[15]

As we all know, when God found out what the two of them had done, he was furious; he punished not only the two human beings but also the serpent for their disobedience.

And that is the point of the tale: human immorality is a function of human disobedience of an authoritative command. Human beings are culpable for the commission of wrongs not because they are ignorant that what they are doing is wrong, but because they *know* they are doing wrong. Indeed, if they were ignorant of the wrongfulness of their act, this would excuse them from culpability. Eve and Adam knew that they were not supposed to eat of the fruit of the tree of knowledge; if they had been ignorant of the command, God would have been filled with sorrow rather than fury at their deed (assuming that the ignorance itself wasn't something for which they were culpable). So their knowledge is central to their culpability.

However, not only knowledge of the command, but also knowledge of the command's *authority* is central to our finding them at fault. Adam and Eve are not culpable out of indifference to an imperative which they happen not to find in their interest to follow. They know they are *supposed* to follow the command – i.e., that it is authoritative over them, that it is supposed to rule them. While the tale represents them as having no knowledge of good and evil, and thus no knowledge of moral commands generally until they eat the fruit, it does establish that they had knowledge of God's authority, and hence of the authoritativeness of his commands. (Is knowledge of God's authority moral knowledge? Part of the point of the tale may be that knowledge of this authority is not moral knowledge, so that God's authority is prior to and higher than the authority of morality.) If they had been ignorant of his authority, their ignorance would once again undercut their culpability for the act they took. If I don't know that an imperative issued by someone gives me a better reason to act than my wishes give me, then (even though I act incorrectly) I am the appropriate subject of further education rather than blame (assuming, again, that my ignorance is something for which I am not culpable).

Finally, Adam and Eve's culpability is a function of the fact that the wrongdoing was *chosen* rather than caused. Eve was not pushed, compelled, or under duress when she ate the fruit. The snake, of course, encouraged her to do so, but, in the words of Dante, Eve herself "let Desire pull Reason from her throne."[16] In other words, she chose the action, aware that it was forbidden by an authoritative command applicable to her.

The Genesis story therefore presents the following four elements as necessary conditions of the culpable mind:

[15] Genesis 3:1–7.

[16] *Inferno*, Canto V, quoted by Donald Davidson in "How is Weakness of the Will Possible?", in *Essays in Actions and Events* (Oxford: Clarendon Press, 1980), p. 35.

1. Making the decision to choose the action.
2. Choosing it in the knowledge that the action is forbidden by a command.
3. Choosing it in the knowledge that the action is forbidden by a command that is applicable to oneself and authoritative in this situation (i.e., it gives one the best possible reason to act in the situation).

These three elements presuppose the fourth:

4. Having both the capacity to make choices and the capacity to have knowledge of authoritative commands.

These last two capacities are necessary conditions for judging someone a moral agent.[17] A person who is either unable to choose how to act despite knowing the authoritativeness of the commands (e.g., a kleptomaniac) or unable to understand the way in which these commands are authoritative (e.g., a sociopath) cannot be considered a moral agent, and hence cannot be appropriately blamed for behavior that is not in accord with those commands. We may very well want to do something about such people – lock them up, execute them, put them into therapy – but they are not people whom we should blame or punish.[18]

But, readers might protest, if this analysis makes immorality a function of such an informed choice, doesn't it portray wrongdoing as a case of knowing the better but choosing the worse, and haven't innumerable discussions of incontinence shown that such a characterization of human action is highly problematic at best, and perhaps incoherent?

This account does indeed portray culpable wrongdoing as a case of knowing the better and doing the worse, but the preceding section on the defiance of reason aimed to establish that such a portrayal need not be understood as an incoherent account of human action. The view that I will henceforth call the "defiance" account of moral culpability incorporates these four features in a coherent and (I will argue) plausible way. In a nutshell, the view is that a culpable agent is one who chooses to defy what she knows to be an authoritative moral command in the name of the satisfaction of one or more of her wishes, whose satisfaction the command forbids. She is disobedient in the face of knowledge that obedience is expected, and a rebel in the sense that she is attempting to establish something more to her liking as authoritative over her decision-making, rather than these moral commands. Just

[17] I am indebted to Peter Arenella for pressing me to make this idea explicit in my analysis.

[18] In "The Legal and Moral Responsibility of Organizations" (in *Criminal Justice: Nomos XXVII*, eds. J. Roland Pennock and John W. Chapman, [New York: New York University Press, 1985] pp. 267–86), Susan Wolf suggests that sociopaths, although incapable of understanding or being responsive to moral authority, are capable of the kind of responsibility (call it 'practical') which is the foundation of tort law. "We use," she says, "the practical sense when our claim that an agent is responsible for an action is intended to announce that the agent assumes the risks associated with the action. In other words, the agent is considered the appropriate bearer of damages, should they result from the action, as well as the appropriate reaper of the action's possible benefits" (p. 276). One can, according to Wolf, be capable of being practically responsible but not morally responsible; sociopaths may be one example of such an agent, organizations may be another. If she is right, there is a difference between being a moral agent and being (to coin a name) a "practical agent." One might also say, as we shall discuss in the next section, that the criminal law takes seriously the question whether or not the lawbreaker is a moral agent, whereas the tort law requires practical agency.

like irrational people, immoral people know the better but do the worse because they believe they can install a new reason-giving authority over their actions that transforms the worse into the better.

I want to argue that such defiance is a distinctively human phenomenon, which normally occurs whenever following a command – which one knows is authoritative in the circumstances – interferes with the perception of what is required to achieve or do something else that one wants. In this situation, a human being has the capacity to "overthrow" the authority in her own mind, and to install a new authority which sanctions the action she wishes to take. Indeed, the previous discussion of irrationality was meant to suggest that defiance of norms generally – including rational as well as moral norms – is a distinctively human capacity, which marks out human beings from other animals and which traditional religious thinkers would consider to be the central element in their fallen natures.

How is it distinctive of human beings? Don't dogs, horses, and monkeys display the ability to break rules, sometimes even exhibiting something approximating shame when they do so? However, the defiant mental act that I claim is distinctive in human beings is not just the act of disobeying a command; it is the choice which leads to the disobedience. Specifically, *it is the choice to supplant what one knows to be an authoritative rule with a different authority that sanctions the act one wishes to take*. Or, to put it another way, it is a rebellion against that which is taken to have final evaluative authority in the situation, in order to install a new evaluative authority which evaluates the action one wishes to take as better and not worse.

Contrast this with the disobedience of a horse. When a horse disobeys his rider's command to canter, the horse is simply doing what he prefers until the rider can use punishments and rewards to induce him to prefer the behavior preferred by the rider. So what the horse does is always determined by his desires. Unless we human beings are badly wrong in our understanding of equine mental life, there is no perception of an 'ought to obey' in the horse's head which can act as a reason-giving authority that competes with his desires. But it is the ability to understand and act from the idea that "I ought to obey" – an ability which involves the appreciation of a moral command as authoritative – that distinguishes a human being from an animal. And it is our ability to challenge that authority and install a reason-giving authority that is more amenable to our interests which makes human beings' disobedience of commands distinctive.

My point is that to be morally culpable, one must be able to recognize the authority of morality even while trying to overthrow it. So wrongdoers are rebels, but rebels always understand the authority of that which they seek to depose. This is why they are, and see themselves as, rebels – people who must depose, bring down, vanquish an authority that they oppose and wish to replace.

In the name of what do they rebel? Normally, one opposes morality for the sake of self-interest, which may or may not be rationally tutored. This is why the question "Why are we immoral?" is so naturally answered by saying "Because we're selfish." A legal norm might also come to oppose the moral authority, and the agent might be tempted to serve that norm, rather than the more important moral norm. Whatever the source of temptation, the agent gives in to it when she installs that source over morality as her reason-giving authority.

As in the case of the discussion of irrationality, the combative language used to state this view may already have some readers worried that it only fits the very worst immoral people. How can the mental state of the reluctant moral offender, or the offender guilty of only a minor moral offense, be understood as some kind of defiant act?

But such a worry misunderstands the account. The defiance view is not a portrait of human character but an analysis of the "culpable act" inside the head of the agent which occurs whenever a person is guilty of a blameworthy but non-negligent action. The view does not attribute to those who are guilty of a wrongdoing the wholesale rejection of the authority of morality on every occasion. Nor does it attribute to them certain emotional attitudes characteristic of political rebels, such as anger, hatred, hostility, or resentment towards the authority they defy, although it is consistent with the view that the culpable agent have any of these emotional attitudes. All that the view says about the morally culpable agent is that inside her there was an act of "insubordination" resulting in the performance of the prohibited action, and it is that insubordination which constitutes her culpability. Specifically, what makes her the appropriate subject of blame is the choice to install as authoritative something that condones what she wishes to do, rather than to allow the relevant authoritative moral command to prevail. That act of insubordination can be done regretfully, sorrowfully, or even happily – the point is that it is *this* act which constitutes being at fault. It can be a rare occurrence in a person's life or a common one; it can occur when the directives of the moral authority are not terribly serious, or when they are very serious indeed; and it can be accompanied by a variety of emotional states. But it is this defiant act that is the basis of all morally culpable action.

So the person who is a decent member of our community but who nonetheless decides, while in a great hurry to get her shopping done at the mall, to sneak into a parking space someone else has been patiently waiting for – that person is, at that moment, defying the claims of morality and obeying the commands of her own wishes. And Peter, who betrayed his friend Jesus three times before the cock crowed and who wept with guilt after his betrayals, nonetheless believed (regretfully, sorrowfully, tearfully) when he denied he knew Jesus that it was more important for him to satisfy his desire to stay alive than it was to be loyal to his friend and the religious views to which he had previously committed himself.

So, like those who defy reason, people who are culpable for moral wrongs obey what they take to be the authority of their own wishes in defiance of the authority of the moral imperatives proscribing the actions that the satisfaction of their wishes require. Take our parking-space thief. She believes that:

a') taking the space herself rather than letting the other person have it (where this other person was there first) was immoral (albeit mildly so; it was at least rude).

b') that, given the authority which the dictates of morality have, she is supposed to have better reason to refrain from this immoral behavior than to engage in it so as to satisfy her desires.

c') that the authority of morality can be defied in this case, because her own wishes are too important to "lose" to it.

Unless one is insensible, everyone knows (a'). Knowing (b') might, however, not be possible for some people, who are thereby precluded from being moral agents. Someone who cannot understand the authority of morality cannot be expected to conform her actions in accord with it when the moral dictates oppose her desires. This seems to be exactly the right thing to say about sociopaths. "Although sociopaths can achieve an intellectual understanding that cheating, stealing, murdering, etc., are *considered* to be immoral, they cannot understand why they ought not to act in these ways."[19] We might say that attributing to someone the knowledge of morality's authority is the same as attributing to him a conscience; sociopaths, therefore, lack consciences.[20] Although we lack, as moral philosophers, a good theory of what moral authority is (to the point where some doubt that it exists at all), still, if such a theory were at hand, it would tell us how one who qualifies as a moral agent has access, cognitively or emotionally, to the authority of moral commands.

In popular parlance, (c') constitutes the parking-space thief's belief that she can and should "get away with it" if she decides on the immoral action. It is interesting to note that, in *Paradise Lost*, Milton portrays Eve as someone who believes (c'), and who is thereby emboldened to eat the forbidden fruit. In Milton's poem, before she picks the fruit she reasons:

> Here grows the cure of all, this fruit divine,
> Fair to the eye, inviting to the taste,
> Of virtue to make wise: what hinders then
> To reach, and feed at once both Body and Mind?[21]

Eve believes there is nothing hindering her from successfully challenging God's authority, and so she eats the fruit. And all her human progeny, who are prone to immoral deeds, are represented as being inclined to reach the same conclusion about their chances of successfully defying the authority that is giving them the commands they dislike. What distinguishes moral skeptics from moral objectivists is that skeptics seriously entertain the idea that the authority of morality can be successfully challenged, whereas objectivists (perhaps out of faith alone) insist that it cannot.

The defiance account describes one kind of choice which all immoral agents share that marks them out as morally culpable. But can it help us to grade the extent to which any agent is immoral?

[19] Wolf, "The Moral and Legal Responsibility of Organizations," p. 278.

[20] Wolf says the same, *ibid.*

[21] *Paradise Lost*, Book IX (New York: Doubleday, 1969), p. 212.

In answering this question, it is important to note that the defiance view denies that any offender is "devilish" in the way Kant described – and the way he refused to believe any of us were.[22] That is, immoral people are not portrayed as people who defy the authority of morality out of some kind of unmotivated hatred of that authority. Instead, they are portrayed as rebels against the authority of morality who aim to substitute as authoritative something they prefer to it. As they fight against the moral authority, they may come to despise it insofar as it persists in interfering with their ability to follow the imperatives of their preferred authority, but they have no fundamental unmotivated antipathy to cooperative, other-regarding behavior. In fact, even the devil himself turns out not to be devilishly defiant on Kant's way of construing the term! The devil, remember, rebels against God not because he finds God intrinsically hateful, but because he prefers himself as ruler of the world (although, as he continues to fight and lose the battle for supremacy with God, he is generally represented as coming to despise his rival).[23]

Hence, the defiance view is not as negative as it might be in its portrayal of human immorality. Still, I believe it leaves room for distinguishing grades of immorality, which are, in essence, represented as degrees of rebellion. The point of the defiance account is that all immoral people (i.e., all people who are morally culpable) are rebels; but there is a difference between rebels who are sorry about having to rebel and rebels who have no qualms about their rebellion, and there is a difference between petty rebellion and major insubordination. We look both to the severity of the offense and to the emotional and intellectual attitudes attending its performance to form a judgment of just how immoral a person has shown herself to be by performing the immoral action. In forming that judgment, I suspect that determining the severity of the offense usually takes precedence, and judgments about emotional attitudes are used to mark out distinctions among those who have challenged the same authoritative command. For example, we would say that two people who, in similar circumstances, betray their friends in order to advance their careers have both engaged in an offense of the same seriousness, but the person who feels no sorrow as he betrays his friend is worse, in our eyes, than the betrayer who is plagued by a bad conscience.

[22] See Kant's *Religion Within The Limits of Reason Alone*, trans. Theodore M. Greene and Hoyt H. Hudson, ed. John Silber (New York: Harper and Brothers, 1960), pp. 52–53.

[23] Because Kant wished to avoid characterizing people as devilish in this sense, he shied away from using the word 'rebel' to describe evil people. For example, he says in the *Religion Within The Limits of Reason Alone* that "Man (even the most wicked) does not, under any maxim whatsoever, repudiate the Moral Law in the manner of a rebel (renouncing obedience to it)" (p. 31). Instead, he maintains that "Man (even the best) is evil only in that he reverses the moral order of the incentives when he adopts them into his maxims," (p. 31) but this kind of "insubordination" (which is different from flat-out renunciation) is characterized as rebellion later on in the *Religion*, when Kant notes that were we to remove the incentive of inclination from human nature, then "though it is true that this rebellion is often stilled, the rebel himself is still not conquered, and exterminated" (p. 51n). The critical debate about whether or not Kant is right to reject the idea that we are devilish in his sense fails to take account of the way in which he does acknowledge a genuinely devilish rebellion in the hearts of all (sinful) human beings. See Silber, pp. cxxivff and cxxixff; Allen Wood, *Kant's Moral Religion* (Ithaca: Cornell University Press, 1970), p. 212n; and Philip Quinn, p. 9 and n. 3.

Those who are familiar with Kant's analysis of immoral behavior in the *Religion* will see strong similarities between his treatment of it as an act of insubordination in one's ranking of motives for action and my account of it as the defiant choice of something other than morality as the authority governing one's choice of action in the situation.

Why isn't the former betrayer better characterized as indifferent, rather than defiant? Some readers may worry that my account of culpability seems to leave out a perfectly good category of wrongdoer: i.e., the kind who violate moral commands without in any way flinching, who appear to have no loyalty to those commands and even express contempt for them. These people seem indifferent to the demands of morality, not defiant of them. But what does it mean to call them 'indifferent'? Does it mean that they are outside the scope of moral imperatives? That is, do those imperatives issue directives that give them *no reason to act* in the way directed? If this is so, such people made no mistake in their action, although they acted in ways we dislike. If we called them 'immoral', the description could only be a reflection of our dislike; it could not convey, as it does in the defiance account, our judgment that the wrongdoer's action has been a mistake not only from our point of view but also from his. Accordingly, if they made no mistake acting as they did, they are best described as 'amoral', where this label designates those who do not act morally and who are not the sort of creature to whom the moral imperatives apply. We may want to do something about these people – they can be greatly disruptive of societal harmony. But our response to them could not be condemnatory, retributive, or desert-based.

Suppose, however, that someone said of such people: "Well, of course they believe they are outside the scope of morality, and so act in ways that we see as indifferent to the authority that commands them, but we don't believe that this is true. We do see these commands as applying to them: they are assuming that they are independent of morality's rule when in fact they are not. Hence, we can correctly say of them that they should have done otherwise, and hence that they are immoral, without finding in them an explicitly defiant act."

But this way of conceiving of these agents does render them defiant in a sense: they are acting as if they are independent of morality's rule when they are not. Now do they understand that they are at least supposed to be ruled by morality, or do they not? If they *do* know about the claim these directives make to rule them (e.g., if they are aware of and can understand the force of the kinds of admonishments of immoral behavior made by parents, Sunday School teachers, judges, and so forth), then there is, in their heads, a defiant act after all. Although they take no interest in the commands, they are aware of their authority, and they are defying it. On the other hand, if they do not know about their authority then either they are themselves responsible for putting themselves in this state or else some other, external cause is responsible for their being in this state. If they put themselves in it – if they were authors of their own moral insensitivity – we have some grounds for holding them culpable for the actions committed because of that insensitivity. But if something else was the author of it (e.g., a severely impoverished childhood, a mental illness), then they are *ignorant*; why should we blame them for actions which reflect an ignorance that was not their doing? As we have discussed, ignorance excuses an agent from culpability. So, oddly enough, an account of an "immoral" agent as purely indifferent actually destroys what is necessary for that agent to be immoral.

Interestingly, one can find this very account of our blaming practices (in the context of legal norms) given by the Supreme Court of West Germany:

> As a free and moral agent and as a participant in the legal community, the individual is bound at all times to conform his behavior to law and to avoid doing the wrong thing. He does not fulfill his duty merely by avoiding that which seems to him clearly to be the wrong thing; rather he must attempt to determine whether that which he plans to do is compatible with the legal imperatives of the system. He must resolve his doubts by reflection or investigation. This requires that he apply his moral sensibility .... If despite the moral sensitivity that can fairly be demanded of him, the individual does not perceive the wrongfulness of the contemplated action, then his mistake is to be viewed as ineluctable; the act would be, for him, unavoidable. In a case of this sort, the individual cannot be blamed for his conduct.[24]

Of course, some kind of response to the harmful acts of those "morally insensitive" people who believe themselves to be part of a different moral realm is highly appropriate, but not a blaming response coupled with retribution. We can either work to remedy their ignorance about moral authority, or, if a remedy seems impossible, we can work to neutralize the threat they pose to others (e.g., through incarceration or execution). But it is not fair to respond to them as individuals who could have acted morally, because in an important sense, they were not able to do so.

However, as the discussion above indicated, there is one kind of morally insensitive agent whose insensitivity is a function of his ignorance; on the defiance view, it does make sense to blame this agent. This is that agent who, although now incapable of conforming his actions to the demands of morality, chose to perform actions and to develop in ways that made such insensitivity likely, and was *fully aware of the risk he was taking*. Such a person now acts immorally out of ignorance, but he is himself responsible for that ignorance in the sense that he chose it knowing he should not. We would call him culpably ignorant.[25] Aristotle insists, for example, that people who appear unaware that what they are doing is wrong are actually people who are

> responsible for becoming men of that kind, and ... make themselves responsible for being unjust or self-indulgent, in the one case by cheating and in the other by spending their time in drunken bouts and the like, for it is activities exercised on particular objects that make the corresponding character .... Now *not to know* that it is from the exercise of activities on

[24] 2BGH 194 (March 18, 1952). Translation by George Fletcher, *Comparative Criminal Theory* 72 (2nd ed. 1971, mimeo, UCLA); in Kadish and Paulsen, p. 124–5.

[25] See Holly Smith, "Culpable Ignorance," *Philosophical Review*, vol. 92, no. 4 (October, 1983), pp. 543–571. Aquinas considers the culpably ignorant to include every non-negligent performer of immoral actions. See *Summa Theologica*, First Part of the Second Part, Question 6, Article 8, "Does Ignorance Render an Act Involuntary?"

particular objects that states of character are produced is the mark of a thoroughly senseless person.[26]

So of course they do know what they are doing, in which case they have chosen to make themselves into people who are morally insensitive; in virtue of that choice, they are culpable for being morally insensitive later.

Indeed, perhaps we are sometimes inclined to judge morally monstrous people – i.e., people who are incapable of understanding moral norms – as culpable despite their inability to act from these norms, because we believe that earlier in their lives they chose to engage in activities that they knew would likely turn them into moral monsters, and that they did so anyway, in defiance of that knowledge, in order to satisfy their desires. If they become incapable of being ruled by moral considerations thereafter, they are ignorant, but nonetheless culpably so – by virtue of this prior defiant act. Note that it is because we can trace their immoral actions to a defiant act that it becomes possible for us to call them culpable. Indeed, insofar as it seems appropriate to call such people indifferent to morality, the defiance account will allow that there is some truth to that description. But this kind of indifference is a function of a prior defiant act, and is not itself the source of their culpability.

Other wrongdoers appear indifferent to morality in a different way, but still in a way that the defiance account illuminates. Consider that there is a difference between understanding morality's authority but consistently opposing it, and accepting that authority most of the time but fighting it off on occasion – say, when its commands oppose certain important wishes. Occasional disobedience of an authority one normally believes deserves obedience is different from full-scale disobedience of directives whose claim to be authoritative one *knows about* but never accepts. The second sort of rebel, one might say, is attempting to declare himself amoral in a society that (he knows) insists on seeing him as persistently disobedient of his proper ruler. He is attempting to make himself indifferent to the claims of morality. Because such a person continually fights to gain his independence from the authority that in his view makes a false claim to rule him, he is unlike and, from a moral point of view, worse than rebels who only occasionally fight against a realm that, on other occasions, they have admitted is entitled to govern them. We judge the former to be worse, from a moral point of view, than the latter, because the latter has significantly more allegiance to the moral authority than the former.

The cagey reader may now be aware that she can make an interesting attack on the defiance account of immorality in light of these last remarks. Why do immoral people defy the moral authority? Presumably they do so because they think they can "get away with it" – their rebellion, they think, will be successful in the sense that any costs they pay because of their defiant action will be outweighed by the benefits from it. Let me be vague about what "costs" and "benefits" refer to here, because different moral philosophers committed to the objective authority of morality will have different ways of cashing out what they are (for example,

[26] *Nicomachean Ethics*, 1114a 3–11; my emphasis; translation is that of W. D. Ross in *The Basic Works of Aristotle* ed. Richard McKeon (Chicago: Random House, 1941).

Aristotle would talk of human flourishing, Kant would talk of the persistent indictment of reason one would feel following the defiance). For present purposes, choose your favorite way of cashing out these terms. Now are moral rebels right to think they can get away with their rebellion and escape without paying any significant costs? Presumably any moral theorist committed to the authority of morality would argue that they cannot do so in any situation over which the moral authority is sovereign.

Now it may well be correct to conclude that the authority of morality has limits – that there are jurisdictions in life over which it does not rule.[27] One might also think that, either because of one's disposition or early training, one may be inclined to exaggerate the scope of morality's authority. In a situation where morality was not the ultimate authority, one's refusal to act morally would be a good thing, because it would show that one was trying to get out from under a ruler whose rule in this situation was inappropriate. Properly speaking, one is not being defiant of morality in such a case because one cannot rebel against something that has no final right of command (although it might *feel* rebellious to the agent who is struggling to overcome what she suspects is her own false sense of morality's authority).

But in situations in which morality is sovereign, moral theorists (e.g., Kantians) committed to the objective authority of morality would insist that the agent's belief that she could successfully defy its rule is false. And it is the falsity of this belief that the agent doesn't know: in this case, the defiance analysis of immorality represents such a person as ignorant of the fact that a rebellion against the authority of morality cannot succeed. Why doesn't this ignorance excuse this person from culpability?

To answer this question, consider that, on the defiance view, *the defiance itself is what makes the person culpable*, whereas the defier's ignorance of the impossibility of succeeding is the explanation of her defiance, and thus, of her culpability (and that which renders it intelligible). That is, it explains why the defiance occurred, but it does not explain away the defiance – and ignorance only excuses when it explains away the defiance. Or, to put it in another way, when ignorance excuses, it is because the fact of the ignorance shows the agent was not defiant after all. When we say "Mary was reasonably ignorant that the man she shot was a human being and not a deer, so we can't find her guilty of murder," or "Joan had no idea that her words to the visitor brought back painful memories, so we can't blame her," we're attributing to the agent an ignorance of something relevant to her assessment of what the authoritative commands told her to perform; because she was so ignorant, she is not acting out of defiance of those commands. In contrast, the ignorance attributed to the culpable agent on the defiance view is an explanation of her defiance – it explains why she thought it made sense to engage in it; this explanation, however, in no way forces us to redescribe her choice to act contrary to the moral rules as not defiant after all. Indeed, it assumes and must assume that defiance in order to explain it. And it is the defiance which makes her culpable.

[27] For an argument to this effect, see Susan Wolf, "Moral Saints."

But why is our assessment of immorality entirely a function of the culpable agent's decision to defy the moral rules? This is, I find, a deep and difficult question. What are we trying to do or say when we label someone immoral? On the defiance view, it seems that we are making a negative evaluation of culpable people because of their decision to give allegiance to something other than the authority that deserves it. And this evaluation shows our own allegiance to the moral authority they flouted. But if it is their allegiance which we are attacking, then our attack is not fended off by any claim that the immoral agent thought she could succeed in evading the rule of morality. That ignorance explains why she thought she could succeed in switching her allegiance, and so explains why she acted immorally. But it does not touch or explain away the (in our eyes) awful fact that she no longer wanted to be committed to the right ruler. And it is that failure of commitment that we are denouncing.

If this way of understanding our moral assessments of people is correct, then there are still mysteries that need to be unraveled. Suppose a person persists in acting morally, not because she respects the moral authority, but only because she is in some way afraid of it. If she could persuade herself that she could get away with defying it, she would defy it. Is such a "closet defier" already in an important sense immoral, since she lacks the allegiance to moral authority which marks out the good from the bad?

And what about the claim made by a long line of defenders of morality's authority that defiance of it is bound to fail: is such a claim really true? The defiance account of immorality assumes what moral philosophers have struggled unsuccessfully to justify for many years: the inescapable authority of moral commands. Perhaps one reason why this has been a favorite and persistent topic in moral philosophy for hundreds of years is that it is the central element upon which our blaming practices rest, and so it must be justified if those blaming practices are to be judged legitimate.

III. Defiance of Law

It is relatively straightforward to apply this account to legal culpability. Take the tax cheat: he knows

a") that the legal system commands him not to commit the action, i.e., that it is illegal.

b") given the authority which legal commands have, he is supposed to have better reason to refrain from illegal behavior than to engage in it in order to do something else he wishes.

Nonetheless, he also believes

c") the authority of the law can be defied, and something else that condones what he wishes can be enthroned in its place, thereby allowing him to act so as to satisfy them.

Given his belief in (c"), our law-breaker believes he can "get away with it." It is (c") which is the defiance that constitutes legal *mens rea*, and which the legal system is looking for when it tries in court those who have committed illegal acts.

Thus, I am proposing that an important component of the criminal law is the defiance conception of culpability. The Model Penal Code gives us criteria for culpability that are, in essence, signs of a defiant mind: e.g., knowledge, purposiveness, and recklessness (where the last assumes a defiant choice of the action knowing the risks). And the excuses and justifications recognized by the law make sense as mental states in which no defiance has occurred.

In particular, those who are excused from legal culpability will be found not to have believed (c"). For example, the man who, misled by incompetent IRS consultants and government pamphlets, fails to pay enough tax doesn't believe (c"). His action is explained by his ignorance of the tax law – an ignorance that cannot be traced to any defiance of the law's authority on his part. And the driver who takes proper and sufficient care in her operation of a motor vehicle and who hits and kills a drunken pedestrian who has inexplicably hurled himself in front of her car in no way kills the person because of her defiance of the law's authority in order to satisfy her wishes.

Normally, however, ignorance of the law is not an excuse, because a legal system expects people to do their best to understand the legal rules of that system, and communicates that expectation to the citizenry. Hence, if someone complains that he did not know the rule, the legal system is unimpressed because it believes this person knew he should have learned of the rule but nonetheless failed to do so. In the words of one judge, "everyone is conclusively presumed to know the law."[28] He is culpably ignorant, and his culpable failure to remedy his ignorance makes him defiant of the authority of the legal system, and hence legally culpable. (So the taxpayer who did his best to comply with the law but who failed to do so because the tax code was either ambiguous or inadequately promulgated by the state such that he could not find out what the relevant tax rules were would be unfairly penalized for his failure to comply with those rules.)

As I have already mentioned, not only illegal acts of commission but also acts of recklessness are analyzed neatly by this approach. A reckless offender is another example of one who is culpable in the manner of those who are culpably ignorant. Even if he doesn't mean, for example, to drive the power boat into the dock full of people, and even if he points out, correctly in our view, that his boat was going too fast for him to control, nonetheless we believe that he had to know, as he chose to go at that high speed, that he was taking the risk that he would be unable to control the boat and possibly endanger others' lives. The fact that he did so anyway is a sign of his defiance of legal (and, in this case, also moral) pronouncements against taking that kind of risk. He is therefore culpable for running the boat into the dock not because he wanted to perform it in defiance of legal and moral imperatives (he wanted no such thing) but because he wanted to do that which entailed *risking* the kind of harm ruled out by legal and moral imperatives, so that he undertook the risk in defiance of these imperatives.

[28] Judge Buttles, *State v. Woods*, Supreme Court of Vermont, 1935, 107 Vt. 354, 179 A 1, in Kadish and Paulsen, p. 110.

But what, the reader may wish to know, is legal authority? This famous question is one that some theorists have had trouble answering.[29] To the extent that one denies there is any authority attaching to law *qua* law, one would say either that the lawbreaker is defiant of the authority of morality upon which one supposes legal commands rely, insofar as they have any force upon us – which is the view of any classic natural law theorist – or that she is defiant of reason, in the sense that she performs the illegal action knowing she may suffer a penalty that she finds unacceptable. On this latter view, the authority of the law (and particularly the criminal law) derives from reason, because laws are imperatives backed by negative sanctions designed to secure a certain deterrent goal. The lawbreaker, on this view, is not defying any special authority that legal rules have, but he is being irrational (assuming that an expected utility calculation, properly performed and of which he is capable, would tell him not to violate the legal rule).

Those who insist, however, that the law does and should have a special authority will want to see the legal offender as defiant not only of reason but also of that special "positivist" authority. Why would someone want to defy the law? She might do so because she was motivated by self-interested considerations that the law opposed, or because she was motivated by what she took to be her moral duty, which conflicted with the legal requirements. Those who insist that the law has its own special authority must defend the strength and scope of that authority, in order to explain when refusal to obey the law for moral or self-interested reasons is legitimate, and when it is condemnable defiance of the proper authority. The question of which authority ought to take precedence when the legal and moral authorities are in conflict is a particularly thorny one. The conscientious objector insists that citizens must serve morality first and the law second; Hobbes is one philosopher who thought that this way of rating the two authorities was a recipe for civil strife, and who therefore insisted that legal authority come first. ("How many throats has this false position cut, that a prince for some causes may be deposed!"[30]) We have located an important point at which philosophizing about the nature and extent of the state's authority is necessary.

Nonetheless, as the quote from the West German Supreme Court shows, a legal system normally does not want to diverge too far from morality; its architects even expect that people understand and assume the authority of morality in the system's own pronouncements and expectations of their appropriate behavior. It may even be that legal systems require that people understand and respect the authority of morality if its punitive response to them explicitly aims at making a moral point, e.g., if the punishment is intended as moral retribution, moral education, or both.

However, the state may actually want to avoid constructing its legal code in strict conformity to morality for certain important reasons. For example, even quite vicious behavior, such as libel or slander, can be merely a tort and not a criminal

[29] See Elizabeth Anscombe, *On the Source of the Authority of the State* in her *Collected Works, Volume III: Ethics, Religion and Politics* (Minneapolis: University of Minnesota Press, 1981), pp. 130–55; Joseph Raz, *The Authority of Law: Essays in Law and Morality* (Oxford: Clarendon Press, 1979); and Leslie Green, *The Authority of the State* (Oxford: Clarendon Press, 1988).

[30] Hobbes, *De Cive, The English Works of Thomas Hobbes*, vol. ii, ed. W. Molesworth, preface, pp. xi–xii.

offense in situations where the state is concerned to pursue other values, such as the protection of free speech.[31]

Although the defiance view of legal culpability fits the facts well, it does not fit them perfectly. There are decisions (e.g., *Regina v. Prince*[32]) concerning mistake in law that suggest that the law is much more inclined toward "strict liability" than the defiance account would allow. In *Regina v. Prince*, a man married a woman who was under age without knowing it, and with the reasonable belief that she was not. It seems improper to claim that such a person is defiant of the law. Finding him guilty anyway might be justified on grounds of pursuing a deterrent goal, and, in general, the state's interest in deterring harm may lead it to convict even non-culpable (in the sense of non-defiant) offenders in the interest of making them an example for those who are contemplating the same action.

Are those people convicted of criminal negligence convicted on deterrent grounds alone? They are not if they are judged "advertently negligent," because such people really do fit the *mens rea* test of guilt. This form of negligence is essentially the same as recklessness; one who is guilty of it knew that she was risking an unacceptable level of harm when she undertook her action, but flouted that knowledge and did so anyway. She therefore displayed a defiant act prior to her crime. But an "inadvertently negligent" agent is someone who did not know that she should have done otherwise, and yet (we think) could and should have known better. There appears to be no defiant act inside the agent, but only an ignorance that we find culpable. Is that finding based entirely on the thought that conviction would have desirable deterrent consequences for this individual (or for others in the community)?

Perhaps not entirely. If we take an Aristotelian attitude towards this inadvertently negligent person, we believe that, although she did not know that what she was doing was wrong, that ignorance was a function of her faulty character – a character for which she bears primary responsibility and which she knew better than to develop in this way. So we locate the defiance not at the time of the act, but earlier, during the process of character-formation. Thus a man who is convicted of gross criminal negligence after killing a pedestrian at a crosswalk while driving 30 miles over the speed limit in a rainstorm may be legitimately culpable: not because we *now* find in him any defiance of a legal rule whose authority he understood in this situation, but because earlier in his life he had developed the character of an irresponsible driver in defiance of what he knew to be the authoritative legal and moral norms mandating safe and responsible motoring.

The inclination to try to see cases of inadvertent negligence as cases of advertent negligence or recklessness derives, I believe, from the desire to find the subjective

[31] It may also be that the stringent conditions needed to convict people of certain crimes (e.g., treason) in some legal systems – conditions that require finding not only the defiance which I call *mens rea* but also a certain kind of reason for that defiance – reflect the society's concern to control the power of the state in situations where it might be inclined to overreact and use its power excessively or arbitrarily. I am indebted to discussions with David Dolinko on this point.

[32] *Regina v. Prince*, L. R. 2 Crim. Cas. REs. 54 (1876). The defendant was convicted of marrying a girl under the age of sixteen, in violation of Victorian English Law, despite the fact that he was judged to have the "reasonable belief" that she was 18.

element of defiance of the relevant norm in any person convicted of a legal offense. To convict someone who is genuinely and reasonably unaware of the criminal nature of his actions in order to secure greater deterrence of social harm violates the conditions of fairness in judgment and response implicit in the defiance account. Indeed, it seems to be a (mild) instance of resorting to terror to gain social control. Now perhaps the state is sometimes justified in pursuing convictions on these grounds (although that is controversial) because it must not only exact retribution but also secure a high degree of protection for its citizens through the deterrence of certain forms of behavior. Nonetheless, these convictions offend our sense of justice – which is created, I would argue, by our acceptance of the idea that genuine culpability requires a defiant mind.

Conclusion

Although defiance is critical to behavior that we standardly criticize, condemn, and take action to stop, I wonder whether or not it is also critical to our success as individuals and as groups. A readiness to "take on the world" may well be what is necessary to invent new machines, concoct ambitious dreams such as going to the moon, or fight off self-doubt occasioned by racist, or sexist, or class-based perspectives on one's abilities. It may even be (as I have suggested elsewhere) that defiance is a necessary part of certain emotions such as resentment and hatred.[33] To appreciate how our capacity to defy authoritative norms may have helped us survive – as individuals, as a people, as a species – might enable us to become reconciled to something that exponents of various sorts of norms would argue that we ought bitterly to regret. And perhaps it is because we do see this capacity as important to our survival that it becomes hard to shake the thought that the first two human beings were impressive in the way they took on God.

Philosophy, University of California, Davis

[33] See *Forgiveness and Mercy* (written with Jeffrie Murphy), ch. 2 (Cambridge: Cambridge University Press, 1986).

CHOICE, CHARACTER, AND EXCUSE*

By Michael S. Moore

Introduction

Freud justified his extensive theorizing about dreams by the observation that they were "the royal road" to something much more general: namely, our unconscious mental life. The current preoccupation with the theory of excuse in criminal law scholarship (including my own) can be given a similar justification, for the excuses are the royal road to theories of responsibility generally. The thought is that if we understand why we excuse in certain situations but not others, we will have also gained a much more general insight into the nature of responsibility itself. Nowhere has this thought been more evident than in the century-old focus of criminal law theoreticians on the excuse of insanity, a focus that could not be justified by the importance of the excuse itself.

In this paper I wish to isolate two theories of excuse, each of which instantiates its own distinctive theory of responsibility. One is what I shall call *the choice theory of excuse*, according to which one is excused for the doing of a wrongful action because and only because at the moment of such action's performance, one did not have sufficient capacity or opportunity to make the choice to do otherwise. Such a choice theory of excuse instantiates a more general theory of responsibility, according to which we are responsible for wrongs we freely choose to do, and not responsible for wrongs we lacked the freedom (capacity and opportunity) to avoid doing. The second I shall call *the character theory of excuse*, according to which one is excused for the doing of a wrongful action because and only because such action is not determined by (or in some other way expressive of) those enduring attributes of ourselves we call our characters. Such a character theory of excuse instantiates a more general theory of responsibility, according to which the primary object of our responsibility is our own character, and responsibility for wrongful action is derivative of this primary responsibility, our actions being proxies for the characters such actions express.

These abbreviated formulae require much clarification, some of which I undertake in the succeeding parts of this paper (sections I and II). I then compare the merits of the two theories in section III, concluding that the choice theory is correct. Before undertaking any of these tasks, however, something needs to be said about what the excuses are and what a theory of the excuses should look like. The balance of this introduction is devoted to these questions.

* This essay has benefited greatly from the comments and suggestions made by the contributors to this volume. My attention was drawn to the character theory by Peter Arenella's work, and my reasons for rejecting that theory were sharpened by my long-term discussions with Larry Alexander, Heidi Hurd, Sandy Kadish, Herbert Morris, Stephen Morse, and Jeremy Waldron.

First, what are the excuses? Do we seek a theory of moral excuse or one of some distinctively legal excuse? My interest is in the moral excuses, although my ultimate interest is in developing a theory of what ought to be our legal excuses. The connection between the moral excuses and what ought to be the legal excuses is a very tight one on the punishment theories I shall here presuppose to be correct. If one is either a retributivist or a holder of the mixed theory of punishment (of the side-constraint type), so that in either case moral responsibility is at least a necessary condition to legal liability to punishment, then wherever there is a moral excuse (and thus an absence of moral responsibility), there should also be a legal excuse (and thus an absence of legal liability).[1] The substantive criminal law of England and America by and large reflects this dependence of legal excuse upon moral excuse, so that where there is a moral excuse there not only ought to be, but often *is*, a legal excuse as well; however, defending this last, doctrinal proposition is no part of the present undertaking.

Even focusing immediately on moral excuse leaves an ambiguity that requires clarification. The most obvious kinds of moral excuse are the excuses we have for violating moral norms. I also intend to include another kind of moral excuse, however: namely, the excuses morality requires for violating legal norms. Often a condition is an excuse in both these senses, such as insanity or duress. Sometimes, however, morality contains excuses that make sense only in relation to legal norms. Mistake of law is one such moral excuse, for although it is morality that demands that actors without a fair opportunity to acquaint themselves with the laws of their jurisdiction be excused, such an excuse makes sense only in relation to a legal norm.

I have elsewhere classified the moral excuses – and correspondingly, what ought to be legal excuses – into three groups.[2] (1) The first consists of those excuses that show some actor not to have violated some moral or legal norm. This may be because (for instance) although it was movements of his body that were part of the causal sequence that brought about the harm, he didn't will such movements; it may be because, although he did will the movements of his body that allowed the wrong to take place, he didn't himself do the wrong because someone else did; or it may be because we think moral norms to prohibit certain intentions, not certain actions, and he lacked the mental state such norms prohibit, even though his

[1] A retributivist about punishment believes that moral responsibility is not only a necessary condition of state punishment, but that it is a sufficient condition as well. The moral responsibility of an actor makes it not only not unfair to punish him; it also gives everyone else the duty to see that he is punished. A mixed theorist of the side constraint type, by contrast, believes that the moral responsibility of an actor is necessary to state punishment, but not sufficient. On the mixed theory, we neither have a duty to punish the guilty nor is their guilt a sufficient justification for punishment. Some other rationale, such as crime-prevention, typically is used by mixed theorists to complete their justification of punishment. I have defended the retributivist theory of punishment in Michael S. Moore, *Law and Psychiatry: Rethinking the Relationship* (Cambridge: Cambridge University Press, 1984), pp. 233–43, and in Michael S. Moore, "The Moral Worth of Retribution," ed. F. Schoeman, *Responsibility, Character, and the Emotions* (Cambridge: Cambridge University Press, 1987), pp. 179–219. For a discussion of the mixed theory of punishment where moral innocence acts as a side constraint on the pursuit of the utilitarian goal of crime-prevention, see *Law and Psychiatry*, pp. 237–38, 240–42.

[2] Michael S. Moore, "Causation and the Excuses," *California Law Review*, vol. 73, no. 4 (July 1985), pp. 1091–1149.

behavior would have been the appropriate means to satisfying such an intention had he possessed it.[3]

(2) Other excuses admit that the actor did the wrongful act, but deny his responsibility anyway. On the view that moral and legal norms prohibit actions, not intentions, then mistake and ignorance belong here.[4] These are often called "cognitive" excuses, because it is cognition, not volition, that is defective. The other branch of this class of excuses are volitional, in the sense that the actor knew what he was doing but didn't have the willpower to stop himself from doing it. Duress, necessity, provocation, and addiction are common examples of this branch of excuse.

(3) The last category of excuses consists of those excuses in which it is unclear whether moral norms were violated or not. These I call the status excuses, because it is the general condition of the agent (his status) that determines whether or not he is excused. Infancy, insanity, diminished capacity, and intoxication[5] are the main examples. What such conditions commonly betoken is that the individuals in them do not and cannot function well enough for us to confidently liken their "actions" and "intentions" to the actions and intentions of sober, sane adults.

A *theory* of this heterogenous range of excusing conditions should be a general statement that accurately describes all or most of the particular conditions we are confident morally excuse, and that itself has some intuitive plausibility to it in light of some yet more general theory of moral responsibility we think to be true. The two competing theories of excuse I wish to examine make both of these claims for themselves, and it is to these theories that I turn.

I. The Choice Theory of Excuse

What I call the choice theory of excuse is also called the "capacity conception of responsibility," the "responsibility principle," the "voluntarism principle," the "Kantian theory of responsibility," the "value of choice" theory of excuses, the "voluntariness principle," the "personhood principle," and my own earlier label, the "disturbed practical reason" theory of excuse.[6] An early expression of the

[3] The moralist who adopts the Catholic doctrine of double effect will take the view that those norms of morality we think of as "absolutes" – deontological constraints – generalize over intentional actions and not simply over actions. See, e.g., Thomas Nagel, *The View From Nowhere* (New York: Oxford University Press, 1986), p. 179.

[4] Argued for in Moore, "Causation and the Excuses," p. 1097, and in R.B. Brandt, "A Motivational Theory of Excuses in the Criminal Law," eds. R. Pennock and J. Chapman, *Nomos XXVII: Criminal Justice* (New York: New York University Press, 1985), pp. 165–98, at pp. 166–67.

[5] I classify intoxication on a particular occasion differently than addiction (a tendency to become intoxicated) on the following assumption: that being addicted, if it excuses, excuses because of a compelling desire that operates within an otherwise undisturbed mind; whereas being intoxicated, if it excuses, excuses because the intoxicated subject is generally incapacitated from reasoning. On this view intoxication, but not addiction, operates like insanity and infancy – as an excuse of general incapacity (status).

[6] See, respectively, to the labels used in the text: Nicola Lacey, *State Punishment* (London: Routledge, 1988), p. 62; Hyman Gross, *A Theory of Criminal Justice* (New York: Oxford University Press, 1979), p. 137; Sandord H. Kadish, "Excusing Crime," in his *Blame and Punishment* (New York: MacMillan, 1987), pp. 81–106, at p. 88; Michael D. Bayles, "Character, Purpose, and Criminal Responsibility," *Law and Philosophy*, vol. 1, no. 1 (April 1982), pp. 5–20, at p. 6; T.M. Scanlon, Jr., "Quality of Will and the Value of Choice" (unpublished manuscript, 1988), p. 42; George Fletcher, *Rethinking Criminal Law* (Boston: Little, Brown,

theory can be found in Blackstone[7] when he said that the legal excuses of his time could be "reduced to this single consideration, the want or defect of *will*. An involuntary act, as it has no claim to merit, so neither can it induce any guilt: the concurrence of the will, when it has its choice either to do or avoid the act in question, being the only thing that renders human actions praiseworthy or culpable."

Despite its long history and its many current adherents, the choice theory's classical modern expression is to be found in the writings of Herbert Hart.[8] In examining legal excusing conditions, Hart thought:

> What is crucial is that those whom we punish should have had, when they acted, the normal capacities, physical and mental, for abstaining from what it forbids, and a fair opportunity to exercise these capacities. Where these capacities and opportunities are absent, as they are in different ways in the varied cases of accident, mistake, paralysis, reflex action, coercion, insanity, etc., the moral protest is that it is morally wrong to punish because 'he could not have helped it' or 'he could not have done otherwise' or 'he had no real choice.'[9]

Such a theory of excuse is itself but an instance of a more general principle of moral responsibility: "what the law has done here is to reflect, albeit imperfectly, a fundamental principle of morality that a person is not to be blamed for what he has done if he could not help doing it."[10]

This theory of excuse, and its accompanying, more general theory of responsibility, was given two quite different justifications by Hart. Hart's early justification, found in his seminal 1957 paper, "Legal Responsibility and Excuses,"[11] arguably was a kind of rule-utilitarianism. The function or value of having duress, insanity, automatism, etc., be excuses to criminal liability was to maximize "the efficacy of the individual's informed and considered choice . . ."[12] Hart more fully described the good that excuses achieved in the criminal law:

> On this view excusing conditions are accepted as something that may conflict with the social utility of the law's threats; they are regarded as of moral importance because they provide for all individuals alike the satisfactions of a choosing system. Recognition of excusing conditions is

1978), p. 804; Joshua Dressler, *Understanding Criminal Law* (New York: Mathew Bender, 1987), at p. 185; Joshua Dressler, "Reflections on Excusing Wrongdoers: Moral Theory, New Excuses, and The Model Penal Code," *Rutgers Law Journal*, vol. 19, no. 3 (Spring 1988), pp. 671–716, at p. 701; Moore, "Causation and Excuse," pp. 1148–49; Moore, *Law and Psychiatry*, pp. 85–90.

[7] Sir William Blackstone, *Commentaries on the Laws of England*, Chitty ed., vol. IV (London, 1826), p. 20.

[8] See the essays collected in H.L.A. Hart, *Punishment and Responsibility* (Oxford: Oxford University Press, 1968).

[9] *ibid.*, p. 152.

[10] *ibid.*, p. 174.

[11] H.L.A. Hart, "Legal Responsibility and Excuses," ed. S. Hook, *Determinism and Freedom* (New York: New York University Press, 1958), and reprinted in *Punishment and Responsibility*, pp. 28–53. (Subsequent references to this essay are to the reprinted version.)

[12] *ibid.*, p. 46.

> therefore seen as a matter of protection of the individual against the claims of society from the highest measure of protection from crime that can be obtained from a system of threats. In this way the criminal law respects the claims of the individual as such, or at least as a *choosing being*, and distributes its coercive sanctions in a way that reflects this respect for the individual.[13]

Hart's idea here was that choice is a power that people prefer and whose exercise provides substantial satisfactions. It is therefore a good that competes with the good that is crime-prevention. The goodness of choice to people is largely due to the power we all want to predict the future.[14] As Scanlon puts Hart's point here: "The most obvious reason why choice has value for me ... is simply instrumental: I would like what happens (e.g., what appears on my plate) to conform to my preferences ..."[15] The way that the excuses of the criminal law further the good that is choice is by protecting unfree, unimpeded choice from criminal sanction; only my free choices will be sanctioned, and knowing that, I can maximally predict what will follow upon my decisions. As Scanlon puts it, if I can "believe that if what happens depends on my subjective response under given conditions then the result is likely to coincide with what I want."[16]

This rationale for having the excuses we do is arguably utilitarian, for it balances off the maximization of one good most people prefer, crime-prevention, against the maximization of another such good, the good that is free choice. It becomes a *rule*-utilitarian rationale once one says, as Hart did, that the attainment of the goodness of choice is not balanced against the attainment of the goodness of crime-prevention in one overall calculation of the good; rather, such calculations are assigned their own "levels" of appropriate domain. The doctrines necessary to achieve a satisfactory level of free choice (once set by separate calculation) then operate as a constraint on the maximization of the good that is crime-prevention.

Hart's second and later justification for the choice theory of excuse – and the way he is usually read today – grounds it in considerations of fairness and justice that are not themselves products of utilitarian calculation. That is, the excuses and the "could have done otherwise" principle they instantiate are seen as deontological, or non-consequentialist, side constraints that constrain the maximization of any utilitarian goals, crime-prevention and choice-maximization included. As Hart himself later recognized, there are constraints "which civilized moral thought places on the pursuit of the utilitarian goal by the demand that punishment should not be applied to the innocent ..."[17] One of those constraints is "that out of considerations of fairness or justice to individuals we should restrict even punishment designed as a 'preventative' [i.e., utilitarian punishment] to those who had a normal capacity and a fair opportunity to obey."[18]

[13] *ibid.*, p. 49 (emphasis in original).
[14] *ibid.*, p. 49.
[15] Scanlon, "Quality of Will," p. 25.
[16] *ibid.*
[17] Hart, *Punishment and Responsibility*, p. 80.
[18] *ibid.*, p. 201.

As important for our purposes as the justification of the choice theory of excuse is the meaning of the theory. What does it mean to say, "one is responsible only for *free* choice," or that "one is responsible if he *could* have done otherwise"? Although Hart made fruitful beginnings in the unpacking of these terms, more detail than he himself provided is needed if we are to understand the choice theory of excuse.

Take the word "could" in the "could have done otherwise" principle. There are three readings of "could," only one of which is intended by the principle. The first is the weak, or behavioral, sense of "could." On this reading, our abilities (what we *can* do, or, counterfactually, what we *could* have done) are measured by what we actually do. If on some occasion we do run a mile in under four minutes, then on that occasion we *could* run a mile in under four minutes; if on some occasion we run a mile in over four minutes, then on that occasion we *could not* run a mile in under four minutes. This weak or behavioral sense of "could" is obviously not what is wanted in the principle, because it trivializes our abilities into merely alternative descriptions of our behavior. In this sense of "could," a broken clock *could* tell the correct time twice every 24 hours (because it did so); a mechanically perfect clock that was set too fast *could not* tell the correct time (because it did not do so). These are not only not idiomatic usages of "could"; they are nonsensical, because they eliminate the idea of general ability presupposed by "can" and "could." Put simply: it has to be possible that I *can* do some things I do not in fact do.

The second reading of "could" is the strong, or incompatibilist, sense of the word. On this reading, we *can* do some action A only if A is not caused by factors exernal to the will of the actor. On this view, "I could have run a mile in four minutes" means not only that there were no causes sufficient to prevent me from doing it, but also, had I done it, that there would have been no causes of that doing of it (other than my willing to do it, which itself must be uncaused).

I doubt that this is an ordinary or idiomatic sense of the word "could," despite a defense of this sense of the word by no less an ordinary language philosopher than J.L. Austin.[19] Notice that to use this sense of the word in the statement about an accurately set, perfectly functioning clock, "it can tell the correct time," attributes free wwll to the clock. In any case, the issue here is not a question of linguistic usage but of morals:[20] is the incompatibilist sense the right sense to be plugged into the "could have done otherwise" principle in order to make that principle true? I have elsewhere argued in some detail that it is not.[21] Not wanting to devote this essay to another defense of my compatibilist metaphysics, let me therefore only mention the incompatibilist sense of "could" in order to put it aside. The choice theory of excuse as Hart and I have construed it does not require any libertarian metaphysics in order to make it true.[22]

[19] J.L. Austin, "Ifs and Cans," ed. H. Morris, *Freedom and Responsibility* (Stanford: Stanford University Press, 1961).

[20] Argued for in Moore, "Causation and the Excuses," pp. 1143–44.

[21] *ibid.*

[22] A libertarian in metaphysics (as opposed to political theory) believes that human actions are uncaused by any factors external to the will of the actor. A compatibilist, as I am here using the word, believes that choice and causation are compatible, so that the statements "he chose to do that" and "his choice was caused by factors themselves unchosen by him" can both be true of some actor and his action. Correspondingly, an

What is required is a third, compatibilist, reading of the principle, which is this: "he could have done otherwise" is elliptical for "he could have done otherwise if he had chosen to." His choice, in other words, was not made *impossible* by factors over which he had no control; his choice was a cause of his behavior (even if it itself was caused). Moreover, his choice was not made *very difficult* by factors over which he had no control; his choice was what lawyers call an *intervening cause*, intervening between the factors that caused it and the action it caused.[23]

We arrive, then, at the crux of the interpretation of the choice theory of excuse. What makes choices impossible or very difficult? Notice the implausibility of the incompatibilist answer to this question (just to give my favorite dead horse a few more lashes): the incompatibilist thinks that the factors that *cause* choice, being themselves unchosen, *preclude* choice. Discover, for example, that will (choice) is caused by certain complex sorts of brain states,[24] and, presto, you have really discovered that choice was impossible or very difficult: i.e., that either there is no choice (idiomatically, "really no choice") or that all choices are hard choices (idiomatically, "no real choice"). This seems about as plausible to me as saying that once you discover the causes for Lake Michigan (glaciation, etc.), the lake disappears.

Be that as it may, I said we were putting aside incompatibilist views, for (when coupled with deterministic metaphysics) they make *all* choices impossible and thus all actions excused on the choice theory of excuse. Hart's answer was different. What makes choices impossible or very difficult is either an incapacity in the agent or the lack of fair opportunity to use a non-defective capacity. Hart thus subdivides the ability presupposed by his sense of "could" into two components. One relates to the equipment of the actor: does he have sufficient choosing capacity to be responsible? The other relates to the situation in which the actor finds himself: does that situation present him with a fair chance to use his capacities for choice so as to give effect to his decision?

An example perhaps is helpful here. Imagine that someone who is accused of stealing in order to get money with which to purchase heroin proffers his addiction to heroin as an excuse. There are two versions of his excuse that are relevant on the choice theory as Hart construes it. One would be defective capacity: at the time of stealing, his reason was overcome by the compelling desire (construed as a reason-unhinging emotional storm) for heroin. The other would be lack of fair opportunity: at the time of stealing, he was not in the grip of any compelling desire

---

incompatibilist believes that choice and causation are incompatible in the sense that the two statements just mentioned cannot both be true. (Notice that, on the choice theory of responsibility, a compatibilist about choice and causation will also be a compatibilist about responsibility and causation.)

[23] For an analysis of the notion of an intervening cause, see H.L.A. Hart and A.M. Honoré, *Causation in the Law* (Oxford: Oxford University Press, 2nd ed. 1985). As Hart and Honoré analyse it, for a human action to be an intervening cause it must be "voluntary" in their extended sense of that word, which means not done in ignorance, not done in compulsion, not done while insane, etc.

[24] On the neurophysiology of willing, choice, and self-directed action, see Benjamin Libet, "Unconscious Cerebral Initiative and the Role of Conscious Will in Voluntary Action," *The Behavioral and Brain Sciences*, vol. 8, no. 4 (Fall 1985), pp. 529–66. See also Myles Brand, *Intending and Acting* (Cambridge: MIT Press, 1984).

or other emotion; rather, he coolly foresaw that if he did not get money for heroin, he would not get heroin, and that if he did not get heroin, he would eventually suffer the extremely unpleasant consequences of withdrawal symptoms. His opportunity to avoid stealing was thus less than for the rest of us, for (unlike the rest of us) not stealing had extremely unpleasant consequences for him.

If addiction were an excuse for stealing, on the choice theory of excuse one or other of these variants would have to be true. That addiction is so implausible as an excuse for stealing is due to the implausibility of either of these claims being true. The defective capacity version depends on what many now regard as an implausible psychological story,[25] and the lack of fair opportunity version depends on a morally implausible view of how diminished our opportunities must be in order to excuse choices made in such circumstances. Thus, that addiction is a poor candidate for an excuse to stealing is something the choice theory of excuse can explain as well as it can explain why it is a candidate for an excuse at all.

Consider duress as a second example of excuse that allows us to delve more deeply into the nature of the choice theory of excuse. One is legally and morally excused for doing an illegal and wrongful act if the doing of it was caused by the threat of a third party to do something unpleasant to the actor unless he complied with the threat. For example, D_1 is threatened with being shot in the knees unless he drives an IRA gunman to the location of a policeman whom the gunman intends to kill.[26]

Put aside any justificatory readings of duress; assume that being shot in the knees is a lesser evil than is the evil of making possible the death of an innocent. D_1's claim can then only be excuse, not justification. There are two readings of D_1's excuse claim on the choice theory. He can tell a psychological story about how hard it was to even think about resisting the threat because his consciousness was flooded by a fear of being shot and a revulsion at the thought of seeing his own blood. Or he can tell a story of how unfair the gunman's threat made D_1's situation of choice, because the threat attached a consequence to D_1's choosing not to help the gunman that is not commonly attached to the choice of the rest of us not to aid terrorists. His first claim is defective capacity; his second, diminished opportunity.

A reason for favoring the opportunity version over the incapacity version of duress can be seen from the following example.[27] D_2 unjustifiably hates another, X, who is in fact an exemplary individual. Much to D_2's delight, X is dying. He can be saved, however, by a rare drug known to T. T threatens D_2 with T's giving the drug to X, and thereby saving X's life, unless D_2 robs a bank with T. D_2 is not otherwise inclined to rob the bank – he does not need the money – yet the thought of X being given the drug and not dying is more than he can stand. After days of not being able to keep the picture of X's happy, smiling, healthy face out of his mind, D_2 reluctantly agrees to rob the bank with T.

[25] See, e.g., Herbert Fingarette, *Heavy Drinking: The Myth of Alcoholism as a Disease* (Berkeley: University of California Press, 1988), reviewed by me in *Ethics*, vol. 99, no. 3 (April 1989), pp. 660–61.

[26] Cf. Lynch v. Director of Public Prosecutions, [1975–1] All Eng. Rep. 913.

[27] Other reasons for favoring the opportunity versus the capacity version of the duress excuse as it is reflected in current criminal law doctrine are given by Dressler, "Some Reflections," pp. 708–12.

Common intuition – at least if a decade-full of criminal law students is any guide – tells us that D_2 is not excused for the bank robbery. Yet, on the capacity version of the duress defense, why not? D_2 was seemingly as incapacitated by his hatred of X as D_1 was by his fear of his own injury. D_2's faculty of reason apparently did not have the same capacity to make choices as does the reason of those not under such emotional distraction.

To reject D_2's proffered excuse is to reject the idea that this kind of (internal) incapacity can, by itself, excuse. The intuition that guides this rejection is the intuition that people like D_2 are responsible. This intuition of a larger responsibility has apparently motivated both Sandy Kadish's recent favoring of the opportunity version of excuses[28] and Stephen Morse's disfavoring of what he calls the "internal compulsion" type of excuses.[29] Kadish and Morse, like Aristotle before them,[30] are worried that recognizing fears, cravings, instinctual desires, strong passions, or other internal states as excuses unduly reduces one's true responsibility. The child's "something made me do it" is taken to be a bad imitation of an excuse, not the general form of an internally incapacitating excuse.

Freud had a similar insight about the proper extent of one's responsibility in the face of fears like those of my hypothetical D_1 and D_2. In discussing the responsibility of each of us for the content of one's dreams, Freud recognized the temptation to subdivide the self and to attribute the bad stuff to a "not-me," an it or id within me but not identical to me. Freud rejected such a narrow notion of responsibility, disdainfully leaving "it to the jurist to construct for social purposes a responsibility that is artificially limited to the metapsychological ego."[31]

Freud had his finger on what I take to be bothering Kadish, Morse, and Aristotle: D_1's and D_2's responsibility are too circumscribed on the capacity version of the duress excuse because the *self* who is being held responsible (or excused) is itself too narrow. We – the persons or selves who are the subjects of responsibility – are more than the faculty of reason that does battle with the faculty of emotion; we are our emotions as much as we are our reason.

Resolving this worry about internal factors operating as incapacitating excuses thus involves us in some deep questions that go to the heart of the choice theory of excuse. One is the question already mentioned: what self-boundaries does the theory presuppose? Does the responsible self who chooses include any emotions, or is the responsible self who chooses only to be identified with the conscious will, against which all emotions are alien and potentially disturbing (incapacitating) factors? The example of D_2 should incline the choice theorist strongly towards Freud's view: some emotions, at least, have to be included within the self who

[28] Kadish, "Excusing Crime," pp. 101–2, 104–6.

[29] Stephen Morse, "Psychology, Determinism, and Legal Responsibility," ed. G. Melton, *Nebraska Symposium on Motivation 1985: Volume 33* (Lincoln: University of Nebraska Press, 1986), pp. 35–85.

[30] Aristotle, *Nichomachean Ethics*, bk. III, ch. 1, in Richard McKeon, *Introduction to Aristotle* (Chicago: University of Chicago Press, 1973), pp. 387–88.

[31] Sigmund Freud, "Moral Responsibility for the Content of Dreams," in *Standard Edition of the Works of Sigmund Freud*, ed. James Strachey (London: Hogarth Press, 1961), vol. 19, pp. 131–34. I discuss this passage from Freud and others on responsibility in Moore, *Law and Psychiatry*, pp. 343–48.

chooses. D_2's hatred of X is part of him; it cannot be seen as an alien factor that incapacitates *him* from deciding whether or not to rob the bank.

Such an extended view of self may seen unavailable on the choice theory of responsibility, for it may seem that to hold people like D_2 responsible for their actions requires a prior judgement holding them responsible for being who they are (viz., people with these kinds of emotions). This would mean that we are ultimately judging D_2 for his bad character, and – only in light of that judgment – then judging the culpability of his choice.

Whether this is so depends on a second fundamental question the choice theorist about responsibility and excuse must answer: does our choosing agency, the will, include those of our emotions that are part of our self, or are such emotions not part of such agency even though they are part of us? Such a question makes sense because our subpersonal agencies (of perception, cognition, etc.) are not coextensive with our personal selves;[32] it is thus possible that an emotion can be part of us and yet not part of our processes of choice. If this possibility is in fact realized in a case such as D_2, then when we hold D_2 responsible, it is not for his choice to do evil (for his choice was a hard one, given the emotion alien to it), but for the fact that he is evil in his emotional makeup.

If we think through what choosing to act (willing) is, we will find it difficult to keep emotions like D_2's hatred of X separate from D_2's choice to help T with the bank robbery. In its narrowest sense, willing is the initiation of those motor responses we call basic actions – acts like moving one's finger, raising one's arm, and the like.[33] Yet the choice that is the touchstone of responsibility for the choice theorist includes much more than this. It includes the deliberative processes that lead up to the initiation of bodily movements. It is here that intentions and plans are formed in light of the actor's desires and beliefs. It is here that the actor chooses his actions under more complex descriptions than simply "moving my body": descriptions such as "taking my revenge on X" or "eliminating that hateful X." Choice, to be morally interesting, must include not only the initiation of basic actions but also the formation of the intentions and beliefs that guide and motivate the doing of basic actions. We choose our plans (complex actions), and not simply the (basic) actions that execute them.

If this is what is meant by "choice," then some emotions will necessarily have a place in this process. As Sabini and Silver observe: "the emotions are connected to cognition, connected to desires and plans . . ."[34] On this view, the emotions are not invaders of our processes of reasoned deliberation, nor are they preemptors of such

[32] I discuss Dan Dennett's distinction between personal versus subpersonal levels of explanation in *Law and Psychiatry*, pp. 274–75. By "subpersonal agency," I mean those centers of functioning posited to exist at the subpersonal level by the approach to mind known as "homuncular functionalism." A homuncular functionalist believes that the nature of a person's actions and thoughts are best approached by subdividing them into the "actions" and "thoughts" of subpersonal agencies each of who "do" only a part of what the whole person does. See *ibid.*, 414–45; see also Michael Moore, "Mind, Brain, and Unconscious," eds. C. Wright and P. Clark, *Mind, Psychoanalysis and Science*, (Oxford: Basil Blackwell, 1988), pp. 141–166.

[33] On the distinction between basic and complex actions, see Moore, *Law and Psychiatry*, pp. 67–77.

[34] John Sabini and Maury Silver, "Emotions, Responsibility, and Character," ed. F. Schoeman, *Responsibility, Character, and the Emotions* (Cambridge: Cambridge University Press, 1987), pp. 164–75, at p. 168.

processes. Rather, our emotions are both products and causes of the judgements we make as we decide what to do. When we get angry, for example, our anger can itself be caused by judgment: e.g., that an innocent person has just suffered undeserved punishment. Such anger reflects our judgment that something immoral has just taken place.[35] Further, such anger at unjust treatment need not make reasoned choice more difficult. It may instead make choice easier by highlighting what we otherwise might have missed. Anger at injustice is at least as effective as reciting Kant when keeping the priority of justice before one's mind as one decides how to respond.

If all of this is true, then it may seem that Kadish and Morse are right: internal factors like emotions cannot be said to incapacitate our choices, except by an impermissibly narrow view either of who we are or of what our choosing agency consists.

As much as I agree with this in cases like D_2 – where the emotion in question clearly seems both part of him and part of his choice to allow X to die – if all emotions are treated in this way, then there is no incapacitation of choice story to be told about D_1 either. True, D_1 may invoke the 'lack of fair opportunity' branch of excuse, whereby he is excused by his comparative lack of opportunity to avoid doing evil. Yet the diminished opportunity branch excuses D_1 without regard to how hard he found the choice; doesn't the D_1 who is "overcome" by his fear of being shot and his revulsion at the thought of his own blood have some excuse in addition to diminished opportunity?

I don't know the answer to this question. It doesn't matter much in cases of duress, because the diminished opportunity branch of the excuse is available in any event. The answer matters a lot to alleged excuses such as provocation, pathological gambling, or obsessional neurosis, where there is no plausible diminished opportunity story to be told. Common-sense morality seems to reflect the idea that some emotions incapacitate choice, and thus excuse. Such an idea is based on a psychological view that holds that some emotions are not "judgment-connected" in the two ways described before: (1) such emotions are not caused by judgments and so do not take intentional objects (these emotions are decribed as "blind rage" or "free-floating anxiety"), and (2) such emotions cause behavior in the way that anger or fear causes our heartbeats to increase: namely, not by motivating a choice to act but by causing action directly without the mediation of choice and judgment.

My doubts about common-sense morality here stem from my doubts about its psychological suppositions. Are any emotions truly free of corresponding judgments that justify them to the agent whose emotions they are? Is any rage truly blind, or any anxiety without its object? Do the emotions that allegedly cause action by "short-circuiting" choice ever proceed except by a chosen letting go, a chosen self-indulgence?

35 Being caused by judgment, such emotions obey laws of proportionality, keeping feeling proportional, both in type and intensity, to its object. (Grieve over a dead goose too long and it won't take a Freudian to surmise that the real object of your feeling is something else, something more appropriate to the nature and depth of your feelings.)

A complete exposition of the incapacity branch of the choice theory of excuse would have to answer these questions. Since my purpose is merely to sketch the choice theory for purposes of contrasting it to the character theory, I fortunately can leave them open. We still need to clarify the diminished opportunity branch of the theory before we turn to the character theory of excuse. Think again of my example of the unjustifiably hateful bank robber (D_2). Why cannot such a bank robber make out the diminished opportunity version of the duress excuse? After all, his opportunity not to rob the bank was less than ours: if he did not rob it, this would have had the consequence that his old enemy X would have survived.

What this brings out is the sense of "unfair opportunity" being used in the opportunity branch of the theory. Our opportunities to avoid wrongful action are not *unfairly* diminished simply because they are diminished. The "cost" to D_2 of not robbing the bank should not have been regarded as a cost at all; in reality, it was a benefit that X not die. That D_2 did not so regard it made it psychologically harder for him (the narrow "him") to refrain from robbing the bank. But D_2's *fair* opportunity is not measured by his psychological difficulties, but rather by the objective facts of the matter. Objectively D_2 had a fair opportunity not to rob the bank, even if subjectively he experienced it as a hard choice.[36]

This may raise a doubt about the opportunity branch of the choice theory of excuse: namely, how it differs from justification.[37] For to lack a *fair* opportunity to avoid doing wrong, there must be some (objectively regarded) evil that one is avoiding, and that may seem to imply that one is justified in doing wrong. Yet the opportunity branch of excuse does not collapse into justification in this way. The fair opportunity idea could be called the "failed justification" idea of excuse. Even though an actor does more bad than good in his action (and is thus not justified), he nonetheless may have lacked a fair opportunity to avoid doing wrong if he acted to prevent some substantial evil. Loss of one's bodily integrity by being shot in the knees is such a substantial evil; the survival of a good person is not such a substantial evil, explaining why D_1 but not D_2 may avail himself of the excuse of duress on the fair opportunity construal of it.

II. The Character Theory of Excuse

The choice theory just examined has come to be regarded as the traditional or orthodox view of excuse. There has recently arisen something of a chorus that is critical of the choice theory and instead puts forward a character theory of excuse.[38] This excuse theory is grounded in a general view of moral responsibility. On this general view, the ultimate object of our responsibility is our own character. Our responsibility for actions is derivative of our more fundamental responsibility for character.

[36] Just as D_1 has a diminished opportunity sort of excuse, even if he experienced his choice as an easy one.

[37] I owe the thought to Jeremy Waldron.

[38] The character theory of excuse is normally attributed to David Hume, who held that "actions are objects of our moral sentiment, so far only as they are indications of the internal character." David Hume, *An Enquiry Concerning Human Understanding* (LaSalle: Open Court, 1949), p. 108. Perhaps the foremost modern exponent of the character theory of excuse has been Richard Brandt. See Richard Brandt, *Ethical Theory* (Englewood Cliffs: Prentice-Hall, 1959), pp. 465–74; Brandt, "Blameworthiness and Obligation," ed. A.

On this view, the excuses, in both law and morality, serve a kind of filtering function. We are *prima facie* morally responsible and legally liable for wrongful and illegal acts, but we are only *prima facie* responsible and liable because we do not yet know whether such wrongful acts were truly expressive of our characters. If they are, we are actually responsible and liable; if they are not, we are neither. The excuses, in such a case, serve to filter out wrongful actions for which we are not responsible because they are not expressive of our character. In such a way the excuses reconcile the ultimate nature of moral responsibility – it is for character, not action – with the surface features of our moral and legal ascriptions: namely, that they are for actions and not character.

This theory of excuse, and the conception of responsibility that stands behind it, are both in considerable need of clarification. Let us begin with the more general conception of responsibility and work towards the filtering function of the excuses. First of all, what is it we are responsible for when we are said to be responsible for our *characters*?[39] The most initially tempting answer may be what I shall call the backward-looking behavioral answer. On this view, the character traits we ascribe to people are simply general descriptions of past actions. To be courageous is to have acted courageously in the past, to be honest is to have acted honestly in the past, etc.

One might also call this the verificationist idea of character, because it takes usual evidence of character – past behavior – to be character itself, in the usual reductionist style of verificationism. What's wrong with this idea of character is what is wrong with verificationism generally: such reductions eliminate what they were supposed to explain. Take Michael Dummett's famous question about courage: can X have been a courageous man, when he is now dead and in his entire life no occasion ever arose that called for courageous behavior?[40] Unlike Dummett, I think the answer to this question to be rather obviously "yes,"[41] showing that character is not *identical* to past behavior (conceding that character is often *evidenced* by past behavior).

Melden, *Essays in Moral Philosophy* (Seattle: University of Washington, 1958), pp. 1*ff.*; Brandt, "The Ultilitarian Theory of Excuse," *Philosophical Review*, vol. 78, no. 3 (July 1969), pp. 337–61; and Brandt, *A Motivational Theory of Excuse.* For other defenses of the theory, see also Fletcher, *Rethinking Criminal Law*, pp. 799–802; Robert Nozick, *Philosophical Explanations* (Cambridge: Harvard University Press, 1981), pp. 387–84, 394–96; Bayles, "Character, Purpose, and Criminal Responsibility"; George Vuoso, "Background, Responsibility, and Excuse," *Yale Law Journal*, vol. 96, no. 7 (June 1987), pp. 1661–86; Lacey, *State Punishment*, pp. 67–78; and the as yet unpublished work of Tim Scanlon ("Quality of Will") and Peter Arenella ("In Praise of Blaming: The Centrality of Character," 1989). As Scanlon discusses ("Quality of Will," p. 13), the theory is implicit in Peter Strawson's general analysis of responsibility in terms of our reactive attitudes "not simply at what happens to us or to others as a result of what is done, but at the attitudes of agents towards ourselves or others as revealed [in] their actions." See P.F. Strawson, "Freedom and Resentment," ed. G. Watson, *Free Will* (Oxford: Oxford University Press, 1982), pp. 59–80. Gary Watson also explores this aspect of Strawson's thought in Watson, "Responsibility and the Limits of Evil," ed. F. Schoeman, *Responsibility, Character, and the Emotions* (Cambridge: Cambridge University Press, 1987), pp. 256–86, particularly at p. 265.

[39] For discussion of character, see particularly Brandt, *Ethical Theory*, "Blameworthiness and Obligation," and "The Utilitarian Theory of Excuse." See also Brandt, "Traits of Character: A Conceptual Analysis," *American Philosophical Quarterly*, vol. 7, no. 1 (January, 1970), pp. 23–37.

[40] Michael Dummett, *Truth and Other Enigmas* (Cambridge: Harvard University Press, 1978), pp. 14–16.

[41] See Brandt, "Traits of Character," p. 26.

This suggests a second sense of character; I shall call it the forward-looking behavioral sense. On this view, our traits of character name dispositions to future behavior. Such traits thus can sensibly be attributed to persons whose behavior never realizes them, because such persons can be *disposed* to act in certain ways even if they never do so act because the occasion never arises.

Gilbert Ryle held this dispositional view of character traits.[42] Ryle thought that persons as well as other objects possessed dispositions in his sense: namely, that certain predictions were true of them. A greedy person will (or would), in certain circumstances, act greedily; a soluble object will (or would), in certain circumstances, dissolve in water. But such dispositions are mere behavioral constructs, a part of an agent only in the sense that such predictive and counterfactual statements are true of that agent.

The problem with this view of character is that it is still too exclusively behavioral. Character, on this view, still doesn't say much about the person whose character it is. To remedy this, why not say, as Quine did against Ryle,[43] that every disposition like greediness requires there to be a dispositional *state* of greediness? Further, that the nature of this state may be physiological, so that certain brain states always underlie greedy behavior; and/or the nature of this state may be reflected in our mental experiences, so that greediness involves certain characteristic emotional experiences and attitudes.[44] We don't adopt a purely behavioral view of solubility or brittleness (Ryle's example of dispositions in natural objects), seeking a physical nature to the *states* such dispositions require; so why be so parsimonious about the physical or phenomenological nature of the states that the character traits of persons require?

Character, on this enriched dispositional view, then becomes logically independent of both the past behavior that typically evidences it and the future (or counterfactual) behavior that will (or would) typically manifest it. Unlike the characters conceived of by Dummett and Ryle, character as I conceive it can *cause* the past behavior that evidences it and will or could cause the future or hypothetical behavior that manifests it – just because character so conceived is logically independent of such behaviors.

We now need to examine more carefully the nature of states of character like greediness, honesty, etc., in order to reveal an ambiguity on which the character theorist about responsibility needs to take a position. We know little of the physiology of character, so let us stick with its phenomenology. Freud and contemporary Freudians such as Morris Eagle[45] and Herbert Fingarette[46] have studied the ways in which we constitute our sense of ourselves through owning up

[42] Gilbert Ryle, *The Concept of Mind* (London: Hutcheson, 1949).

[43] Willard Van Orman Quine, *Word and Object* (Cambridge, Mass.: MIT Press, 1960), pp. 222–25. See also David Papineau, *Theory and Meaning* (Oxford: Clarendon Press, 1979), p. 182.

[44] For my general views on how phenomenology interacts with physiology and behavior to get at the deep nature of mental states, see Michael S. Moore, "Mind, Brain, and the Unconscious."

[45] Morris Eagle, "Anatomy of the Self in Psychoanalytic Theory," ed. M. Ruse, *Nature Animated* (Dordrecht: Reidel, 1983), pp. 133–61. For a commentary on Eagle, see Michael S. Moore, "The Unity of Self," pp. 163–202 of the same volume.

[46] Herbert Fingarette, *Self-Deception* (London: Routledge and Kegan-Paul, 1969).

to, or disowning, various emotions, desires, or behaviors. The phenomenological sense of the id is of the "not-me," the ego-alien emotions, thoughts, etc., that (1) come unbidden by my will; (2) are experienced as not-me; and (3) cohere neither with the other emotions, etc., that we have nor with the picture we have of what we are like. Sometimes we repress such ego-alien entities into unconsciousness, and sometimes we defend our view of ourselves through other defense mechanisms like projection. In any case, "we" select some subset of all the traits "we" in some sense possess, and cohere that subset into a view of who "we" are. (The scare quotes are there because one 'we' is arguably different from another.)

One of Freud's persistent theses about this kind of self-inflicted division of self was that the items typically experienced as ego-alien were instinctual desires and emotions such as sex and aggression. This same tendency can be seen in Gary Watson's discussion of character as well, dividing character into appetitive versus evaluational character.[47] Appetitive character is not what we identify as ourselves, but rather as what intrudes upon or potentially disturbs our selves; our self is to be found in that reflective, evaluative self that picks and chooses which of the desires, emotions, thoughts, etc., are worth being considered part of the self.

The choice faced by the character theorist is this: how broadly does he wish to identify character? Does the character of a person include only that which he reflectively identifies as "me"? This would be a narrow and subjective view of character, for it excludes those actions, thoughts, and feelings that the person himself subjectively experiences as ego-alien. Or does the character of a person include not only those items *he* identifies as part of his sense of self, but also those he experiences as an *id*? This we shall call the broad and objective view of character, since it includes more items and does so on a nonsubjective basis.

As we saw earlier, the choice theorist had to decide whether an emotion such as the hatred of D_2 for X was part of D_2's self, and if it was, whether such emotion was part of that part of D_2 that I called D_2's choosing agency. The character theorist faces a similar decision. If his intuition also is that people like D_2 are responsible, then the character theorist must argue that, no matter how ego-alien may be D_2's experience of his hatred for X, nonetheless (1) D_2's hatred is part of his self, and (2) the character trait that D_2's hatred instantiates is part of D_2's character (so that D_2's action can be expressive of D_2's character and thus not excused on the character theory of excuse). This would commit the character theorist to the broad, objective view of character whereby a person's character includes more than that with which he identifies. This allows the character theorist to say (quite plausibly, to my mind) that someone such as Bulstrode in George Eliot's *Middlemarch* has a character marred by greediness, even though Bulstrode's sense of who he is excludes greediness.

Aside from clarifying what character theorists should mean by "character," one thing the discussion thus far reveals is that a commonly perceived difference between the character and the choice theories does not exist. It is commonly thought that the choice theorist cannot hold a person responsible for those of his

[47] Gary Watson, "Free Agency," *Journal of Philosophy*, vol. 72, no. 8 (April 1975), pp. 205–20.

actions that stem from strong emotions because such emotions impede choice (and should thus excuse on the choice theory of excuse), whereas the character theorist can easily hold such persons responsible for such actions because (on the character theory) responsibility for actions is only a proxy for responsibility for the emotional makeup such actions express. Yet, as we have seen, this difference can only exist if we make asymmetrical assumptions about the two theories: namely, we stick the choice theorist with a narrow view of choosing agency while we allow the character theorist the broad view of character. Whereas if we allow each theorist the most plausible assumptions about what choosing and character include, this difference disappears.

One last nuance in our usage of "character" needs attention here in order to keep clear the real differences that do exist between the two theories. Sometimes our talk of character is not about character *traits* or *attributes*; indeed, such talk does not use "character" to name universals of any kind. Rather, we talk of characters doing things, and what we mean to designate is some particular agency. When we speak of characters in novels, we think in this way of character as a particular – in this case, the whole person in the novel. Sometimes we even speak of characters as particular agencies within the person. Bernard Williams notes this usage in his discussion of multiple-personalitied persons.[48] What we seem to mean when we talk of different characters (personalities) operating within one person is that character names a particular, an agency within one person that itself chooses actions. Such a character (as a particular) can itself have a character (as a set of universals).

There is nothing wrong with this usage of "character." I come neither to praise nor to condemn such usage; only to bury it for purposes of this enquiry. For this cannot be what the character theorist on responsibility can mean by "character," on pain of collapsing his theory into the choice theory. If "character" simply names our choosing agency, then responsibility for character is simply responsibility for choice, and there is no debate to have about which is the correct theory of responsibility. For the two theories to be as different as they seem to be, there must be a metaphysical difference between that aspect of our selves we call our character and that part we call our agency of choice. One can heighten the difference between the two theories by claiming that either character or will *constitutes* the self exclusive of the other; to maintain any difference at all between the two theories, however, one must see a metaphysical difference between character and will.

If we are clear about what character is, we next need to inquire whether and in what sense we can be *responsible* for our characters. One debate a choice theorist could have with a character theorist about the excuses is whether there is a responsibility for character at all.[49] If there is not, if there is only responsibility for actions, then the excuses cannot have as their function the isolation of actions expressing bad character; if one is not responsible for one's character, then responsibility for action cannot be derivative of that responsibility.

[48] Bernard Williams, *Problems of the Self* (Cambridge: Cambridge University Press, 1973), pp. 15–18.

[49] This appears to be the point at which Nicola Lacey believes the two theories of excuse diverge. See Lacey, *State Punishment*, p. 68.

This route to denying the character theory of excuse (by denying the character conception of responsibility that lies behind it) is not one I adopt. For I think it is obvious that, in some sense, we are responsible for being the kind of people that we are – i.e., for our characters. This includes responsibility for traits like greediness and honesty, emotions like love, gratitude, guilt, and envy, desires and ambitions, etc. There is a morality of virtue versus vice, not only for academic ethicists but also reflected in the common judgments of daily life. We morally judge our own and others' general moral worthiness all the time.[50]

There is room for disagreement as to exactly how, and in what sense, we are each responsible for our characters. With regard to the "how" question, there are two possibilities: (1) we are responsible for our characters because we *chose* to become persons with such character, or (2) we are responsible for our characters because we *are* (at least in part) our characters. The first possibility, of course, collapses the character conception of responsibility back into a choice conception of responsibility; on this view, the character theory of excuse becomes the idea that we hold persons responsible only for those choices (actions) expressive of their character, *and* we hold persons responsible only for those attributes of character that are themselves freely chosen. Choice ultimately is what matters on such a view, even if character mediately explains why we are responsible for some of our choices.

Despite the distinguished lineage of this first view in Aristotle,[51] there are two reasons to doubt its correctness. One is an empirical worry: do we really have much capacity to mold our characters? We do have some such capacity. We do form "second-order desires"[52] or "ego-ideals" about what kind of person we would like to become, and we have some causal power to effect changes in ourselves in conformity with such desires or ideals. Yet the social science on this issue gives little encouragement to thinking we have much of this power.[53]

Secondly, there is a conceptual worry: who is the "he" who is choosing character? Does he himself have any character, and, if so, was it chosen too? To the character theorist who grounds responsibility for choice and action in responsibility for character, a characterless chooser is an odd legitimator of responsibility for the character he chooses; yet a chooser of character who already possesses character before he chooses invites an infinite regress.[54]

[50] Consider but one example: the moral judgment Morgan Forster invited us to make of Henry Wilcox in Forster's novel, *Howard's End.* Forster persuasively presents Henry as having a fatally flawed character because of his failure "to connect," which defect was itself due to Henry's having a mind like "an unweeded garden." We rightly blame Henry for his flawed character, quite independently of the fact that that character leads him to do actions that are themselves clumsily hurtful to himself and others.

[51] Aristotle, *Nichomachean Ethics*, pp. 395–99. For explications of the Aristotelian view, see Charles Taylor, "Responsibility for Self," ed. A. Rorty, *The Identities of Persons* (Berkeley: University of California Press, 1976), pp. 281–99.

[52] Harry Frankfurt's description of our power to mold our own characters. Harry Frankfurt, "Freedom of the Will and the Concept of a Person," *Journal of Philosophy*, vol. 68, no. 1 (January 1971), pp. 5–20; Frankfurt, "Identification and Wholeheartedness," ed. F. Schoeman, *Responsibility, Character, and the Emotions* (Cambridge: Cambridge University Press, 1987), pp. 27–45.

[53] See Dressler, "Some Reflections," pp. 695–96 for doubts on these grounds.

[54] Seen clearly by Vuoso, "Background, Responsibility, and Excuse," p. 1676; Susan Wolf, "Sanity and the Metaphysics of Responsibility," ed. F. Schoeman, *Responsibility, Character, and the Emotions*, pp. 46–62; and Gary Watson, "Responsibility and the Limits of Evil," p. 281.

One might attempt to alleviate both these worries by what might be called the weak Aristotelian view.[55] This view concedes that our characters are formed initially by processes over which we have little choice or control; however, our responsibility for character comes from our later choices to *maintain* these already formed character traits. Patty Hearst, for example, may have had little choice in the processes that caused her to have the beliefs, desires, emotions, and dispositions that she had on emerging from the Symbionese Liberation Army's closet.[56] Responsibility for that character became hers, however, by the passage of time during which she maintained and/or failed to change those attributes of character. After some period of time, "Tania" was the character for whom Patty was responsible.[57]

The weak Aristotelian view at least sounds empirically more plausible. Even so, the weak view cannot accommodate all the attributes of self that intuitively are the proper subject of moral judgement. Take the emotions, for example. There seems very little that we can do about willing our emotions into or out of being. (Thus the oddness of questions like "why don't you love me?", as if not loving someone was a choice for which one was responsible.) Yet we do hold people responsible for their emotional makeup, including the presence or absence of particular emotions on particular occasions.[58] This inclines me to think that it is the second possibility that captures our responsibility for our character: we are responsible for our character because we are, in part, constituted by our characters.

Since we by-and-large do not choose to become or remain who we are, the sense in which we are *responsible* for our character no doubt differs from the sense in which we are responsible for our actions, which we do choose. "Responsibility" may not even be the right word here, for it is a kind of aesthetic morality that governs our assessments of character. Someone who lacks good character is poorly made, a defective being for a being of his or her kind. Unlike most aesthetic judgments, however, our judgments of character have moral overtones. We shun those with bad characters, avoid their friendship, and disadvantage them in various ways. Moreover, we feel entitled to so treat them because they deserve no better. To the extent that such persons did not choose their character, they are to that extent morally unlucky in being the defective creatures they are. The morality of the virtues, like that governing actions, has a good deal of moral luck built into it.

All of this should be a welcome conclusion to a character theorist about excuse, for if he avoids the conclusion that we are responsible for our character only insofar as we choose our character, then he has conceded nothing to the priority of choice

[55] See, e.g., Nozick, *Philosophical Explanations*, p. 396.

[56] For those too young to remember the Patty Hearst story, the 18-year-old Ms. Hearst was kidnapped by a group of would-be revolutionaries who subjected her to physical abuse, isolation, and indoctrination. At some point it appeared that this heiress to the conservative Hearst family empire succumbed to this indoctrination and believed in the justice of the revolutionary cause. She renamed herself "Tania" and appeared (complete with commando garb and assault rifle) in bank films as a voluntary participant in the revolutionary group's bank robbery.

[57] So argued by Dan Dennett, "Mechanism and Responsibility," ed. T. Honderich, *Essays on Freedom of Action* (London: Routledge and Kegan Paul, 1973), pp. 175–80.

[58] See the discussions of this in Moore, *Law and Psychiatry*, pp. 343–47, in Bernard Williams, "Morality and the Emotions," in his *Problems of the Self*, pp. 207–229, and in Sabini and Silver.

over character as the touchstone of responsibility. We should also be clear that such an answer also concedes nothing to the priority of character over choice, however. Thus far, all that has been established is that we have two different sorts of moral judgments that we appropriately make about persons: we hold them responsible for the actions they choose to do, and we hold them responsible for being the sort of people that they are. Although I have just rejected the claim that moral judgments about character are merely a disguised form of moral judgments about choice, that rejection says nothing in favor of the claim that moral judgments about choice are merely a disguised form of moral judgments about character. And it is this latter claim that the character theorist about excuse must establish.

Before we assess this crucial claim of the character theorist on its moral merits, we have one last clarificatory question to explore about the claim itself. This is the question of the sort of relationship that the character theorist asserts to exist between character and action that makes an actor responsible for action. The character theory of excuse variously asserts that we are excused from responsibility for our actions when those actions do not *manifest*, *express*, *reveal*, or *indicate* bad character; when such actions are not the *result* of, not *determined by*, *explained by*, or are not *attributed to* bad characters; when such actions are not an *exercise* of a character defect; or when such actions are not *evidentiary of* bad character.[59] We need to be clearer about what is meant by these expressions.

Three different sorts of relations might be meant by them. The first would be a logical relation between character and actions that are "in character." On this view, the relation between someone's greedy action on a particular occasion and his greedy character is the logical relation between a particular and the universal that it instantiates. Such a view of the relation commits one to a behavioral view of what character is, and that is sufficient reason for the character theorist to avoid it.

Preferable on this ground is a second view of the relation, which is that it is a causal relation. A greedy action, on this view, is in character for a person only if that action was caused by that person's greedy character. This view of the relation presupposes a nonbehavioral view of what character is, but that is a virtue – not a defect – of this relational view. There is a problem with this second view, however; it stems from the non-discriminating nature of the causal relation. Greedy character in a person can cause any number of behaviors besides greedy actions. My greed can cause my heart rate to go up (e.g., I get excited when I see large amounts of money). It can cause overtly generous behavior (e.g., Bulstrode in *Middlemarch*, who compensates for his greediness by overtly generous behavior). Indeed, any given character trait can probably cause virtually any kind of behavior on a given occasion. For example, suppose Van Gogh was greedy; his greed could have caused him to cut off his ear (e.g., by way of punishment of himself for not being paid enough for a picture).

George Vuoso, who sees the problem, attempts to contain the promiscuity of the causal relation by the pragmatics of explanatory utterance.[60] Vuoso attempts to

[59] All such expressions may be found in Nozick, *Philosophical Explanations*, p. 383; Bayles, "Character, Purpose, and Criminal Responsibility," p. 7; Brandt, "A Motivational Theory of Excuse," pp. 165, 169, 170, 171; Lacey, *State Punishment*, p. 66; Fletcher, *Rethinking Criminal Law*, pp. 799, 801.

[60] Vuoso, "Background, Responsibility, and Excuse," pp. 1672–73.

limit the causal relation to those instances when it would be appropriate to say "that character trait explains the action." Yet we might well say that about any of the foregoing examples, and I doubt that a character theorist holds them to be examples of actions "in character" for the greedy person.

If not, the character theorist has need of a more discriminating relation. The evidentiary relation is his best bet. Some act A will evidence some trait C if and only if not only C causes A, but also states of type C typically cause events of type A. Effects are evidence of their causes only when there is some general connection between the *class* of events that includes the effect and the *class* of events that includes the cause. Evidentiary inference is the more discriminating relation sought by the character theorist. Then acts of refusing to give to charities, forcing poor debtors to pay, paying employees as little as possible, etc., are acts "in character" for the greedy person; lopping off one's ear, or giving away all of one's money, are not acts "in character" for some greedy person even if they happen on some occasion to be caused by his greed.

This last clarification allows us to pinpoint what are and are not the differences between the two theories of excuse. One difference that does not exist is the difference between "historical" and "mesh" theories.[61] That is, one cannot contrast the character theory to the choice theory on the ground that the first is concerned only with the "mesh" (or logical fit) of action with the actor's character and not with any historical inquiry into an action's genesis. The nonbehaviorist account of character, and the evidentiary account of the relation between character and actions "in character" makes the character theory focus on an action's genesis too.

The difference between the two theories has to be in the kinds of causes of action they each find to be the touchstone of responsibility: character or choice. Whether there is any difference between the two theories boils down to the question of whether there is any difference between a person's character and his choices. On the assumption that choices are possible only if a person has and exercises a choosing agency (will), the question is whether there is a difference between a person having a character and a person having a will. The evidentiary relation just discussed seems to isolate just such a difference: any action evidences the possession of a will, because a will can typically will anything and still be a will. But as we have seen, while a character *can* cause any action, to be possessed of a character precludes the possibility that one's character can *typically* cause any class of actions equally well. Characters, to be characters, can only typically cause some classes of actions, but not others. Character in this sense is inherently general, requiring typical causal connections to classes of actions; will and the choices that issue from it are in this sense particular, being equally capable of causing any particular act and not being tied to any general class of actions.

[61] For the contrast between "historical" versus "mesh" theories of responsibility, see John Martin Fischer, "Responsiveness and Moral Responsibility," ed. F. Schoeman, *Responsibility, Character, and the Emotions*, pp. 81–100, at 103–5. Fischer is a choice theorist (his "reasons-responsiveness" test being his way of measuring free choice) who criticizes certain character theorists (Frankfurt, Watson) for being ahistorical in the sense indicated in the text.

III. Character versus Choice as the Touchstone of Responsibility and Excuse

Perhaps the place to start in assessing the moral merits of the two theories of excuse is with the main arguments put forward by the character theorists in favor of their theory. Unfortunately, of the five main arguments, four are irrelevant to the moral issue I wish to raise. Let me mention them, if only to put them aside.

One is the argument that proceeds from utilitarian (or, more broadly, consequentialist) theories of punishment. Richard Brandt[62] and Nicola Lacey[63] both make arguments of this type in favor of the character theory of excuse, Brandt from his rule-utilitarian theory of punishment and Lacey from her non-utilitarian but consequentialist theory of punishment. Briefly, the argument is that the preventive goals of punishment do not require its infliction on those whose actions have not manifested bad character, because such persons are not dangerous nor can their punishment have any significant deterrent effect. It is not clear to me that the character theory of excuse would better serve crime–prevention goals than would the choice theory. But in any case, the argument for me is a non-starter since it proceeds from an unacceptable theory of punishment. At the very least, moral innocence should operate as a side constraint on the pursuit of goals like crime prevention; what we need is a theory of excuse that tells us when someone is morally innocent. These utilitarian and consequentialist arguments do not tell us that, so we may put them aside.

A second argument, one that also does not address the moral issue about excuses focused for us by the mixed and retributivist theories of punishment, is the argument of Michael Bayles and others which is designed to show how well the character theory fits the legal excuses that presently exist in American law.[64] This is an exercise in doctrinal exegesis that is relevant to deciding what theory of excuse our present law comes closest to instantiating. It is not an exercise capable of answering the normative question of which theory of excuse our law ought to recognize.

A third argument in favor of the character theory is by far the major consideration which in fact motivates character theorists to adopt their theory.[65] This is the argument that proceeds from hard determinist premises. The assumption is that the choice conception of responsibility is in trouble because it is hostage to the questionable truth of libertarian (Strawson: "panicky") metaphysics; if determinism turns out to be true, the choice conception is assumed to have the unhappy implication that no one is responsible for anything. Whereas, the

[62] See particularly Brandt, "A Motivational Theory of Excuses," pp. 184–94.

[63] Lacey, *State Punishment*, pp. 65–72.

[64] Bayles, "Character, Purpose, and Criminal Responsibility."

[65] See Lacey, *State Punishment*, pp. 65, 73; Vuoso, "Background, Responsibility, and Excuse"; Strawson, "Freedom and Resentment"; Scanlon, "Quality of Will"; Watson, "Responsibility and the Limits of Evil"; Fletcher, *Rethinking Criminal Law*, pp. 801–2; Nozick, *Philosophical Explanations*, pp. 393–96. Of the character theorists, only Richard Brandt and Peter Arenella see clearly that a characterological conception of responsibility has no advantage over a choice conception in answering the hard determinist. See Brandt, "A Motivational Theory of Excuse," p. 172; Arenella, "Character, Choice, and Moral Agency," *Social Philosophy & Policy*, vol. 7, no. 2 (Spring 1990).

character theorist thinks, responsibility can be preserved by his theory even in the face of determinism. So long as he rejects Aristotle's notion that we are responsible for our characters because we choose them, and sticks to the idea that we are responsible for our characters because we are our characters, he escapes any threat from determinism. For his idea of responsibility does not depend on an actor's choices being free. Rather, he can happily admit that responsible choices are caused by character, and that character in turn is caused by factors not themselves chosen by the actor. By *his* idea of responsibility, the actor is responsible for any actions in character just because he is his character. This is known in the trade as the "character-stop" answer to determinism.[66]

There is nothing wrong with the character-stop strategy. This is why that part of morality known as the theory of the virtues is not hostage to the falsity of determinism. However, the character theorist overlooks the fact that the choice conception of responsibility has an answer just as good to the hard determinist: we are at least in part the agency that chooses whether to act or not; that agency's choices can themselves exist even if caused by factors external to the will; it would make choice a very peculiar event if it has to be uncaused in order to exist; there is no persuasive argument showing that choices have this peculiar feature; and the fact that some people find such arguments persuasive can be explained in ways having nothing to do with the truth of the arguments in question. I and others have sought to draw this argument out in detail, and the conclusion – that compatibilism between choice and causation is true – is far from being problematic and worrisome within philosophy, but is now a kind of philosophical orthodoxy. As one not very sympathetic philosopher has recently observed, "compatiblism, as a philosophical position, has become complacent."[67]

Any argument for the character theory proceeding from that theory's supposed advantage in answering hard determinism had better first show why the philosophical orthodoxy about compatibilism is false. Since none of the character theorists undertake this uphill struggle, we should ignore arguments for the character theory built on this shaky metaphysical base.

A fourth argument for the character theory proceeds from a very general intellectual fashion prevalent today. This I have elsewhere called "interpretivism."[68] Briefly, the idea is that moral questions (if not the explanatory questions of social and even natural science) are interpretive questions, questions that seek the best interpretation of various social practices. To ask what responsibility is, or when a person is responsible, is to ask what the best interpretation of the "blaming stories" prevalent in our society might be. The character theory of excuse appears to be favored by interpretivists because such a theory requires "more story" than

[66] For a contemporary use of the character-stop argument, see Nozick, *Philosophical Explanations*, pp. 395. The character-stop argument has not been without its critics. See, e.g., John Hospers, "Meaning and Free Will," *Philosophy and Phenomenological Research*, vol. 10 (1950), pp. 307–30.

[67] Ferdinand Schoeman, "Introduction," *Responsibility, Character, and the Emotions*, p. 5. Schoeman appears to favor the character theory of excuse (see *ibid*., pp. 2–3), perhaps because he is not so convinced of the truth of compatibilism.

[68] Moore, "The Interpretive Turn in Modern Theory: A Turn for the Worse?," *Stanford Law Review*, vol. 41, no. 4 (April 1989), pp. 871–957.

does the choice theory. That is, to see whether an action expresses the agent's character requires a longer, more complete narration of what sort of person, in general, he is; whereas to see whether an action was freely chosen by an agent seemingly requires a more limited enquiry into his capacities and opportunities at the moment of acting.

It is hard to get a handle on just what this argument comes to. Even if one's metaethics commits one to viewing moral reasoning as storytelling and -retelling, why should one prefer "more story"? Are not "short stories" an appropriate genre? The interpretivists here sound like the psychiatrists of the 1950s who criticized the M'Naughten definition of insanity on the ground that it did not allow them to tell their psychiatric stories.[69] In both cases, we should like to know why the stories someone wants to tell are better because they are closer to some relevant truth.

It is a fifth kind of argument in favor of the character theory of excuse that raises the relevant issues. Consider George Fletcher's nonutilitarian appreciation of the need for this kind of argument:

> An inference from the wrongful act to the actor's character is essential to a retributive theory of punishment. A fuller statement of the argument would go like this: (1) punishing wrongful conduct is just only if punishment is measured by the desert of the offender, (2) the desert of the offender is gauged by his character – i.e., the kind of person he is, (3) and therefore, a judgment about character is essential to the just distribution of punishment.[70]

It is the second premise, of course, that the character theorist must defend.

Despite her consequentialist leanings (and her resulting disavowals of any intent to answer the question of moral blameworthiness), Nicolas Lacey presents some defense of this essential premise. She defends the moral view that "it is unfair to hold people responsible for actions which are out of character . . . fair to hold them so for actions in which their settled dispositions are centrally expressed."[71] In order to test the moral correctness of these conclusions, we should construct examples of two kinds: (1) an actor freely chooses to do wrong (i.e., he had the capacity and a fair opportunity not to so choose), and yet the action is "out of character" for that actor; (2) an actor's behavior is good evidence for a settled disposition (character) of a bad kind, and yet he has not (yet) chosen to act on that disposition. If Lacy is right, we ought to find it fair to punish the second but not the first, because the first but not the second has a moral excuse. However, I shall contend that we rightly find it fair to punish the first but not the second, because we rightly think the second but not the first to have a moral excuse.

[69] See the discussion in Moore, *Law and Psychiatry*, p. 228. Because the M'Naughten test required that a defendant be unable to know either the nature and quality of his action or that it was wrong in order to be excused by reason of insanity, many psychiastrists were frustrated by the lack of fit of their "stories" (psychiatric explanations) and the story the law required them to tell. In criticizing the M'Naughten test on this ground, what they overlooked was why the law should care that their story didn't fit the law's concerns about responsibility and blame.

[70] Fletcher, *Rethinking Criminal Law*, p. 800.

[71] Lacey, *State Punishment*, p. 68.

As an example of the first kind, consider the well-publicized killing of Bonnie Garland by her jilted boyfriend, Richard Herrin.[72] Bonnie was an undergraduate at Yale; Richard was a graduate student there. Richard had not had much experience with women, and he found Yale a lonely and alien place. He had grown up in the *barrio* of East Los Angeles, but had succeeded at getting good grades and was, by all accounts, a stunning success. He early and heavily committed himself emotionally to Bonnie once a romance had begun between them. Before too long, she found his neediness off-putting and sought to break off the relationship. Like many people whose kindness makes them weak and unintentionally cruel, she couldn't bring herself to break it off with Richard cleanly. He accordingly felt misled, hurt, and frustrated by her attempt to let him down gradually.

Staying over at her parents' house one night, Richard decided he couldn't stand it any more. He went down to the basement, looking around for something with which to kill her. He found a claw hammer and proceeded upstairs to her room with it. Finding her asleep, he beat her to death with the hammer. He had planned to commit suicide after the act, but found he could not bring himself to do it and instead sought out some Christian counseling.

Richard had the capacity not to choose to kill Bonnie, and he had a fair opportunity to exercise that capacity. Nonetheless, he chose to kill her. For that, to my mind, he fully deserved the eight to twenty-five year sentence he received for Bonnie's killing. Yet a character theorist should find this conviction unfair, for the act was out of character for Richard. Richard himself felt that way about his sentence:

> Herrin: I feel the sentence was excessive.
>
> Gaylin (a psychiastrist interviewing Herrin in prison): Let's talk about that a little.
>
> Herrin: Well, I feel that way now . . . Considering all the factors that I feel the judge should have considered: prior history of arrest, my personality background, my capacity for a productive life in society – you know, those kinds of things – I don't think he took those into consideration. He looked at the crime itself . . . This being my first arrest and considering the circumstances, I don't think I should have been given eight to twenty-five years.[73]

Richard wanted credit for an otherwise good – even, in some ways, exemplary – life. He felt it was unfair to have eight years of his life taken from him because of a momentary choice that was at odds with who he really was and how he both had lived and would live his life. His choice to kill Bonnie in the middle of a sleepless night must have looked, in retrospect, like an unbelievable action for him.

Yet is there any doubt at all that Richard Herrin was seriously culpable for his choice? No matter how out of character this act was for him behaviorally, no matter how alien it seemed to him phenomenologically, *he* horribly violated another's

[72] The facts below are taken from William Gaylin, *The Killing of Bonnie Garland* (New York: Penguin Books, 1983).

[73] *ibid.*, p. 325.

rights at a single point in time. His generally good character puzzles us, because we don't understand very well how a generally kind, non-violent (if somewhat weak) individual could do what he did. But such explanatory puzzlement is not accompanied by a similar puzzlement about his responsibility: his clear choice to do evil is sufficient to make him very culpable.

Character theorists have two responses to such examples. They might deny that someone like Herrin is culpable. Or they could deny that Herrin's action was really out of character. I shall first deal with the second kind of response.

A character theorist might think that Richard Herrin really did have bad character that was evidenced by his choice to kill Bonnie – but it was a *hidden* character defect. Yet the character theorist has to be careful here, lest "hidden character defect" become her label for "free choice." "Character," as we have seen, has to mean something considerably more general than merely a disposition to do the particular act done – on pain of this kind of collapse of the character theory into the choice theory. By "bad character," Lacey (for example) means a settled hostility to, rejection of, or indifference to the values of the community that the criminal law exists to protect and foster.[74] Richard Herrin had no such settled hostility, indifference, or rejection, so presumably he would be included by Lacey in the category of those excused: "To punish those who have exhibited no such hostility [to the values protected by the criminal law] would be to fly directly in the face of those values themselves. . . ."[75]

Any theory of excuse that has an implication that people like Richard Herrin ought to be excused is a bad theory of excuse. Those character theorists opting for the first response above (denying that Herrin was responsible) obviously disagree. Their disagreement seems to me to be motivated by two intuitions, one metaphysical and the other moral. The metaphysical intuition is that it wasn't really Richard that did the killing, because who Richard is is guided by his character so that an act truly out of character was no act of Richard's. Lacey appears to adopt this idea when she holds that the criminal law should "respond punitively only to actions which are in a real sense [the actor's] *own* . . ."[76] She appears to equate this with actions centrally expressive of settled features of the actor's character. Elsewhere, Lacey elaborates that the criminal law should "treat seriously the individuality and sense of identity of each citizen by responding punitively only to actions which are genuinely expressive of the actor's relevant disposition: with which the agent truly identifies, and can call her own."[77] If this means what it seems to mean – what I have called the metaphysical intuition that actions we do are not *our* actions unless they are in character for us – then it is hostage to a very problematic theory of personal identity. This is the theory that holds character to swamp both spatiotemporal contiguity and unified consciousness as the touchstone of personal identity.[78] On this theory, we are only our

[74] Lacey, *State Punishment*, pp. 189–90.

[75] *ibid.*, p. 189.

[76] *ibid.*, p. 71.

[77] *ibid.*, p. 77.

[78] For a discussion of these three factors as determining personal identity, see Michael Moore, "The Unity of the Self," ed. M. Ruse, *Nature Animated* (Dordrecht: Reidel, 1982), revised and reprinted as chapters 3 and 11 of Moore, *Law and Psychiatry*.

character, a conclusion that has two startling implications. First, when "we" radically change our character over time, we literally become someone else – not just another kind of person, but a different person. Second, multiple-personalitied persons are not single persons with multiple characters; they are rather many persons with one character each. This allowance of the possibility that many persons can inhabit one body – either over time or even at one time – raises havoc with some basic metaphysical, moral, and legal ideas that are difficult to imagine giving up.[79] One of those ideas is just the sort of thing Lacey is apparently willing to abandon: namely, how we individuate and attribute basic actions to persons. Normally we do this by the body involved in the action: one movement by one body, one basic action. Yet multiple persons (characters) acting through one body could yield a variety of possibilities: several actions, if the movement was in character for several characters; one action, but by "someone" other than the person at home at the time the action was performed; or no action, if the action was not in character for any of the characters sharing one human body. These implications are so unacceptable that we should not think of character as exclusively constituting the identity of persons – and if we do not think this, then we cannot think that an action out of character is no action of ours.[80]

The moral intuition that may motivate denials of culpability like Herrin's is a kind of "there but for the grace of God go I" intuition, for isolated acts of violence like Herrin's may well seem possible for any of us in the right circumstances. Yet it would still be us, even if we slipped like Herrin slipped . . . We are all basically good, we hope. Yet if we think about how we would view ourselves in this circumstance, would it in fact be excusing of ourselves, as Richard excused himself? Wouldn't it rather be that we felt guilty unto death for our horrible violation of another? Far from leading to conclusions of excuse, for me this thought-experiment yields a judgment of very heavy culpability when someone like Herrin steps out of his otherwise good character to perform a wrongful act.[81]

I said that there were two kinds of examples with which to test the choice versus character theory of excuse on moral grounds. I now turn to the second kind of example, where there is behavior revealing bad character, but no free choice to do wrong. Virtually any preventive detention example will do – e.g., Dallas Williams, in whom psychiastrists detected violent character traits even though Williams had not yet acted upon them.[82] May someone like Williams fairly be punished even though he has done nothing wrong?

[79] I explore some of these in *Law and Psychiatry*, pp. 147–52.

[80] Perhaps Lacey intends a less metaphysical defense here. To speak of a "sense of identity" is not necessarily to speak of personal identity, for who we *think* we are need not coincide with who we are in fact. Yet then Lacey has no basis for saying that an action out of character is not our action. Rather, such a phenomenological observation can only generate the conclusion that we have disowned (not identified with) one of *our* own actions.

[81] I pursue this thought-experiment in the context of justifying a retributive theory of punishment in Moore, "The Moral Worth of Retribution," pp. 212–16.

[82] See Jay Katz, Joseph Goldstein, and Alan Dershowitz, *Psychoanalysis, Psychiatry, and Law* (New York: Free Press, 1967), pp. 526–35 for the history of the real Dallas Williams.

The question is a hard one for the character theorist. After all, he thinks that we are ultimately responsible for our characters and that action-responsibility is only a derivative of this more basic character-responsibility. If this is true, then why not punish people directly for bad character, since that is the locus of their just deserts? Why punish bad character indirectly, only through punishing actions expressive of it? George Fletcher seeks to answer this question in terms of a value distinct from the justice of the guilty getting their just deserts: namely, privacy.

> The limitation of the inquiry to a single wrongful act follows not from the theory of desert, but from the principle of legality. We accept the artificiality of inferring character from a single deed as the price of maintaining the suspect's privacy ... Disciplining the inquiry in this way ... secures the individual against a free-ranging enquiry of the state into his moral worth.[83]

I mention Fletcher's argument because it illustrates a kind of argument that cannot establish what the character theorist needs to establish here. Much of the literature on "punishment for thoughts alone" is persuasive on why it would be undesirable for various reasons to dispense with the *actus reus* requirement of the criminal law.[84] But our moral question has only to do with the *fairness* of dispensing with the *actus reus* requirement. That punishment would be *deserved* because of bad character alone is something the character theorist seems committed to, however much other values prevent punishment of this class of deserving persons.

Nozick sees the need to escape this seeming implication of the character theory – namely, that people with bad character do deserve punishment directly for their character and not for actions, if any, expressing that character.[85] Yet Nozick's escape is only a statement of the conclusion needed by him: "It is through actions that correct values are flouted; the actions constitute the flouting. ... Since it is flouting that is to be punished, actions are required."[86] Stated this tersely, Nozick's argument says little more than his conclusion. If flouting is a kind of action, then Nozick is by definition correct that only actions can constitute flouting: but why is the action of flouting required for a just punishment? Alternatively, if flouting is not necessarily a kind of action, why isn't the possession of bad character a flouting of the values that show it to be bad?

If the character theory were correct, the answer given to Moliere's Robespierre (when the latter asks why he is being condemned to death) should not be jarring: you are being condemned, Robespierre is told, "because you lack grace." Yet the answer is jarring precisely because no one deserves to be punished for being a poor specimen of humanity. The aesthetic kind of responsibility that we admittedly do have for so much of our characters as are unchosen cannot fairly lead to

[83] Fletcher, *Rethinking*, pp. 800–801.

[84] For example, Lacey's argument in *State Punishment*, p. 199. The criminal law's "*actus reus* requirement" forbids punishment for bad states of mind or bad character; it is necessary for punishment that the defendant performed a forbidden action.

[85] Nozick sees the question clearly (*Philosophical Explanations*, pp. 380–82) before giving his own answer (*ibid.*, pp. 383–84).

[86] *ibid.*, p. 384.

punishment, because we could not have avoided possessing these aspects of ourselves. A choice theorist – even one such as myself who admits that there is such a think as responsibility for unchosen character – can readily say this, because he conceives of the existence of two independent kinds of (and bases for) responsibility. I have yet to see how the character theorist can deny that character-responsibility alone makes it fair to punish, given his notion that character-responsibility is basic and act-responsibility only derivative.

Both kinds of examples point to the choice theory of excuse, for only it excuses where there is no choice, no matter how much bad character may be exhibited (the second kind of example); it doesn't excuse where there is a free choice, however much out of character it may be (the first kind of example). I accordingly reject the character theory of excuse on these moral grounds.

While I find these moral thought-experiments to be conclusive against the character theorist, the latter is not without her own troublesome counterexamples. Her best stem from our apparent responsibility for negligence. The character theorist may think that people who negligently cause harm are morally responsible. Taking that judgment to be secure, she then claims (1) that such responsibility for negligent conduct cannot be squared with the choice theory, and (2) that such responsibility is just what one should expect on the character theory.[87] I shall address each of these two claims separately before returning to the underlying assumption that negligence generates responsibility.

Responsibility for negligence *is* difficult to square with the choice conception of responsibility for the obvious reason that a negligent actor does not choose to do the complex act (such as killing) that is forbidden. True, such an actor does choose to do some basic action, such as moving his finger on the trigger of his gun; and it also may be true that he chooses to do more complex acts (such as hitting a target) through his doing of the basic act of moving his finger. But in the sense of choice earlier described, he does not choose to do the complex action forbidden by morality and law (such as killing the man standing behind the target) because his mind was not adverting to that aspect of his action.[88]

Herbert Hart's attempt to reconcile responsibility for negligence with the choice conception of responsibility results in a considerable alteration of the choice conception. Hart argued that although the negligent actor did not choose to do a

[87] Lacey makes both of these points: she concludes that "negligence liability ... sits unhappily with traditional conceptions of responsibility in the criminal law" (*State Punishment*, pp. 105–6), and that "the link with a possible rationale for negligence liability is obvious" (*ibid*, p. 66) on the character theory of responsibility.

[88] A choice theorist who rejects my notion of choice might deny that we ever do hold people responsible for unchosen actions. Negligence, he might say, is not a *mens rea* requirement like knowledge or recklessness; rather, it is a criterion of wrongful action. As such, the injunction "don't kill negligently" is a shorthand for all the injunctions aimed at more particular actions, such as "don't shoot at a target without first ascertaining whether someone is behind it or not." And those latter acts, he might conclude, are chosen under every aspect that makes them wrongful. The lesser responsibility for negligent (as opposed to intentional) killing is not due to the differential presence of choice, but the differential wrongness of the acts chosen.

Tempting as this line may be, it slurs over the crucial fact that someone who only negligently kills (e.g., by shooting at a paper target without checking for persons behind it) does not choose just that feature of his action that makes it wrongful; in the example given, he does not make a choice one way or the other about checking. It simply doesn't occur to him to check, although it should have.

wrongful act, he had the capacity and a fair opportunity to have chosen not to do it, and is therefore fairly blamable for his non-exercise of that capacity.[89] So long as we individualize the standard by which we judge an actor's behavior so that we can say of him, "he could have done otherwise, given his capacities,"[90] then, Hart urges, we may blame negligent actors with as much confidence as we do intentional wrongdoers.[91]

In accommodating responsibility for negligence in this way, Hart, as he recognized, shifted the touchstone of responsibility from choice to capacity.[92] A choice to do a wrongful act then becomes only one way in which the actor's capacity to avoid evil goes unexercised; inadvertence is another. My objection to this shift is a moral one: it relegates choice to a subsidiary role in our responsibility assessments that our judgments won't support. What makes the intentional or reckless wrongdoer so culpable is not unexercised capacity – although that is necessary – but the way such capacity to avoid evil goes unexercised; such wrongdoers are not even trying to get it right. Their capacity goes unexercised because that is what they choose. Choice is essential to their culpability, not one way among others that they could have been seriously culpable.

Does this mean that when we blame for negligence we blame for character (the second of the character theorist's two claims here)? Interestingly enough, although the choice theorist cannot easily accommodate responsibility for negligence, neither can the character theorist. For the character theorist must bridge two gaps in order to link her theory with responsibility for negligence. The first is the gap between the failure of a negligent actor to advert to the risk that made his action negligent *at the time of that action*, on the one hand, and the *general tendency* of such an actor to be inadvertent about such risks, on the other. Thus, Lacey (for example) urges that we may infer of the actor who makes an unreasonable mistake of fact that "this is a person who systematically, characteristically makes unreasonable mistakes causing danger to the interests of others . . ."[93] This may indeed be an inference we may sometimes draw, but the fact is ignored that we hold negligent actors responsible irrespective of whether one can draw such an inference or not. Put simply, judgments of negligence don't depend on any general traits of carelessness; an isolated act of negligence suffices for responsibility for the harm that act causes.

The second gap is between the actor who does "systematically, characteristically make unreasonable mistakes" and the bad character of such an actor. Lacey thinks we can infer from the presence of such mistake–proneness in a person that that person had a "genuine practical indifference to the interests protected by the criminal law," such as the interests of others in their bodily integrity.[94] Again, this

[89] H.L.A. Hart, "Negligence, *Mens Rea*, and Criminal Responsibility," in *Punishment and Responsibility*, pp. 136–57. I earlier adopted Hart's view in *Law and Psychiatry*, pp. 81–84.

[90] A point on which Hart's view of the moral idea of negligence diverges considerably from present law on the subject. See "Negligence, *Mens Rea*, and Criminal Responsibility," pp. 152–57.

[91] *ibid.*, p. 152.

[92] *ibid.*, p. 140.

[93] Lacey, *State Punishment*, p. 66.

[94] *ibid.*

is indeed sometimes an inference we can draw about a careless person, because a general attitude of indifference to others does sometimes explain such carelessness. But one can be careless – even characteristically so – without having a bad character in this sense. Such carelessness can be due to awkwardness and stupidity as easily as indifference. And, again, we blame for carelessness irrespective of *why* one is careless.[95]

Thus responsibility for negligence fits poorly with either conception of responsibility. When we attribute moral responsibility to someone for a negligent act, we cannot base such attribution either on a judgment of culpable choice or of culpable character. Negligent actors may often have both, but to be negligent they need have neither. What this suggests to me is that perhaps negligence by itself does not merit any moral blame,[96] and that its presence in the law has to be explained on purely utilitarian grounds.

Negligence does not exhaust the kinds of moral thought–experiments the character theorist might use to support her theory. The criminal law we have suggests several others.[97] All of such thought–experiments will be of one of the two kinds I earlier distinguished, where bad choice is present but bad character is not or where bad character is present but bad choice is not. (The latter is where negligence allegedly falls.) Unlike my own thought–experiments, of course, the character theorist's will assume there is responsibility in the second sort of situation but not in the first.

In thinking through such thought–experiments, two things should be borne in mind. One is that it is not enough to show that *usually* an inference of bad character can (or cannot) be drawn when moral excuse fails (or succeeds). A theory of excuse has to do better than this, and tell us what it is that always makes us responsible and, in its absence, always excuses us. Secondly, it is not enough to show the presence or absence of bad character whenever an excuse fails or succeeds; one must also show that the presence or absence of bad choice does not stand in that same relation to the excuse in question. After all, bad choices are usually made by bad people, and bad people usually make a lot of bad choices, so it shouldn't be surprising if the two theories overlap greatly when they excuse. Still, they do not always excuse in the same situations. Moreover, even when both theories yield the same conclusions about responsibility, it is important that we understand the reasons on which these conclusions are based. If I am right in this essay, we excuse because culpable choice is lacking, not because the action fails to manifest bad character.

Law, University of Pennsylvania

[95] The extent to which this last statement is true depends upon the degree to which we individualize the standard of care by virtue of which we judge an actor negligent. If morality is like Anglo-American law here, ignoring the different degrees to which people are hasty, awkward, and stupid, then our judgments of carelessness are blind to these different explanations of carelessness.

[96] A conclusion that should be agreed to by character theorists too. See Bayles, "Character, Purpose, and Criminal Responsibility," pp. 10–11, who sees that "on the basis of one careless act, the inference to a careless attitude is less valid," sees that such carelessness "does not indicate an attitude of indifference to standards of care," and concludes that, on the character theory, "the basis for blame [for negligence] is much less sure."

[97] See Dressler, "Reflections," p. 693, n.107, for a partial list of where the law appears to take character into account. See also Bayles, "Character, Purpose, and Criminal Responsibility."

CHARACTER, CHOICE AND MORAL AGENCY: THE RELEVANCE OF CHARACTER TO OUR MORAL CULPABILITY JUDGMENTS*

By Peter Arenella

Introduction

Should a person who cannot appreciate the moral significance of legal norms qualify as a blameworthy actor simply because he has the capacity to comply with them for non-moral reasons? Such a person may lack any empathy for other human beings and view moral norms as arbitrary restraints on his self-interested behavior: does he nevertheless deserve moral blame when he makes an instrumentally "rational choice" to breach a norm governing his action? Should our answers to these questions depend on whether we believe that the actor is morally responsible for lacking these moral emotions and understandings? In short, must we concern ourselves with those aspects of the agent's character – his goals, desires, values, emotions, and perceptions of what courses of action are available to him – that motivate his rational choices? Or are questions about what motivates the actor to exercise his capacity for rational choice irrelevant to our judgments concerning his moral culpability for violating some governing norm?

One way of thinking about such questions is to ask what attributes a person must possess to qualify as an appropriate addressee of moral norms and a suitable object of moral blame. Must a moral agent have the capacity to respond to moral norms as a reason for his choices? Must he also be able to control those aspects of his character that impair his capacity to make moral choices?

Most legal theorists insist that moral agents do not need such capacities to be fairly blamed for violating the minimal moral restraints that the criminal law imposes on their self-interested acts. These scholars claim that the actor's capacity for rational self-determined action is alone sufficient to justify treating him as someone worthy of moral address and evaluation. In their view, moral agents are simply beings whose powers of rational choice give them the capacity to comply with governing norms. Accordingly, individuals who could not have chosen to comply with the law for a moral reason still qualify as moral agents as long as they are capable of responding to non-moral reasons for obeying the law. When such an actor makes a rational choice to engage in conduct that breaches the governing norm, he deserves moral blame because he could have chosen to comply with it.

* I would like to thank David Dolinko, John Fischer, Jean Hampton, Stephen Morse, Stephen Munzer, Steven Shiffrin, Ken Simons, Stephen Yeazell, and John Varat for their helpful comments on earlier drafts of this essay. I owe a special debt of gratitude to Robert Goldstein and Lucie White for their remarkable intellectual generosity.

This essay argues that the rational choice model of moral responsibility does not adequately justify those judgments of criminal culpability that impose moral blame[1] on the criminal. It does so by attacking that model's "thin" account of a moral agent's attributes and its premise: that deserved attributions of moral blame do not depend on any assumptions about the actor's capacity for moral choice.

Moral theorists generally agree that moral blame is appropriate when three conditions are satisfied: (1) a moral agent (2) must breach some governing moral norm (3) under circumstances [e.g., fair attribution conditions[2]] that gave the moral agent a fair opportunity to avoid its breach. This paper offers an internal critique of the rational choice model's account of these three elements of moral culpability.

I shall argue that choice theorists have paid insufficient attention to the first two conditions of moral culpability and how they relate to each other. Consequently, they have frequently ignored differences between moral and legal norms that should bear on any defensible account of moral culpability.[3] Most choice theorists begin their analysis of moral blame by offering a legalized version of the last

[1] Not all violations of criminal law conduct rules constitute breaches of some independent moral norm. Consequently, establishing that the criminal defendant is morally responsible for breaching a legal norm does not justify an attribution of deserved moral blame unless the actor's conduct also breaches some governing moral norm. See text accompanying notes 2–3 below; see also note 3 below and text accompanying notes 21–22 below. This essay thus concerns criminal culpability judgments for "mala in se" crimes whose commission constitutes a breach of both moral and legal norms.

[2] A word about terminology. I have deliberately avoided using the term "moral act-responsibility" to describe this third condition; even though choice theorists themselves believe that their account of this third condition justifies holding individuals morally responsible for their acts. My central thesis is that one cannot make ultimate sense of moral responsibility for action unless one recognizes that this concept rests on a logically prior and independent conception of moral agency. Accordingly, I have used the term "fair attribution conditions" to convey the choice theorists' claim that satisfaction of this requirement establishes that the defendant deserves moral blame because the defendant's breach of a norm can be fairly attributed to him.

[3] One striking illustration of this claim can be found in the work of retributivist choice theorists who appear to assume that the actor's moral responsibility for breaching a legal norm concerning morally neutral conduct establishes his moral culpability.

These theorists acknowledge a discrepancy between legal and moral blame whenever the law does not require proof that the specific breach of the governing norm can be fairly attributed to the actor. See note 21 below. However, most of these theorists do not discuss whether it is appropriate to impose moral blame for the breach of legal norms fairly attributed to the actor that violate no independent moral norm. Those theorists who do touch on this question tend to blur the distinction between breaches of legal and moral norms.

Consider Professor Kadish's treatment of the problem.

> To blame a person is to express a moral criticism, and if the person's action does not deserve criticism, blaming him is a kind of falsehood and, to the extent the person is injured by being blamed, unjust to him. It is this feature of our everyday moral practices that lies behind the law's excuses ....
>
> It may be argued that though this may be true of excuses in everyday moral judgment, it is not true of the criminal law, because it is not intrinsic to judgments of criminality in our society that they express a moral fault. But this is surely mistaken. Certainly not all criminal conduct is independently immoral. In some cases the law attaches criminal penalties as well to conduct that, apart from its being prohibited, is not immoral. But in either case criminal conviction charges a moral fault – if not the violation of a moral standard embodied in the criminal prohibition, then the fault of doing what the law has forbidden. Sanford H. Kadish, "Excusing Crime," in *Blame and Punishment* (New York: MacMillan, 1987), p. 87.

condition concerning fair attribution conditions. Their model explains when the actor's breach of a legal norm can be fairly attributed to her as something that she had a fair opportunity to avoid. They then derive their conception of moral agency from their account of the capacities presumed by such fair attribution conditions.

This "fair attribution" view of moral agency does not explain why adults are worthy of moral address and evaluation, because it ignores the special attributes an individual needs to understand and use moral norms as a reason for his action. A discussion of cases concerning moral psychopaths, actors who fail to behave like "reasonable persons," and brainwashed defendants will demonstrate that individuals need far more than rational choice abilities to respond appropriately to moral norms, including those that only impose minimal restraints on their self-interested acts.

I shall suggest that the individual's capacity for moral responsiveness encompasses several distinct but interrelated abilities to react to moral norms in thought, feeling, perception, and behavior. In assessing whether individuals deserve moral blame for their acts when they lack such attributes or fail to exercise them competently, we should consider whether these agents can control those aspects of their character that impair their capacity for moral responsiveness. Only a character-based conception of a moral agent's necessary attributes can explain how this capacity for moral responsiveness is developed and why it is sometimes fair to blame actors who fail to exercise this capacity.

This essay is part of a larger project that demonstrates the extent to which we depend on descriptive and normative conceptions of character to help us interpret and defend the moral significance of human action. One objective of that project is to show how these character constructs infuse our cultural blaming stories about the normative significance of our chosen acts. By suppressing this link between character and choice, rational choice theorists offer an impoverished account of moral blame that does not accurately reflect the meaning of moral culpability embedded in our actual blaming practices. My goal in this essay is to show how this intimate link between character and choice also infuses the most persuasive theoretical account of a moral agent's necessary attributes.

I. A Brief Overview of the Rational Choice Model

One of the major distinctions between the criminal law and other legal methods of constraining people's behavior is that a criminal conviction often conveys a message of moral as well as legal censure of the actor for engaging in such activity. Legal liability to significant punishment usually depends on a demonstration that the actor was morally responsible for his crime. And most courts, legislatures, and

---

Left unexplained is why this latter "fault" of doing what the law has forbidden should qualify as a breach of some independent moral norm that subjects the actor to deserved moral blame. Certainly, it is not always a moral fault to deliberately violate a legal norm that prohibits morally neutral conduct. Thus, demonstrating that an actor intentionally violated a legal norm that he could have chosen to obey can not, by itself, establish that he deserves moral blame for what he has done unless one collapses the distinction between legal and moral censure. See text accompanying notes 21–22 below.

commentators agree that our criminal culpability judgments for serious non-regulatory offenses "rest" on notions of deserved "moral blame" for engaging in such conduct.

Retributivist theorists offer deontological justifications for requiring a link between criminal responsibility and moral culpability. Justice to the individual requires that he be rewarded and punished on the basis of what he deserves. The criminal actor does not deserve blame and punishment if he could not have avoided violating the law's dictates. Thus, retributivist theorists require a demonstration of the actor's moral responsibility to establish his moral culpability for committing the crime.

Many retributivists justify their "just deserts" principle in part by relying on Kant's categorical imperative that a moral agent must be treated as an "end" in himself. Blaming a morally culpable wrongdoer treats him as an end because we are respecting and appropriately responding to his rational and voluntary choice to do wrong.[4] It is "right" to give people what they deserve and the "good" of this practice lies in the fact that justice is being done, regardless of whether blaming the individual generates desirable or undesirable social consequences.

Utilitarians, in contrast, do not insist on any necessary connection between criminal liability and judgments of moral culpability. After all, criminal liability does not always require a demonstration that the actor engaged in morally objectionable conduct, and utilitarians approve of the criminalization of morally neutral conduct when such a practice will promote our social welfare.[5] Consequently, they do not link their defense of the law's moral responsibility requirement to any general principle concerning the actor's moral culpability.

Most utilitarian theorists embrace a mixed value theory of punishment that treats the moral responsibility requirement as a useful side-constraint on the law's goal of crime-prevention. The criminal justice system maximizes social utility when it reaches an optimal balance between two competing social objectives: the maximization of individual autonomy and the minimization of crime. These two "social goods" are in ultimate conflict, because whatever coercive measures we use to promote the latter goal will interfere with the former. Requiring a demonstration that the actor could have acted differently promotes our social welfare by maximizing the utility of individual choice within a coercive legal framework.[6]

Pure utilitarian theorists treat the retributivist's conception of "just deserts" as a disguised social utility requirement.[7] Limiting our legal blaming judgments to those criminal actors who could have acted otherwise if they had chosen to do so reassures the "law-abiding" segment of the community that their individual choices will be respected and valued. In addition, the moral responsibility requirement is critical to the deterrent value of the criminal law's most efficient

[4] See generally Michael Moore, *Law and Psychiatry: Rethinking the Relationship* (Cambridge: Cambridge University Press, 1984), pp. 233–43.

[5] See H.L.A. Hart, *Punishment and Responsibility* (Oxford: Oxford University Press, 1978), pp. 37–39.

[6] *ibid.*, p. 49. Finally, some utilitarian theorists have also offered nonconsequentialist justifications for accepting this side-constraint so that it operates to limit the pursuit of any utilitarian goal. *ibid.*, p. 80.

[7] See Louis M. Seidman, "Soldiers, Martyrs, and Criminals: Utilitarian Theory and the Problem of Crime Control," *Yale Law Journal*, vol. 94, no. 2 (December 1984), pp. 315–49.

sanction: moral stigma. Imposing such moral censure when the public *believes* it is not deserved undermines the sanction's deterrent efficacy.[8] In short, while utilitarian theorists do not insist on any necessary link between criminal liability and moral culpability, they do assume that the law's moral responsibility requirement will reassure the public that the criminal actor deserves moral blame when he is convicted of a serious non-regulatory offense.

While retributivist and utilitarian theorists offer different normative explanations for why the criminal law should require a demonstration of the actor's moral responsibility, prominent members from both camps rely on the rational choice model to explain the law's judgments of moral responsibility.[9] Michael Moore's essay in this volume illustrates both the substance and the methodology of this model.[10]

Moore argues that a choice theory of excuse is superior to a character theory of excuse in accounting for the moral excuses underlying our legal blaming judgments. According to the choice theory of excuse, "one is excused for the doing of a wrongful action because and only because at the moment of such action's performance, one did not have sufficient capacity or opportunity to make the choice to do otherwise."[11] Thus, even if the actor's wrongful act was "out of character" for him because it did not reflect some morally objectionable character defect, the actor is morally responsible for doing the act if he had the capacity and a fair opportunity to comply with the law's dictates.[12]

Like all choice theorists, Moore assumes that "the excuses are the royal road to theories of responsibility generally."[13] Accordingly, he derives a general account of moral agency from a choice excuse theory that identifies the conditions under which the criminal act can not be fairly attributed to the actor. Human beings are suitable objects of moral blame solely because we possess the capacity to make rational and voluntary choices about our acts.[14]

Choice theorists' definitions of rationality focus predominantly on the actor's instrumental reasoning abilities. Thus, their conception of the actor's rational

[8] See Schulhofer, "Just Punishment In An Imperfect World," *Michigan Law Review*, vol. 87, no. 6 (May 1989), pp. 1263–93, at p. 1271.

[9] Hart, *Punishment and Responsibility*; Moore, *Law and Psychiatry: Rethinking the Relationship*; Hyman Gross, *A Theory of Criminal Justice* (New York: Oxford University Press, 1979); Sanford H. Kadish, "Excusing Crime," in *Blame and Punishment* (New York: MacMillan, 1987), pp. 81–106; Joshua Dressler, *Understanding Criminal Law* (New York: Matthew Bender, 1987); Joshua Dressler, "Reflections on Excusing Wrongdoers: Moral Theory, New Excuses, and The Model Penal Code," *Rutgers Law Journal*, vol. 19, no. 3 (Spring 1988), pp. 671–716.

[10] Moore, "Choice, Character, and Excuse." I shall use Moore's work throughout this essay to illustrate both the strengths and weaknesses of the rational choice model for two reasons. First, he is a retributivist who believes his model demonstrates the actor's moral culpability for engaging in criminal conduct. Second, his work, in my judgment, offers the most articulate, detailed and subtle account of the rational choice model in the legal literature.

[11] *ibid.*, text accompanying note 1.

[12] *ibid.*, text accompanying notes 71–75.

[13] *ibid.*, text accompanying note 1.

[14] While the "choosing self" might include some of the emotions and desires that motivate these choices, the salient moral characteristic of the choosing self remains this capacity for rational and voluntary choice. *ibid.*, text accompanying notes 33–35; see also text accompanying notes 41–46 below.

choice capacity focuses primarily on whether the actor can make choices to act that are sensibly and logically connected to achieving his identified goals.[15] Neither the source nor the content of the actor's goals, desires, and values that motivate his choice are relevant to any assessment of whether he qualifies as a moral agent as long as they appear intelligible to us. Stephen Morse exemplifies this view when he suggests that "judgments about the intelligibility or rationality of goals can be made as long as we recognize that few goals are rational or irrational in an ultimate sense and make a general presumption in favor of rationality."[16]

This "thin" theory of rationality permits choice theorists to define the moral agent's capacities for rational and uncompelled action in the abstract without tying those capacities to the unique character of the individual possessing them. Thus, choice theorists can evaluate whether the actor is a proper object of our blaming judgments without ever asking whether the actor can be fairly held accountable for the goals, desires, values, and emotions that motivate his rational choices. Moral agents are simply beings whose rational choice powers explain why their *acts can be fairly attributed* to them because they had the power to have acted otherwise.

This *minimalist* account of a moral agent's necessary attributes serves two major functions for rational choice theorists. First, it permits them to offer an account of moral responsibility that is compatible with a "soft determinist" view of human action. Since such accounts assume sane adults possess the freedom to act in a manner that effectuates their reasoned choices,[17] choice theorists can argue that their conception of moral agency rests on a defensible view of our human powers that does not treat human beings as uncaused choosers.[18]

[15] Irrationality about the means-ends relationship may arise where the actor has an empirically unjustifiable and unintelligible belief that the means he uses can produce his goal. For example, a crazy person who is thirsty may suffer from the delusion that imbibing sand will quench his thirst. His goal is intelligible to us, but the means he has chosen to reach it are "irrational." Instrumental irrationality may also occur where the actor has a sensible goal, understands that a particular action will not be an effective means to accomplish it, but takes that action anyway. Thus, a person who was dehydrated and who knew that sand is not something one drinks would be considered "irrational" if he "drank" the sand to quench his thirst. None of these examples of deficient "practical reasoning" capacities depend on any assessment of those aspects of the agent's character that motivate his rational choices.

[16] Stephen Morse, "Psychology, Determinism, and Legal Responsibility," ed. Gary B. Melton, *Nebraska Symposium on Motivation 1985: Volume 33* (Lincoln: University of Nebraska Press, 1986), pp. 35–85, at p. 60.

[17] Both "soft" and "hard" determinists assume that individuals have this minimal degree of autonomy. Soft determinists argue that this degree of autonomy is sufficient to justify holding individuals morally responsible for their acts even if they lack the greater autonomy to revise their "will." In contrast, most "hard" determinists insist that moral responsibility requires a greater degree of autonomy over the causal forces in our character that shape our will. In essence, hard determinists agree with Aristotle that moral responsibility for action derives from moral responsibility for character, but they rely on a deterministic account of human action to show why what we are is not up to us.

[18] In contrast, compatibilists are not eager to defend the claim that individuals can be fairly blamed for their characters. See Dressler, "Reflections on Excusing Wrongdoers," pp. 695–96. In theory, a soft determinist could argue that the individual is morally responsible for those aspects of his character that are a product of his rational and voluntary choices. But, since Freud, legal theorists generally do not link either character development or character change to a simple process of conscious rational choice. *ibid.* Thus, both rational choice and character-based conceptions of moral agency are vulnerable to the critique of "hard" determinists who insist that the most significant causes of human action lie beyond our conscious control.

Second, the minimalist account suppresses the issue of moral agency from scrutiny and legal dispute. Since the choice model's instrumental account of rationality does not require any substantial assessment of the rationality of the actor's goals, desires, and values – or how he came to possess them – the criminal law can treat most criminal defendants as blameworthy moral agents without ever addressing the background conditions that might have impaired their ability to respond appropriately to societal moral norms. All the defendant needs to qualify as an appropriate addressee of these norms is the capacity for instrumental reasoning and the ability to act without compulsion. Consequently, few criminal defendants will be able to establish a "capacity" excuse that denies their status as a moral agent, because all but the very young and the very crazy possess the capacity for rational self-determined action.

Since the law automatically views them as blameworthy moral agents, these defendants can only litigate the question of whether they deserve moral blame for their acts by claiming a "fair opportunity" excuse that denies their moral act-responsibility. Choice theorists offer different formulations of the cognitive and volitional excuses that negate the individual's fair opportunity to avoid violating the law's dictates. But most accounts of these excuses adopt a narrow time-frame that focuses on whether the circumstances immediately preceding the criminal act prevented the defendant from complying with the law's dictates. Very few criminal defendants escape blame by relying on such narrowly drawn cognitive and volitional excuses.

II. Some Problematic Cases for the Rational Choice Model

The rational choice model arguably imputes blame to some actors (e.g., moral psychopaths and "brainwashed" defendants) for reasons that raise troubling questions about the model's account of moral culpability. Moreover, the rational choice model arguably could exculpate some defendants whom the law blames: those individuals convicted of negligence crimes and those who lose affirmative defenses because of their failure to behave like "reasonable persons."

This section considers whether moral psychopaths, individuals who fail to act like "reasonable persons," and "brainwashed" actors deserve moral blame for their crimes. I suggest that choice theorists' minimalist account of a moral agent's necessary attributes prevents them from addressing the issues that make these cases so morally problematic.

1. The moral psychopath: must moral agents appreciate moral norms and possess the capacity to use them as a reason for their action?

According to rational choice theorists, a moral agent's only necessary attributes are his instrumental reasoning ability and his capacity to make choices about his acts. Thus, psychopaths who make a "rational choice" to commit a crime qualify as moral agents as long as they "know" that society views their conduct as morally objectionable. Although some of these individuals view moral norms solely as arbitrary restraints on their self-interested acts and see other human beings only as objects to manipulate, these "facts" do not negate their moral agency.

But why should such individuals qualify as appropriate addresses of *moral* norms if, through no fault of their own, they lack the capacity to appreciate the norms' significance? And why do such psychopaths deserve our moral blame if they therefore lack the capacity to use moral norms as motivating reasons for their actions?

The choice theorist's response is that deserved attributions of moral blame do not depend on any assumptions about the agent's ability to act on the basis of moral motivations. The psychopath's understanding of the legal significance of his actions combined with his instrumental reasoning capacity gives him the ability to comply with the governing legal norm for non-moral reasons. Since he can choose to comply with the law when he believes doing so will promote his self-interest, he deserves moral blame when, instead, he chooses to breach the governing legal norm.

Admittedly, the psychopath's choice to comply with legal norms may be a harder one than that faced by other moral agents who can rely on moral as well as prudential reasons to obey the law. But the psychopath's choice to comply is not unduly difficult as long as he retains the ability to avoid breaching the governing norm. His moral culpability lies in his capacity to have acted differently,[19] even though no moral reason could have prompted him to act differently.

This rational choice account is flawed in two different respects. First, by equating the actor's moral culpability with his act-responsibility, rational choice theorists derive a general conception of the circumstances under which individuals deserve moral blame solely from a conception of fair attribution conditions that can equally well apply to morally neutral, blameworthy, and praiseworthy acts. Consider the following hypothetical.

> During World War II, the Nazi regime enacts a law through the properly constituted legal authority that makes it a crime for anyone deliberately to conceal a Jewish person in his home. German law requires proof beyond a reasonable doubt that someone has purposely committed this proscribed conduct without any *legally recognized justification or excuse.* German courts have concluded that defendants charged with this crime cannot raise the legal justification defenses of necessity and defense of another because their application would frustrate the state interests promoted by this statute. On the other hand, German law applies all of the excuse defenses such as duress and insanity to this crime.

[19] That choice theorists tend to assume that deserved attributions of moral blame follow automatically from a demonstration of the actor's moral act-responsibility can be seen in the examples they use to illustrate circumstances where the criminal law severs the connection between legal and moral blame. Their examples include strict liability crimes, the law's rejection of excuses concerning the actor's nonculpable mistake or ignorance about the legal norm he has breached, and restrictions on the scope of excuse defenses that seem motivated more by administrative concerns (e.g., "slippery slope" objections, difficulty of proof, fabrication risks) than moral excuse principles. What unites all of these examples is that they concern the unfairness of blaming someone for an act or a breach of a legal norm that he could not have avoided committing. In all of these examples, the unfairness has nothing to do with whether the norm breached was a moral norm or with whether the actor had the capacity to understand its moral significance.

> A German citizen, Fran Kliber, deliberately hides a Jewish neighbor in her attic. She knows she has committed a crime and does her best to conceal her actions from the authorities. The Gestapo uncovers her crime through legally valid procedures and prosecutes her. All legal procedural requirements (including a fair trial where she is represented by counsel) are satisfied, and she is convicted.

Choice theorists would agree that Fran is morally responsible for the breach of this legal norm. She is a legally sane actor who made a rational and voluntary choice to engage in conduct that she knew was prohibited by German law. But her moral act-responsibility cannot by itself demonstrate that she deserves moral blame. Indeed, her ability to choose whether to comply with this legal norm provides a *partial* explanation for why she deserves praise for what she has done. Even though we can fairly attribute a breach of legal norms to her, she deserves moral praise for the conduct[20] that the law blames her for committing.

This simple point underscores why one cannot derive a general conception of when individuals deserve *moral* blame solely from a conception of fair attribution conditions that applies to the breach of any norm, regardless of its moral value. Choice theorists may concede this point but correctly note that it does not undermine their central claim: the agent's instrumental reasoning and choice capacities explain why he qualifies as a moral agent who deserves moral blame *when* he chooses to engage in morally objectionable conduct.

But this modification does not correct a second flaw in the rational choice account of moral agency: its assumption that the capacity to be moved by moral reasons for action is not a necessary condition of moral agency. Even where the chosen act is morally objectionable, the actor's rational choice to commit it does not provide sufficient grounds for attributing deserved moral blame to the actor. Our judgments about moral act-responsibility presuppose that we are dealing with a moral agent whose capacities extend beyond those needed to satisfy fair attribution conditions.

To illustrate this point, consider why we do not treat young children as full moral agents. We certainly treat them as potential addressees of moral norms, because we assume most children will gradually develop the capacity to understand their normative significance and abide by their dictates. And when they make a rational and voluntary choice to engage in morally objectionable conduct ("I knew it was bad to take her toy from her but I really wanted it and I didn't think you'd catch me Daddy because I thought you were upstairs"), we may hold them accountable to some sanction to teach them the significance of the rule they have broken.

But we do not treat young children as full moral agents, despite their capacity for practical reason and their freedom to act on the basis of their reasoned choices. The

[20] Even if we assumed that all citizens were under some *prima facie* moral obligation or duty to obey duly enacted laws, the text's conclusion that Kliber merited moral praise for violating this law could be sustained. Even if the duty to obey the law created a reasonably strong moral "ought" that applied to this law from an unjust regime, strong countervailing moral reasons justify Kliber's breach of the legal norm that would defeat any *prima facie* moral obligation she had to comply.

six-year-old who took the toy while "knowing" it was a bad thing to do made a practical judgment about whether the satisfaction of getting it outweighed the risk of getting caught and punished. He has not had sufficient time and experience to internalize moral norms as something worthy of his respect. Nor does he have sufficient empathy and understanding for the feelings of other human beings as separate selves that would provide him with the moral comprehension and motivation to act on the basis of moral reasons that place constraints on his self-interested acts.

Young children do not qualify as moral agents because they have not yet fully developed this capacity to respond appropriately to moral reasons for action. This capacity for *moral responsiveness* presupposes that moral agents appreciate the normative significance of the moral norms governing their behavior. It also assumes that moral agents can exercise *moral judgment* about how these norms apply in a particular context. Acting on the basis of moral judgment also requires *moral motivation*: the capacity to use the applicable moral norm as the basis for acting.

Through no fault of their own,[21] some psychopaths lack these capacities and understandings. Their decisions whether to violate a governing moral norm are much like the six-year-old's: they involve balancing the gratification of getting what is wanted against the risk of apprehension and punishment. Psychopaths can make instrumentally rational choices about whether to comply with governing legal norms, but some cannot appreciate the normative significance of the moral norms that inform some of these legal rules.

For utilitarian theorists, the psychopath's practical reasoning capacities and his freedom to effectuate his reasoned choices may provide sufficient grounds to justify attributing a breach of a legal norm to him. After all, if we assume he was given a "fair opportunity" to exercise these capacities, our psychopath could have acted otherwise had he chosen to do so. Utilitarian choice theorists may argue that satisfying this fair-attribution condition is sufficient justification for imposing legal censure on the actor. Limiting our legal blaming judgments to criminal actors who possess this capacity should reassure the law-abiding community that their individual choices will be respected and valued. Moreover, the deterrent value of our legal blaming judgments should not be impaired as long as the public *believes* the psychopath deserves moral censure for his chosen act.

[21] Alternatively, a choice theorist might reject the premise that the moral psychopath lacks these moral understandings and moral emotions "through no fault of his own." According to this view, the psychopath deserves moral blame for his rational choice to violate the law in part because he is morally responsible for lacking the appropriate moral motivation to comply with legal norms that prohibit morally objectionable conduct.

But such a response raises further difficulties for the rational choice theorist. First, it concedes too much ground to a character-based conception of moral agency by implying that what motivates the actor's rational choices is relevant to our judgments about deserved moral blame. Second, the psychopath would not deserve blame on rational choice grounds for lacking appropriate moral understandings and motivations unless he made some earlier choice to deprive himself of these moral capacities. While some adult moral agents do make rational and voluntary choices to destroy their moral capacities by becoming addicted to drugs or alcohol, this explanation would not fit many moral psychopaths who fail to develop these moral capacities and understandings in their childhood when they are not considered responsible moral agents.

However, the appearance of desert is insufficient for a retributivist choice theorist who must show why this moral psychopath actually *deserves* moral blame for his crime. These theorists insist that the psychopath's freedom to have acted differently provides a sufficient basis for imputing blame to him. His capacity to respond appropriately to prudential reasons for complying with moral norms qualifies him as a blameworthy moral agent. His ability to have done otherwise gives him a fair opportunity to comply with governing norms, even if he faces a more difficult choice than other moral agents who can rely on moral as well as prudential reasons for making the right choice.

What these theorists never explain is why this ability to have done otherwise coupled with the actor's capacity for instrumental reasoning is a sufficient test for moral agency. Older children and many insane actors possess these two attributes, yet we do not treat them as fully accountable moral agents. Why should someone qualify as a moral agent if he lacks the capacity to deliberate about whether he *should* have acted differently? Choice theorists assume that the only salient moral issue is how "hard" it is for the moral psychopath to comply with governing norms. But if a deserved attribution of moral blame is at issue, the moral nature of the choice should matter as well as its degree of difficulty. Neither the psychopath's instrumental reasoning ability nor his capacity to respond to prudential reasons for action justifies treating him as an appropriate addressee of moral norms when the general significance and purpose of such norms lie beyond his "affective" understanding.

Of course, most criminal actors do not fit the extreme picture of the moral psychopath that I have painted here. Accordingly, even if rational choice theorists conceded that moral agents must have some capacity to use moral norms as a reason for their choices, most sane adult offenders would still qualify as blameworthy agents.

These choice theorists might also remind us that the type of moral norms that are violated by "core" crimes of violence against human beings impose very minimal restraints on our self-promoting acts. Since any account of a moral agent's necessary attributes must vary with the rigors of the moral demands being made of the agent, choice theorists can argue that a minimalist conception of moral agency suitable for our legal blaming judgments need not presuppose all of the moral capacities I have described above.

Finally, even if they concede that moral agents must have some minimal capacity to make moral choices, choice theorists may characterize this additional attribute as a minor modification of their model. The next two subsections suggest otherwise. I shall argue that only a character-based conception of moral agency can explain how individuals acquire this capacity for moral responsiveness[22] and why it is sometimes fair to blame actors who fail to exercise this capacity.

[22] Of course, some individuals never develop this capacity because of bad constitutive luck. These individuals would not qualify as moral agents, nor are they morally responsible for the conditions that prevented them from attaining this status.

2. The capacity to think, feel, and act like a "reasonable person": the moral agent's capacity for critical self-reflection and self-revision

A. The "Negligence" Problem. Should an actor's inadvertent negligent behavior[23] that breaches a governing moral norm serve as an appropriate basis for imputing some degree of moral blame? Choice theorists divide on this question. "Subjectivists" insist that the actor's conscious awareness of at least the risk of wrongdoing is the *sine qua non* of moral culpability. Thus, negligent actors are not morally culpable because they are not consciously aware of the risk that their conduct could breach some norm.[24] Their lack of awareness prevents them from making a rational and voluntary choice to engage in behavior that risks breaching the norm.

Other choice theorists rely on Hart's explanation that it is fair to blame the negligent actor as long as he had the "capacity" to act like a reasonable person.[25] According to this view, the actor deserves moral blame for failing to exercise this capacity at the time he engaged in negligent conduct.

While Hart did not offer a detailed account of the abilities and motivations that would inform this capacity to behave reasonably, Michael Moore provides an excellent description of them in his earlier work, *Law and Psychiatry*. To behave in a non-negligent manner, the reasonable person must embody

> those qualities of character that we think persons should possess, and those capacities of mind that we think all persons do possess. The average reasonable man is benevolently motivated – he counts all persons' interests as equal to his own; he is thus neither unduly selfish nor unrealistically altruistic. In addition, he knows the true worth of things and is able to compare the value of life with the dollars and cents cost of altering the design, say, of an automobile. He is also capable of calculating what actions are likely to lead to what results and even to assign relative probabilities to each. He is, in other words, a preeminent practical reasoner, finding the morally and legally correct major premises . . . and forming the accurate means/end beliefs . . . for his minor premises . . . . It is because people have the capacity to reason this way that they can be said to be culpable when they do not do so.[26]

The law presumes all responsible individuals possess the capacity to behave reasonably. What Moore does not explain is how the choice theorist's minimalist

[23] The criminal law distinguishes between recklessness and negligence on the basis of whether the actor was consciously aware of the risk that his conduct would violate some legal norm. Recklessness requires that the actor consciously disregard a substantial and unjustifiable risk that his conduct will violate a legal norm, whereas negligence only requires proof that he should have been aware of the risk. See American Law Institute, *Model Penal Code and Commentaries* (*Official Draft and Revised Comments*), Part I §§ 1.01–2.13 (A.L.I. Institute: Philadelphia, 1985), pp. 225–26.

[24] Glanville Williams, *Criminal Law: The General Part*, (London: Stevens and Sons, 2d ed. 1961), pp. 122–23.

[25] See H.L.A. Hart, "Negligence, *Mens Rea* and Criminal Responsibility," in *Punishment and Responsibility*, pp. 136–57.

[26] Moore, *Law and Psychiatry: Rethinking the Relationship*, p. 83.

account of a moral agent's necessary attributes can generate this capacity. An account of the agent's instrumental reasoning abilities cannot by itself explain our capacity to form the morally correct desires and rationally correct emotions that we need to reason and act non-negligently. In *Law and Psychiatry*, Moore acknowledged this point.[27] He conceded that a non-instrumental account of rational desires and emotions must inform any account of the agent's capacity to act like a reasonable person, but his version of a moral agent's necessary attributes did not provide one.

In his essay in this volume, Moore takes a new position. He now argues that a choice theorist should not accept Hart's defense of negligence because it shifts "the touchstone of responsibility from choice to capacity," relegating "choice to a subsidiary role in our responsibility assessments."[28] Moore apparently recognizes that any adequate explanation of the capacities one needs to behave reasonably would require a more ambitious account of a moral agent's necessary attributes than that offered by choice theorists.

B. Must Moral Agents Have the "Capacity" to Behave Like a Reasonable Person? Moore's rejection of negligence as an appropriate basis for attributing any moral blame because of its inconsistency with rational choice premises might seem insignificant to many legal theorists. After all, basing criminal liability on the actor's inadvertent negligence is "the exception, not the rule."[29] Moreover, negligence crimes have always generated controversy among legal scholars who insist on a connection between criminal liability and the actor's moral culpability.

But questions concerning the linkage between a moral agent's necessary attributes and the various abilities, traits, and powers one needs to behave reasonably can not be confined – and thereby dismissed – to issues concerning the fairness of negligence crimes. Both our legal and moral norms presuppose that most of us have the capacity to think, feel, value, interpret, and react like reasonable persons. That we expect moral agents to have these abilities can be seen in our excuses that do not exempt responsible actors from blame if they fail to behave reasonably in light of the facts and moral duties imposed on them.

Our legal excuses that concern the moral agent's moral act-responsibility support this claim. Unlike moral agency excuses such as insanity that permit a completely subjective inquiry into the defendant's capacities, our moral act-responsibility excuses usually incorporate reasonable person standards into their doctrinal criteria.[30] If the defendant failed to think, feel, interpret, and react as a reasonable person would have in the same situation, he loses the full excuse.

[27] *ibid.*, p. 104.

[28] Moors, "Choice, Character, and Excuse," text accompanying note 92.

[29] See *Model Penal Code and Commentaries*, p. 226, § 2.02(3) which creates a presumption that some consciousness of wrongdoing is required for any crime where the legislature has not explicitly placed a mental state requirement in its definition of the offense.

[30] The traditional common law rule concerning mistaken self-defense claims requires an assessment of whether the defendant had a "reasonable belief" that the use of force was necessary to repel some unlawful threat of imminent physical harm. Thus, if the defendant makes a negligent assessment of the facts that are needed to support this defense, he loses a full affirmative defense in most jurisdictions. See People v. Goetz, 497 N.E.2d 41 (N.Y. Ct. of Appeals 1986).

Of course, there are powerful utilitarian rationales why the criminal law incorporates "reasonable person" standards into some of its excuse defenses. But these standards could also reflect the judgment that people are morally culpable when they fail to interpret and react to a situation like a reasonable person should.

Consider the following two cases. X threatens to punch T in the stomach unless T shoots Y, an enemy of X's, in the leg. T is an extremely timid person who has always had an excessive aversion to any form of physical pain. Terrorized by the thought of the imminent assault, he reluctantly shoots Y. Contrast this case with one where X's threat to pour corrosive acid on Z's hands leads Z to shoot Y in the leg.

Both T and Z made an instrumentally rational choice to shoot Y to avoid harms to themselves; both could assert the excuse defense of duress. In most jurisdictions, only Z could be excused from blame for his choice. The law requires not only that the defendant be coerced by some unlawful threat of physical harm to commit a crime but also that a "person of reasonable firmness" would have succumbed to the same threat.[31] T cannot successfully raise the duress defense because a person of reasonable firmness should not give in to such a minor threat.

But how does the rational choice model explain T's moral culpability for being so easily coerced by a minor threat? Both T and Z chose to protect their own self-interest at the expense of a moral innocent, Y. Both subjectively experienced themselves as succumbing to an external threat that overbore their will to resist. The only distinguishing feature between the two cases[32] is that a person of reasonable firmness would not have given in to the threat facing T, but might have given in to the threat facing Z. Thus, T's moral culpability appears to lie solely in his failure to have acted like a reasonable person should have in the same situation.

Notice that we are not dealing with a "negligence" crime, yet T's moral culpability depends on a showing that he deserves moral blame for failing to act like a reasonable person. We are back to the question of what attributes a moral agent must possess that give him this capacity, a question that Moore agrees cannot be answered by relying on the agent's rational choice capacity.[33]

Full excuses such as duress require the defendant to show not only that he was coerced to commit the crime but that "a person of reasonable firmness in his situation would have been unable to resist." *Model Penal Code and Commentaries*, § 2.09(1), p. 367. Thus, if a person of reasonable firmness would have realized that the person making the threat lacked the ability or will to carry it out, the defense is not available even if the actual defendant made a negligent assessment of these facts because he was so intimidated by the threat. *ibid.*, p. 374, n. 50.

Even the partial excuse of provocation that reduces an intentional killing from murder to voluntary manslaughter requires proof that a "reasonable person" would have lost his normal self-control capacities if subjected to the provocation that prompted the defendant to kill. See Arenella, "The Diminished Capacity and Diminished Responsibility Defenses: Two Children of a Doomed Marriage," 77 *Columbia Law Review*, vol. 77, no. 6 (October 1977), pp. 827–65, at pp. 850–52.

[31] See *Model Penal Code and Commentaries*, § 2.09(1), at p. 367.

[32] Moore does offer an alternative "failed justification" account for duress excuses that I shall examine in the last section of this essay. See text accompanying notes 39–40 below.

[33] See note 28 above. It is highly unlikely that T made some earlier rational choice to become an excessively timid person. Thus, the choice theorist must argue that T's excessive aversion to physical discomfort constituted a "predisposition" to succumb to such a threat, but that he retained the capacity to choose to act inconsistently with this character defect. This behavioral view of our character traits as simple

C. Explaining Why Moral Agents Possess The Capacity To Behave Reasonably. A character-based conception of moral agency could be used to explain why moral agents possess the capacity to think, feel, interpret, and behave like a reasonable person. This model would assume that moral agents can exercise some modest degree of control over those aspects of their character that motivate their rational choices. But this form of control is not the simple exercise of the agent's rational choice to act inconsistently with his timidity on a specific occasion. A character-based model would concede that T's excessive aversion to physical suffering motivated his choice, and that he could not simply have made a rational choice to act inconsistently with this character defect when threatened by X.

Instead, this character-based model would locate his moral culpability in his earlier failure to do something about a character defect that clearly could impair his ability to make the right moral choice in certain circumstances. We blame him for not acting like a reasonable person because we believe he is morally responsible for not doing something about those defective aspects of his character that prevent him from acting like one.

But what makes this ealier failure culpable? It is possible but unlikely that T made some earlier rational choice not to work on his character defects. It is more likely that he gave this aspect of his character little thought if it did not frequently get him into difficulty. What makes his earlier failure culpable might well hinge on a negligence-based argument that refers to his capacity to have done something that he never consciously considered.

What gives him this capacity? A character-based model of moral agency must presuppose that moral agents have some capacity for critical self-reflection about those aspects of their character that make it difficult for them to make the right moral choice. Moreover, moral agents must also have some modest capacity for self-revision that permits them at least to modify the intensity of those aversions and desires that impair their capacity to act like reasonable persons. These attributes would explain why T has some moral culpability for succumbing to this minor threat. While he may not have been able to act inconsistently with his excessive timidity at the time of the threat, he deserves some moral blame for his earlier failure to do something about this character flaw.

D. Choice Theorists' Rebuttal. I have suggested that our moral culpability judgments presuppose that moral agents can exercise some control over those aspects of their character that motivate their choices. Choice theorists frequently respond to such claims by arguing that they misconstrue the kind of blaming judgment incorporated into the law's account of legal blame. They argue that the moral theory needed to justify our legal blaming practices need not concern itself with even a limited version of a character-responsibility theme because the defendant's moral character defects are not the object of the law's moral critique.[34]

---

predispositions to act assumes we can isolate the actor's timidity from both his "rational choosing capacity" and his other desires, aversions, emotions, and interpretations of what his options are at the moment he acts. The last section of this essay will offer reasons for rejecting this reductionist view of our character traits. See text accompanying notes 41–45 below.

[34] Dressler, "Reflections on Excusing Wrongdoers," pp. 695–98; Moore, *Law and Psychiatry: Rethinking the Relationship*, pp. 110–11; Gross, *A Theory of Criminal Justice*, pp. 76–77.

These theorists point out that the criminal law is concerned primarily with discouraging the commission of *acts* that risk or cause some significant social "harm." Accordingly, the criminal law does not reach a broad range of morally objectionable conduct that reflects "bad character" but does not risk causing such harm. When the state does criminalize morally objectionable conduct, that conduct usually violates moral norms that impose minimal restraints on our self-regarding acts. In sum, we do not impose legal blame on people with "bad" characters who have not committed any criminal act. And we do impose legal blame on individuals with "good" characters who have made a culpable but uncharacteristic choice to commit a crime.

This description of our legal blaming practices concerns the type of moral blaming judgments made by the criminal law. It demonstrates that the criminal's act, and not his character, is the primary object of the law's moral judgment. It also shows that the defendant's "bad" moral character is not a necessary – much less a sufficient – condition for imposing legal blame. But why are these two "facts" about our legal judgments of blame inconsistent with a character-based conception of moral agency?

Apparently, choice theorists assume that a character-based model implies that we can *only* impose moral blame on individuals for acts that reflect or express some morally objectionable character defect. For example, Moore relies on this assumption to show why a character-based model of moral responsibility cannot offer an adequate justification of the law's negligence judgments. After all, argues Moore, one can be negligent on a specific occasion even though one is generally a careful and attentive person. Moreover, even individuals who characteristically act negligently and make unreasonable mistakes may not have "bad characters."[35]

The flaw in this argument is that it conflates two separate and independent elements of moral culpability analysis: (1) what attributes the actor needs to qualify as a moral agent who has the capacity to act like a reasonable person, and (2) whether an act-based or character-based moral judgment best reflects the type of moral blame imposed by our legal blaming judgments.[36] We might blame criminals for their choice to violate minimal act-regarding norms, but the culpability of their choice might depend on our assumption that moral agents can control those aspects of their characters that motivate such choices.

Similarly, relying on a character-based conception of moral agency to explain why it is fair to blame individuals for their failure to act like a reasonable person does not limit our legal blaming judgments to acts that reflect morally objectionable traits of character. A character-based model of moral agency would explain why individuals can be held accountable for what motivated their negligent judgments and behavior. If the individual is generally a careless and inattentive person, he is

[35] Moore, "Choice, Character, and Excuse," text accompanying notes 93–95.

[36] To be fair to Moore, he makes these negligence arguments in reply to character theorists such as Nicola Lacey who argue that we should only impose legal blame for criminal acts that do reflect some morally objectionable character trait. See generally Nicola Lacey, *State Punishment* (London: Routledge, 1988); Michael Bayles, "Character, Purpose, and Criminal Responsibility," *Law and Philosophy*, vol. 1, no. 1 (April 1982).

held accountable for failing to control a character defect that can cause him to act in a negligent manner. But sensitive and attentive actors who uncharacteristically engage in negligent behavior also deserve moral blame for failing to exercise their character strengths because of some momentary distraction.

In sum, a character-based conception of moral agency does not suggest that we can only impose moral blame for acts that reflect some well-established character defect. It simply provides an explanation for why we believe that all moral agents, regardless of their character flaws, have the capacity to act like reasonable persons.

Of course, choice theorists can deny the linkage I have indicated here between the capacity to act reasonably and moral blame for crimes that require a demonstration that the actor made a rational choice to breach (or risk breaching) a legal norm. And they can still argue that blaming an individual solely for his failure to act like a reasonable person is a morally indefensible practice. But we are then left with a theory of moral culpability that neither describes nor justifies many of our actual blaming practices.

The next section returns to a situation where the actor does make a rational choice to breach some governing norm. It suggests that even in this context, to demonstrate that the agent deserves moral blame for making the wrong choice, we must show why the agent deserves blame for those aspects of his character that impair his ability to make the right moral choice.

3. *Brainwashing and rational choice*

One way of comparing the rational choice and character-based conceptions of moral agency is to see which model offers a better explanation for why we find some cases so morally problematic. The Patty Hearst case provides such a situation. We may disagree about whether she deserves moral blame for what she did, but which model provides us with a better account of the morally relevant questions raised by her case?

"Revolutionaries" kidnapped the eighteen-year-old heiress to the Hearst empire and transformed her value system into that of a "freedom fighter" after weeks of isolation, abuse, and indoctrination. After adopting their "world view" as her own, she renounced her past, took on the new name of "Tania," and joined her former captors in criminal activity. After her arrest and some counseling, Patty insisted that she had been brainwashed into becoming "Tania" and should therefore be excused from any criminal liability.

A rational choice theorist has difficulty explaining what is morally problematic about blaming her. Her brainwashing defense does not fit comfortably within the duress defense,[37] because her former captors apparently did not need to coerce

[37] Some common law formulations of duress require that the defendant have faced some "imminent" threat of unlawful physical harm in order to raise the defense of duress. Many jurisdictions would not permit this defense if the actor had a reasonable opportunity to avoid committing the criminal act without subjecting himself to the threatened danger. In contrast, the Model Penal Code duress provision is drafted broadly enough to permit a defendant in Hearst's situation to raise the defense. See *Model Penal Code and Commentaries, Part 1*, pp. 375–84. But as the authors of the commentary to this section note, "it may be very difficult to persuade a jury that an act willingly performed at the time was truly the product of unlawful force and would have been performed by a person of reasonable firmness subjected to similar conditions." *ibid.*, p. 377.

"Tania" into committing these crimes. Moreover, rational choice theorists cannot seriously consider her claim, that she does not deserve moral blame because she was not morally responsible for becoming "Tania" – at least not without modifying their claim that choice, not character, is the morally significant cause of action that justifies attributions of deserved moral blame.

After all, the normative appeal of her brainwashing excuse lies in her claim that she was not morally responsible for those aspects of her character (e.g., "Tania's" values, desires, goals, and her construction of social reality) that motivated her rational choices to commit these "revolutionary" crimes. But choice theorists insist that what motivates actors to engage in instrumental reasoning about what they want to do should not affect judgments about deserved moral blame unless the actors' goals, desires, and values seem unintelligible to us. Robbing banks to pay for revolutionary activities certainly qualifies as an intelligible goal.

Since their instrumental account of rationality does not require any meaningful assessment of the "rationality" of Hearst's new goals, desires, and values or how she came to possess them, rational choice theorists cannot adequately address the question that makes this case so troubling: is she morally responsible for the values, goals, and desires that motivated her choice to violate governing moral norms? While some rational choice theorists might want to exempt Hearst from blame, their account of an appropriate excuse could not rely solely on how the brainwashing impaired her capacities for rational choice.

Consider one version of such an excuse. Hearst would not deserve moral blame for her crimes unless they occurred after she had been given sufficient time to "choose" whether or not to maintain her new "Tania" character. Under this account, we might hold her morally responsible for the new values, desires, and goals that motivated her choice to commit these crimes, but only after and because she had "chosen" to maintain these new aspects of her character.

But why should her subsequent "choice" have any normative significance unless it occurred in a context which enabled her to exercise some critical self-reflection about what had happened to her? For example, if she remained with her former captors for a year before she decided to commit crimes with them, but never received any "deprogramming" assistance from others, why should the mere passage of time make a moral difference? Even if the mere passage of time did give her a "fair opportunity" to choose whether to maintain these new characteristics, the normative significance of her choice to "internalize" these new values hinges on her presumed capacity to reflect about the type of person she wants to be. This capacity for critical self-reflection is one of the attributes that a character-based conception of moral agency presupposes; it is not a capacity that can be explained solely by referring to a moral agent's ability to engage in instrumental reasoning about the best means to reach any end.

This section's cases concerning moral psychopaths, the capacity to behave like a reasonable person, and the brainwashed actor raise three essential questions. First, do deserved attributions of moral blame depend on any assumptions about the agent's capacity to respond appropriately to moral norms as a reason for acting? If they do, must moral agents have some ability to control those aspects of their character that impair their ability to make the right moral choices? Finally, what types of powers and capacities must moral agents possess to exercise sufficient control over their characteristic motivations? Choice theorists' "thin" account of our practical reason and their "fair attribution" view of moral agency prevent them from adequately addressing these questions.

This essay's final section provides further evidence that these three questions cannot be ignored in any defensible account of why moral agents deserve moral blame for their actions. It does so by examining the choice theorists' claim that character-based moral judgments do not infuse their own conception of moral agency.

III. Character, Choice, and Moral Agency

Choice theorists insist that the actor's moral culpability does not depend on any prior assumption about the agent's moral responsibility for those aspects of his character that motivate such choices. This section uses Moore's discussion of a hypothetical duress problem to demonstrate how the culpability of our choices does indeed presuppose this limited version of character-responsibility.

Moore's problem concerns an actor H who unjustifiably hates an exemplary individual V. V is dying but could be saved by a rare drug known only to T. T threatens to give this drug to V unless H helps T rob a bank. H has no inclination to rob this bank, but he is obsessed with the thought that his hated enemy V will survive unless he aids T. H therefore reluctantly agrees to rob the bank with T. Is H morally responsible for the crime, or does he deserve the excuse of duress?

Our common intuition does not support an excuse claim under these facts. But Moore's analysis of how choice theorists justify that intuition suggests that character-responsibility themes are embedded in choice theorists' most coherent accounts of their rational choice principles.

Choice theorists have two excuse options to apply to this hypothetical. Perhaps H lacked the "capacity" to comply with the law here because his practical reasoning powers were overwhelmed by his emotional hatred of V. This capacity excuse would establish that H was not capable of acting like a moral agent at the time of the crime. Alternatively, a choice theorist could suggest that T's threat coupled with H's hatred of V denied H a "fair opportunity" to comply with the law's dictates. The "fair opportunity" excuse treats H as a moral agent, but denies his moral responsibility for the robbery because the circumstances did not give him a fair chance to exercise his unimpaired moral-agency capacities.

Moore correctly points out that most choice theorists are not eager to treat such "internal disability" cases as raising capacity excuse claims. Instead, they prefer to characterize H's problem as presenting a "fair opportunity" excuse claim and deny it. According to Moore, H still had a fair opportunity to choose to comply with the law despite the fact that such a choice was psychologically harder for him than for most of us because of his hatred for V. Choice theorists use an objective criterion to measure what constitutes an unfair diminution of our opportunities to avoid wrongful action. "[To lack] a fair opportunity to avoid doing wrong there must be some (objectively regarded) evil that one is avoiding."[38] Since V's survival is a social good, there was no objective cost being imposed on H's choice to avoid violating the law.

I do not dispute Moore's assumption that duress as a moral excuse presupposes some normative baseline which we use to measure the degree of difficulty of choice. But why should a "substantial evil" standard serve as that baseline for a moral excuse that concedes the actor has no moral justification for what he has done?

One possible explanation for using a "substantial evil" standard is that it enables us to make a character-based moral judgment about the actor's failure to resist the threat. Perhaps we should not hold actors morally responsible for succumbing to external threats that constitute substantial harms to the choosing agent and that would overwhelm the resistance of most reasonable persons. In H's case, the choice not to rob the bank would cause him substantial psychological harm. But any person of reasonable moral character would not suffer any harm by making such a choice. If this is the case, the substantial evil criterion actually serves as a proxy for evaluating whether the individual's succumbing to the threat reflected a morally objectionable character trait for which we hold the agent morally responsible.

Even more revealing is Moore's account of why H does not merit a "capacity" excuse. After all, it is certainly a plausible psychological story that H's hatred for V unhinged his practical reasoning abilities when T "threatened" to save V if H did not help T rob the bank. Moore correctly points out that most choice theorists reject these internal incapacity claims because they are "worried that recognizing fears, cravings, instinctual desires, strong passions, or other internal states as excuses unduly reduces one's true responsibility."[39] Their fear is well-founded. Recognizing such internal incapacity excuses would dramatically diminish the scope of moral responsibility. But why is it fair to hold H morally responsible for his crime if his hatred unhinges his practical reason?

In his earlier work, Moore answered this question by viewing the "self" encompassed by moral agency as a disembodied will that has the power to choose whether or not to succumb to the person's characteristic impulses, desires, emotions, and values.[40] According to this account, H's hatred for V would predispose him to succumb to T's threat, but moral agents choose to act "out of character" all the time. H merits no capacity excuse, because he retains this power to choose to act in contravention of what his emotions predisposed him to do.

Most choice theorists have taken a similar tack by defining the agent's capacities for rational and uncompelled action in the abstract without tying them to the unique character of the individual possessing them.[41] This approach adopts a very narrow conception of the moral self who does the choosing: a disembodied practical reasoner who is isolated from the values, goals, and desires of the individual's character.

[38] Moore, "Choice, Character, and Excuse," text accompanying notes 37–38.
[39] *ibid.*, text at note 30.
[40] Moore, *Law and Psychiatry: Rethinking the Relationship*, p. 88 ["characters are themselves constructs created by generalizing about what one does when one's choices are unconstrained."]
[41] Dressler, "Reflections on Excusing Wrongdoers," p. 701.

This narrow version of the moral self also presupposes a behavioral view of the person's character traits as predispositions to act that constitute "external" constraints on the moral self's choosing capacity. According to this view, character trait attributions are simply descriptions of either a pattern of action in the past or a prediction of future behavior based on a posited disposition to act.

Both descriptive and normative conceptions of character, so conceived, are not logically independent of a person's actions. Moral judgments about a person's character constitute nothing more than normative evaluations concerning a consistent and coherent pattern of action over time. Acts derive their moral value from the moral self's rational choice to comply with the governing moral norm; a choice that may require the disembodied practical reasoner to act inconsistently with what his "character" disposed him towards doing.

This account of moral blame only makes sense if we can defend its two essential premises: that we can separate the choosing self from what motivates its choices and take a behavioral view of a person's character traits. Neither premise is defensible; when combined, they generate an account of our moral behavior that defies both our common sense and current tenets of moral psychology.[42]

Some of our character states, including emotions like hatred, can constitute motivations to act because of a particular set of values, feelings, desires, or aversions.[43] Thus, a character trait attribution can describe an emotional state reflecting attitudes, experiences, and desires that may cause the individual to perform some act and that would typically cause others with the same set of feelings, values, and motivations to act in a similar fashion. Moreover, a moral character trait may refer to far more than a simple disposition to do the act required by some moral rule. It may also encompass dispositions to feel the appropriate emotions and moral motivations to do what the governing moral norm requires. The moral agent cannot simply make a rational choice to experience the appropriate moral sentiments when he wishes to act morally. These moral emotions are the product of prior moral education, experience, and deliberation by the agent about what he should strive to be.

If this motivational view of some of our character traits provides a more accurate psychological account of how they operate than the behavioral view, then choice theorists will have a difficult time defending their continued treatment of character trait attributions as a proxy for some form of behavioral description about a person's past acts or future act-dispositions.[44] But once choice theorists stop relying on their outmoded behavioral view of character, their narrow conception of the moral self as a disembodied practical reasoner who can simply choose to ignore some "external" predisposition to act collapses from within.

[42] See Richard Brandt, "Traits of Character: A Conceptual Analysis," *American Philosophical Quarterly*, vol. 7, no. 1 (January 1970), pp. 23–37.

[43] *ibid.*

[44] Adopting this motivational view of character traits might also lead theorists to reject the idea that "character" as a general descriptive construct can be derived simply by looking at a person's consistent pattern of action over time. Instead, a motivational view of some of our character traits might support a more holistic and integrated conception of character that referred to the way an individual's relatively consistent and coherent values, emotions, desires, and aversions interact with each other over time to generate that person's goals, motivations, and interpretations of his social reality.

Moore acknowledges this last point in his essay in this volume. He recognizes that he defined the choosing self too narrowly in his earlier work. In his discussion of why H does not merit a capacity excuse, he now describes the "choosing" self as encompassing not only the conscious will but "some" of our emotions – including H's hatred.

> Choice, to be morally interesting, must include not only the initiation of basic actions but also the formation of the intentions and beliefs that guide and motivate the doing of the basic actions .... If this is what is meant by "choice," then some emotions will necessarily have a place in this process.[45]

I agree. Ironically, Moore's expansion of the "self," encompassed by our view of moral agency to include those emotions and values that motivate our reasoned choices, brings him much closer to the character-based conception of moral agency that he and other choice theorists have rejected.

While Moore broadens his image of the moral, choosing self, he does not see the implications of this shift for his theory of culpability. Treating moral agents as something more than radically unsituated practical reasoners does not explain *why* they deserve moral blame for the emotions and values that motivate their rational choices. Moore appears to believe that once emotions are no longer seen as "alien" to the moral agent's choosing self, their mere inclusion into the choosing self domesticates them. ("On this view, the emotions are not invaders of our processes of reasoned deliberation, *nor are they pre-emptors of such processes.*"[46]) But that many of our emotions have cognitive components and that they can be both products and causes of our decisions to act does not establish that we can control their impact on our choices simply by choosing to act inconsistently with them. Nor does their inclusion into a broader definition of the choosing self prevent some emotions, like hatred, from completely overwhelming our practical reason.

One implication of these competing views of character and character traits is that they establish very different baselines from which to evaluate whether a person's action was "in" or "out" of his moral character. If moral character refers to a consistent and coherent pattern of moral action over time, then a person can be described as acting "out of character" whenever he does something that is inconsistent with this pattern. Thus, a greedy person is someone who has acted greedily in the past or someone whom we predict will act greedily in the future if given an occasion to do so. If this person does something that appears generous, we describe the action as "out of character." Depending on our knowledge of that person's past acts and our evidence about his present predispositions, a potentially broad range of future behavior on his part could qualify as being morally "out of character."

In contrast, if we use the broader motivational view of moral character as our baseline, a far smaller category of actions will be described as morally "out of character" even if the person had never acted like that before. If we have a reasonably complete picture of a person's moral character, most of his moral and immoral future actions will reflect some enduring moral character trait – even if what we learn is new information about how that trait motivates behavior under new and unusual circumstances.

I do not mean to suggest that, once we adopt a broader conception of what moral character traits encompass, one can never act out of moral character. While all of a person's actions tell us something about that person's personality, the information might not tell us anything significant about the person's moral character that distinguishes him from anyone else for purposes of making a judgment of moral blame.

[45] Moore, "Choice, Character, and Excuse," text at notes 33–34.

[46] *ibid.*, text at notes 34–35.

The choice theorist still must explain why the psychologically plausible story that H's hatred severely limited his capacity to respond appropriately to governing norms does not excuse him. While Moore broadens his view of the moral self that does the choosing, he still treats H's choice capacity as his only salient moral characteristic. Unfortunately, it is not clear that we choose some of the strongest emotions that motivate our choices, nor is it clear that we can simply choose not to feel or act on the basis of such emotions.

I do not mean to suggest that all of our emotions are "irrational," or that we are "stuck" with those passions that interfere with our deliberations about whether we should engage in morally objectionable conduct. A character-based conception of moral agency could shift the focus of moral inquiry from H's "choice" to succumb to T's threat to his earlier opportunities to do something about his hatred for V. It could accept H's claim that his hatred prevented him from responding appropriately to the governing moral norm against theft *at the time of his act.* But we would hold H morally responsible for allowing this character defect to fester to the point that it unduly interfered with his capacity to respond appropriately to the governing moral norm.

The object of our legal blaming judgment would remain his criminal act of robbing the bank. We would not blame him for hating V, but we would hold him morally responsible for a morally objectionable act that was motivated by this hatred. A character-based moral judgment about his moral culpability for not doing something about his hatred for V would contribute to our judgment of his criminal culpability.

This limited version of a character-responsibility theme suggests that when our criminal acts do reflect some established feature of our characters, our moral culpability does not lie exclusively in our rational choice to do wrong. The ultimate basis for our culpability may lie in our failure to do something about those aspects of our character that make it so difficult for us to avoid engaging in morally objectionable conduct.

This character-based conception of moral agency suggests that the normative significance we attribute to our rational choices stems in part from this limited version of a character responsibility theme. It could be used to generate an alternative model of moral responsibility that rejects the stark dichotomy between our being and our doing presupposed by the rational choice account. Such a character-based model would certainly not treat all judgments about choice as disguised moral judgments about character. Nor would it only impose blame for acts that reflect some relatively enduring aspect of the agent's character. Choice theorists have mistakenly made these criticisms of all character models by conflating two independent (albeit related) elements of moral culpability analysis: why humans qualify as moral agents and what types of moral judgment (character- vs. act-based) that may be imposed on them.

But even if this character-based conception of moral agency helps to explain the normative significance we attach to our rational choices, we must still show why it is fair to hold individuals morally responsible for their motivational character traits. Why is H morally responsible for failing to do something about his hatred for V?

What powers and self-understandings must moral agents possess before we can hold them morally responsible for failing to control how their character defects motivate their rational choices? And does such an account of a moral agent's attributes rest on a defensible vision of human nature?

A comprehensive treatment of such questions merits its own essay. However, this paper's critique of the rational choice model suggests some of the additional attributes a moral agent would need to respond appropriately to moral reasons for action. A capacity for *moral responsiveness* presupposes that moral agents appreciate the normative significance of the moral norms governing their behavior. It also assumes that moral agents can exercise *moral judgment* about how these norms apply to a particular context. Acting on the basis of moral judgment requires *moral motivation*: the desire to use the applicable moral norm as the basis for acting.

Finally, moral agents must be able to act on these moral motivations, despite conflicting desires and impulses. This latter ability is only possible if the moral agent can control or revise those aspects of her character that impair her ability to appreciate or comply with applicable moral norms on any particular occasion. Thus, moral agents must have some modest capacity for *critical self-reflection* and *self-revision.*

This capacity for moral responsiveness encompasses several distinct but interrelated abilities to react to applicable moral norms in thought, feeling, perception, and behavior. Assessing whether this account of a moral agent's attributes rests on a defensible vision of human nature requires theorists to consider how we acquire and develop these moral capacities. In short, moral theorists must attend to questions of moral psychology.

If they do so, they will discover how dependent we are on other human beings for both the development and exercise of our moral capacities. The capacities of critical self-reflection and self-revision are not simply some individual *properties* that some individuals have the moral luck to possess. Their acquisition and development depend on an interpersonal process between the agent and other human beings. The ability to control one's character is a process that often requires some form of socially created *transformational opportunity* being made available to an individual who has the capacity to take advantage of it. Thus, a character-based conception of moral agency reveals the extent to which we neither choose nor control the process that determines whether we become full moral agents.

Finally, we are left with the specter of determinism. Most theorists who take the concept of moral culpability seriously still express strong reservations about whether people are morally responsible for their characters as well as their actions. It is one thing to argue that people exercise sufficient control over their actions to be held accountable for them. It is quite another to claim that people choose their motivational traits or have the ability to control them simply by choosing to do so. Thus, many determinists might challenge the moral legitimacy of this character-based conception of moral agency by arguing that some of its attributes do not rest on an accurate vision of human nature.

To be responsible for those aspects of our character that motivate our choices, it would seem that we must either be able to control how these motivational traits initially develop or have the power to revise relatively established features of our personality. But few of us believe the former proposition, and proof of the latter claim concerning our power to remake ourselves is fraught with difficulties that both soft and hard determinists are eager to point out. It may be ennobling to believe in the existential claim that what we are is always up to us, but the evidence supporting this strong version of human autonomy will always be open to serious question.

One point of this essay is to explain why moral theorists must confront questions about the extent to which we can control those character traits that motivate our choices. Choice theorists suppress too much of the importance of character in our renditions of praise and blame. To be sure, it is difficult to defend the ways we lend moral stature to ourselves, and puzzles surround the meanings we create when we blame and excuse. But if we minimize the role of character in that story and persist in the illusion that we are only blaming the rational choices of disembodied rational agents, we will create a moral theory that neither describes nor justifies our actual blaming judgments. Better that we see the story we are telling ourselves. Perhaps the discrepancy between our vision of why we qualify as moral agents and the real-life conditions that make it so difficult for some criminal defendants to develop into full moral agents might motivate us to do something about those conditions. If we acknowledge that discrepancy, we may, at least, come to see the moral ambiguity of our blaming judgments when we fail to offer transformational opportunities to those we judge.

Law, University of California at Los Angeles

RECONSIDERING THE RELATIONSHIP AMONG VOLUNTARY ACTS, STRICT LIABILITY, AND NEGLIGENCE IN CRIMINAL LAW

By Larry Alexander

Introduction

This essay, as will become obvious, owes a huge debt to Mark Kelman, particularly to his article "Interpretative Construction in the Substantive Criminal Law."[1] That debt is one of both concept and content. There is rich irony in my aping Kelman's deconstructionist enterprise, for I do not share his enthusiasm for either the "insights" or the political agenda of the Critical Legal Studies movement. I do not believe that either the law in general or the criminal law in particular is radically indeterminate, rife with internal contradictions, or an expression of the interests of a dominant economic class. And although, like Kelman, I believe that the freedom/determinism, act/character, and rule/principle dichotomies must ultimately be dealt with in order to have a completely satisfactory account of criminal law, I also believe that these dichotomies loom just as large in other areas of law and in normative theory generally.[2] They are problems for Crits as well as for liberal-legalists.

In any event, my intentions in undertaking this deconstructionist enterprise are modestly reformist, not revolutionary. I do not intend to shift any paradigms, but to work with well-established ones. I will assume that criminal law seeks to accomplish some blend of retributive response to and deterrence of culpable choices, choices to defy moral norms that are also legal norms.[3] (I omit consideration of criminal laws premised on immoral norms.) I will also assume that a culpable choice is one that reflects negatively on the values held by the chooser. Beyond these quite modest assumptions, I need not and will not venture in this paper, realizing, of course, that much has and can be written about the proper aims of punishment and the proper account of culpability.

[1] *Stanford Law Review*, vol. 33 (April 1981), pp. 591–673. See also Mark Kelman, *A Guide to Critical Legal Studies* (Cambridge: Harvard University Press, 1987), pp. 15–185.

[2] See Mark Hager, "Against Liberal Ideology," *American University Law Review*, vol. 37 (Summer 1988), pp. 1051, 1057–58.

Briefly, the freedom/determinism dichotomy refers to the philosophical issue of whether determinism prevails throughout nature, including the realm of human action, or whether human action is indeterministic is some sense, and what resolution of these questions entails for moral responsibility. The act/character dichotomy refers to the issue of whether moral responsibility is ultimately a function of how we act or a function of what kind of character we have. The rule/principle dichotomy refers to the issue of whether we should be guided in each of our acts by our ultimate moral principles, or whether we should be guided by rules that are more determinate than those principles but that lead to some acts that from the standpoint of the principles would be judged to be morally wrong.

[3] See Jean Hampton, "*Mens Rea*," *Social Philosophy & Policy*, vol. 7, no. 2 (Spring 1990).

My focus will be on three principles of Anglo-American criminal law. The principles are:

(1) The "voluntary act principle": there can be no criminal liability in the absence of a voluntary act. (For example, if one is blown by a hurricane into another person, one cannot be convicted of criminal battery because one did not "batter" the other "voluntarily.")
(2) The "strict liability principle": criminal liability can be predicated solely on a voluntary act and need not be predicated additionally on a showing of a culpable mental state or negligence (though whether it should be so predicated is controversial). (For example, in many jurisdictions, exceeding the speed limit is an offense regardless of the care taken by the driver to avoid doing so.)
(3) The "negligence principle": as an alternative to strict liability, criminal liability can be predicated solely on a voluntary act plus negligence (though whether it should be so predicated is controversial). (For example, in all jurisdictions, if one causes another's death by acting without adverting to a risk to others that a reasonable person would not impose, one is criminally liable for negligent homicide.)

My purpose in this paper is to explore the relationship among these three principles. I will conclude that principles (1) and (2) – the voluntary act principle and the strict liability principle – are in tension with one another. Construing the voluntary act principle to reflect its most promising normative rationale results in a direct conflict with the strict liability principle. Conversely, construing the voluntary act principle so as to render it consistent with the strict liability principle renders the former principle virtually empty. I will also conclude that principles (2) and (3) – the strict liability principle and the negligence principle – cannot be differentiated non-arbitrarily and that they therefore collapse into each other. Ultimately, the conclusion I am led to is that the voluntary act principle, taken to the fullest extent that its rationale suggests, requires us to reject the other two principles: that is, principles that envision crimes predicated on strict liability and negligence. On the other hand, the considerations behind the strict liability and negligence principles are valid and probably should limit the application of the voluntary act principle.

I. The Standard Account of the Voluntary Act, Strict Liability, and Negligence Principles

A. The Voluntary Act Principle

According to the commentators, it is the law in all Anglo-American jurisdictions that "no person is guilty of a crime unless she commits a voluntary act."[4] The voluntary act principle is usually treated by courts as implicit in criminal statutes, though several states have followed the Model Penal Code and made the principle an explicit part of their criminal codes.[5]

[4] Joshua Dressler, *Understanding Criminal Law* (New York, Oakland, and Albany: Matthew Bender, 1987), p. 65.

[5] *ibid.*

The voluntary act principle, as illustrated by § 2.01 of the Model Penal Code, requires that the criminal defendant have engaged in a willed bodily movement[6] (or, in the case of criminal omissions, to have failed to perform certain bodily movements which defendant could have performed had she so willed[7]). The Model Penal Code states that "a person is not guilty of an offense unless his liability is based on conduct that includes a voluntary act [or omission]."[8] An "act" is defined as a "bodily movement."[9] "Voluntary" is defined negatively by examples of involuntary conduct, including external physical compulsion (a push, for example), reflexes, convulsions, unconscious behavior, and behavior undertaken in a state of altered consciousness.[10] As H. L. A. Hart concludes:

> We know now what the general doctrine [that all criminal responsibility must be voluntary] means: It defines an act in terms of the simplest thing we can do: this is the minimum feat of contracting our muscles. Conduct is "voluntary" or "the expression of an act of will" if the muscular contraction which, on the physical side, is the initiating element in what are loosely thought of as simple actions, is caused by a desire for those same contractions. This is all the mysterious element of the "will" amounts to: It is this which is the minimum indispensable link between mind and body required for responsibility even where responsibility is strict.[11]

If the requirement of a voluntary act, defined as a willed bodily movement, is a fundamental principle of Anglo-American criminal law – and, indeed, in the United States, arguably a constitutional requirement[12] – what is its rationale? Put differently, what fundamental value does the voluntary act principle serve?

Douglas Husak has examined the voluntary act principle in terms of what it exempts from criminal liability (e.g., forced and reflex movements, unconscious movements, thoughts, and status offenses) and what it does not (e.g., omissions), and he concludes that the principle is an expression of the judgment that it is unfair to blame or punish one for conduct that is not fairly subject to one's control.[13] I believe Husak is correct. The above examples of things exempted from liability have very little in common except that their exemption is appropriate according to this judgment. In any event, I shall accept but not defend this view of what value the

[6] Performance of a mental ritual might also qualify. See Leo Katz, *Bad Acts and Guilty Minds: Conundrums of the Criminal Law* (Chicago and London: University of Chicago Press, 1987).

[7] Dressler, *Understanding Criminal Law*, pp. 67–68; H.L.A. Hart, *Punishment and Responsibility* (New York: Oxford University Press, 1968), pp. 95–96, 150–51; Rollin Perkins and Ronald Boyce, *Criminal Law* (Mineola: Foundation Press, 3rd ed. 1982), p. 837.

[8] *Model Penal Code*, § 2.01 (Proposed Official Draft 1962).

[9] *ibid.*, § 1.13(2).

[10] *ibid*, § 2.01.

[11] Hart, *Punishment and Responsibility*, p. 99.

[12] The United States Supreme Court held that the federal constitutional prohibition of "cruel and unusual punishments" prevented criminalizing the status of narcotics addiction. Robinson v. California, 370 U.S. 660, 82 S.Ct. 1417, 8 L.Ed.2d 758 (1966). The orthodox interpretation of the *Robinson* decision is that it rests on the distinction between punishing statuses and punishing acts. See, e.g., Dressler, *Understanding Criminal Law*, pp. 73–77.

[13] Douglas Husak, *Philosophy of Criminal Law* (Totowa: Rowman and Littlefield, 1987), ch. 4.

voluntary act principle is meant to express, and I shall also accept but not defend the value itself. I am primarily interested in what acceptance of the voluntary act principle as glossed by this value entails as regards the strict liability and negligence principles.

B. The Strict Liability Principle

Although most criminal offenses require some form of culpable mental state or negligence with respect to the proscribed conduct or results, some do not.[14] Usually, though not always, these "strict liability crimes" carry light penalties.[15]

Strict liability crimes, which are my concern in this paper, must be distinguished from ordinary crimes, the seriousness of which can be enhanced by strict liability elements – that is, elements the defendant does not intend to bring about and is unaware exist. (For example, assault upon a peace officer is frequently treated as an aggravated form of criminal assault, even where the actor is completely unaware that her victim is a peace officer.) These strict liability punishment-enhancing elements raise interesting problems in the theory of punishment, particularly the problem of whether one who is culpable to some extent can fairly be subjected to a "lottery" that will determine his level of punishment. (In other words, the presence or absence of the punishment-enhancing strict liability element can be viewed as a matter of chance from the standpoint of the culpable actor: hence, the notion of a punishment "lottery.") This problem is one that runs through large areas of criminal law, particularly the distinction between attempted crimes, where the actor tries but fails to bring about the criminal harm, and crimes where the criminal harm does result.[16]

I am also not dealing with the strict liability element regarding the existence of the various criminal offenses themselves. The general rule is that one is strictly liable for acting in ignorance of, the criminal law,[17] though at its boundaries the rule is subject to constitutional limitations.[18] The rule permits the punishment of some defendants who, though they intended, or knew, or were reckless or negligent with respect to the conduct they engaged in or the results they brought about, were faultless with respect to their ignorance that such conduct or results were forbidden. I deal here only with strict liability offenses where the strict liability is

[14] Perkins and Boyce, *Criminal Law*, pp. 896, 899.

[15] Wayne LaFave and Austin Scott, *Criminal Law* (St. Paul: West Publishing, 3rd ed. 1986), p. 242.

[16] David Lewis, "The Punishment That Leaves Something to Chance," *Philosophy & Public Affairs*, vol. 18, no. 1 (Winter 1988), pp. 53–67; Steven Sverdlik, "Crime and Moral Luck," *American Philosophical Quarterly*, vol. 25, no. 1 (January 1988), pp. 79–85; Andrew Ashworth, "Criminal Attempts and the Role of Resulting Harm Under the Code, and in the Common Law," *Rutgers Law Journal*, vol. 19, no. 3 (Spring 1988), pp. 725–810; Yoram Shachar, "The Fortuitous Gap in Law and Morality," *Criminal Justice Ethics*, vol. 6, no. 2 (Summer/Fall 1987), pp. 12–36; Note, "Chance, Freedom, and Criminal Liability," *Columbia Law Review*, vol. 87, no. 1 (January 1987), pp. 125–41; Judith Thomson, "The Decline of Cause," *The Georgetown Law Journal*, vol. 76 (1987), pp. 137–50; Paul Rothstein, "Causation in Torts, Crimes, and Moral Philosophy: A Reply to Professor Thomson," *The Georgetown Law Journal*, vol. 76 (1987), pp. 150–67; Stephen Schulhofer, "Harm and Punishment: A Critique of Emphasis on the Results of Conduct in the Criminal Law," *University of Pennsylvania Law Review*, vol. 122 (January 1974), pp. 1497–1607; Andrew Ashworth, "Belief, Intent, and Criminal Liability," eds. J. Eekelan and J. Bell, *Oxford Essays in Jurisprudence* (Oxford: Clarendon Press, 3rd ed. 1987).

[17] See *Model Penal Code*, § 2.04(3).

[18] See Lambert v. California, 355 U.S. 225, 78 S.Ct. 240, 2 L.Ed.2d 228 (1957).

with respect to the conduct or result, and not with respect to the law itself. My conclusions, however, will have some bearing on the issue of ignorance of the law.

Strict liability crimes such as speeding, which are punishable despite lack of intent, knowledge, or negligence, though relatively common, are quite controversial among jurists and commentators.[19] They are surely inconsistent with any version of retributivism that absolutely condemns punishment of the non-culpable. Of course, such a strong version of retributivism is arguably inconsistent with any system for imposing punishment based upon an ascertainment of culpability that is subject to error – i.e., any system for imposing punishment.[20] What is distinctly problematic about strict liability crimes is that even when they are enforced without error, they still may result in punishment of the nonculpable: those who have not chosen to defy the governing norms.

Nonetheless, strict liability crimes do serve some retributive and consequentialist values at the same time that they disserve other retributive values. Strict liability crimes serve the retributive value of seeing that the culpable do not go unpunished in that by omitting the necessity to prove culpability beyond a reasonable doubt, they make it easier to convict the culpable.[21] In addition, strict liability crimes deter unwanted conduct (which produces undeserved suffering, arguably a desert-based value if not a retributive one[22]) in two ways: first, they deter would-be culpable actors who might otherwise engage in harmful conduct believing, whether correctly or incorrectly, that the prosecution will be unable to prove their culpability;[23] second, they deter the innocent by creating incentives to take extraordinary care to avoid harmful conduct. Finally, strict liability crimes cost less to investigate and prosecute.[24]

Although strict liability crimes are controversial, their existence is generally considered to be consistent with the voluntary act principle. And they are also generally regarded as distinguishable from crimes on negligence with respect to conduct or result.

C. The Negligence Principle

Criminal liability is frequently predicated on negligence, which is conduct that creates an unreasonable risk of harm to an interest protected by the criminal law (negligence as to result), or an unreasonable though sincere belief that one's

[19] See M. Bayles, *Principles of Law: A Normative Analysis* (Dordrecht, Boston, Lancaster and Tokyo: D. Reidel Publishing, 1987), pp. 295–300; Jerome Hall, *General Principles of Criminal Law* (Indianapolis: Bobbs-Merrill, 1960) pp. 342–51; LaFave and Scott, *Criminal Law*, p. 248; Perkins and Boyce, *Criminal Law*, p. 905; Henry M. Hart, "The Aims of the Criminal Law," *Law and Contemporary Problems*, vol. 23 (Summer 1958), pp. 401, 422–25; Frances B. Sayre, "Public Welfare Offenses," *Columbia Law Review*, vol. 33, no. 1 (January 1933) pp. 52, 82; Richard Singer, "The Resurgence of *Mens Rea*: The Rise and Fall of Strict Criminal Liability," *Boston College Law Review*, vol. 30, no. 2 (March 1989), pp. 337, 403–8.

[20] See Larry Alexander, "Retributivism and the Inadvertent Punishment of the Innocent," *Law and Philosophy*, vol. 2, no. 2 (August 1983), pp. 233–46.

[21] LaFave & Scott, *Criminal Law*, p. 247.

[22] See Note, "Criminal Liability Without Fault: A Philosophical Perspective," *Columbia Law Review*, vol. 75, no. 8 (December 1975), pp. 1517, 1564.

[23] *ibid.*, p. 1537.

[24] *ibid.*, p. 1537. For a rejoinder to this student note's claims on behalf of strict liability, see Richard Singer, "The Resurgence of *Mens Rea*: The Rise and Fall of Strict Criminal Liability," pp. 403–8.

conduct is not conduct which, under another description, is proscribed by the criminal law (negligence as to conduct). Negligent homicide is an example of a crime based on negligence as to result – i.e., the creation of an unreasonable risk of death that in fact eventuates in a death. Bigamy is an example of a crime that can be based on negligence as to conduct, as (for example) in those cases where one unreasonably believes in the validity of a prior divorce. The Model Penal Code's definition of criminal negligence is representative:

> *Negligently.* A person acts negligently with respect to a material element of an offense when he should be aware of a substantial and unjustifiable risk that the material element exists or will result from his conduct. The risk must be of such a nature and degree that the actor's failure to perceive it, considering the nature and purpose of his conduct and the circumstances known to him, involves a gross deviation from the standard of care that a reasonable person would observe in the actor's situation ....[25]

To be negligent, one need not advert to (in the sense of "be aware of") the unreasonable risk one is creating with respect either to proscribed result or to the proscribed nature of one's conduct. Indeed, adverting to such risks converts one's negligent conduct to recklessness. True negligence is inadvertent creation of unreasonable risks. What distinguishes negligence from strict liability is that the negligent actor's unawareness of the risk is a failure to meet the objective "reasonable person" standard.[26]

Criminal punishment of inadvertent negligence is just about as controversial as the existence of strict liability crimes.[27] All of the arguments in favor of strict liability crimes are available on behalf of making negligence a basis of criminal liability. In addition, many theorists contend that negligence, unlike strict liability, betokens culpability, especially when the "reasonable person" of the negligence standard is relativized to the reasonable person "in the actor's situation."[28] Essentially, those who deem negligence culpable argue that failure to advert to a risk that one had a fair chance to perceive (had one only tried) is culpable, even though it does not entail a conscious choice to produce or unreasonably to risk harm.[29]

[25] *Model Penal Code*, § 2.02(4)(d).

[26] See Note, "Element Analysis in Defining Criminal Liability: The Model Penal Code and Beyond," *Stanford Law Review*, vol. 35 (April 1983), pp. 681, 696.

[27] Bayles, *Principles of Law*, pp. 295–300; Hart, *Punishment and Responsibility*, pp. 132–40; James Brady, "Punishment for Negligence: A Reply to Professor Hall," *Buffalo Law Review*, vol. 22, no. 3 (Spring 1972), pp. 107–22; George Fletcher, "The Theory of Criminal Negligence: A Comparative Analysis," *University of Pennsylvania Law Review*, vol. 119, no. 3 (January 1971), pp. 401–38; Jerome Hall, "Negligent Behavior Should Be Excluded from Penal Liability," *Columbia Law Review*, vol. 63, no. 4 (April 1963), pp. 632–44; Richard Wasserstrom, "H.L.A. Hart and the Doctrine of Mens Rea and Criminal Responsibility," *University of Chicago Law Review*, vol. 35 (1967), pp. 92–126.

[28] See Hart, *Punishment and Responsibility*, pp. 147–149; Glanville Williams, *The Mental Element in Crime* (Jerusalem: Magnes Press, Hebrew University, 1965), pp. 54–60; Fletcher, "Theory of Criminal Negligence," p. 417; Hall, "Negligent Behavior," pp. 632–36; J.W.C. Turner, "The Mental Element in Crimes at Common Law," *Cambridge Law Journal*, vol. 6, no. 1 (1936), pp. 31, 44–48.

[29] See authorities in note 27; LaFave and Scott, *Criminal Law*, p. 234.

II. Deconstructing the Distinction between Strict Liability Crimes and Violations of the Voluntary Act Principle

A. A Case

In 1977, the Kansas Court of Appeals had before it the case of one Mr. Baker, who had been convicted at trial of driving 75 miles per hour in a 55 miles per hour zone.[30] The pertinent Kansas speeding law was conceded by all to be a strict liability offense. Mr. Baker did not deny that his car was going 75 in a 55 zone, or that he was driving it. Mr. Baker did deny, however, that his driving 75 was a voluntary act on his part.

What happened, apparently, is that Mr. Baker's cruise control stuck in the "accelerate" position, causing his car to accelerate beyond the posted speed limit. His attempts to deactivate the cruise control by hitting the "off" button and the brakes did not initially succeed. Because the speed of the car was temporarily out of his control, he argued that his speeding was not a voluntary act.

Although the Kansas court purported to accept the voluntary act principle, it nonetheless affirmed Baker's conviction. In the key passage of its opinion, the court argued:

> We have no doubt that if defendant were able to establish that his act of speeding was the result of an unforeseen occurrence or circumstance, which was not caused by him and which he could not prevent, that such would constitute a valid defense to the charge. But, the evidence proffered suggests a malfunction of a device attached to the motor vehicle operated by the defendant over which he had or should have had absolute control. Defendant does not suggest that the operation of the motor vehicle on the day of his arrest was anything but a voluntary act on his part, not that anyone other than himself activated the cruise control, which may have caused his excessive speed. ...[31]

The court went on to distinguish cases from other jurisdictions in which the defendant was merely a passenger in the car,[32] in which the brakes failed without warning,[33] or in which the accelerator broke.[34] The court argued that

> Unexpected brake failure and unexpected malfunction of the throttle on an automobile, both being essential components to the operation of the vehicle, differ significantly from the malfunction of a cruise control device to which the driver has voluntarily delegated partial control of the automobile. We believe it must be said that defendant assumed the full operation of his motor vehicle and when he did so and activated the cruise control attached to that automobile, he clearly was the agent in causing the act of speeding. ...[35]

[30] State v. Baker, 1 Kan. App. 2d 568, 571 P.2d 65 (1977).
[31] *ibid.*, pp. 570, 571 P.2d, pp., 67–68.
[32] People v. Shaughnessey, 66 Misc.2d 19, 319 N.Y.S.2d 626 (1971).
[33] State v. Kremer, 262 Minn. 190, 114 N.W.2d 88 (1962).
[34] State v. Weller, 4 Conn. Cir. 267, 230 A.2d 242 (1967).
[35] State v. Baker, 1 Kan. App. 2d, p. 573, 571 P.2d, p. 69.

B. What Baker Reveals: The Time-Framing Problem in Strict Liability Offenses

If you are not particularly satisfied by the Kansas court's explanation of why Mr. Baker's punishment does not violate the voluntary act principle, or the court's grounds for distinguishing other similar cases, there is a good reason: the voluntary act principle and the strict liability principle are in conflict with one another, and the resolution of that conflict depends on a quite arbitrary decision with respect to determining the relevant voluntary act. The problem is, to borrow Mark Kelman's useful term, one of "time-framing."[36]

Time-framing refers to the temporal boundaries of the criminal conduct: when that conduct can be said to begin and end. Turning to *Baker*, when did Baker's criminal conduct begin? (When it ended is of no concern here.) If it began when his car accelerated past 55 miles per hour, then it looks as though Mr. Baker's claim that he did not act voluntarily was correct. One of the paradigms of involuntary action is compulsion by an external force, such as a push. Being propelled by an out-of-control car surely looks like being pushed, insofar as the voluntary act principle is concerned. Undoubtedly, that is why the New York case cited by the *Baker* court deemed the defendant not to have acted voluntarily when he was but a passenger in the car.[37] If the criminal conduct that is the subject of the strict liability offense of speeding began at the time the speed passed 55 miles per hour – or, indeed, at any time after the defective cruise control was switched on – then Mr. Baker cannot be convicted without violating the voluntary act principle.

On the other hand, suppose we say Mr. Baker's criminal conduct began with his choice to activate the cruise control, or his choice to go driving – with any choice that preceded the cruise control's being activated. Surely his conduct at these earlier times was voluntary, and it led to his car's exceeding the speed limit.

Moreover, all strict liability crimes that are predicated on resulting harm will be involuntary if we time-frame narrowly – if we begin the story only after the defendant has acted, and all that remains is for the harmful results of that action to occur. Therefore, it makes sense, or so it seems, to time-frame more broadly and begin Mr. Baker's story early enough to find a voluntary act. Indeed, the same point holds true of strict liability crimes defined in terms of conduct, not results. For one can always claim that what one voluntarily chose was conduct X (say, marrying someone who is single), which is innocent conduct, and that the fact that conduct X was the same as conduct Y (say, marrying someone who is in fact already married), which is proscribed conduct, was a result out of one's control once one chose to engage in conduct X.

On the other hand, if we time-frame too broadly we make the voluntary act principle vacuous. After all, all conduct engaged in by adults will be traceable to some voluntary act in their past (unless they have been incapable of acting voluntarily since infancy). If the voluntary act principle is to have any normative bite at all, criminal conduct cannot be time-framed too broadly.

[36] Kelman, "Interpretative Construction in the Substantive Criminal Law," p. 593.

[37] See People v. Shaughnessey.

How then do we choose the proper time-frame for strict liability crimes, given that too narrow a time-frame will threaten strict liability and too broad a time-frame will empty the voluntary act principle of its content?

The answer is that any choice is going to be completely arbitrary. Remember that we are dealing with strict liability crimes, which by definition do not require any culpability. Therefore, we cannot use a culpable choice as the touchstone of the commencement of the story. If Mr. Baker's choice to switch on the cruise control had been a culpable choice, no one would believe that the voluntary act principle was in issue in his case. (Consider the Jekyll-and-Hyde choice to render oneself an involuntary actor as part of a criminal scheme, for example, taking a potion that one knows will later induce homidical automatism: there is no question but that the culpable choice satisfies the voluntary act requirement despite involuntariness at the time of the homicidal conduct.) But culpability cannot be required to satisfy the voluntary act principle without at the same time undermining the strict liability principle.

How else can arbitrariness in time-framing be avoided? Perhaps by requiring that the defendant's earlier, voluntary choice be the "proximate cause" of the conduct or result in question. Causation-in-fact is always going to be present and thus cannot be used to distinguish proper and improper time-framing. But proximate causation is not a question of fact. To the extent it is meaningful at all, it represents a choice to ascribe responsibility for certain results of conduct to those whose choices were causes-in-fact of those results or that conduct.[38] But if it is such a choice, on what values will it be based? As I see it, the proximate cause determination can be based on either the values underlying having strict liability crimes or the values underlying the voluntary act principle. Since those values lead us to time-frame differently, building them into proximate causation as a basis for time-framing won't help us with our problem, but will just relabel it.

Let me amplify this point. The voluntary act principle reflects the belief that it is wrong to punish people for events not fairly subject to their control. The strict liability principle contemplates punishment of the nonculpable in order to achieve deterrence and other values. The more broadly we time-frame in searching for a voluntary act that is the proximate cause of the strict liability conduct or result, the more we trample on the value expressed by the voluntary act principle, but the more we serve deterrence and other values associated with strict liability. The truly guilty will not escape punishment through a failure to prove voluntariness, nor will anyone be tempted to commit a crime by the prospect of escaping punishment on that ground.

Of course, sometimes time-framing choices will be limited by the semantics of the criminal statutes. In other words, it may be impossible to stretch a statute that by its terms, say, proscribes "dangerous operation of a motor vehicle" to reach

[38] Perkins and Boyce define proximate cause as an actual cause which is not so remote in the causation chain that the court will not recognize it as a legal cause of the event in question. It is a question of "fact and degree." Perkins and Boyce, *Criminal Law*, pp. 774–77. LaFave and Scott add, "one might logically . . . be harder on those who intended bad results which differ from what they intended, than on those (morally less at fault) whose conduct amounts only to reckless or negligent creation of risks of bad result." LaFave and Scott, *Criminal Law*, p. 283.

those who are merely passengers. But there will be lots of cases where the time-framing issue will not be resolvable on semantic grounds. In those cases, the time-framing problem will leave the voluntary act principle and strict liability in tension.

To see if I have fairly stated this dilemma, let us look at a sample of cases and see if the problem that surfaced in the *Baker* case is pervasive. In *State v. Kremer*[39] and *State v. Weller*,[40] the failed brake and failed accelerator cases cited by the *Baker* court, the difference in result between those cases and *Baker* is obviously the result of a difference in time-framing – at least if we absolve Mr. Baker of any culpability in activating the cruise control. In all three cases, the defendants voluntarily put their cars in operation. In all three cases, the cars had defects that caused harm. In all three cases, the defendants acted nonculpably. In *Baker*, however, the court chose to time-frame more broadly than did the courts in *Kremer* and *Weller*, with the inevitable result that it found a voluntary act to be subjected to strict liability where the other courts found none.

There have been a relatively large number of cases involving unconscious behavior. Sometimes the courts look to the voluntary acts that preceded and led to the unconscious behavior and convict the defendant. At other times they look only at the unconscious behavior itself and acquit. In *People v. Decina*,[41] for example, the New York appellate court upheld the conviction for negligent homicide of a driver who had an epileptic seizure while driving and killed four children. The court focused on defendant's decision to drive while knowing that he was subject to such seizures. That decision, unlike the speed and direction of the car at the fatal moment, was surely voluntary. Moreover, it was, at least in the eyes of the majority, a culpable decision as well.

In *Government of the Virgin Islands v. Smith*,[42] on the other hand, the Court of Appeals reversed defendant's conviction for involuntary manslaughter arising out of an automobile accident, because the trial court had failed to instruct the jury properly regarding the burden of proof on the issue of whether the defendant had an epileptic blackout at the time of the accident. The strong implication of the court's decision is that a reasonable doubt as to the defendant's consciousness would mandate acquittal.[43]

These two cases can perhaps be distinguished on the ground that Decina, but not Smith, was culpable in choosing to drive. Smith's seizure might have been his first, whereas Decina knew he was subject to seizures. But suppose the crimes charged in these cases had been strict liability crimes. Presumably, then, the culpability of the choice to drive would be immaterial to the charge. The only pertinent question according to the orthodox account would be whether Decina and Smith acted voluntarily. And it looks as though only a difference in time-framing could account for the opposite conclusions reached by the two courts.

39 See State v. Kremer.

40 See State v. Weller.

41 2 N.Y.2d 133, 157 N.Y.S.2d 558, 138 N.E. 2d 799 (1956).

42 278 F.2d 169 (3rd Cir. 1960).

43 See also People v. Freeman, 61 Cal. App. 2d 110, 142 P.2d 435 (1943); People v. Hardy, 33 Cal. 2d 52, 198 P.2d 865 (1948); People v. Newton, 8 Cal. App. 3d 359, 87 Cal. Rptr. 394 (1970); Hill v. Baxter, 1 Q.B. 277 (1958).

Or consider the case Kelman uses to make this point, *Martin v. State*.[44] In that case, the appellate court reversed Martin's conviction for public intoxication because, while drunk, he had been taken out of his house and into public by the police. As Kelman demonstrates, the voluntariness of Martin's public intoxication depends upon whether his saga is broadly time-framed to begin with his decision to drink excessively or is narrowly time-framed to begin only with his being taken onto the street by the police. If we are not interested in Martin's culpability – that is, if being intoxicated in public is a strict liability crime – we are left completely without guidance in choosing the appropriate time-frame.

Finally, consider the strange case of *People v. Newton*.[45] There Newton, a passenger on a flight from the Bahamas to Luxembourg, was carrying a loaded .38 caliber revolver. The flight was diverted to New York City, where Newton was arrested for possessing a loaded firearm without a license. The court released Newton from custody, because it did not find his violation of the New York statute to have been voluntary. Yet there was no indication that Newton was not in voluntary possession of the gun when he got on the plane. Nor was it inconceivable, as opposed to improbable, that he would end up in New York, not Luxembourg. (It could hardly be inconceivable, since it happened.) Therefore, it we dismiss any concern with culpability, and focus on voluntariness, it is difficult to see why Newton acted more involuntarily then Decina. Moreover, we are entitled to suspect that the court would have found Newton to have acted voluntarily if, for example, Bahamas to Luxembourg flights frequently made unscheduled stops in New York City, a fact that might affect Newton's culpability but not the voluntariness of his act. In other words, the court made a time-framing choice in deeming Newton to have been an involuntary actor, but it appeared to do so on grounds relevant to culpability, presumably immaterial to strict liability.

My conclusion is that the voluntary act principle and the strict liability principle are completely opposed to one other. We can square strict liability crimes like Baker's with the voluntary act principle by broadening the time-frame, but in doing so we strip the voluntary act principle of its power to limit punishment. On the other hand, if we give the value behind the voluntary act principle full force, we are driven to find a choice the actor made that led to the harm and – most importantly – of which we disapprove. In other words, we are driven to find a culpable choice and thus to abandon strict liability.[46]

But before concluding this section, let us look more closely at this last point. Is finding a culpable choice really the only way to give expression the value behind the voluntary act principle? Jeffrie Murphy thinks not:

[44] 31 Ala. App. 334, 17 So. 2d 427 (1944).

[45] 72 Misc.2d 646, 340 N.Y.S. 2d 77 (1973).

[46] For earlier hints in the literature that strict liability and the voluntary act principle are strange bedfellows, see M. Budd and A. Lynch, "Voluntariness, Causation, and Strict Liability," *Criminal Law Review* (January 1978), pp. 74, 75, footnote 6. See also Husak, *Philosophy of Criminal Law*, p. 140 (obliquely making this point). And see Killbride v. Lake, 1972 N.Z.L.R. 590.

> Why do we feel a requirement to excuse the man whose actions are involuntary? Not merely for utilitarian reasons, surely.... A penal code so Draconian as to punish even epileptics might have high general deterrence and little disutility (as long as most of us could be fairly sure of not becoming epileptic). So another important reason against holding liable here is justice or fairness. And we always feel the pressure to take account of justice or fairness – even in strict liability cases. We may hold a man liable without fault in some areas and thus punish him even if he was not negligent – even if he took all reasonable care. But we would surely object to this on grounds of justice (no matter how high the general utility) if the man did not have fair warning that this was an area of conduct in which he might have to expect this sort of thing. A drug manufacturer is under danger of strict liability prosecution for any faultless adulteration in his product. But we do not object to this as much as we otherwise might as long as he is given fair warning to choose to do something else with his life if he is not willing to assume this kind of risk. If he does many things to protect his product and fails, then we can always say that he could have done more. ...
>
> But compare strokes, seizures, and the like. We do not have any capacities to exercise when these are operative. And thus, by no stretch of the imagination can we regard their punishment as fair. When one is suffering a seizure, normal capacities just do not enter the picture. ...[47]

Murphy needs a concept of "fair warning" that does not equate to culpability. I deny that there is such a concept. In one sense, we are all aware – we have been fairly warned – that whatever we voluntarily do at this moment may lead to further conduct or results that are out of our control once we act: consequences that we do not intend to bring about or do not believe have a substantial and unreasonable likelihood of occurring. If we are held liable for their occurrence, have we been "fairly warned"? If Murphy says yes, then he can have no objection to punishment of epileptics; after all, we are all aware when we drive of the possibility of heretofore undisclosed epilepsy. If Murphy says no, then where is the line to be drawn short of a choice that is culpable? If we don't want anyone to drive because of the remote risk of epilepsy or automatism, we should deem anyone's choice to drive to be culpable and punish it. On the other hand, if we want only those to refrain from driving who are aware of a risk of seizures that is higher than normal by a certain amount, then we will deem their choice to drive culpable and proscribe it. It is difficult to understand why one whose risk of seizures is higher than normal but lower than the level of culpability should be deemed to have had "fair warning" if he drives as permitted but suffers a seizure, whereas if someone whose risk is (prior to the occurrence) assessed as normal suffers a seizure and is punished, he lacks "fair warning." We have reasons for permitting the taking of certain risks and reasons for proscribing the taking of certain risks. A "fair warning" is one that

[47] Jeffrie Murphy, "Involuntary Acts and Criminal Liability," *Ethics*, vol. 81 (1971), pp. 332, 340–42.

acquaints actors with what risk-taking is proscribed and permitted. The lottery concept of fair warning which attaches to strict liability is too weak to rule out punishment of epileptics who are unaware of their epilepsy.[48] The only alternative concept of fair warning is one parasitic on standards of culpability: the voluntary act principle requires fair control, and fair control requires not just choice but a reason to choose the preferred conduct – i.e., a choice between the culpable and the nonculpable.

III. Deconstructing the Distinction between Negligence and Strict Liability

A. A Case

In *State v. Williams*,[49] the defendants, a husband and wife, were convicted of negligent homicide in the death of their infant son. As the Washington Court of Appeals described them, the defendants were full-blooded Indians, one of whom had a sixth-grade education and one of whom had an eleventh-grade education. Their infant son, William, died from gangrene caused by the failure to treat an abscessed tooth. The court summed up the evidence presented at trial as follows:

> Dr. Gale Wilson, the autopsy surgeon and pathologist for the King County Coroner, testified that the child died because an abscessed tooth had been allowed to develop into an infection of the mouth and cheeks, eventually becoming gangrenous. This condition, accompanied by the child's inability to eat, brought about malnutrition, lowering the child's resistance and eventually producing pneumonia, causing the death. Dr. Wilson testified that in his opinion the infection had lasted for approximately two weeks, and that the odor generally associated with gangrene would have been present for approximately 10 days before death. He also expressed the opinion that had medical care been first obtained in the last week before the baby's death, such care would have been obtained too late to have saved the baby's life. Accordingly, the baby's apparent condition between September 1 and September 5, 1968, became the critical period for the purpose of determining whether in the exercise of ordinary caution defendants should have provided medical care for the minor child.
>
> The testimony concerning the child's apparent condition during the critical period is not crystal clear, but is sufficient to warrant the following statement of the matter. The defendant husband testified that he noticed the baby was sick about two weeks before the baby died. The defendant's wife testified that she noticed the baby was ill about a week and a half or two weeks before the baby died. The evidence showed that in the critical period the baby was fussy; that he could not keep his food down; and that a cheek started swelling up. The swelling went up and down, but did not disappear. In that same period, the cheek turned "a bluish color like." The defendants, not realizing that the baby was as ill as it was or that the baby

[48] See discussion in text accompanying note 16 *supra*.

[49] 4 Wash. App. 908, 484 P.2d 1167 (1971).

> was in danger of dying, attempted to provide some relief to the baby by giving the baby aspirin during the critical period and continued to do so until the night before the baby died. The defendants thought the swelling would go down and were waiting for it to do so; and defendant husband testified that from what he had heard, neither doctors nor dentists pull out a tooth "when it's all swollen up like that." There was an additional explanation for not calling a doctor given by each defendant. Defendant husband testified that "the way the cheek looked, ... and that stuff on his hair, they would think we were neglecting him and take him away from us and not given him back." Defendant wife testified that the defendants were "waiting for the swelling to go down." ... The evidence showed that the defendants did not understand the significance or seriousness of the baby's symptoms. However, there is no evidence that the defendants were physically or financially unable to obtain a doctor, or that they did not know an available doctor, or that the symptoms did not continue to be a matter of concern during the critical period. Indeed, the evidence showed that in April 1968 defendant husband had taken the child to a doctor for medical attention.[50]

Based on this evidence, the trial court found:

> That both defendants were aware that William Joseph Tebafunda was ill during the period September 1, 1968 to September 12, 1968. The defendants were ignorant. They did not realize how sick the baby was. They thought that the baby had a toothache and no layman regards a toothache as dangerous to life. They loved the baby and gave it aspirin in hopes of improving its condition. ... They knew that medical help was available because of previous experience. They had no excuse that the law will recognize for not taking the baby to a doctor.
>
> The defendants Walter L. Williams and Bernice J. Williams were negligent in not seeking medical attention for William Joseph Tabafunda.
>
> That as a proximate result of this negligence, William Joseph Tabafunda died.[51]

The Court of Appeals affirmed the conviction, stating:

> In our opinion, there is sufficient evidence from which the court could find, as it necessarily did, that applying the standard of ordinary caution, i.e., the caution exercisable by a man of reasonable prudence under the same or similar conditions, defendants were sufficiently put on notice concerning the symptoms of the baby's illness and lack of improvement in the baby's apparent condition in the period from September 1 to September 5, 1968 to have required them to have obtained medical care for the child. The failure so to do in this case is ordinary or simple negligence, and such negligence is sufficient to support a conviction of statutory manslaughter.[52]

[50] *ibid.*, p. 917–19, 484 P.2d, p. 1174.
[51] *ibid.*, p. 910–11, 484, P.2d, p. 1170.
[52] *ibid.*, p. 919, 484 P. 2d, p. 1174.

B. Framing the Concept of the Reasonable Person: The Impossibility of Distinguishing Negligence and Strict Liability

Everyone would agree that if the Williamses would have been criminally liable solely upon proof that the baby died of a treatable disease while in their custody, the liability would be strict liability. On the other hand, had there been proof that the Williamses were aware of the presence of a substantial risk that William had a life-threatening illness, everyone would agree that they were culpable and that their culpability was greater than negligence. But if negligence is a form of culpability that, unlike strict liability, rests not on what actually was the case – that William was seriously ill – and, unlike recklessness and higher forms of culpability, rests not on what was sincerely believed, on what *does* negligence rest?

The standard answer is that negligence rests on what the defendant should have known, or, put differently, what a reasonable person in the actor's situation would have known.

I am going to argue in this section that the concept of the "reasonable person in the actor's situation" is indeterminate and, from the standpoint of the purposes of punishment, wholly arbitrary. There is no moral difference between punishing for inadvertent negligence and punishing on the basis of strict liability, and the lack of a moral difference evidences itself in the inability to draw a distinction between strict liability and negligence on any basis other than arbitrary stipulation.

To see this, consider how the standard of the "reasonable person in the actor's situation" – RPAS – might apply in the *Williams* case. There are two clear boundary lines for the concept. On the one hand, if the RPAS were someone appraised of all the facts about the world that bore on a correct moral decision – particularly, that William had an abscessed tooth and needed medical treatment to avert a life-threatening complication – then it is clear what the RPAS would do: take William to the doctor.

At the other possible conceptual boundary, if the RPAS were someone with all of the beliefs that the Williamses actually held, including the belief that medical treatment was unnecessary for William's condition, then it is also clear what the RPAS would do: exactly what the Williamses did. After all, if because of your education, acculturation, and experiences, you don't perceive the baby's problem as a "possible medical emergency," but only as a "toothache," you act as the Williamses acted. Put somewhat differently, where action falls below the standard of recklessness – the *conscious* disregarding of a substantial and unjustifiable risk – the action will appear reasonable to the defendant and thus to the RPAS if the RPAS has exactly the same beliefs as the defendant.

The two possible boundaries that provide the frame for characterizing the RPAS present us with this dilemma, then. If the RPAS knows all the facts, the RPAS will always choose the action that averts the harm (in the absence of a justification, of course). but if this is the standard of the RPAS, then every case of strict liability will also be a case of negligence as defined by the RPAS standard. If the RPAS knows that Baker's cruise control will malfunction, the RPAS will not activate it. On this version of RPAS, Baker is not strictly liable, but negligent.

If the RPAS knows only what the defendant knows, however, there is never any negligence either, only recklessness: The RPAS will always act as the defendant acted where the defendant is not conscious of the risk, and will act differently only where the defendant *is* conscious of the risk, i.e. reckless.

At either conceptual boundary, therefore, RPAS collapses negligence into either strict liability or recklessness. The question, then, is where between those boundaries the RPAS is to be located.

Any location will be morally arbitrary. Between the boundaries, any RPAS will be a construct that will include some beliefs of the actual defendant together with beliefs that the constructor inserts. Which beliefs are inserted other than the ones the defendant actually had will determine whether or not the RPAS would act as the defendant acted. But there is no standard that tells us which of the beliefs of the actual defendant should be left intact and which should be replaced by other (correct) beliefs. The RPAS standard, cut loose from the alternative moorings of the defendant's actual beliefs or of the world as it really was at the time defendant acted, is completely adrift in a sea of alternative constructions, none of which is more compelling than the others.[53]

Some commentators at this point assert the possibility that the RPAS is like the actual defendant in all material aspects, but that the RPAS "would have" adverted to and properly assessed the risks because the actual defendant "could have" averted to and properly assessed them.[54] But there is an equivocation here in the reference to what the defendant "could have" adverted to and assessed in the defendant's situation. If we take the defendant at the time of the "negligent" choice, with what he is conscious of and adverting to, his background beliefs, etc., then it is simply false that the defendant "could have" chosen differently in any sense that has normative bite. For while it may be true that the defendant "could have" chosen

[53] Consider the following defense of combining objective and subjective factors in determining negligence: "A second source of resistance to admitting negligence as a basis of criminal liability is the assumption that legal negligence determinations must remain wholly objective, i.e., exclusively determined by reference to what a reasonable or prudent person would have thought or done in the circumstances. Such fully objective tests have the weakness that they will not be sensitive to those respects in which an individual accused may be disadvantaged, through no fault of his own, as compared with a person or reasonable prudence. But in the absence of good arguments for retaining these objective tests, it seems reasonable to revise Canadian law so that the test of negligence combines an appeal to publicly accepted objective standards of reasonable care with an individualized test of fault or culpability, permitting evidence of the individual's lack of capacity or opportunity to meet those standards to tell against a verdict of negligence." Brenda Baker, "Mens Rea, Negligence, and Criminal Law Reform," *Law and Philosophy*, vol. 6, no. 1 (April 1987), pp. 53, 82.

This attempt to weld objective and individualized tests together demonstrates a basic confusion. There is either the accused as we find him, with whatever kinds of problems of memory, prior education, prior choice, etc., that explained the particular choice on the particular occasion – i.e., that explained the particular case of inadvertent negligence – or there are other people with other character traits that we might want to deem to be ordinary reasonable people, purely fictitious people who would or would not have made the choice that the defendant did. There is no way of combining the real defendant and some objective defendant. The only real question is: what is the explanation of why the person did not advert to the risk in the particular case? The relevance of any other question is hard to discern. For example, the relevance of what somebody else would have chosen had that person adverted to the risk is of dubious relevance to the question of what we should do with an individual who did not advert to the risk.

[54] Hart, *Punishment and Responsibility*, p. 148; Baker, "Mens Rea, Negligence, and Criminal Law," pp. 83–85; Fletcher, "Theory of Criminal Negligence," p. 417.

differently in a sense relevant to the free will/determinism issue, it is false that in that situation, defendant had any internal reason to choose differently from the way he chose.[55] The Williamses were free to take their baby to the doctor; however, they had no reason of which they were aware for doing so.

To have such a reason, a defendant will have to advert to that to which he is not adverting. But one has no control at such moments over what one is adverting to or is conscious of; try thinking of what you aren't thinking of, but should be.[56] The "could have adverted to the risk" position is directly at odds with the voluntary act principle as a reflection of the value of restricting punishment to choices over which defendant had fair control.

Finally, let us consider a hypothetical case that tests the conclusion that this section is heading toward – namely, that inadvertent negligence is not culpable action.[57] Suppose that the Williamses had not been poor and relatively uneducated, but had been well-to-do and well-educated. Suppose they were ambitious social climbers who were hosting a large party that they hoped would be the social event of the year. Preoccupied for several days with the preparations, they failed to get treatment for their infant, William, with the same result as in the actual case. Are we really willing to say that in such circumstances, the Williamses would be morally blameless merely because they never actually adverted to the risk that their baby needed medical attention?

If we feel that the hypothetical Williamses are more deserving of moral censure than the actual Williamses, the feeling is probably the product of one of two possible inferences that we have made. One possible inference, a very natural one, is that the hypothetical Williamses are people with quite unadmirable character traits. Specifically, the hypothetical Williamses seem shallow and excessively self-centered. Nonetheless, if we believe that culpability rests on choice, not character,[58] then bad character traits are by themselves insufficient for deeming the Williamses culpable.[59]

The other possible inference supporting the hypothetical Williamses culpability is that their inadvertence to the risk to their child was the product of past culpable

[55] Bayles, *Principles of Law*, p. 299.

[56] See *ibid.*

[57] This hypothetical case is courtesy of Michael Moore.

[58] See Michael Moore, "Choice, Character, and Excuse," *Social Philosophy & Policy*, vol. 7, no. 2 (Spring 1990).

[59] Although I am assuming throughout this essay that culpability in the criminal law is and should be choice-based, not character-based, and I am thus agreeing with Michael Moore on this point – see *ibid.* – I believe that choice and character are two paradoxically-related sides of the same culpability coin. Choice, apart from what it reveals about character, seems inadequate as a basis for praise or blame. But character that has not been chosen – that is a matter of luck – likewise seems inadequate as a basis for praise or blame. See Thomas Nagel, "Moral Luck," in *Mortal Questions* (Cambridge: Cambridge University Press, 1979), pp. 24–38. And punishing someone for possessing a bad character, when, through luck, that person has never been in a circumstance in which his character would cause him to make a culpable choice, is also troubling. See *ibid.* I believe the inseverability of act and character in judgments of culpability is revealed in many of the examples in Moore's essay, despite Moore's conclusion that those examples favor choice-based judgments over character-based ones. Nevertheless, it seems evident from the standard categories of *mens rea* – purpose, knowledge, recklessness, and (though not a mental state) negligence – that Anglo-American criminal law rests on a choice-based notion of culpability, whether or not such a notion is independent of or intertwined with a character-based notion.

choices (past recklessness). The Williamses might have realized when deciding to throw this party that they would likely become preoccupied with it and oblivious to more important concerns. I deal with the general topic of negligence as the product of past culpable choices in the next section. For present purposes, it is sufficient to note that while this inference supports a negative moral judgment of the Williamses, it does not support a negative moral judgment of their present inadvertence to William's condition and failure to seek treatment. The negative moral judgment it supports is directed toward a past reckless choice, not the present negligence.

I conclude that inadvertent negligence does not denominate a category of culpable action distinguishable from the concededly nonculpable category of strict liability. The concept of the RPAS, if it falls between the defendant's beliefs and the actual facts, is a morally arbitrary and morally empty construct. To adjudge a defendant "negligent" by such a standard is not to say anything about her actual culpability. Recklessness is the lowest form of actual culpability,[60] whereas negligence is just an arbitrarily drawn subcategory of strict liability. It has the same time-framing problems that strict liability has, since at some point the harm is out of defendant's control, and prior to that time there will always be a voluntary act so long as we go back far enough and do not require culpability. And, therefore, as strict liability is in conflict with the voluntary act principle, so too is negligence.

C. Negligence as the Product of Past Culpable Choices

If negligent acts are themselves non-culpable and thus indistinguishable on that ground from acts that result in strict liability, at least some negligent acts might still be the products of *past culpable choices*. In other words, there may be a sizable subclass of negligent acts where the failure of the defendant to advert to the risk was caused by some prior culpable – and hence fully voluntary – choice of the defendant.[61]

For example, suppose that at some point before the baby became ill, the Williamses were invited to attend a free class for parents on how to recognize medical emergencies of children. Suppose that the Williamses realized that, given this class's importance relative to alternative uses of their time, they should attend this class, and that not to do so would be to take a substantial and unjustifiable risk

[60] See Richard Singer, "The Resurgence of *Mens Rea*: The Rise and Fall of Strict Criminal Liability," p. 406.

Recklessness in the Model Penal Code is defined as a conscious choice to disregard "a substantial and unjustifiable risk." *Model Penal Code*, § 2.02(2)(c). The most plausible interpretation of this provision is that to be reckless, the actor need only be aware of the magnitude of the risk; she need not be aware that it would be legally characterized as "substantial and unjustifiable." Failure to avoid the known or believed risk must, however, manifest culpability – in the language of the Code, "a gross deviation from the standard of conduct that a law-abiding person would observe." *ibid.*

Actually, the Code's definition of recklessness suggests conduct somewhat more culpable than the minimum possible degree of culpability. If an actor knowingly takes *any* unjustifiable risk, no matter how substantial, the actor may be culpable, depending upon whether the choice bespeaks callousness.

[61] Ronald Milo, *Immorality* (Princeton: Princeton University Press, 1984), p. 83; Michael Zimmerman, "Negligence and Moral Responsibility," *Nous*, vol. 20, no. 2 (June 1986), p. 199; Holly Smith, "Culpable Ignorance," *The Philosophical Review*, vol. 92, no. 4 (October 1983), p. 543.

of failing to perceive a medical emergency. Nonetheless, they do not attend the class, but watch television instead. And suppose that had they attended the class, they would have learned about abscessed teeth, gangrene, etc., and would likely have recognized the need to seek prompt medical treatment for William.

Given that scenario, the Williamses made a culpable choice that led to their fatal inadvertence to their baby's medical needs. Punishing them for the death of their baby is consistent with the voluntary act principle and is not really a form of strict liability, since it is their voluntary and culpable choice to watch television rather than go to the class on medical emergencies that led to the result for which they are punished.

There are all sorts of problems with this approach for squaring the punishment of negligence with the voluntary act principle. First, in tracing the negligent act to the prior choices that led to the crucial failure to advert to the risk, we may find a prior choice that was culpable – but we may not. Second, if we do find a prior choice that was culpable, it may be quite remote in the causal chain.[62] Third, and perhaps related to the second point, the degree of culpability displayed by that prior culpable choice may be quite disproportionate to the punishment specified for the negligent act. An act of very minor culpability, such as cutting language classes for soldiers stationed in a foreign country, might lead to a major harm, such as rape (through misunderstanding "no" and "yes").[63] On the other hand, many quite reckless choices will produce only minor harms. And, as I said, many prior acts will not be culpable at all.

Where does all this lead insofar as criminal liability for negligence is concerned? The present approach can be characterized as a conclusive presumption of a past culpable choice that proximately caused the pertinent inadvertence.[64] But underlying the presumption is the fact that negligence may not betoken any prior culpable choice at all, much less a prior choice exactly as culpable as the present offense.

Four other approaches more consistent with the voluntary act principle suggest themselves. First, we might extend the criminal codes to include many new crimes that identify specific types of culpable choices that unjustifiably risk producing harmful failures to advert to risk. For instance, we might make it a crime for new

[62] Holly Smith offers the hypothetical case of the secretary asked by her boss to survey the blood types of the office staff as part of an experiment and who culpably fails to do so. As a result, a worker dies from massive bleeding who would have been saved by a transfusion by the paramedics had they known his blood type in time, which they would have had the secretary conducted the survey. The secretary is culpable. Her culpable choice caused the death in fact. But the culpable choice did not "proximately" cause the death. Holly Smith "Culpable Ignorance," pp. 550–51.

Actually, Holly Smith's example is just an illustration of the general problem of having liability turn on causation rather than solely on culpable choice. See authorities cited in note 16 *supra*. Of course, to the extent that we require that culpable choices be expressed in actions, there is always a "proximate cause" issue in relating the culpable choice to the action that expresses it. In other words, even if all criminal liability were to be based on "attempts" regardless of whether the attempts produced harm, we would still need some notion of proximate cause to distinguish "attempts" from mere intentions. I owe this point to Leo Katz.

[63] *Cf.* United States v. Short, 4 C.M.A. 437, 16 C.M.R. 11 (1954) (an assault with intent to commit rape case where an intoxicated soldier failed to understand a Japanese woman's "no," although we don't know if he skipped any language classes).

[64] Kelman, "Interpretive Construction in the Substantive Criminal Law," pp. 606–11.

parents to fail to take classes on children's medical emergencies. Obviously, this approach has the drawback of greatly proliferating the number of crimes while at the same time failing to reach all of the virtually limitless types of reckless choices.

The second approach is the one commonly taken with intoxication.[65] Intoxication itself is not criminalized. But when it leads people to engage in otherwise criminally reckless or harmful conduct unaware (because of the intoxication) of the risks they are creating, the criminal law treats the intoxication as a substitute for recklessly risking whatever harm was caused or put at risk. In other words, the choice to become intoxicated is treated as if it were an all-purpose reckless choice that enters the defendant in a form of punishment roulette. If his intoxication leads to no untoward consequences, he escapes punishment altogether. If it leads him to commit what, were he sober, would be a minor crime, he receives a small amount of punishment. And if it leads him to commit what, were he sober, would be a serious crime, he receives much more severe punishment.

This approach to intoxication could be extended to particular types of culpable conduct that frequently produce unwanted inadvertence to risk. We would specify these types of conduct in advance, and then state in the codes describing negligent crimes that inadvertence shall not negate criminal liability if it is caused by the prior voluntary choice to engage in one of these types of conduct. This approach has the problem of the first approach of having to specify the particular forms of conduct that lead to unwanted inadvertence to risk when the number of such forms is virtually limitless. It also raises the question of the justice of punishment lotteries that mete out unequal punishments to acts of equal culpability.[66]

A third approach one could take would be to authorize courts to look at all of the defendant's prior choices whenever the defendant claims that he failed to advert to a risk with which the criminal law is concerned, not just at specific, predefined culpable choices. If the court finds any culpable choice that "caused" the present inadvertence – no matter how serious or trivial the culpability – the court would impose the punishment prescribed for a negligent commission of the particular crime. This approach avoids the problem of specifying the culpable triggers in advance, but it replaces it with that of determining whether a past culpable choice "proximate caused" present inadvertence, and the related problem of how far back in time the court should go in looking for a pivotal culpable choice. The approach also has the "lottery justice" problem of the previous approach.

The final approach is the same as the third, except that it dispenses with a set level of punishment for inadvertence and scales the punishment to the degree of culpability of the causative culpable choice, perhaps limited upwards by the punishment specified for reckless commission of the crime involved. This approach has all of the problems of the third approach, except that the lottery is eliminated among those culpable acts that led to the inadvertence. The lottery is retained insofar as those who make culpable choices that produce no unwanted inadvertence still escape punishment altogether.

[65] See *Model Penal Code*, § 2.08(2).

[66] See Lewis, "The Punishment That Leaves Something to Chance."

CONCLUSION

Here are the final results of the previous analysis:

(1) The negligence principle collapses into the strict liability principle if the former is construed without reference to any prior culpable choice.
(2) If the negligence principle is construed without reference to any prior culpable choice, both it and the strict liability principle are inconsistent with any nonvacuous construction of the voluntary act principle.
(3) If the negligence principle is construed to require finding a prior culpable choice, it is consistent with the voluntary act principle.
(4) There are several approaches to dealing with negligence on this latter construction of the negligence principle. None preserves all the positive values of strict liability (or negligence construed as a form of strict liability). That is, all of the approaches will result in some culpable defendants escaping punishment who would not escape punishment under strict liability (or negligence construed as a form of strict liability). All of the approaches will be weaker deterrents than strict liability (or negligence construed as a form of strict liability), since, under these approaches, more culpable defendants will believe (rightly or wrongly) that they will escape punishment. And all of the approaches will be more expensive to operate than strict liability (or negligence construed as strict liability).[67]
(5) All of the approaches involve either lottery justice or a proliferation of crimes in the criminal codes.

I don't have any solution at hand for the conflict between the value of fair control that lies behind the full-bodied voluntary act principle – a value that requires some culpable choice before one can be criminally punished – and deterrence and the other values which are served by strict liability and negligence crimes.[68] The conflict between culpability-based punishment and consequence-based punishment pervades the criminal law, and this area is just one of many examples. I do proffer, however, one modest recommendation: that is that we bring the conflict between culpability and consequence-based punishment into the foreground and drop misleading references to the three principles regarding voluntary acts, strict liability, and negligence, as if they were all distinct from one another and harmonious. They are neither.*

Law, University of San Diego

[67] See Kelman, "Strict Liability: An Unorthodox View," *Encyclopedia of Crime and Justice*, ed. S. Kadish (New York: The Free Press, 1983), vol. 4, p. 1517.

[68] I, of course, have completely omitted any discussion of the strict liability presented by the absence of a defense for nonculpable ignorance of the criminal law. See, e.g., *Model Penal Code*, § 2.04(3).

* My thanks to Elaine Alexander, Kevin Cole, Jean Hampton, Paul Horton, Leo Katz, Evan Lee, Michael Moore, and the editors of *Social Philosophy & Policy* for their helpful suggestions and insightful criticisms.

THE GENDER QUESTION IN CRIMINAL LAW*

By Stephen J. Schulhofer

Over the past decade, both the doctrine and the practice of criminal law have come under intensely critical review by feminist scholars and reformers. The territory under reexamination by or because of feminists spans the problems of women as witnesses, defendants, and prisoners in the criminal justice system; it extends to the situation of women as potential victims and offenders in diverse offense circumstances. Crimes in which the defendant or victim is typically female (e.g., prostitution, rape) are predictable subjects of feminist concern, but attention has extended as well to the dynamics of women's experience (arguably distinctive and certainly neglected) in connection with such offenses as assault, shoplifting, drug offenses, and even armed robbery.

Feminist criticism and reform efforts have focused for the most part at the level of specific rules or particular areas of practice. In this paper I want to comment on the structure of the feminist critique and to compare its underlying assumptions to those of criminal law as it has been traditionally understood and practiced. In at least some of its prominent versions, feminism entails orientations and commitments incompatible with those of the received criminal law tradition. To the extent that this is true, criminal law, constructed and expounded almost exclusively by males, can fairly be characterized (descriptively) as "sexist" or at least "gendered" (that is, male-oriented) in its core assumptions. Moving to normative ground, I suggest that if the descriptive claims of the feminist movement are true to any substantial extent, then criminal law – conceived in terms seemingly uncongenial to a large part of our population – would require thorough reexamination. I offer some very tentative thoughts about where such a reexamination might lead, with a particular focus on the law of self-defense and rape.

1. Conceptions of Feminism

Before proceeding further, I need to be at least a little bit clear about what I mean by "feminism." While feminists are united by their interest in studying and remedying women's disadvantaged – or (more strongly) oppressed – condition, there are many distinct (and, in some ways, opposed) strands in feminist thought. I want to identify three different kinds of feminism. The first I will call the

* I presented portions of this paper at workshops at the University of Chicago and New York University Law School. I benefited from the reactions of participants on those occasions, and from comments on the manuscript by Mary Becker, Albert Alschuler, Sanford Kadish, Cass Sunstein, Michael Vitiello, and the contributors to this volume.

perspective of *equal treatment*, the second the perspective of *different norms*, and the third the perspective of *different situations*. My way of organizing the debate provides only a rough way of sorting assumptions. It glosses over important differences among feminists, but it will be sufficiently discriminating to make my principal points.

The perspective of *equal treatment* views women as fundamentally equal to men. While not insensitive to differences in the power and opportunities of women in many of the situations of contemporary life, equal treatment feminists worry that rules intended to accommodate those differences, to adjust for disadvantage, or to promote affirmative action will perpetuate negative stereotypes, reinforce adverse cultural messages, and therefore operate to the ultimate disadvantage of women.[1] Equal treatment feminists direct their attention to rules that impose distinctive disadvantages on women: e.g., lower pay for equal work or – in the criminal law – corroboration requirements and special jury instructions applicable only to the testimony of rape complainants. But they tend to support legal standards that are not overtly discriminatory and to assume that women can function effectively in terms of the prevailing criteria of merit and success. They would oppose rules implying categorically different treatment for women as well as most forms of affirmative action, however benign in motivation.

The perspective of *different norms* asserts a distinct difference between the conceptions of morality that dominate the thinking of men and of women. The prevailing (i.e. "male") concept of morality is seen as grounded in a liberal conception of abstract rights held by autonomous individuals who are equal in native capacity and powers of self-protection. This prevailing morality is said systematically to ignore considerations of connection and caring, complexities of context, and responsibilities to an ongoing network of relationships.[2] Yet these excluded or deemphasized considerations are said to be precisely the ones that (for better or worse[3]) dominate the moral universe of (most) women. The implication is that an ostensibly neutral system of abstract rights and responsibilities involves gender bias in its very structure, and that the elimination of sex discrimination requires a radical change in the methodology of moral and legal analysis.[4]

The perspective of *different situations* emphasizes crucial differences in the life situations of women and men. Among feminists who share this perspective, there are important disagreements about what those differences are, what their source is,

[1] E.g., Wendy M. Williams, "The Equality Crisis: Some Reflections on Culture, Courts and Feminism," *Women's Rights Law Reporter*, vol. 7 (1982), p. 175.

[2] Carol Gilligan, *In a Different Voice: Psychological Theory and Women's Development* (Cambridge: Harvard University Press, 1982).

[3] Catherine MacKinnon argues that the different voice described by Gilligan is "the voice of the victim." "Feminist Discourse, Moral Values, and the Law – A Conversation" (panel discussion), *Buffalo Law Review*, vol. 34 (1985), pp. 11, 27.

[4] Consider Leslie Bender, "A Lawyer's Primer on Feminist Theory and Tort," *Journal of Legal Education*, vol. 38, pp. 3, 10–11:

> Our legal system ... resolves problems through male inquiries formulated from distanced, abstract, and acontextual vantage points, while feminism emphasizes relationships, context, and factual particulars for resolving human problems.

and where the cure lies. Some emphasize relatively discrete aspects of women's situation (e.g., only women bear children) and therefore stress easily bounded affirmative action remedies (e.g., mandatory availability of maternity leave). Others suggest that the problems of acculturation, role stereotyping, and power imbalance are so pervasive that women are systematically subordinated. This "dominance" perspective calls for profound changes in culture and in legal categories.[5] Of particular relevance to criminal law is the perspective these feminists offer on the incidence of force and aggression in interpersonal relations. Many feminists argue that the prevailing ("male") conception of normality has been systematically blind to the intimidation that colors a woman's experience of the world. A comment by Elizabeth A. Stanko expresses a viewpoint about aggression that is undoubtedly foreign to the experience of many men:[6]

> To be a woman – in most societies, in most eras – is to experience physical and/or sexual terrorism at the hands of men. Our everyday behaviour reflects our precautions, the measures we take to protect ourselves. We are wary of going out at night, even in our own neighbourhoods. We are warned by men and other women not to trust strangers. But somehow they forget to warn us about men we know: our fathers, our acquaintances, our co-workers, our lovers, our teachers. Many men familiar to us also terrorise our everyday lives in our homes, our schools, our workplaces.... [T]he *daily* possibility of being threatened by male behaviour is one message women constantly receive.

The equal treatment perspective offers no profoundly threatening challenge to prevailing legal doctrine; its reform agenda has been successful over a broad front. Not so for the other two strands of feminist thought. When feminists claim that women hold a different conception of normality and of morality, that women see their material and normative surroundings differently from the way men do, their position is heard as truly radical by many – both women and men. In effect, such feminists assert that women and men live in different worlds. It should not be surprising that traditional legal scholars find such assertions factually implausible and conceptually difficult to integrate into prevailing paradigms. Many, predictably, greet such assertions dismissively or with derision. Predictably, too, reactions of that kind serve to reinforce the feminist's conviction that there is indeed a wide and perhaps unbridgeable gulf between male and female world views. To assess the feminist critique of ostensibly "male" and assertedly improper criminal law conceptions, one must at some level consider whether the claim about the profound difference in women's norms and in women's situations is in any sense *true*.

Consider first the claim that a woman's conception of the relevant criteria of moral judgment differs from that of men. The inevitable citation here to the work of Carol Gilligan too often overlooks Gilligan's own ambivalence about whether the

[5] Catharine A. MacKinnon, *Feminism Unmodified* (Cambridge: Harvard University Press, 1987), pp. 32–45.

[6] Elizabeth A. Stanko, *Intimate Intrusions* (London: Routledge & Kegan Paul, 1985) pp. 9, 11.

"different voice" of caring and connection is, empirically, a *woman's* voice: that is, a morality for which women systematically express a greater affinity than do men.[7] Any difference here is unlikely to be completely bipolar, since attention to community and to the value of ongoing personal relationships are present (and, in some instances, heavily emphasized) in traditional (male-authored) political theory.[8] And in the law, abstract rules stand in constant tension with intuitive community norms and highly contextualized standards, both in formal doctrine and in the various customs and enforcement practices that give shape to the "real" law-in-action. I will have more to say about this feature, with specific reference to criminal law, in a moment.[9]

With respect to possible empirical difference in male-female patterns of moral reasoning, Gilligan's book is no more than suggestive, and subsequent empirical work has produced inconsistent findings. All of the researchers agree that most individuals, male or female, use *both* "voices" (the ethic of rights and the ethic of care). With respect to the crucial question of whether women tend to emphasize the ethic of care more than men do, a recent study by Gilligan herself suggests a definite affirmative answer.[10] Gilligan and her collaborators asked men and women to describe moral conflicts they had experienced personally. The researchers then characterized each response as "predominantly care oriented" or "predominantly justice [rights] oriented." They found that 75 percent of the women predominantly exhibited a "care" orientation, while only 14 percent of the men did. However, because the interview subjects each addressed different personal dilemmas and because the women conceivably could have been more likely to experience dilemmas that presented "caring" types of concerns, the study does not necessarily show that men and women would use different "voices" to reason about the *same* moral problems. Several studies suggest that responses to moral dilemmas are, in fact, affected far more by the character of the issues than by

[7] See Gilligan, "In a Different Voice," at p. 2:

> The different voice I describe is characterized not by gender but by theme.... Its association with women... is not absolute, and the contrasts between male and female voices are presented here to highlight a distinction between two modes of thought and to focus a problem of interpretation rather than to represent a generalization about either sex.

See also "Feminist Discourse," at pp. 47–48 (remarks of Carol Gilligan).

[8] Much modern political theory does have a decidedly individualistic emphasis, whether its orientation leans to the right – e.g., Robert Nozick, *Anarchy, State and Utopia* (New York: Basic Books, 1974) – or to the left – e.g., John Rawls, *A Theory of Justice* (Cambridge: Harvard University Press, 1971); Bruce A. Ackerman, *Social Justice in the Liberal State* (New Haven: Yale University Press, 1980). Nonetheless, attention to the importance of community and ongoing networks of relationships is central to the work of countless important figures in the history of social and political thought, especially within the conservative tradition. Edmund Burke and Talcott Parsons are only two of the most obvious examples. Among more recent examples from the political left are Michael J. Sandel, *Liberalism and the Limits of Justice* (Cambridge: Cambridge University Press, 1982) and Duncan Kennedy, "The Structure of Blackstone's Commentaries," *Buffalo Law Review*, vol. 28, pp. 205 (1979). See also Alasdair MacIntyre, *After Virtue* (Notre Dame: University of Notre Dame Press, 2d ed. 1984).

[9] See text at note 33 below.

[10] Carol Gilligan, S. Langdale, N. Lyons, and M. Murphy, *The Contribution of Women's Thought to Developmental Theory* (Washington: National Institute of Education, 1982). I am grateful to my colleagues Albert W. Alschuler and Mary Becker for discussion of this and related studies.

the gender of the respondents.[11] Among studies that test whether women tend to emphasize the ethic of care more than men reasoning about the same problem, most of the studies find either no difference between the sexes[12] or "at best minimal" differences.[13] To judge by the reception of Gilligan's work among academics, the notion that the voice of caring is distinctively female does have great resonance for many women, including feminists who have applied Gilligan's work to law.[14] Within the framework of a critical theory rife with concern about socially constructed stereotypes, however, such intuitions cannot be unproblematic.

Perhaps the best we can say at this point is that we do not know whether Gilligan and the feminists who extrapolate from her work are right. But for my purposes, the possibility of a systematic difference in moral priorities and in the criteria of moral reasoning is intriguing and filled with important implications for the criminal law. On that basis it seems prudent, even for the skeptical outsider, to assume that there may be some truth in this charge.

A larger question is whether, even if differences in moral reasoning exist, such differences have any bearing on the question of which principles of criminal responsibility are jurisprudentially correct.[15] Certainly, the fact that a moral view is held by most or all women (or men) does not make that view correct; "is" is not "ought."[16] But one would have to have enormous faith in the possibilities for objective moral knowledge to deny the importance of distinctive moral intuitions and patterns of reasoning if they were shown to dominate the thinking of large segments of our population. Since I take as given the interplay between reason and intuition in the construction of moral truth, which (at least in part) is always historically and socially contingent,[17] the Gilligan claims pose a substantial and intriguing challenge to our understanding of the appropriate elements of justice in

[11] Mary K. Rothbart, Dean Hanley, and Marc Albert, "Gender Differences in Moral Reasoning," *Sex Roles*, vol. 15, nos. 11/12 (1986), p. 645.

[12] William J. Friedman, Amy B. Robinson, and Britt L. Friedman, "Sex Differences in Moral Judgments? A Test of Gilligan's Theory," *Psychology of Women Quarterly*, vol. 11 (1987), pp. 37–46.

[13] Maureen R. Ford and Carol R. Lowery, "Gender Differences in Moral Reasoning: A Comparison of the Use of Justice and Care Orientations," *Journal of Personality and Social Psychology*, vol. 50, no. 4 (1986), pp. 777, 783; M. Brabeck, "Moral Judgment: Theory and Research on Differences Between Males and Females," *Developmental Review*, vol. 3 (1983), pp. 274–91.

[14] See especially Suzanna Sherry, "Civic Virtue and the Feminine Voice in Constitutional Adjudication," *Virginia Law Review*, vol. 72 (1986), p. 543; Leslie Bender, "A Lawyer's Primer on Feminist Theory and Tort," *Journal of Legal Education*, vol. 38 (1988), pp. 3, 10–12; Carrie Menkel-Meadow, "Feminist Legal Theory, Critical Legal Studies, and Legal Education or 'The Fem-Crits Go to Law School'," *Journal of Legal Education*, vol. 38 (1988), p. 61; Robin West, "Jurisprudence and Gender," *University of Chicago Law Review*, vol. 44 (Winter 1988), p. 1.

[15] George Fletcher forcefully raised this point when discussing my paper. See also his influential book *Rethinking Criminal Law* (Boston: Little, Brown, 1978).

[16] For a useful discussion in the context of the Gilligan debate, see Lawrence A. Blum, "Gilligan and Kohlberg: Implications for Moral Theory," *Ethics*, vol. 98 (April 1988), pp. 472–91. For a feminist perspective, see Donna Haraway, "Situated Knowledges: The Science Question in Feminism and the Privilege of Partial Perspective," *Feminist Studies*, vol. 14, no. 3 (Fall 1988), p. 575.

[17] See Stephen J. Schulhofer, Book Review, *California Law Review*, vol. 68 (1980), p. 181. Jeffrie Murphy suggested a more rigorous formulation of this approach at the conference: within contractarian premises, the Rawlsian methodology of "reflective equilibrium" implies that an enlargement of the community whose reflective intuitions count will likely change the analysis of what radically *un*situated parties would accept behind the veil of ignorance.

punishment. To say that is not, of course, to foreordain the outcome of that challenge. It is precisely the objective of this paper to explore to what extent a reconsideration of the criminal law in light of the feminist challenge should lead to changes in its working doctrines.

The second set of claimed differences, relating to the extent of violence and aggression, goes to the heart of the criminal law. There must be something very wrong with traditional assumptions and with traditional categories for understanding what constitutes unacceptable aggression if the perspective of feminists like Elizabeth Stanko is anywhere close to the truth. Is it?

Questions about the actual incidence of violence become difficult to answer empirically when they focus on low-visibility aggression against powerless or stigmatized victims, such as battered wives and children. The available (problematic) data suggest shockingly high figures – perhaps 10–15 percent of all women are victims of marital rape,[18] and 38 percent of all girls are victims of child sexual abuse.[19]

In any event, the questions are not entirely empirical, since they turn in part on what kind of behavior is *regarded* as aggressive. Although it is clear that not all women accept the Stanko view (and not all men reject it), the tendency to see pervasive, unacceptable aggression appears markedly more common among women than among men.[20] Many men assume that sounding a "wolf whistle" at the approach of a bypasser in the street or making a pass at a perfect stranger on a bus can be innocuous or even flattering to the woman. Professor Menachem Amir reports "general assumptions ... that some aggression is an expected part of the male role in sexual encounters."[21] Expected (and desired) by whom? Part of what may be "wrong" with the Stanko claims is that a considerable amount of aggression

[18] Irene Hanson Frieze, "Investigating the Causes and Consequences of Marital Rape," *Signs*, vol. 8 (1983), p. 532; Diana E. H. Russell, *Rape in Marriage* (New York: MacMillan, 1982).

[19] Diana E. H. Russell, "The Incidence and Prevalence of Intrafamilial and Extrafamilial Sexual Abuse of Female Children," *Child Abuse and Neglect*, vol. 7 (1983), p. 137. The most recent review of the literature reports:

> [P]revalance estimates for child sexual abuse rang[e] from 6 percent to 62 percent for females and from 3 percent to 31 percent for males. The lowest rates suggest that child sexual abuse is not an uncommon experience. The highest rates suggest a social problem of staggering dimensions. There are a variety of explanations for variations in estimated prevalance rates. Studies vary in the restrictiveness of their definitions of child sexual abuse, they vary in their sample selection strategies, and they vary substantially in methodology.

James Gabarino, "The Incidence and Prevalence of Child Maltreatment," in *Family Violence* (*Crime and Justice: A Review of Research*, vol. 11) ed. Lloyd Ohlin and Michael Tonry (Chicago: University of Chicago Press, 1989), pp. 219, 240.

[20] A comparison of male and female perceptions in this area appears to be a fruitful issue for systematic research. I performed my own very unscientific survey among 75 first-year law students. Neither men nor women had homogeneous reactions to the Stanko quote. For example, among women 12 percent described it as largely false and another 24 percent as partly false. Yet 64 percent of the women described the Stanko view as largely or entirely true, while only 42 percent of the men did so. (The validity of the poll is clouded by the fact that it was taken some months *after* class discussion of feminist views on rape. Many of the respondents – especially male respondents – indicated that they now gave much more credence to the feminist perspective than they had before.)

[21] Menachem Amir, *Patterns in Forcible Rape* (Chicago: University of Chicago Press, 1971), p. 130.

may be obvious, but just not considered inappropriate (by some men and women) in situations ranging from encounters between strangers through jobs, dates, and even marriage.[22]

Under these conditions, claims about male-female differences in perceptions about aggression remain quite problematic, even when buttressed by corroborating empirical surveys. The perceptions themselves may be (in part, *must* be) an artifact of social conceptions of normality. And these social conceptions in turn not only produce but in part *are produced by* the law that we have, including the categories we use to conceptualize impermissible behavior. To that extent, citizens (male and female) who reject the feminist view may be victims of false consciousness (or adaptive preferences). Conversely, those who accept the feminist view may simply be "too sensitive" – or they may themselves be captured by the particular consciousness that takes shape from concepts and assumptions legitimated and reinforced within the social communities of feminism.

The problem for criminal law is to determine what kind of behavior should be understood as aggressive, as well as the extent to which aggression is acceptable (and to whom). Against this background, it becomes question-begging for criminal law scholars to dismiss views like those of Stanko on the ground that they are empirically unsubstantiated or analytically irrelevant to the categories we use in thinking about issues of violence and sexual misconduct. The world view of these feminists needs to be reckoned with. And if that world view is at all widely shared, then the categories themselves need to be rethought.

To summarize, what I have in mind as a feminist critique of criminal law includes (among many diverse elements) two particularly central ideas. The first is that the prevailing concept of normality in regard to force and aggression is one-sided ("male-sided"); it has been systematically blind to the pervasive intimidation that colors a woman's experience of the world. That concept of normality reflects and in turn perpetuates the pervasive and profound subordination of women. The second idea is that the prevailing concept of morality is also one-sided in its preoccupation with autonomy and rights and its blindness to the elements of caring and connection that assume relatively great importance in the moral thinking of women. These ideas, despite their undeniably debatable character, deserve to be taken quite seriously. Any useful rethinking of the criminal law must proceed from the premise that a woman's situation, in terms of her conception of morality and normality, may indeed be profoundly different from that of a man.

II. Organizing Assumptions of Criminal Law

Before entering into the concrete controversies relating to the law of self-defense and rape, I want to remain at a general level just long enough to contrast the central ideas of feminism with several organizing principles of traditional criminal law. These principles need to be made explicit here, because they help locate what makes the feminist critique so hard for mainstream (male) scholars to assimilate.

[22] Stanko herself makes a similar point. Stanko, *Intimate Intrusions*, pp. 9–11.

To comment on these organizing principles, I will have to abstract from a good deal of detail; some qualifications and exceptions will be related to footnotes. In law, general principles are inevitably vulnerable to counterexample. Nonetheless, my claim is that these principles organize and dominate criminal law's doctrinal complexity and that they are so central that we usually just take them for granted (when we notice them at all).[23]

The first principle is that criminal law is *judgmental.* It accuses. In the event of conviction, it does not (immediately, or perhaps ever) forgive. Rather, it condemns, it blames, and it punishes.

These accusatory, judgmental features of criminal law are a bit muted in the legal systems of continental Europe, where criminal law proceeds along the lines of a somewhat more community-oriented, "family," or helping model.[24] (Interestingly, those societies are not noted for being less patriarchal or less misogynist than we are. Evidently, the connections between male domination of culture and social practice on the one hand and the importance of allegedly "male" concepts in legal doctrine on the other is more problematic than some legal feminists have allowed.) The judgmental features of the criminal law are also considerably muted at the sentencing stage, or at least they used to be, under the regime of the rehabilitative ideal. Recently that approach has given way to the more rights-oriented punishment philosophy of "just deserts." (Again, we are struck by the problematic character of the connection between culture and legal constructs that legal feminists inspired by Carol Gilligan have posited. Just when women's voices have become more audible and more accepted in our culture and in our law, legal doctrine in sentencing and many other areas[25] has become more individualistic, abstract, and rights-oriented than ever.) In any event, the traditional posture of our formal mechanisms for the adjudication of guilt remains heavily rights-oriented, accusatory, and judgmental.

The second principle is that criminal law is *demanding.* Criminal law prohibitions are not addressed solely, or even primarily, to people who can easily comply. Robbery prosecutions bear mainly on the very poor, those who face the strongest of temptations. Homicide prosecutions often concern those who have acted under the most substantial external or internal pressures. And the point I am making is not limited to statistical patterns in enforcement. It is deeply embedded

[23] In support of the propositions to be discussed in the paragraphs that follow, I have drawn primarily upon *Model Penal Code, Proposed Official Draft* (Philadelphia: American Law Institute, 1962); Sanford H. Kadish and Stephen J. Schulhofer, *Criminal Law and Its Processes* (Boston: Little, Brown, 5th ed. 1989); Wayne LaFave and Austin Scott, Jr., *Criminal Law* (St. Paul: West, 2nd ed. 1986).

[24] For an excellent discussion of the "family" or community-oriented assumptions of continental Europe's non-adversarial systems of criminal procedure and a comparison with the more individualistic, rights-oriented, or "arm's length" orientation of adversarial procedure, see Mirjan Damaška, "Evidentiary Barriers to Conviction and Two Models of Criminal Procedure," *University of Pennsylvania Law Review*, vol. 121 (1973), pp. 506, 563–84. Further discussion of the contrast between these two organizing conceptions of procedure and their manifestation in different cultures can be found in Karl Llewellyn, *Jurisprudence* (Chicago: University of Chicago Press, 1962), pp. 439–50; John Griffiths, "Ideology in Criminal Procedure or a Third "Model" of the Criminal Process," *Yale Law Journal*, vol. 79 (1970), p. 359.

[25] Juvenile justice and civil commitment regimes are perhaps the most obvious examples. See text at note 64 below.

in the structure of existing (traditional) criminal law doctrine. Social and economic circumstances that strongly predispose to crime ("rotten social background") do not afford a defense.[26] Duress excuses only in very limited circumstances of extreme, overbearing compulsion; lesser pressures afford no excuse, even when they render the decision to comply very difficult.

Impaired mental capacity provides several clear illustrations of the principle. When a defendant suffers from an identifiable mental abnormality short of "mental disease" (severe neurosis or personality disorder, for example), such diminished mental capacity provides no affirmative defense. Many jurisdictions exclude evidence of such mental impairment even when it would be logically relevant to rebut a required element of an offense. The upshot: defendants with impaired capacity, for whom compliance may be very difficult, are held to precisely the same standard as defendants who enjoy normal powers of self-control. Indeed, impairment short of "mental disease" affords no excuse even when it *totally* deprives the defendant of the capacity for self-control.

My claim – that the law is unwilling to vary its standards for defendants with diminished capacities of self-control – requires some qualification to the extent that such defendants may gain mitigation of punishment at the sentencing stage. In principle, their reduced culpability should mean a reduced sentence. And often this principle wins out: for example, in those jurisdictions that allow diminished capacity as a partial defense, or in the rules that almost everywhere permit reducing murder to manslaughter when the defendant acts in response to serious provocation. Even here, note that the partial defense of provocation is available only if a *reasonable person* would have been likely to lose the power of self-control. The defense is situational rather than character-specific; in fact, it is crafted to insure that defendants with less than normal capacities for self-control do *not* gain mitigation of sentence. More generally, the problem is that reduced culpability also means *increased* dangerousness. Should the drug addict who commits a robbery or burglary receive a shorter sentence because the acute need to support his habit reduces his capacity to avoid criminal conduct? Or should he receive an increased sentence because he is harder to deter and more likely to offend again? In practice, sentencing judges respond primarily to the latter consideration, so that the term of confinement is, if anything, longer.[27]

Similar conclusions can be drawn with respect to impairments that do rise to the level of "mental disease." Only a minority of jurisdictions now accept the Model Penal Code proposal that mental disease should excuse whenever it substantially impairs the capacity either to appreciate the wrongfulness of the conduct or to exercise self-control. On the contrary, severely impaired capacity for self-control generally is *not* sufficient to establish the defense. Even in those jurisdictions

[26] See Stephen J. Schulhofer, "Just Punishment in an Imperfect World," *Michigan Law Review*, vol. 87, pp. 1263, 1282–92 (May 1989).

[27] See, for example *United States Sentencing Commission, Guidelines Manual* §5K2.13 (1988), providing that diminished capacity may warrant a reduced sentence, but only if the situation involves (1) a non-violent offense, (2) the reduced mental capacity does not result from voluntary use of drugs or alcohol, *and* (3) the defendant's criminal history does not indicate a need for incarceration to protect the public.

(probably a minority) that accept "irresistible impulse" as a basis for an insanity defense, a defendant who lacks substantial capacity for self-control, as a result of mental disease, is still held responsible; a successful defense requires the jury to conclude that the impairment be *complete*. And under the more prevalent *M'Naghten* test, even a *total* impairment of volitional controls is insufficient to establish the defense; only a cognitive impairment will do.[28] In all these ways, traditional criminal law demands compliance (and punishes non-compliance) even in the case of those for whom compliance is demonstrably quite difficult.

A final illustration, from the law of intoxication, makes the point in perhaps its starkest form. Voluntary intoxication is a defense only under quite limited circumstances. But what if the defendant has been tricked into swallowing a mind-altering drug? Such involuntary intoxication can be a defense if it produces legal insanity (e.g., an inability to know right from wrong) or if it negates a required element of the offense (as when it triggers hallucinations that result in a decisive mistake of fact). In other cases, even *in*voluntary intoxication affords no defense. A defendant who becomes loud, emotional, and unruly and then commits an assault because of drugs secretly forced upon him has no defense. But for the drugs, he would not have committed the assault, and the drug consumption was wholly beyond his control. Nonetheless, he is held responsible.[29] The premise is that even though circumstances beyond his control made compliance much harder for him than for the average citizen, he still retained some residual capacity for self-control and therefore can still be blamed for his improper choice. (Punishment of the impoverished ghetto dweller is justified on the same ground.)

The short of it is that in criminal law, empathy for the defendant is not the strong suit. One must add, of course, that the relatively uncompromising position of legal doctrine is substantially softened in practice by prosecutorial discretion, plea-bargaining, and the jury system. Nonetheless, in countless, deeply engrained ways, criminal law doctrine demands compliance even from those (and one could say *particularly* from those) for whom compliance is extremely difficult.[30]

[28] The *M'Naghten* rule provides that to establish an insanity defense "it must be clearly proved that, at the time of committing the act, the party accused was labouring under such a defect of reason, from disease of the mind, as not to know the nature and quality of the act he was doing; or, if he did know it, that he did not know he was doing what was wrong." M'Naghten's Case, 8 Eng. Rep 718 (House of Lords, 1843). Illustrative of the recent trend back to the narrow *M'Naghten* approach, which requires complete impairment of cognition and excludes impairment of control as an independent basis for the defense, are United States v. Lyons, 731 F.2d 243 (5th Cir. 1984) and the statutory formulation adopted by Congress in 1984, 18 U.S.C. §20. It must be added that, as in other areas considered in this paper, actual enforcement attitudes of prosecutors and juries soften these requirements to some extent. Severely impaired capacity for self-control is probably often understood to reflect on a defendant's capacity to know (or fully "appreciate") the wrongfulness of his conduct; truly *complete* impairment of cognition (if such a thing exists at all) is probably seldom required in practice.

[29] See, e.g., *Model Penal Code*, §2.08.

[30] The highly demanding character of the substantive rules seems largely inconsistent with the principle of keeping the severity of punishment proportional to moral fault. The reasons for this approach must therefore be located primarily in the criminal law's social protection function and, in particular, in the non-availability of alternative institutions to serve that function when "mental disease" is absent. See Schulhofer, "Just Punishment."

In terms of the feminist critique I previously described, these central elements of criminal law – its pervasively judgmental and demanding features – would be described as highly "male" characteristics. From the feminist perspective, criminal law doctrine seems gendered to its very core. The implications of the feminist critique are thus ultimately quite far-reaching. They lead to questions about whether criminal law's core commitments to an allegedly "male" conception of rights and responsibilities ought to be altered or abandoned.

A third feature of the criminal law is also relevant. Criminal law is *pacifist.* There is an irony here because the mode of the criminal law – its procedure and style – is abstract and aggressive. But substantive criminal law *doctrine* is pacifist. By that I mean that it rejects violence as a solution to interpersonal problems. Some important countercurrents qualify this generalization. The law-in-action tolerates violence much more than the law on the books. The law on the books sometimes departs from pacifist principles too, but we usually recognize such departures as compromises or imperfections deserving of criticism. (As another section of this paper shows, the departures are more pervasive – and the need for criticism more profound – in the law of rape.) The general theme still holds – the criminal law commands respect for the fundamental humanity of the other even when that other is an egregious wrongdoer. Force can be used only when necessary. Deadly force can be used *only* to prevent death or great bodily harm and, in many jurisdictions, only if there is no possibility of retreat.[31] So, in principle, the law requires that the attacked party submit to a non-deadly beating rather than defend with deadly force. The laws prefers retreat and loss of honor to the unnecessary taking of life. And it generally construes the requirements of retreat and necessity very strictly.

One example will vividly illustrate these commitments. In a Nebraska case,[32] two prisoners – Schroeder and a much bigger convict – were locked in a cell. The larger cellmate said that in the morning he was going to rape Schroeder, and then went to sleep. In this situation, a "snitch letter" to the guards does not offer much protection. If anything, it would expose Schroeder to even more serious reprisals. So, during the night, Schroeder stabbed the sleeping cellmate. The court held that there was no need to instruct the jury on self-defense here, because the threat of harm was not imminent: Schroeder could have waited till morning to see what his cellmate might do. This is quite an extreme result in terms of its insistence upon a truly imminent threat. On the facts of this case, the result is probably wrong. Nonetheless, the case reflects the law's heavy presumption against resort to deadly force. Criminal law requires sacrifice of property, honor, and pride as well as acceptance of non-serious personal injury before it will tolerate the sacrifice of human life.

This pacifist feature of the law could also be regarded as, in effect, "gendered." The rules on necessity and retreat are not Rambo's rules. This core principle

[31] There are several qualifications to the retreat requirement and other rules mentioned here. For example, about half the states have no retreat requirement at all; in others, the retreat requirement is generally inapplicable when the person resorting to self-defense is in her own home.

[32] State v. Schroeder, 199 Neb. 822, 261 N.W.2d 759 (1978).

resonates best with the ostensibly "feminist" conceptions of connection and community.[33] Yet it is not always compatible with the tactical particulars of the feminist reform agenda. Indeed, at precisely the point where criminal law begins to approximate the feminism of the "different norms" approach, it collides most forcefully with the feminism of different situations, which sometimes sees violent self-help as an appropriate means of redress for women who have been systematically oppressed in the private sphere and systematically denied the protection of public remedies.

To develop the tensions between the commitments of the various feminisms on the one hand and those of the criminal law on the other, I want now to consider the specific issues raised in connection with the law of self-defense and rape.

III. Self-Defense

What standards should govern the disposition of cases in which a battered spouse kills her abuser? How can we eliminate sex discrimination in these cases? The questions produce intense disagreement in the courts and among feminists themselves. For Lenore Walker and many of the feminist litigators who have built on her work, the law's refusal to recognize the special circumstances that propel some battered women to homicide reflects the inexcusable sex bias of the criminal law.[34] Other feminists are ambivalent; they worry that Walker's work, and litigation strategies based on it, will perpetuate inaccurate, negative stereotypes about women, and will prove tactically self-defeating to boot.[35] Finally, some argue that most women have the capacity to escape abusive relationships and that it is important for feminists forcefully to condemn those who fail to do so. This instinct emerges with particular clarity when the battered woman's failure to seek outside help leaves a child at risk.[36]

[33] The mixture of rights-oriented and community-oriented principles in a body of doctrine such as criminal law raises larger questions about the explanatory power of Gilligan's paradigms in a legal setting. Similar problems have been mentioned in connection with the uncertain correlations between feminist culture and the allegedly female orientation of legal constructs over time and across different legal systems. See text at notes 24 and 25 above. An exploration of the relevance of the Gilligan hypothesis to law could profitably examine such comparisons in detail. In addition, it seems essential to consider the interpenetration of substantive doctrine, which generally (though not uniformly) is abstract and rights-oriented, with procedure, where plea bargaining and the jury system interject important elements of ad hoc, highly contextual decision-making.

[34] Lenore E. Walker, "A Response to Elizabeth M. Schneider's Describing and Changing," *Women's Rights Law Reporter*, vol. 9 (1983), p. 223.

[35] Elizabeth M. Schneider, "Describing and Changing: Women's Self-Defense Work and the Problem of Expert Testimony on Battering," *Women's Rights Law Reporter*, vol. 9 (1983), p. 200.

[36] Commenting on the situation of Hedda Nussbaum – a terribly abused woman whose husband Joel Steinberg was recently convicted of murdering their adopted daughter – Susan Brownmiller writes ("Madly in Love," *Ms.*, April 1989, pp. 56, 64):

> Many of us old-warrior feminists ... thought that Nussbaum should have been standing trial as well, for reckless endangerment of a child, at the least ... Feminist analysis of the Steinberg-Nussbaum case must center on moral responsibility for the death of six-year-old Lisa. The battery of Hedda Nussbaum cannot be denied, but her complicity must also be acknowledged. The movement to aid battered women ... must also cease to excuse every battered woman who engages in criminal behavior, with the argument that she is, after all, merely a victim of the patriarchy, socialized into her feminine passivity, brainwashed into robotry by an evil man. The

Too often, the debates tend to discuss the battered spouse situation as a unitary phenomenon. The particulars of the context are secondary to some feminists (in the nature of quibbles about *how* she was tortured), but the details assume great importance for other feminists and can be crucial for the courts, which are perhaps particularistic to a fault. The focus on detail reflects the courts' traditional preoccupation with confining the boundaries of any defense suggestive of the inevitably powerful "blame the victim" strategy, said to be "the oldest, most common and most successful tactic in homicide cases."[37] Special sensitivity to the taking of human life also plays a central role here:[38]

> It is difficult enough to justify capital punishment as an appropriate response of society to criminal acts even after the circumstances have been carefully evaluated by a number of people. To permit capital punishment to be imposed upon the subjective conclusion of the individual that prior acts and conduct of the deceased justified the killing would amount to a leap into the abyss of anarchy.

Against the background of these concerns, the touchstone for the courts is always necessity: a self-defensive killing can be found legally justified only when it is strictly necessary. To start with the traditional criminal law perspective on the battered spouse problem, we therefore need to look closely at both the nature of the abuse and the circumstances of the killing.

A. The Variations in Context

Walker defines a battered woman as one "in an intimate relationship with a man who repeatedly subjects ... her to forceful physical and/or psychological abuse." "Repeatedly" is defined as "more than once," and "abuse" is defined as including any of six behaviors, from life-threatening violence to "extreme verbal harassment and expressing comments of a derogatory nature with negative value judgments" and "restriction of her activity through physical or psychological means."[39] This approach includes as battered women the wife whose husband subjects her to derogatory comments twice in two years, the spouse who is slapped across the face six times in six months, and the woman who suffers severe bruises, internal injuries, or broken bones from severe beatings inflicted every week throughout her marriage. The breadth of Walker's definition has obvious value from the perspective of the clinical psychologist interested in questions of research and treatment. It seems flagrantly overbroad from the perspective of traditional self-defense categories, which it is in part intended to challenge.

> point of feminism is to give women the courage to exercise free will, not to use the "brainwashed victim" excuse to explain away the behavior of a woman who surrenders her free will ... [B]attery defines a sustained relationship over many years between two people. With rape there may be no exit. In battery the exit signs may be flashing, but a woman may still refuse to walk out the door ... Hedda Nussbaum – white, middle class, with excellent editorial skills – chose to stay in her bondage with Joel.

[37] Jahnke v. State, 682 P.2d 991 (Wyo. 1984) (concurring opinion).

[38] *ibid.*

[39] Lenore E. Walker, *The Battered Woman Syndrome* (New York: Springer, 1984), p. 203.

Similarly, the context in which the woman's act of killing takes place can be extremely important. It is useful to focus on four possible variations:

(1) The woman who kills in the heat of a serious battering incident (i.e. a "confrontational" killing).

(2) The battered woman who files for divorce, moves out, and gets an order of protection, but is repeatedly pursued and beaten by her husband. Eventually, in desperation, she kills him.

(3) The battered woman who kills her spouse while he sleeps.

(4) The battered woman who gets a hired killer to shoot her spouse – days or weeks after a battering incident.

Battered spouse killings appear to be distributed in significant numbers among all four of these categories, with a surprisingly high percentage of killings in the non-confrontational settings. One survey of 87 reported battered spouse killings found that only one-third took place during a battering incident. In 18 cases (21 percent), the battering husband was killed while asleep or nearly asleep and five women (6 percent) arranged to have their spouses killed by others.[40]

B. *Traditional Law and the Feminist Challenge*

In terms of traditional self-defense doctrine, the four cases just described present radically different kinds of claims. In the first case, the killing in a confrontational setting, the wife *might* have a valid claim of self-defense. To succeed, she would have to show that her use of deadly force was reasonably necessary to avoid an imminent threat of death or great bodily harm. Under the traditional test, she would need to show all four of these elements – that is, she would have to believe (1) that the threat is imminent, (2) that the threat is of great bodily harm, (3) that deadly force is a necessary response. Additionally, (4) all three of those beliefs (as to imminence, great bodily harm, and necessity) would have to be reasonable.

Though the four required elements could be satisfied in the first case, the claim becomes progressively weaker in the other three. In the last case, that of the contract killing, there is not only an obvious opportunity to escape, but also strikingly clear evidence of premeditation. In traditional terms, a self-defense claim in the last case seems unthinkable.

Feminist research and criticism has shown basic continuities among these four ostensibly distinct situations. Abuse within marriage is now known to be frequent,[41] and it sometimes takes extremely violent forms. Abuse is frequent in

[40] Charles P. Ewing, *Battered Women Who Kill* (Lexington: D.C. Heath, 1987), p. 34. Ewing's sample, drawn from newspaper accounts, does not purport to be representative.

[41] See, e.g., Murray A. Straus, Richard J. Gelles, and Suzanne K. Steinmetz, *Behind Closed Doors* (Newbury Park: Sage Publications, 1980), p. 32 (28 percent of married couples report at least one instance of physical assault during their relationship, with 16 percent reporting one such instance within the past year). The empirical problems of estimation in this area are, of course, enormous. An excellent recent review of the literature reports similarly substantial figures; for example, a Kentucky survey found that 21 percent of the women respondents (and two-thirds of those recently separated or divorced) had been physically attacked by a male partner at least once. See Irene Hanson Frieze and Angela Browne, "Violence in Marriage," in *Family Violence* (Crime and Justice: A Review of Research, vol. 11, pp. 163, 179.

part because abused women have great difficulty leaving the relationship. The difficulties of leaving are in part social and economic. Women lack the resources to move out, to support themselves and their children. Shelters are not available. Husbands often threaten violent reprisals if they flee. Women who do move out are frequently pursued by battering husbands. And police assistance or court orders of protection often prove inadequate to protect such women. In a number of cases, police have actually counseled abused women *not* to file a complaint, on the ground that doing so would expose them or their children to the risk of even more serious injuries.[42]

Some of the difficulties of leaving are less tangible; they flow from a series of interrelated, partly perverse messages transmitted by our culture. The culture teaches that the good wife remains with her husband. It teaches that the good mother remains with her children. It even teaches (or did, until very recently) that some amount of physical intimidation and threatening, perhaps even an occasional slap across the cheek, is normal and nothing to worry about.[43]

A third set of reasons for not leaving is largely psychological. Lenore Walker's research on the battered wife syndrome suggests a theory that abused women experience a cycle alternating between violence and "loving contrition." The result, reinforced by the material obstacles to leaving the relationship, is what Walker calls "learned helplessness"[44]: Abused women are said to suffer greatly lowered self-esteem and to experience an inability to take action to protect themselves. They become gripped by passivity and fear. As a result, even when escape from an abusive relationship is objectively possible, abused women become unable to seek help.

This approach, if accepted, has two important implications. First, women who face no immediate threat can begin plausibly to claim that the four elements of a traditional self-defense claim are satisfied. The use of deadly force begins to appear reasonable or even necessary in that situation.[45] In fact, use of deadly force becomes necessary precisely because the abusive male is *not* threatening them, for it is only then that the woman has any opportunity to defend herself.

Second, in thinking about the different kinds of non-confrontational cases just mentioned, the Walker approach turns traditional intuitions inside out. In traditional terms, the strongest (or least weak) of the non-confrontational cases was that of the woman who filed for divorce, fled, and sought outside help. But such behavior does not fit the typical pattern of learned helplessness. Expert testimony about battered spouse syndrome could be ruled inadmissible, or prosecution

[42] See "View of Abused Women is Changing, Some Say," *New York Times*, Jan. 30, 1989, p. 7, col. 2.

[43] Straus, Gelles, and Steinmetz (*Behind Closed Doors*) report that 31 percent of husbands and 25 percent of wives rated one spouse slapping the other as either "necessary," "normal," or "good" under some circumstances. Some of the more recent surveys show from 80–90 percent of respondents (male and female) indicating that it is "never okay" for a husband to slap his wife; yet a 1985 survey found 24 percent approval for a husband slapping a wife for having a sexual affair. See Frieze and Browne, "Violence in Marriage," pp. 165–66.

[44] Walker, *The Battered Woman Syndrome*, p. 86.

[45] See Kit Kinports, "Defending Battered Women's Self-Defense Claims," *Oregon Law Review*, vol. 67, no. 2 (1988), p. 393 (arguing that the defendant's actions should be tested from the perspective of the "reasonable battered woman," and that from this perspective the use of deadly force can be found necessary).

experts could testify that the defendant, even if abused, did not display the battered wife *syndrome*, and therefore could be expected to avoid resort to deadly force.[46]

Conversely, my last variation, that of the contract killing, begins to look like the strongest case of all. The utter passivity, the inability to act even when the abuser is sleeping, the apparent dependence on the intervention of a male support figure, all reinforce a diagnosis of battered wife syndrome. In fact, Lenore Walker is very explicit in challenging traditional assumptions about contract killing. She writes with irritation that under the traditional approach, "hiring someone else to kill an abusive mate is seen as evidence of premeditation, even though many women, because of sex role conditioning or other factors, cannot use sufficient force to protect themselves."[47] Walker concludes that this traditional view is just evidence of the criminal law's "[b]iases ... against women."[48]

The Walker approach has won extraordinarily rapid and widespread acceptance in the courts. Testimony on battered wife syndrome is now widely admitted, even in cases in which the abusive spouse was killed while sleeping, or ambushed by a hired killer.[49] Recently, in two Illinois cases prosecuted before testimony about battered spouse syndrome became available, Governor Thompson freed women who had been convicted for using contract killers to murder their husbands.[50]

C. Limitations of the Walker Approach

There are many important details that bear on the proper resolution of cases like those just described. Here I want to raise some rather general points. The feminist strategy associated with Walker's research is problematic in part because it accepts (for understandable tactical reasons) the normative universe of the received criminal law tradition. Accepting that universe, these feminists have tried to show how battered women meet the necessity standard in circumstances under which a man would not.

The feminist strategy, to the extent that it accepts the traditional criminal law paradigm, is vulnerable on three counts. First, Walker's cycle theory and theory of learned helplessness rest on very fragile empirical foundations.[51] Her interviews

[46] The latter strategy was followed, successfully, on remand in *Kelly*, one of the leading cases upholding the admissibility of testimony on battered spouse syndrome. See Schneider, "Describing and Changing," p. 205 n. 59.

[47] Walker, "Response."

[48] *ibid.*

[49] E.g., State v. Norman, 366 S.E.2d 586 (N.C. App. 1988) (error for trial court to reject expert testimony on battered spouse syndrome in case of wife who shot sleeping spouse). Similarly, the *New Republic* recently reported a case in which Lenore Walker's expert testimony was admitted at trial in a contract killing case. There are also a number of important holdings to the contrary. The *Norman* decision itself was recently reversed on appeal to the state supreme court. State v. Norman, 324 N.C. 253, 378 S.E.2d 8 (1989). See also State v. Stewart, 763 P.2d 572 (Kan. 1988) (error to give self-defense instruction where wife shot sleeping spouse); State v. Martin, 666 S.W.2d 895 (Mo. Ct. App. 1984) (not error to exclude Walker's expert testimony in a $10,000 contract killing case). For a helpful review of the many cases, see Kinports, "Defending Battered Women's Self-Defense Claims."

[50] See *New York Times*, "View of Abused Women."

[51] See Note, "Battered Woman Syndrome and Self-Defense: A Legal and Empirical Dissent," *Virginia Law Review*, vol. 72 (1986), p. 619.

were built upon leading questions designed to elicit data to fit a preconceived model, and the interviewers who interpreted subject responses were not shielded from Walker's own expectations about what the responses should show. In addition, the data leave unclear whether there were long periods of rapport between the periods of violence and whether the women felt powerless (or capable of escape) during such periods when intimidation was in abeyance. Perhaps most important, the data give no indication of what kinds of harm women feared at particular stages of the "cycle of violence" and do not specify which groups of women experienced all (or which portions) of the cycle. Indeed, Walker's own data imply that at most only 58 percent (and conceivably as few as only 23 percent) of her battered women experienced all three phases of the cycle.[52] The empirical underpinnings of Walker's research thus fail to support the aspects of her theory that become crucial when a self-defense claim is at issue – namely, whether battered women typically experience a cycle of violence and learned helplessness, whether they live in "constant" fear of their husbands, whether they develop special insight into a spouse's likelihood of using deadly force, and – most important – whether they believe themselves unable to flee or seek help.

A further empirical problem is that, for many cases, Walker's learned helplessness hypothesis becomes largely nonfalsifiable. Often a central issue at trial is the question of whether the defendant really was abused by her husband. Too many women, of course, bear the irrefutable marks of gross physical abuse. But in some cases, prior injury has left no trace, and there is no history of prior hospitalizations or calls to the police. Indeed, the failure to seek medical attention or other outside help is said to be typical of the battered woman.[53] But when a woman has killed and then claims to be a battered woman, the prosecution vigorously attacks the credibility of her testimony on this point and cites her failure to leave as directly in conflict with her claims about abuse. Learned helplessness becomes crucial here, because it explains what might otherwise seem to be inconsistent claims (she was abused and she did not leave) and actually reinforces the credibility of the defendant's testimony. But what is the basis for the diagnosis of learned helplessness? Often, that conclusion is reached precisely because the clinician credits the woman's claim that she was abused and that she did not (and could not) leave. While this posture of trust is understandable for a researcher or clinician (and has led to many useful insights), it can scarcely be transported without qualification into a context in which the patient-defendant has powerful motivations to lie. There are few, if any, independent diagnostic markers to distinguish battered and truly passive, helpless women who kill their spouses from battered but not helpless women who do so. And in the absence of physical injury observed by third parties prior to the killing, there may be little or no basis to

[52] *ibid.*, pp. 639–640 & n. 108.

[53] See Kinports, "Defending Battered Women's Self-Defense Claims," p. 447:

> [M]any battered women cannot substantiate their testimony about the abusive relationship. Indeed, because of their fear and shame, they may not have told anyone about the beatings or even sought medical treatment, or they may have tried to cover up the cause of their injuries.

corroborate the woman's claim that she was battered at all. In these kinds of cases,[54] the credibility of her testimony that she was battered and could not leave is buttressed by the expert's diagnosis of learned helplessness, and the diagnosis of learned helplessness rests on her testimony that she was battered and did not leave.[55]

A second point of vulnerability is of concern primarily within feminism, and it retains much of its force even if the empirical problems can be overcome. The highly individualized, highly contextualized standard sought on behalf of battered women not only legitimates the notion that women (or a significant subgroup of them) are fundamentally different from men, but it does so in a context where those differences carry powerfully negative connotations. The Walker approach sees these women as passive, self-effacing, volatile, and sometimes irrational. In fact, given these features of the Walker approach, it becomes less surprising that this particular strand of radical feminist thought (with all its dubious empirical foundations) was so quickly adopted by male courts.

A third difficulty with the Walker approach is that its attempt to answer the requirements of the prevailing paradigm leads it to a Catch-22. The very dynamic that it uses to satisfy imminence and necessity (learned helplessness and the inability to act) leaves it without an explanation for what the woman *did* – kill her husband. Indeed, in some respects the theory of learned helplessness seems inconsistent with the act of killing.[56] The result is not only a theoretical anomaly but a serious practical obstacle to success in battered spouse litigation.[57] What the defense needs, above all, is a theory that makes the act of killing reasonable. But just as the failure to leave seems atypical, "unreasonable," even incomprehensible for a man, the act of *killing* seems atypical, "unreasonable," even incomprehensible for a woman.

D. Other Feminist Responses to the Problem

The Feminism of the "Different Voice." Responding to their inability to fit the facts of many battered spouse cases within the traditional self-defense paradigm (at least

[54] Walker attempted to measure several independent variables in an effort to differentiate battered women from a partial control group consisting of formerly battered women who were no longer in battering relationships. She hypothesized that the former group would exhibit more learned helplessness than the latter and that the presence of learned helplessness would be signaled by a psychological profile of strong fear, anxiety, and depression (and relatively weaker indications of anger, disgust, and hostility). Walker claims the results of this analysis were "compatible with learned helplessness theory," Walker, *The Battered Woman Syndrome*, p. 89, but in fact differences between the currently battered group (which ostensibly was suffering from learned helplessness) and the control group were small and not consistently in the predicted direction (see pp. 87–89). Nor does Walker analyze the differences for statistical significance.

[55] Consider State v. Kelly, 478 A.2d 364, 378 (1984):

> After hearing the expert, instead of saying Gladys Kelly could not have been beaten up so badly for if she had, she certainly would have left, the jury could conclude that her failure to leave was very much part and parcel of her life as a battered wife. The jury could conclude that instead of casting doubt on the accuracy of her testimony about the severity and frequency of prior beatings, her failure to leave actually reinforced her credibility.

[56] Catharine A. MacKinnon, "Toward a Feminist Jurisprudence" (Book Review), *Stanford Law Review*, vol. 34 (1982), pp. 703, 734.

[57] Schneider, "Describing and Changing."

without fostering pejorative and factually problematic stereotypes of women), some supporters of the battered spouse defense have recognized that what is needed here is, in essence, a *different* paradigm. They advocate relaxation of the traditional requirements of self-defense and recognition of how hard it is for abused women to flee their abusers.[58] In essense, this approach stresses not so much the difference in women's material situation as the difference in their moral universe. The ethic of caring and connection does double service here. First, it works to explain the battered woman's strong ties to her marriage and her children. She cannot leave because her ties to these relationships outweigh her suffering in a way that would be incomprehensible to a man.[59] Second, the ethic of care structures responses to the abused woman's act of self-protection. Because the act is so readily understandable for one in her situation, she merits not condemnation but empathy and support.

Notice how this kind of a feminist program collides with the core assumptions of criminal law. Criminal law, as I have indicated, is judgmental and demanding. Its usual posture is *not* supportive and empathetic. Its aim is not to understand each person in her individuality, but rather to articulate general norms, and to judge and to condemn even when compliance was understandably difficult.

The feminist notion, empathizing with the very real difficulties of compliance, implicitly moves us toward a non-judgmental, caring, and helpful conception of the criminal law. That is not an unattractive vision. But we must recognize that if valid, this approach cannot and presumably should not be confined to the situation of the battered wife. Many potentially violent encounters lend themselves to description in terms of the defendant's great difficulty in escaping threats, invoking lawful assistance, or controlling her impulses. Bernard Goetz could be seen as a victim of Battered New Yorker Syndrome.[60] Arguments for the recognition of numerous like "syndromes" and the various manifestations of "post-traumatic stress disorder" have already been pressed upon the courts, sometimes successfully.[61] A "caring and helping" approach, if generalized to such cases, has understandable appeal. But it inevitably means a radically different conception of "guilt"-determination, sentencing, and dispositions; greatly increased discretion at these stages; and an increase in opportunities for unstructured social intervention. That

[58] E.g., Christine Littleton, "Women's Experience and the Problems of Transition: New Perspectives on Battered Women," *University of Chicago Law Forum*, vol. 1989 (forthcoming); Phyllis L. Crocker, "The Meaning of Equality for Battered Women Who Kill Men in Self-Defense," *Harvard Women's Law Journal*, vol. 8 (1985), p. 121.

[59] See Littleton, "Women's Experience."

[60] Before his now-famous confrontation with several youths on a subway, Goetz had been mugged, had seen the legal system fail to prosecute his assailant, and had been denied a license to carry a gun. See Albert W. Alschuler, "Mediation With a Mugger," *Harvard Law Review*, vol. 99 (1986), p. 1808. No doubt, too, Goetz had no practicable way to escape what he saw as an ever-present threat; unable to afford the regular use of a taxi, he had no choice but to use the streets and subways of New York.

[61] See, e.g., Werner v. State, 711 S.W.2d 639 (Tex. Crim. App. 1986) (upholding the exclusion of evidence suggesting that defendant, the son of a concentration camp survivor, suffered from "Holocaust Syndrome"); Jahnke v. State, 682 P.2d 991 (Wyo. 1984) (upholding the exclusion of expert testimony on battered child syndrome). With respect to post-traumatic stress disorder, especially the so-called "Vietnam Vets Syndrome," see cases discussed in Kadish and Schulhofer, *Criminal Law and Its Processes*, pp. 1012–13.

kind of approach, suggested by a noted English social scientist a generation ago[62] is riddled with problems of ineffectiveness and unfair, overreaching administration.[63] It also implies radically altering or abandoning the concepts of condemnation and blame.

Criminal justice has not eschewed the model of caring and connection simply because its (male) leadership has been acculturated to prefer adversarial struggle. It has rejected the model of caring and connection because there is not, and cannot be, a genuine community of interest between the public at large and the offender who resorts to violence. Efforts to ignore, paper over, or proclaim away this reality are not unprecedented. Indeed, they have been attempted frequently and on a very wide scale. But every one of them – including the juvenile court movement, the *parens patriae* orientation of involuntary commitment programs for the retarded and the mentally ill, and the rehabilitative model for "treating" criminal offenders after conviction – has foundered on the unpleasant fact that conflicting interests are inherent in any criminal justice system that serves society's interests in deterrence and social protection. A system of criminal law premised on caring and connection will simply mask conflict and invite the abuses that vague standards of intervention have produced over and over in ostensibly benign programs.[64] For these reasons, the feminism of different norms, even if well-grounded empirically and useful in many legal contexts, can only be of limited service in designing the framework and doctrines for determining criminal guilt.

The Feminism of Different Situations. Other feminist approaches to the battered spouse problem accept the adversarial, rights-oriented structure of criminal justice norms but want to give them altered content in order to reflect women's different situations and systematic subordination. Catharine MacKinnon criticizes self-defense standards that look to the behavior of a reasonable "person" in the battered woman's situation; for her, the effort to understand that situation while abstracting it from history and experience that is unique to women distorts the reasonableness standard and ultimately renders it incomprehensible.[65] Implicitly, MacKinnon seeks (and the *Wanrow* court accepted[66]) one standard for the "reasonable man," but a distinct standard for the reasonable woman.

Professor La Fond emphasizes a different problem: battered women's self-defense claims are often vulnerable because the abuse, though serious, did not clearly threaten death or great bodily harm. The prevailing paradigm rules out

[62] Barbara Wootton, *Crime and the Criminal Law* (London: Stevens & Co., 1963). Lady Wootton proposed that the criminal process determine, at the guilt-determination stage, only whether the accused had done the proscribed act or physically caused the proscribed harm. If so, dispositional authorities would determine the appropriate treatment in light of the offender's mental and emotional condition, including his *mens rea* at the time of the offense.

[63] See H.L.A. Hart, Punishment and Responsibility (Oxford: Oxford University Press, 1968), pp. 158–185; Sanford H. Kadish, "The Decline of Innocence," *Cambridge Law Journal*, vol. 26 (1968), p. 273; H.L.A. Hart, "Book Review of Wootton, *Crime and the Criminal Law*," *Yale Law Journal*, vol. 74 (1965), p. 1325.

[64] See Francis A. Allen, The Decline of the Rehabilitative Ideal (New Haven: Yale University Press, 1981); Stephen J. Schulhofer, "The Future of the Adversary System," *Justice Quarterly*, vol. 3 (1986), pp. 83, 91–92.

[65] MacKinnon, "Toward a Feminist Jurisprudence."

[66] State v. Wanrow, 81 Wash.2d 221, 559 P.2d 548 (1977).

resort to deadly force in this situation, but this is in part because the paradigm assumes that the typical (male) combatant can ward off lesser threats without resort to deadly force. Since this is systematically untrue of women, who cannot avoid non-deadly abuse simply by punching back, La Fond proposes that resort to deadly force be permissible whenever it is "necessary to protect [the defendant] effectively" against any threat of unlawful physical violence.[67]

Charles Ewing approaches the problem from a different direction.[68] The notion of authorizing a deadly response to assaults that are not life-threatening seems to violate traditional conceptions of proportionality. Ewing avoids this kind of objection by arguing that even in the absence of a risk of fatal injury, repeated battering, in its social and psychological context, threatens the complete obliteration of individual autonomy and self-respect. By widening the understanding of "the self," Ewing suggests that deadly force becomes justifiable in self-defense not only when physical life is at risk but when the psychological self is threatened with destruction. He therefore proposes a theory of "psychological self-defense" that authorizes deadly force where necessary "to prevent the infliction of extremely serious psychological injury," defined as "gross and enduring impairment of one's psychological functioning which significantly limits the meaning and value of one's physical existence."[69]

These suggestions pose a common problem. Each, in a somewhat different way, collides with criminal law's traditionally demanding and pacifist features. MacKinnon's separate standard of reasonableness for women has ample empirical support; from a feminist perspective, it may even be worth the strategic costs that separate standards and potentially negative stereotypes can entail (though this point remains intensely debatable). But criminal law's social protection function has prompted rejection of separate, less demanding standards for discrete groups in countless other contexts in which marked difficulties of compliance can be convincingly demonstrated. Similarly, proposals to authorize deadly force as a response to assaults that do not threaten serious bodily harm violate pacifist principles of proportionality and respect for human life.

I want to argue that the organizing principles of traditional criminal law I have discussed here (whether conceived as "male" or "female") are all principles that we should keep. Criminal law *should be* judgmental, it should be demanding, and it should be pacifist. It goes without saying that I hold no brief for the abusive husbands in these cases. On the evidence, many of them appear to be thoroughly repulsive human beings. But they *are* human beings. And we do not know what produced their situation. We must resist the implication in some of the battered spouse writing that men like this are just animals or that they fully deserve to die for their crimes.

[67] John La Fond, "The Case for Liberalizing the Use of Deadly Force in Self-Defense," *Puget Sound Law Review*, vol. 6 (1983), pp. 237, 280.

[68] Ewing, *Battered Women Who Kill*, p. 79.

[69] For a telling critique of the unworkable vagueness of the Ewing proposal, see Kinports, "Defending Battered Women's Self-Defense Claims," pp. 458–60.

These observations point to a fundamental link between the demanding and pacifist orientations of criminal law. The former may seem harsh and aggressive (perhaps "male"), while the latter is forgiving and opposed to violence (perhaps "female"). But both are premised on rejection of a simplistic either-or, victim-victimizer model of human behavior. Pacifist principles grow out of recognition that even the abusive husband retains his humanity; even he retains some right to consideration and respect. If attacked with lethal force, the victimizer can become a victim. Likewise, the highly demanding features of criminal law doctrine grow out of recognition that condemnation, deterrence, and incapacitation cannot be restricted to those who are victimizers pure and simple; many (perhaps most) offenders are themselves victims – of abusive parents, oppressive environments, stunted education, constricted opportunities, wartime trauma, mental illness, or the like. We can recognize such factors – we can understand, empathize, and *care* – without concluding that we must excuse. Given the almost unlimited potential for conflict that human interaction creates, criminal law standards must be both demanding and pacifist. They are addressed to victimizers who are themselves victims, and they protect victims who may be victimizers as well.

This feature of the human condition, the ambiguous nature of moral character, also helps explain why the criminal law's demanding and pacifist features so often seem "elitist" and meet intuitive popular resistance. The impulse to think in either-or terms is always strong. The battered spouse cannot be an offender because, above all, she is clearly, undeniably, painfully, a victim. The abusive husband who is finally killed cannot be a real victim because he was so clearly, repulsively in the wrong. This way of thinking not only contributes to the appeal of the battered spouse defense, but it underlies other currents opposed to pacifist and demanding principles; for example, rejection of the duty to retreat. But criminal law attuned to social complexity does not attempt to reduce its protagonists to cartoon-like characters in a simplified morality play. Victim and victimizer too often coalesce.

E. Prospects for Battered Women under the Traditional Approach

So far, I have been critical of the feminist strategy to the extent that it attempts either to alter the criminal law's moral paradigm or to fit battered spouses within the existing paradigm by emphasizing the distinctive psychology that characterizes their situation. Does that mean that we should treat the situation of a battered woman as basically comparable to that of an assaulted man? To do that would be to ignore many features unique to the battered spouse context and quite independent of the problematic psychological claims. Criminal law's traditional doctrines and standards can provide an appropriate basis for resolving battered spouse cases, provided they are applied with genuine sensitivity to these unique features.

The inquiry under traditional standards focuses on whether the actions of the person claiming self-defense were reasonable for a person *in that situation.* The problem is to determine which features of the situation should and should not be taken into account. To consider gender itself as part of a person's legally important "situation" would amount to creating a separate standard in the guise of preserving the traditional one. For the reasons already discussed, the focus should *not* be confined to the behavior of the "reasonable battered woman."[70] That approach would import into the standard of reasonableness a special psychological attitude toward flight that, although relevant to *understanding* the behavior of this group of women, falls short of the demanding norm that society properly imposes even upon the disadvantaged.

Similarly, the focus should not be confined to the behavior that would be expected of the "reasonable woman," considered as someone generically distinct from the "reasonable man."[71] The history and experiences of disempowerment that affect all women as a group undoubtedly are relevant for many purposes. They help us understand the problems women encounter, and the remedies they need in many diverse social, political, and legal forums. It might appear that only a blind, heartless, or oppressive law would ever exclude them from consideration. But broad influences on the behavior of a social group, however accurate or important, should not lead to looser standards for the use of force in self-defense; the privilege to use deadly force calls for a demanding standard applicable even to (and especially to) those who have suffered the experiences of disempowerment and the sore temptation to take the law into their own hands.

I want to focus now on those distinctive features of the battered spouse problem that are properly entitled to special emphasis. Here, there are strands of feminism that infuse and guide the analysis. With its commitment to listening to, and truly hearing, the concerns of women in conditions of subordination and oppression, with its commitment to investigating and portraying in rich detail the texture of these environments, the feminism of different situations provides the crucial grounding for a three-dimensional appreciation of the context to which the traditional, fact-specific legal standard must be applied. One striking and distinctive feature of the battering case is that the situation of a spouse subjected to repeated, unpredictable, sometimes low-level (but still potentially serious) violence is quite different from the bounded, one-time encounter for which our traditional conception of self-defense was formulated. The danger is ongoing and pervasive rather than local and acute. Traditional concepts of just how much force was threatened, and of what it would mean to "escape," need to be reformulated for such cases, which have only rough analogues outside the context of domestic violence.

For similar reasons, the traditional insistence on a literally "imminent" infliction of great bodily harm must be abandoned outright. Imminence is relevant only because it helps identify cases where flight or legal intervention will be impossible, so that violent self-help becomes truly necessary. The decisive factor is necessity, not imminence *per se*. Thus, the proper approach is not to insist upon imminence but to require, as proposed in Model Penal Code §3.04, that the use of force be

70 As argued, for example, in Kinports, *ibid.*

71 As argued in MacKinnon, "Toward a Feminist Jurisprudence," and accepted by the court in State v. Wanrow, 81 Wash.2d 221, 559 P.2d 548 (1977).

"necessary on the present occasion." By this test, the act of killing an abusive husband who has just fallen asleep could (sometimes) be justified, just as the act of the male prisoner who stabbed his sleeping cellmate should have been held justified in the *Schroeder* case.[72]

A second distinctive feature of the battered spouse situation is the woman's limited prospect for obtaining help from police and courts. Many battered wives, far from reacting passively, repeatedly seek police assistance, only to find that officers are uninterested, insensitive, or sometimes simply unable (despite genuine efforts) to protect them from a determined abuser. One study of spouse killings found that police had been called to the home at least once in 85–90 percent of the cases; in more than half the cases, police had been called at least five times. A study of women imprisoned for killing abusive mates found that all reported having called the police at least five times before the lethal incident.[73] The unavailability or ineffectiveness of public authority is a problem that, in theory, can arise outside the context of domestic violence,[74] but it is an everyday occurrence within that context. When *shown* in the particular case, it has an obvious, undeniable bearing on the forms of self-help that become reasonable as part of the defendant's situation.

A third distinctive feature of the domestic violence situation may lie closest to the heart of the matter. The battered wife who finally, in desperation, shoots her abusive husband is seldom an intrinsically violent or uncontrolled person. Unlike most others suffering from forms of diminished capacity or post-traumatic stress disorder, the battered spouse is not a person whose "bitterness [has] turned into blasting powder which can be touched off by a spark."[75] Although the possibility cannot be excluded that the battered spouse who kills may once again find herself feeling trapped in an abusive relationship, it seems more likely that counseling and support services will quickly dissipate any tendency toward "learned helplessness." Unlike almost every other "syndrome" situation, therefore, battered spouse cases are not cases in which incapacitation must be a primary concern.

This feature of the problem is hard to classify because it does not bear directly on "reasonableness" or on the contours of the relevant "situation." And advocates of the battered spouse defense do not appear to have emphasized it. Yet this feature seems to explain much of the intuitive appeal of claims for a special battered spouse defense.

The lack of concern about incapacitation must be treated with caution, however, because of the problem of general deterrence. Even when fully assured that a woman who kills her abuser would never again resort to violence, we cannot forgo all punishment if the circumstances afforded the woman some alternative (though perhaps difficult) choice. Particularly in light of the pervasiveness of domestic violence, we cannot safely contemplate allowing abused spouses even a single bite

[72] See discussion in text at note 32 above.

[73] See Frieze and Browne, "Violence in Marriage," p. 205.

[74] Cf. United States v. Contento-Pachon, 723 F.2d 691 (9th Cir. 1984) (error to refuse duress defense where defendant claimed that corrupt Colombian and Panamanian police would afford him no protection against threats of drug dealers).

[75] Judge Bazelon used these terms to describe a ghetto youth who claimed to lack the capacity for self-control because of "rotten social background." United States v. Alexander, 471 F.2d 923 (D.C. Cir. 1972).

at this apple. The battered woman's lack of a violent or explosive disposition is therefore a factor relevant primarily for sentencing. Conviction and some punishment remain appropriate so long as the social and economic circumstances, realistically considered, did afford some reasonable alternative to the use of deadly force.

The ultimate inquiry should therefore remain, as under existing law, whether a reasonable person, in that situation, would have believed themselves at risk of death or great bodily harm and whether such a person would have considered deadly force the only reasonably available remedy.

Such a standard, applied with genuine sensitivity to the full texture of the battered spouse situation, should be adequate to produce acquittal in those cases involving both truly serious abuse and tangible barriers to flight. Many women do successfully escape from abusive mates.[76] Those who instead resort to deadly force should have to prove the concrete circumstances that prevented them from doing likewise. Sometimes, the battered woman has literally no place else to go. She may reasonably fear for the safety of children left behind. After trying to flee, she may have been pursued, beaten, and dragged back. In some instances, battered women who have sought police help have been told not to flee or press charges because both courses would put them at even greater risk. When these features are present, courts and juries can be led to understand that a person in that situation would have reasonably concluded that escape was impossible.

For cases not qualifying for acquittal under this approach, the degree of punishment becomes the important question. In this area, traditional doctrine affords the tools for avoiding excessive punishment, provided that, once again, these tools are applied with genuine sensitivity to context. First, if the battered spouse sincerely believed that escape was impossible and deadly force her only solution, but she was unreasonable in making that appraisal, then it is quite inappropriate to convict her of first degree murder. Since the essence of her culpability is carelessness rather than conscious awareness of wrongdoing, the offense should be treated as comparable to negligent homicide, and the punishment should be reduced accordingly. The Model Penal Code has long recommended this approach for self-defense cases generally.[77] The prevalence of the problem of unreasonable mistake in battered spouse cases makes it particularly urgent that this reform be adopted by jurisdictions (such as Illinois) that have yet to do so.

Second, the battering circumstances will often involve enough "provocation" to reduce the degree of killing from murder to manslaughter, especially under the modern view about cooling time.

Third, whatever the degree of homicide appropriate to the facts, the battering circumstances may suggest mitigation of sentence. In most instances, probation and psychological counseling will deal adequately with any danger of recidivism. A relatively short prison sentence can provide the deterrence and retribution that ordinarily remains appropriate when we conclude that an act of killing was wrong.

[76] See Frieze and Browne, "Violence in Marriage," p. 206-7.
[77] *Model Penal Code*, §3.09.

Since I argue that the battered spouse should not have a privilege to kill unless the very strict, appropriately demanding requirements of traditional self-defense law are satisfied, I want to be concrete about the positive steps that can be taken to help her, consistent with the core principles I advocate here. We need more shelters for women, and more counseling and psychological support – not only for battered wives, but also for the abusers who need to begin to understand the dynamics of their own behavior. And we need more responsive police.

Until reforms of the foregoing kind are made, compliance with the pacifist requirements of criminal law will remain *very* difficult for battered women. Nonetheless, the place for recognizing the extraordinary difficulties battered women face in seeking to avoid the use of deadly force is not in extending to them a special, expanded privilege of self-defense. The way to respond to this situation, most consistent with the orientation and objectives of the criminal law, is strict enforcement and vigorous penalties against aggressive husbands. The woman who flees and is pursued, who calls for help and is turned away, should have a defense. But when the woman's prison is *in*tangible, when the chains are largely psychological (whether in terms of learned helplessness or, more positively, in terms of her bonds of connection to her children and to her marital relationship), then the woman who resorts to deadly force should be punished.

There is one important qualification to this conclusion. I have assumed that the battered woman is not mentally ill. If the learned helplessness phenomenon claimed by Walker can be reliably established (and this would require a far better understanding of psychological dynamics and a much better handle on questions of falsifiability than we are close to having at this point), then the battered woman would lack the mental capacity to do what the law requires; she could be acquitted on grounds of insanity. But if the woman is mentally responsible, and if escape is possible in terms of the social and economic resources reasonably available, then – even though escape may indeed be difficult – the criminal law, unfortunately, has to come down forcefully in favor of the hard choice that minimizes violence and saves lives.

IV. Rape

I want to make some related points about the law of rape. I will focus on a 1982 Massachusetts case, *Commonwealth v. Sherry*.[78] Three defendants, all doctors, made advances to a nurse at a hospital staff party. Two of them grabbed her by the arms and pulled her out of the room, saying "We are all going up to Rockport" (where one of them had a beach house). She protested verbally, but not physically. Later she said that she thought they were just "horsing around." When they got to Rockport, all of them smoked marijuana. Then the three men took off their clothes and started to undress her. She got frightened and protested, but she felt too numb to fight back. One after another, each of the three doctors had intercourse with her. A jury acquitted the defendants on a kidnapping charge, in effect finding that her going to the beach house with them was consensual. But they convicted the defendants of rape.

[78] 437 N.E. 2d 224 (Mass. 1982).

The defendants argued that the victim had consented, or if not, that they thought she had. They requested that the jury be instructed: "Unless you find beyond a reasonable doubt that the accused had actual knowledge of [the victim's] lack of consent, then you must find them not guilty." The trial judge denied the instruction and in effect told the jury that if the acts were done with a threat of force, expressed or implied, and against the victim's will, then a mistake would not be a defense.

The Massachusetts Supreme Judicial Court affirmed the conviction. The court made two points. First, the requested instruction, which required knowledge of nonconsent, was clearly incorrect, because at most only a *reasonable* mistake of fact would arguably afford a defense. Second, the court suggested that mistake of fact might not be a defense even if it were reasonable. In other words, the defendants might be held strictly liable with respect to the presence or absence of consent. Subsequent Massachusetts cases have tended to support the latter view.[79]

This is an impressive victory for the feminist perspective – for putting a very heavy burden on the defendant to be sure about the existence of consent. The result is in accord with that reached recently in several other states, where courts have held that negligence or even strict liability may suffice with respect to the element of consent in rape.[80]

While I have sympathy for the end result – the conviction of the defendants in *Sherry* – I want to argue that the use of a negligence or strict liability standard in this context is a bad mistake. My first objection is the conventional one. Conviction of a serious crime ought to require subjective culpability – in other words, a conscious awareness of wrongdoing. Instances of strict liability do exist in the criminal law, but they are largely confined to two situations: (a) "lesser crime" cases, in which only the degree of punishment is at stake (i.e., the defendant knows she has committed a lesser wrong, but facts of which she was unaware bring her conduct within the terms of a greater offense); and (b) regulatory offenses, in which conviction typically carries no great stigma and little likelihood of incarceration. Strict liability is almost unheard of in the context of traditional *malum in se* felonies when, if the facts were as the defendant believed them to be, he would be committing no crime whatsoever. The danger here is that the strict liability approach, if taken seriously and pursued consistently over time, would in effect risk converting rape into a sort of regulatory offense not requiring fault and carrying at most only a very diluted stigma.

A negligence standard is less radically at odds with criminal law's traditional requirement of fault in serious offenses.[81] A move from subjective awareness to a negligence approach could even be seen as an effort to bring into the *mens rea* area the kind of demanding standards that the law routinely (and properly) imposes with respect to capacities for self-control. But there is an important difference – if a person *knows* that his course of conduct is wrong, it is appropriate to impose heavy

[79] E.g., Commonwealth v. Lefkowitz, 481 N.E.2d 277 (1985).

[80] E.g., People v. Mayberry, 542 P.2d 1337 (Cal. 1975) (negligence); Commonwealth v. Williams, 439 A.2d 765 (Pa. Super. 1982) (strict liability).

[81] See Celia Wells, "Swatting the Subjectivist Bug", *Criminal Law Review*, vol. 1982, p. 209.

pressure for compliance even when (or particularly when) that conduct is hard for him to avoid. The psychological mechanisms, the deterrence possibilities, and the propriety of moral condemnation all become more problematic when we use the threat of heavy sanctions to try to induce thought on the part of those who, by hypothesis, do not advert to the possibility that their conduct may be wrongful. These difficulties tend to support (though not conclusively) the law's traditional preference for conscious awareness of wrongdoing as a prerequisite for conviction in the serious felonies.

If we were to have either a strict liability standard or a crime of negligent rape, then what penalty would be appropriate?[82] We treat criminally negligent homicide as a minor felony or even a misdemeanor, even though the offense requires a *gross* deviation from the standard of care that a law-abiding person would follow. Even if we treat negligent rape as just as serious an offense as grossly negligent homicide, the moral message we want to convey would be greatly diluted, and the penalties provided would be much too low. In this connection, it is noteworthy that in the *Sherry* case each defendant was sentenced to only six months' imprisonment. The penalty is consistent with the trial judge's assumption that they could be convicted without subjective culpability, but the resulting punishment is, in my view, much too low.

My second objection is somewhat less conventional. Focusing on the culpability issue, as most feminists have done here and as mainstream scholars typically do, misses the main problem. Let me illustrate this point by going back to the facts of *Sherry*. The feminist perspective holds that a good-faith mistake is not, by itself, sufficient to warrant acquittal and that defendants should have to show that their mistake was reasonable. But how could the doctors in *Sherry* have made a reasonable mistake? Given the victim's isolation in an unfamiliar setting, her intimidation by three naked men, and her explicit protests, there could not possibly have been (from the feminist perspective) a reasonable mistake. For the same reasons, however, one would have to say that these defendants actually *knew* that the victim was not consenting. At the very least, they were all aware that she *might* not be consenting; hence, they were reckless. In other words, on any appropriate conception of consent, these defendants were *subjectively* culpable and would be convicted whether or not we insist on a negligence standard.

Against this background, why does it make any difference what the mistake standard is? There is one perspective from which these defendants might have made an honest mistake. That is the perspective that "no" does not really mean "no," that women really love indiscriminate sex and just want to feign some initial reluctance. On this view of when a woman's behavior signals consent, the defendants probably would not have had an actual awareness of her non-consent, and they could have been acquitted. But if you hold this view of consent (and of women), you might very well consider that the doctors' mistake of fact was not unreasonable. Indeed, on this view of consent, you might even conclude that the

[82] Professor Estrich proposes a negligence standard but does not address questions of grading and punishment. Susan Estrich, *Real Rape* (Cambridge: Harvard University Press, 1987), pp. 97–98.

victim really *did* consent – that the doctors made no mistake at all. Once one accepts this alternative (hopefully outmoded) conception of what consent means, the defendants could conceivably be acquitted even if they were tried under a strict liability standard.

The point here is not that choice of the *mens rea* standard can never make a difference. Certainly, conviction becomes progressively easier as we move toward the strict liability approach. But we are working at the fringes of the problem. The *Sherry* court's position on mistake of fact standards begs the most important question, or sweeps it under the rug of jury findings about reasonableness. This is really not a debate about *mens rea* standards. Rather, it is (or ought to be) a debate about what we mean by the construct that we call "consent." In most instances, a juror who comes into court with the conception that "no" means "no" will vote to convict in a case like *Sherry*, no matter what the mistake of fact standard is. Conversely, a juror who comes in with the notion that "no" probably means "yes" will acquit, no matter what the mistake of fact standard is. The debate about mistake of fact standards diverts attention from the question of what it is that you have to be mistaken about. Rather than requiring that the mistake be reasonable, and then leaving the jurors to their own conceptions of what is "reasonable" and what is "consent," we need to spell out what the concept of consent means.

Feminists who address this issue are very clear that, in their view, "no" means "no." But this is a point that has to be built explicitly into the formal statutory definition of the offense, rather than being left to being worked out in jury deliberations or in the gradual evolution of our culture.

Secondly, the usual feminist position probably does not go far enough. Why should there have to be a "no"? There are still many cases in which a woman has been beaten into submission, time and again; eventually she simply submits or capitulates to the inevitable, with only her silence or her sobs to express her own preferences. Courts treat such conduct as amounting to consent.[83] When there is no question that her partner can enforce his will if he has to, why should silence be taken as the equivalent of consent? Why should the law in effect *presume* the existence of consent in the absence of an explicit "no"? In this area, the law has yet to catch up with its more general commitment to a pacifist conception of human relations. The pacifist commitment implies that citizens may not presume a privilege to intrude upon the rights of others, but rather must respect the autonomy of each person and stand clear in the absence of a direct, affirmative manifestation of consent. On this basis, anything less than an explicit "yes" should not count as consent. A recent Washington statute captures this approach:[84]

> "'Consent' means that at the time of the act of sexual intercourse there are actual words or conduct indicating freely given agreement to have sexual intercourse."

[83] State v. Alston, 312 S.E.2d 470 (N.C. 1984). Some feminists agree that a woman in this situation can reasonably be expected to express her disinclination openly and firmly. E.g., Vivian Berger, "Not So Simple Rape," *Criminal Justice Ethics*, vol. 7 (Winter/Spring 1988), pp. 69, 75.

[84] Wash. Code Ann. §9A.010(6) (1981).

Once you have this explicit formulation of what consent means, you will rarely, if ever, need a strict liability or a negligence standard in order to achieve the appropriate results. You can preserve the traditional requirement of conscious awareness of wrongdoing.[85] And you can preserve the tough penalties that can and should apply to conscious awareness of wrongdoing. Since the defendants in *Sherry* undoubtedly *knew* that the victim had never affirmatively expressed, by words or conduct, a "freely given agreement to have sexual intercourse," they would *know* that they were raping her. The result is, in effect, a very conventional criminal law position on the importance of *mens rea*, but one that is informed by a feminist conception of what consent means: in other words, what consent means to the woman who is giving it.

Some feminists argue for the fairness of a strict liability or negligence standard in a way that conflates the issues of *mens rea* and substantive consent. In effect, they use our intuitions about the fairness of a strict standard in the latter area to support a strict standard on *mens rea* issues that are conceptually distinct. Thus, Susan Estrich suggests that because a man can fairly be held to understand that "no" means "no," "unreasonable mistakes, no matter how honestly claimed, should not exculpate."[86] The force of this position depends very much on the question of what the "unreasonable mistake" is about. If a man knows that a woman has said no and mistakenly interprets this to mean yes, his unreasonable mistake should not exculpate. But this is because the law requires (or should require) an affirmative expression of consent – and in the case posited, the man *knows* that affirmative consent is not present.

The fairness of giving strict substantive content to our concept (and legal definition) of consent, as in the example just mentioned, is a distinct question from the fairness of imposing strict liability or negligence with respect to mistakes about whether the substantive facts defined as consent are present. Suppose, for example, that the man fully understands that "no" means no, but honestly believes that the woman said "yes" – perhaps because he was mistaken about what the "yes" referred to, or because, as happened in *United States v. Short*,[87] he allegedly misunderstood a Japanese woman's response in her native language. There is still an argument that the carelessness in such cases should be punished. But it is a different argument from the argument for punishing men who claim to think that no means yes. I submit that carelessness in this second group of cases should not be punished as a serious felony. Probably (though I want to be quite tentative on this last point) it should not be punished at all. Cases of the sort just posited rarely arise, and one would prefer to know more about their contexts before making a definitive judgment about whether this sort of negligence poses a problem that needs to be addressed. The more important point, for the time being, is that we can both preserve traditional principles of criminal law *and* further the objectives of the

[85] Compare Lynn Henderson, "What Makes Rape a Crime," *Berkeley Women's Law Journal*, vol. 3 (1988), pp. 193, 216. Her analysis parallels mine in focusing on the content of the "consent" construct but diverges in arguing at the same time for a strict liability standard.

[86] Estrich, *Real Rape*, 103.

[87] 4 U.S.C.M.A. 437 (1954).

feminist reform agenda by insisting on proof of knowledge or recklessness with respect to non-consent (along with the firm punishments that are appropriate in cases of subjective culpability) while focusing our attention on development of a more informed, more sensitive social and legal conception of what consent means.

If you take this approach, it solves one set of problems but creates others. Once a "no" means "no," the next generation of issues will center on when or whether "yes" is sufficient to mean "yes." What happens when the "yes" is produced by intimidation, indirect pressure, or manipulation? Perhaps the hardest set of problems in this area concerns the question of when fraud or misrepresentation should invalidate consent. A 1981 California case illustrates the problems.[88] Two roommates shared an apartment. One of them had a girlfriend who moved in and stayed for a month. The other roommate did not like the arrangement. One night (at 1:00 A.M.) while the first roommate was out, a friend of the second roommate slipped into bed with the young woman (who was sleeping) and began sexually fondling her. She responded, and they continued until she suddenly realized that he was not her boyfriend. She abruptly pulled away. The young man stopped immediately but was charged with attempted rape.

Should this kind of behavior be subject to criminal penalties? I suspect that many men would regard these facts as a bit funny, or at worst as an example of a bad practical joke. To try to get more empathy, one would probably have to ask a man to imagine the roles reversed, to imagine how he would feel if an unknown woman did something like this to him. But many men might still have difficulty understanding what there is to be upset about. What is a woman's perspective on this sort of situation? In the California case, when the woman realized that the person in bed was not her boyfriend, she began screaming hysterically. There is no question that from a woman's perspective, this kind of unwanted sexual contact is extremely intrusive and frightening.

The legal analysis of this case, in terms of existing categories, proceeds much differently. In California, as in most states, what is called fraud in the inducement does not invalidate consent. As a result, sexual intercourse induced by fraud is not regarded as rape. Nor is it regarded as any lesser sexual offense. Thus, the man who obtains consent by false promises – whether of undying love, lavish gifts, or job opportunities and promotions – has not committed rape.[89] Nor has the doctor who convinces a patient that she will die unless she obtains a special serum that must be transmitted by sexual intercourse.[90] In my case of the California woman awakened in her bed, the victim knew that she was engaged in a sexual act (she was not misled about that), so the defendant's conviction was reversed. I submit that this result is wrong. More than that, the result reflects a totally one-sided, male-sided view of the nature of unwanted sexual conduct. I conclude that this ought to be a case of rape: at least some frauds in the inducement are sufficiently serious to

[88] Mathews v. Superior Court, 119 Cal.App.3d 309, 173 Cal.Rptr. 820 (1981).

[89] Compare United States v. Condolon, 600 F.2d 7 (4th Cir. 1979), upholding the wire fraud conviction of a man who posed as a talent agent and falsely represented that he could place women in modeling and acting jobs in return for sexual favors.

[90] Boro v. Superior Court, 163 Cal.App.3d 1224, 210 Cal.Rptr. 122 (1985).

invalidate consent and justify criminal punishment. (The *degree* of punishment, of course, ought to be more stringent when the rape is accomplished by physical violence.)

My point here is not that rape should be treated just like other crimes. I cannot join Professor Estrich in thinking that fraud in obtaining consent to intercourse should be tested by the same standards as fraud in obtaining property.[91] That approach, which amounts to abstracting the concept of fraud from contexts in which its motivations and consequences are quite diverse, strikes me as unsound. My point is just the reverse. We need to look at how fraud works in the context of sexual interaction. Surely not every misrepresentation in the course of courtship or seduction warrants criminal or even civil penalties. But ever since widespread abolition of the civil action for seduction in the 1930's,[92] existing law has tilted to the opposite extreme, immunizing *all* misrepresentation, however egregious.

In this relatively small way, as well as in larger ones, criminal law has simply been blind to the pressures that influence consent and to the unique harms experienced by women in unwanted sexual encounters. The result of reliance on a reasonableness standard is to reflect and reinforce a status quo morality that includes considerable intimidation and exploitation as acceptable (apparently on the ground that they have been acceptable to men). Since we should seek to preserve the traditional (though arguably gendered) premises of the criminal law –

[91] Estrich discusses two cases involving elements of both fraud and fears for physical safety. In one, a man posing as a talent agent lured a high school student to his "temporary studio" with the prospect of helping place her as a model. In the other, a man who posed as a psychologist conducting a sociological experiment lured a young woman to his "office." Estrich argues that apart from the element of intimidation presented by the isolated setting of both incidents, the misrepresentation alone should vitiate consent: "[W]e [should] prohibit fraud to secure sex to the same extent that we prohibit fraud to secure money." Susan Estrich, "Rape," *Yale Law Journal*, vol. 95 (May 1986), pp. 1087, 1120. Similarly, though her book does not discuss fraud problems as such, she asserts there that "[t]he 'force' or 'coercion' that negates consent ought to be defined to include extortionate threats and misrepresentations of material fact." Estrich, *Real Rape*, pp. 102–3. For sharp criticism of Estrich's position on these points, see Berger, "Not So Simple Rape," pp. 76–77.

[92] See, e.g., N.Y. Civ. Rts. Law §80-a. This provision, formerly Civil Practice Act §§61-b, d, was enacted in 1936 in response to concern that young women without financial prospects were using the threat of a suit for seduction as a means of legalized blackmail.

As stated in §61-a of the original legislation:

> The remedies heretofore provided by law for the enforcement of actions based upon alleged alienation of affections, criminal conversation, seduction and breach of contract to marry, having been subjected to grave abuses, causing extreme annoyance, embarrassment, humiliation and pecuniary damage to many persons wholly innocent and free of any wrongdoing, who were merely the victims of circumstances, and such remedies having been exercised by unscrupulous persons for their unjust enrichment, and such remedies having furnished vehicles for the commission or attempted commission of crime and in many cases having resulted in the perpetration of frauds, it is hereby declared as the public policy of the state that the best interests of the people of the state will be served by the abolition of such remedies.

See Aadland v. Flynn, 27 Misc. 2d 833, 837 (N.Y. Sup.Ct., 1961).

Note how the threat that these suits posed to the reputation and resources of propertied gentlemen preoccupied the legislature. The severe harm that breach of promise could cause to young women (who, given the mores of the time, may have been deprived of the prospect of contracting a "respectable" marriage) seems not to have weighed heavily in the minds of the legislators.

Both civil and criminal suits for seduction survive to this day in a few states, but the frequency of enforcement appears to vary from rare to nonexistent. See "Seduction," in *Corpus Juris Secundum*, vol. 79 (1952), p. 953ff.; *ibid.* (1988 Supp.).

its overtly judgmental, demanding, and pacifist features – we need to begin taking seriously in rape law the norms of non-violence and respect for the humanity and personal privacy of others. If we had a woman-centered conception of when male behavior was unacceptably intimidating, if we thought about what constitutes an unwanted intrusion from the perspective of the person intruded upon, then the law of rape would look very different from the way it looks today.

V. Conclusion

Feminist thought combines a variety of conceptually diverse and controversial challenges to criminal law. Gender bias arguably exists not only in attitudes of overt hostility to women and in discriminatory law enforcement practices, but also in the content of legal doctrines and in the very structure and styles of legal and philosophical thought about questions of criminal responsibility. Too often, the issues raised by feminists have simply been ignored or neglected by mainstream criminal law scholars. This paper is, in part, an effort to remedy that neglect: the "gender question," in its many manifestations, deserves to be taken quite seriously and addressed on its merits.

To say that many of criminal law's characteristic doctrines, conceptual structures and modes of procedure are "gendered" is not, however, to say that such features should be consigned forthwith to the scrapheap, as nothing more than relics of an outmoded and intolerable oppression. Criminal law's judgmental, demanding, and pacifist features place it on a collision course with some of the most thought-provoking and attractive strands of feminist thought. Nonetheless, I have sought to show why these traditional principles continue to deserve support.

I have also sought to illustrate a few of the ways in which consistent support for these principles requires significant modifications in legal doctrine, to reflect the revised understanding of the social condition that modern feminism makes available. In the law of rape, traditional insistence on a culpable *mens rea* remains largely sound, but substantive notions of force, consent, and fraud require thorough overhaul to escape the one-sided, male-sided perspectives that have dominated the legal conception of these constructs. And if the law could begin to reflect and promote different attitudes toward the dignity and autonomy of women in the law of rape, it is possible that the problems of domestic violence and the conundrums of spousal self-defense would also begin to look different. The solution in that context is not to fight violence with violence but for the criminal law consistently to adhere to pacifist principles, to condemn violence, and to try to enforce a more humane conception of the acceptable ways to resolve conflict in social life.

THE ASSUMPTION OF RISK ARGUMENT*

BY LEO KATZ

> And Jephthah made a vow to the Lord, and said, "If thou wilt give the Ammonites into my hand, then whoever comes forth from the doors of my house to meet me, when I return victorious from the Ammonites, shall be the Lord's, and I will offer him up for a burnt offering." So Jephthah crossed over to the Ammonites to fight against them; and the Lord gave them into his hands ...
>
> Then Jephthah came to his home at Mizpah; and behold, his daughter came out to meet him with timbrels and with dances; she was his only child; beside her he had neither son nor daughter. And when he saw her, he rent his clothes, and said, "Alas, my daughter! you have brought me very low, and you have become the cause of great trouble to me; for I have opened my mouth to the Lord, and I cannot take back my vow."
>
> *The Book of Judges*

I. SOME PUZZLES

You buy a lottery ticket and you lose. You are sorry, but you wouldn't dream of complaining. Why then do you feel entitled to complain in the following sorts of cases?

(1) You are a shareholder in the Ancient Mariner Company. One day you receive a letter telling you that the company is about to dissolve and that you are entitled to ten dollars for every share you own. The letter also tells you that the managers of Ancient Mariner will soon found a new company, Novum Organum, which will be pursuing a different – and, they hope, more profitable – line of business. The letter asks you to invest in the new venture; indeed, it concludes by saying that unless you indicate differently, the managers will simply reinvest your Ancient Mariner capital in Novum Organum. They enclose Novum Organum's freshly minted prospectus, which carries a bold-face disclaimer on the very first page. The disclaimer, which I take from a very real case, *Holmes v. Carey*, states:

> (i) The present directors do not foresee the possibility of the corporation ever being in a position to pay any dividends or having any assets of determinable value. The continued existence of the corporation is questionable. Bankruptcy may result at any time.
>
> (ii) Anyone considering purchase of this security must be prepared for immediate and total loss.

* I want to thank my fellow symposiasts and the members of the University of Michigan Legal Theory Workshop for some very valuable comments – and Wilhelm and Jacob Grimm whose stories about ill-conceived promises first made me skeptical about the assumption of risk.

(iii) No representation is made that the possibility exists that the corporation can continue to exist.
(iv) No representation is made in this statement that the President and Secretary of the Company have any capability that can benefit the corporation in any way.
(v) In view of the above unfavorable factors, and other unfavorable factors in every part of this offering circular, it would appear that it is self-evident that any prospective purchaser of [Novum Organum] stock should be prepared for immediate total loss.[1]

Let us suppose – quite contrary to the real and undramatic facts of Holmes v. Carey – that ensuing months prove this company to be everything the prospectus promised: incompetent, corrupt, and eventually bankrupt. You lose all your money. You will feel cheated and will want to complain.

But given what is said in the prospectus, why are you still entitled to do so?

(2) You see an advertisement in a newspaper asking you to put your money into an account at your local savings and loan association. It offers you an interest rate far in excess of what you are getting at your local bank. You have a pretty good idea why the S&L is being so generous: rumors abound that it might soon collapse, and that if it collapses the federal government might not make good on its promise to reimburse all depositors. But you take your deposit there anyway. The S&L collapses, and the federal government, as predicted, reneges on its promise.

Again: given those rumors, and given the higher interest rate paid you to bear the risks rumored about, do you have a legitimate complaint?

(3) You enter a bar and immediately notice a brawl in progress. You are fascinated, and give not even a thought to leaving. As fate will have it, one of the brawlers' elbows lands in your jaw, producing the usual consequences – and the usual question: are you entitled to complain?

(4) The mayor of a small town wants to persuade a chemical plant to locate in his town. You and nearly all of the citizenry support him, although you know that there is the distinct risk of a dangerous chemical accident. The mayor campaigns on this very platform and is elected by an overwhelming majority.

An accident occurs. Given your support for the mayor's platform, should you be able to complain?

(5) You are a retired army general. The government is about to adopt some controversial policies. To forestall criticism from certain quarters, it offers all retired officers an increase in their pension if they promise not to criticize the government in public, come what may. You accept the pension increase. When the policies are finally adopted, you are shocked. You write a book vehemently attacking them. The government threatens to sue you for going back on your promise. If they do, do you have anything to complain about?

Those who say that you have nothing to complain about seem to have logic on their side – the logic of what is known as the assumption of risk argument. Whether you buy a risky lottery ticket, invest in a risky stock, make a risky deposit, witness a

[1] Holmes v. Carey, 234 F.Supp. 23, 24 (N.D. Ga. 1964).

risky barroom brawl, invite a risky chemical plant into your neighborhood, or sign a risky government waiver – doesn't each of these amount to an assumption of risk that deprives you of the moral right (and should also deprive you of the legal right) to complain about what happened to you? Why isn't this merely a rhetorical question? Why do our intuitions about these cases waver? To be sure, they don't waver about the lottery case, but they do waver about the five others, even though they seem logically the same. This essay is meant to find out why.

II. An Ubiquitous Argument

Although the assumption of risk argument is associated with tort law, it is in fact ubiquitous, as the above examples show. It certainly seems to have relevance to the criminal law – most notably because it enters into the definition of harm. What's consented to doesn't count as harm: if consented to, the taking isn't theft, the intercourse isn't rape, the tackling isn't battery – even the killing may not be murder. And if the consented-to activity is not in fact certain to result in a taking, or in intercourse, or in a tackling, or in a killing, but only entails that risk – well, then, the victim consented to the risk. Or so it has sometimes been argued.

Statutes of strict liability are often justified by an assumption of risk argument: "Really, now, even a thoroughly circumspect, irreproachably conscientious executive who is held strictly liable for causing a contaminated drug to be shipped through interstate commerce has nothing to complain about. He chose to work in an area he knew was regulated by such statutes. He assumed the risk."

The rule that holds the coconspirator, and occasionally even the accomplice, liable for actions of others that he neither desired nor foresaw is often justified by the assumption of risk: "The defendant knew what he might be getting into and proceeded nonetheless. He assumed the risk."

We invoke the assumption of risk when we punish the person who mistakenly assists an aggressor thinking the man was acting in self-defense; or when we punish the person who acted out of necessity or duress but carelessly let himself be put in such a spot; or when we punish the good samaritan who comes to a dying man's rescue and then botches the job; or when we punish the bank robber who inadvertently, and without negligence, brings about a death and is charged with felony-murder; or when we punish unequally the person who attempts a crime but fails as against the person who succeeds.

Most notoriously, or course, the assumption of risk is the legal economist's old standby. He will advance numerous proposals that at first glance have an air of unfairness about them, but which tend to promote efficiency. Never mind the unfairness, the economist will say, it's only superficial. The putative victim of this unfair arrangement typically has a choice about whether he wants to get into the arrangement or not. As long as he is free to stay away, how can he complain of unfairness?

The most intriguing recent application of this argument is to insider trading. Good arguments can be made that allowing insider trading would promote efficiency – for instance, that it is a good form of incentive compensation for managers. When someone objects that insider trading is unfair, the economist will ask: imagine that a company were founded that announced point-blank, in advance, "We will allow insider trading. If you don't like it, if it strikes you as unfair, if you fear you'll lose out as a result, well then, don't buy our company's stock." How can someone who buys that company's stock be entitled to complain about insider trading? Moreover, even if no such announcement is ever explicitly made, a stockholder knows that a lot of insider trading goes on and that his company's insiders might be engaging in it. Therefore, whether the corporation says anything or not, the shareholder has no good grounds for complaint. He assumed the risk.[2]

The fact that the assumption of risk argument is used in all of these contexts doesn't mean that it persuades. Indeed, in nearly all of these contexts, the argument has a slightly hollow ring to it. But one is hard-put to say why.

III. First Tries

In trying to figure out why the argument sometimes fails, the lawyer's most instinctive inclination is to say: the assumption of risk argument, like all rules or principles, must have some underlying purposes. And like all rules or principles, it probably can be made in many circumstances where those purposes are not really being served. These must be the cases where the argument rings hollow. Therefore, hard cases are best resolved by going back to basics – figuring out whether the purposes of the argument are being served by applying it to such a case. If they are, uphold the argument; if not, reject it.

In fact, the purposes of the assumption of risk argument aren't hard to discern: they are, by and large, the usual reasons for according moral force to someone's consent. First, each person knows what's best for him. Second, as Joseph Raz puts it, "Through consenting a person attempts to fashion the shape of his moral world."[3] The next step is to ask: in which of the many examples mentioned above would acceptance of the assumption of risk argument further those two purposes – getting people what they want and letting them fashion their moral world? But look at any of the examples with which we began, and you will find it no easier to resolve. Figuring out which resolution of a hard case most favors the purposes of the rule usually is no easier than figuring out the applicability of the rule. Telling someone to find an answer to a legal question in this way is often no more helpful than J.P. Morgan's advice on how to make money on the stock market: "Buy cheap, sell dear."

But there have been other, more specific suggestions for why the assumption of risk argument sometimes fails. All of these explanations have some force under the right circumstances. But none accounts for most of the cases with which I began. None cuts to what I think are the central logical and moral difficulties with the argument. Let me briefly review the most promising of those explanations.

[2] See, for instance, Henry G. Manne, *Insider Trading and the Stock Market* (Glencoe: The Free Press, 1966); Dennis Carlton and Daniel Fischel, "The Regulation of Insider Trading," *Stanford Law Review*, vol. 35, p. 857 (1983), and Kenneth E. Scott, "Insider Trading Rule 10b-5, Disclosure and Corporate Privacy," *Journal of Legal Studies*, vol. 9, p. 801 (1980).

[3] Joseph Raz, *The Morality of Freedom* (Oxford: Clarendon Press, 1986), p. 86.

(1) *Paternalism.* You cannot consent to be killed, maimed or tortured. Given that, we may be understandably worried even to let you *risk* having all these things happen to you.

But this argument won't go very far. First, it won't account for cases in which we are reluctant to let you assume a risk to property – as in the case of insider trading, the investment in Novum Organum, or the deposit in a moribund S&L. Second, we fairly often allow someone to risk personal injury, but almost never allow someone to consent to it. So the leap from *consent to injury* to *consent to risk of injury* is probably too quick. The fact that someone is *consenting to injury* may strongly suggest that he is irresponsible and in need of supervision; the fact that someone is *consenting to risk of injury* hardly merits the same inference.

(2) *Duress and lack of choice.* X holds a gun to Y's head, forcing him to sign a contract with Z, assuming an unpleasant risk. The contract isn't voluntarily made, hence it deserves no recognition.

Actually, that's not crystal-clear, given that Z is not in cahoots with X. Why should Z bear the loss flowing from this contract (assuming he didn't know why Y signed)? And perhaps that's why we are at least slightly ambivalent about cases of third-party duress. Still, this one is relatively easy to understand.

Assumption of risk is often said to be vitiated by duress. Sometimes the gunman is the Force of Circumstance rather than some malevolent human being. But none of my examples really involves an undue restriction of someone's available alternatives. So this account won't go very far.

(3) *Uninformed choices.* It is often said that an assumption of risk need not be respected, because the risk-taker wasn't well-informed. This presupposes that there is a difference between well-informed and poorly informed risk-takers. But wherein lies the difference? It would seem as though every poorly informed risk-taker could be recharacterized as a well-informed risk-taker of a slightly larger risk emcompassing the facts the ignorance of which made us call him poorly informed. Conversely, it would seem as though every well-informed risk taker could be recharacterized as a poorly informed risk-taker of a slightly smaller risk. In other words, why not view the purchaser of a stock about which next-to-nothing has been disclosed as the well-informed investor of a very uncertain, open-ended venture? Otherwise, what is to prevent someone from viewing the purchaser of a lottery ticket as an inadequately informed consumer because he doesn't know whether his is the winning ticket?

(4) *Meaninglessness.* Some have suggested the assumption of risk has no moral force because it doesn't mean anything. Anytime anyone complains of some injury, we can plausibly characterize the situation so as to make it look like a thoroughly voluntary assumption of risk; we can equally plausibly characterize it so as to make it look like the opposite. Has the person living next to a nuclear plant voluntarily assumed the risk of radioactive poisoning? He didn't want the plant where it is. That makes the risk seem involuntary. He could have moved away. That makes it seem voluntary. Has a window washer voluntarily assumed the risk that his ropes may break? He has a large family to support and couldn't find an equally well-paying job for a man with his skills. That makes the risk seem involuntary. He could

have taken a lower-paying job all the same. That makes it seem voluntary. If we made a large enough sacrifice, we could avoid the risk of any mishap. That makes it seem voluntary. If it didn't cost us anything, we would not expose ourselves to the risk of any mishap. That makes the risk of any mishap seem involuntary. Whether we call a risk voluntary or involuntary depends mostly, it seems, on whether we like to call the cup half empty or half full. In other words, the assumption of risk argument has no moral force, because it is meaningless.[4]

Is that a good objection? I don't think so. To be sure, the foregoing semantic game can always be played. In purely semantic terms, a risk can always be made to look voluntarily assumed or not, depending on how the fancy strikes us. But the resulting argument will not necessarily persuade. Sometimes it will sound solid, sometimes it will ring hollow. There must be a reason. And why shouldn't it be a morally significant one?

The assumption of risk argument is, of course, just one of many legal concepts that critics have claimed are meaningless. The same claim has been made about nearly every concept of the criminal law's general part: act, omission, causation, intention, knowledge, recklessness, negligence, complicity, attempt, abandonment, impossibility, duress, and necessity. It is alleged that with just a little bit of manipulative effort an act can be turned into an omission, a cause can be turned into an attendant circumstance, an intention can be turned into mere knowledge, an accomplice can be turned into a bystander, and duress can be turned into free choice. In other words, the concepts of the general part are only window-dressing, after-the-fact rationalizations of conclusions reached on other grounds, *political* grounds, dishonest grounds – in any event, hidden grounds.

This argument runs into the problem of infinite regress. It's a bit like the argument that Shakespeare's plays weren't written by the William Shakespeare we all think of, but by someone else entirely, who happened also to be named William Shakespeare, to have been born in Stratford-on-Avon, and to have been in London at around the same time as the other Shakespeare. If judges reach the conclusions they reach on grounds other than their understanding of causation, intention, attempts, and all the other meaningless concepts of the general part, what do they go by? Well, let's assume they go by crass prejudice in favor of some subgroup of the population. They will still have to make decisions as to whether the defendant by his *actions intentionally* or *negligently caused* harm to that group – and, if he didn't, whether he was *attempting* to do so. In short, even to reach prejudiced, dishonest decisions, judges must first figure out the meaning of the allegedly meaningless. If honest decisions are rendered impossible by the meaninglessness of the general part, then so are dishonest decisions: indeed, so is anything which deserves to be called a decision.

(5) *Wrongful threats.* The courts have developed one line of argument that goes quite far in explaining why many applications of the assumption of risk argument fail. Here is a typical example:

[4] For an intriguing presentation of such arguments, see Mark Kelman, "Interpretive Construction in the Substantive Criminal Law," *Stanford Law Review*, vol. 33, p. 591 (1981). I make similarly skeptical arguments about the assumption of risk in *Bad Acts and Guilty Minds* (Chicago: University of Chicago Press, 1987), p. 43.

> A illegally blocks the public sidewalk, so that pedestrians can pass only by walking in the street. In order to pass, B walks in the street, knowing that there is substantial danger of being struck by passing traffic. He is struck and injured by a negligently driven automobile. B is not barred from recovery against A by assumption of risk.[5]

The principle courts invoke is that there is no valid assumption of risk if the defendant's wrongful conduct "has left [the victim] no reasonable alternative course of conduct in order to exercise or protect a right or privilege of which the defendant has no right to deprive him." In the above case, A's blocking of the sidewalk left the victim no reasonable alternative to walking in the street, which is a "right or privilege of which A has no right to deprive the victim."[6]

What is the idea behind this principle? Just this: if someone steals your car and offers to return it to you if you pay him $1000, we wouldn't say that he is (morally or legally) entitled to that money, even though you willingly handed it over to him. That's because he held you to an improper choice: he threatened to do something to you he is prohibited from doing (keeping your car) unless you give him something which you are entitled not to give him (your money). The sidewalk hypothetical is the logical equivalent of this.

If one bears this wrongful threat principle in mind, a lot of problematic cases become easy. Consider this one, invented by Frank Michelman:

> Suppose I buy scenic land along the highway during the height of public discussion about the possibility of forbidding all development of such land, and the market clearly reflects awareness that future restrictions are a significant possibility. If restrictions are ultimately adopted, have I a claim to be compensated in the amount of the difference between the land's value with restrictions and its value without them?[7]

A plausible argument can be made that such a claim doesn't deserve much respect.

> I bought land which I knew might be subjected to restrictions; and the price I paid should have been discounted by the possibility that restrictions would be imposed. Since I got exactly what I meant to buy, it perhaps can be said that society has effected no redistribution so far as I am concerned, any more than it does when it refuses to refund the price of my losing sweepstakes ticket.[8]

Still, one is left uneasy. The wrongful threat principle makes it clear why – because it suggests a different answer. If the state is not entitled to take a certain piece of land without compensation, then it isn't entitled to threaten a would-be purchaser with taking his land away without compensation if he should decide to go through with the purchase – that is, the state is not entitled to put the would-be purchaser to

[5] Restatement of Torts, 2d, Section 496E, Illustration 5.

[6] Restatement of Torts, 2d, Section 496E.

[7] Frank I. Michelman, "Property, Utility, and Fairness: Comments on the Ethical Foundations of 'Just Compensation Law,'" *Harvard Law Review*, vol. 80, pp. 1165, 1238 (1967).

[8] *ibid.*

the choice of not buying that land or buying it subject to the risk of having it taken away from him (which is what a restriction on development amounts to).[9]

The wrongful threat principle explains another tricky case, posed by Jules Coleman.

> Suppose that, having accepted a teaching position at the University of Chicago, you are deciding whether to live in Evanston, where prices are high but where the crime rate is relatively low, or in Hyde Park, where the crime rate is higher but the house prices, though high, are low compared with those in Evanston. Knowing this, suppose you decide to purchase a house in Hyde Park. The difference you pocket between the prices for comparable housing in Evanston and Hyde Park constitutes a kind of *ex ante* compensation. Suppose now that your house is burglarized. Is it at all plausible to say that you had given your consent to the burglary by accepting *ex ante* compensation in the form of a reduced housing price? Could the burglar introduce your consent as a defense in court?[10]

Coleman thinks the answer to this question is obviously no. He doesn't say why, but it seems clear that he is simply applying our principle: the burglar has no right to put the victim to the choice of either not moving into the dangerous neighborhood or of assuming the risk of a burglary – just as the car thief has no right to put the victim to the choice between paying $1000 or losing his car.

The principle also helps to clear up the savings and loan hypothetical posed at the outset.

> You see an advertisement in a newspaper asking you to put your money into an account at your local savings and loan association. It offers you an interest rate far in excess of what you are getting at your local bank. You have a pretty good idea why the S&L is being so generous: rumors abound that it might soon collapse, and that if it collapses the federal government might not make good on its promise to reimburse all depositors. But you take your deposit there anyway. The S&L collapses, and the federal government, as predicted, reneges on its promise.

Here, too, the wrongful threat principle would say that you did not assume the risk of collapse. The government's reneging would be illegal. Hence, putting the depositor to the choice of not investing or not collecting insurance which the bank's contract with the government entitles him to is impermissible as well.

But the argument has its limitations. There are many cases for which it will not account – indeed, just about all of the remaining examples with which I began. Moreover, it may not even work on slight variations of the cases just examined. Consider this variation of Coleman's hypothetical: suppose the burglar is the original owner himself. As to him, the wrongful threat argument is a bit hard to

[9] Richard Epstein makes an equivalent observation in his discussion of Michelman's hypothetical in his book *Takings* (Cambridge: Harvard University Press, 1985), p. 154.

[10] Jules L. Coleman, *Markets, Morals, and the Law* (Cambridge: Cambridge University Press, 1988), p. 357, n. 41.

make. We cannot say that he wrongfully put the purchaser to the choice of either not moving into the dangerous neighborhood or assuming its risks. He put the purchaser to what looks like a much more acceptable choice: that between buying his house and putting up with an occasional burglary from its original owner, or not buying the house.

There is an even deeper problem with the wrongful threat principle. It rests on the idea that when you are confronted with a wrongful choice, something is taken away from you – therefore such choices shouldn't be honored. But on closer inspection, it is by no means clear that something is really taken away from you when you are confronted with a wrongful choice. Return to the case of A's blocking the sidewalk. Suppose A blocked the sidewalk by parking his car on it because he could find no other parking space. We know that if A had done so in order to get his stricken mother to the hospital in time, doing the very same act would not be considered illegal. Indeed, if A had blocked off not just the sidewalk but much of the street, and thus somehow further aggravated the danger to passers-by, this would still be legal if it were done to get some people to the emergency room in time. It is the fact that no such saving purpose motivated A's parking the car on the sidewalk *this* time which renders it illegal. But how does the defendant's doing something illegal *limit* the victim's options when, as we have just seen, it would have been possible for the defendant to act perfectly legally and impose far more unpleasant choices on the victim? It will require some effort to deal with this objection to the wrongful threat principle – but not one which I will here undertake.

So why does the assumption of risk argument sometimes succeed and sometimes fail? In large part, I believe, for the reasons that follow:

(1) *Hidden Symmetries.* In certain (indeed, many) settings, the assumption of risk argument becomes peculiarly indeterminate.

(2) *Collective Consent.* When a group assumes risks, it is often difficult to say which of its members should be deemed to have assumed those risks.

(3) *Victimless Injuries.* Some injuries, though very real, have no discernible victims. Those who at first glance seem to be the victims aren't really – hence, their assumptions of risk shouldn't count for much.

(4) *Ignorance and Incommensurability.* There is a level of ignorance at which it makes sense to say the person who assumed the risk was too ill-informed for his assumption to be binding.

(5) *The Assumption of Risk as a Form of Permission.* Every assumption of risk can be construed as a form of permission. Permissions, however, have some invisible, built-in limitations. This point is remade in a slightly different way in the section that follows: *The Assumption of Risk as a Conditional Promise.*

(6) *Forced Gambles.* Some assumptions of risk involve the acceptance of a small risk in exchange for being relieved of a larger one. Under certain circumstances, we deem these unworthy of being enforced.

(7) *Penal Lotteries.* The use of assumption of risk arguments in the criminal law tends to be misguided for a multiplicity of reasons discussed herein.

IV. Hidden Symmetries

It is worth distinguishing the implicit from the explicit assumption of risk. The implicit assumption of risk occurs where the actor enters a situation fraught with risk and is deemed by virtue of that entrance to have assumed the risk. The explicit assumption of risk occurs where the actor actually declares "I hereby assume such-and-such a risk." (I am not pretending, however, that a gulf separates the two categories – only a gray zone occupied by cases like that of the chemical plant.)

It is the implicit assumption of risk argument that is most commonly invoked and that makes us most uneasy. Oddly enough, what makes us uneasy about implicit assumption of risk arguments will become most apparent if we focus for a moment on corporate law rather than the tort or criminal law — in particular, the law governing corporate acquisitions.

Over the past few years, companies defending against takeovers have devised an astonishing number of clever legal defensive maneuvers. Most of these maneuvers involve inserting a special anti-takeover provision into the corporate charter – that constitution-like document that determines the rights and privileges of the corporation's various investors and managers. These anti-takeover provisions, at bottom, all do the same thing: they impose various burdens on an unwelcome acquirer, so as to render the target indigestible. The simplest and most inoffensive of these is the supermajority provision requiring a would-be acquirer to obtain the consent of 80% of the shares before consummating a merger between the target and the acquiring company. The most ingenious and most obnoxious of these provisions is the "poison pill" requiring the would-be acquirer to pay target shareholders shares in the post-merger company worth three times as much as the shares they gave up.

Many are incredulous when first told about the poison pill. How can this be, they wonder – what permits the target company to simply take assets out of the pocket of the acquiring company and hand them over to its own shareholders? The answer they get usually convinces them: each company is free to promulgate through its charter the rules by which it will be run. The initial rules are promulgated by the founders of the corporation, and subsequent rules are adopted consistent with amendment procedures authorized by the initial rules. It seems only natural that those who decide to purchase the company's stock be subject to these rules – whether they concern the size of the board of directors, the number of authorized classes of stock, or takeover attempts. After all, no one is being forced to make this investment. But this answer isn't as convincing as it sounds.

Acquirers have tried to come up with antidotes to the poison pill. The simplest and most audacious of these would simply be for the acquirer to insert a provision into its own charter, providing essentially that future shareholders who came by their shares as a result of a poison-pill provision would have to give back whatever financial advantage they thus obtained. For instance, the provision might state that any shareholder who has acquired shares in that company at less than market price will receive no distributions of any kind until the amount of distributions withheld equals the difference between the market price of the company's shares and the price at which the shareholder actually bought them.

Consider now a takeover battle that might develop between two such companies. Let us suppose that Company X is on the lookout for a company to acquire. The fact that X is eager to make an acquisition does not mean, of course, that it would itself welcome an acquisition attempt by someone else. On the contrary: eager to forestall just this possibility, X has adopted a poison-pill provision precisely like the aforementioned one. X's management then purchases a small chunk of the would-be target's shares on the open market, and shortly thereafter approaches Y's management to suggest a merger. Y's management says no. Fearful, moreover, that X might try to make a hostile acquisition (by tender offer), they decide on a preemptive strike: they will acquire X before X can acquire them. But they face one critical obstacle: X's poison pill provision. As long as that provision is in place, it is simply too costly to acquire X. A merger with X would mean giving X's shareholders shares in the new company worth three times as much as the shares they are currently holding. That would very nearly bleed Y's shareholders to death. So they adopt the aforementioned antidote provision, forcing X's shareholders to give back whatever amount they manage to extract from Y through their poison-pill provision. The antidote in place, Y begins buying X's shares and to launch a tender offer. It eventually obtains some 30% of X's shares, ousts the incumbent board, takes charge of the company, and proposes a merger. When it does, will its antidote provision enable it to nullify the poison pill?

In effect, what has happened is this: Company X has adopted a provision which says that anyone who interacts with Company X subjects himself to a series of burdensome conditions. Company Y in turn has adopted a mirror image provision which says that anyone who interacts with Company Y subjects himself to a series of burdensome conditions. But the two sets of conditions conflict – one tries to undo the other. Then the two companies interact. Now whose law should govern?

Whatever the answer may be, the assumption of risk approach does not tell us. Or rather, what it tells us is incoherent: it tells us that Y assumed the risk of being subjected to X's poison-pill-infected charter by buying X's shares, and that X assumed the risk of being subjected to Y's antidote-infected charter by buying Y's shares. But both cannot be true at once.

In this particular context, then, the assumption of risk argument makes no sense. But is our difficulty unique to this context, or is it more universal?

Quite universal. Consider one of the puzzling cases with which I began – that of the person entering a bar in which a brawl is in progress. We know that an assumption of risk argument can be made, but we are ambivalent about it. The takeover example suggests why: the argument is indeterminate – rather, it can be invoked symmetrically. While one can argue that you assumed the risk of injury by entering, one can with equal ease argue that the bar owner assumed the risk by letting you in, or that the perpetrator assumed the risk by pursuing his fight without concern for bystanders. Most injuries suffered at sports events are like this. Here, too, one can argue that the spectator assumed the risk of injury by entering, but one can with equal ease argue that is was the event organizer, or perhaps even the players, who assumed the risk of having to compensate spectators by inviting them.

My symmetry argument closely parallels a familiar one from another setting: the argument against the coherence of strict liability rules. An early instance of that argument is found in an invented Greek case, Antiphon's Second Tetralogy: X practices javelin throwing in the gymnasium. Y runs in front of the target just as X is making his throw and is killed. Y's father prosecutes X for accidentally causing his son's death, the governing law being a strict liability murder statute. X's father defends by pointing out that under a strict liability approach, the victim is as much to blame as the javelin-thrower. He also comes close to pointing out under such an approach the number of potential defendants would be absurdly large: it would include the person who enticed the defendant to learn javelin throwing, the other javelin throwers whose actions caused the defendant to throw his javelin no sooner and no later than he did, the people who built the gymnasium . . . and that's just the beginning. Ronald Coase's case of the rancher and the railroad (in his celebrated essay "The Problem of Social Cost") gives us this argument in more modern garb.[11]

Why doesn't this symmetry problem plague and destroy *all* implicit assumption of risk arguments? After all, some applications of the argument do not leave us uneasy, yet it would seem as though the symmetry problem might easily arise there too. We tend to say with some confidence that the person entering a baseball stadium assumes the risk of being hit by a ball, not that the person who invites others into his baseball stadium has assumed the risk that he might be liable for injuries to them. The situation doesn't look indeterminate. How come? There must be some as-yet-unarticulated criterion that allows us to resolve the seeming symmetry. What is it?

It is the act-omission distinction: it was the spectator who entered the stadium – the stadium owner merely *let him enter*. The spectator has committed an act, it seems; the owner merely an omission. The act-omission distinction is often said not to make much sense, to be completely manipulable. Why not say in this case, for instance, that the owner committed the *act* of opening his stadium and inviting spectators in, and that the spectator merely *let the owner's hired performers perform* – in other words, the spectator only omitted. But the act-omission distinction is in fact no less solid than most other concepts of common sense. We have no trouble distinguishing the passer-by who walks past a drowning victim whom he could easily save, silently cheering his enemy's imminent death, and the person who actually holds the victim's head under water. To be sure, both engaged in actions (walking past, holding the head under water) that caused the victim's death, and both desired the victim's death, but there is one crucial difference between them: assume the passer-by didn't exist, and the victim would still have died. Assume the murderer didn't exist, and the victim would not have died. It is this "existence" test which allows us to distinguish act and omission.

The existence test won't always be easy to apply – it usually fails us in precisely those cases where our intuition has the hardest time classifying something as an act or an omission. One such category of case is exemplified by *R. v. Speck*: a young girl

[11] Ronald H. Coase, "The Problem of Social Cost," *Journal of Law and Economics*, vol. 3, p. 1 (1960).

fondles the defendant who endures what she does with great pleasure while utterly immobile.[12] He is charged with the act of gross indecency with a child; he defends on the ground that his was merely an omission. Under the existence test, this would clearly seem to be an act. If the defendant didn't exist, this event would not have occurred. If we are nonetheless tempted to call what he did an omission rather than an act, it is because we are willing to extend the act-omission distinction metaphorically. In a certain metaphorical sense, the defendant's presence in this case was superfluous to what happened; all that was required was the presence of his body. Had he had a fatal heart attack seconds before the girl approached him, things would have gone exactly the same. In other words, we are willing to speak of an omission not merely where things would have gone the same if the defendant hadn't been there *at all*, but also where things would have gone the same if the defendant hadn't been "*all there*". It is the metaphorical extension of the act-omission distinction that leads us to classify the spectator's entrance as an act, and the stadium owner's invitation as an omission.

We can now see incidentally why *explicit* assumption of risk cases are usually easier to decide: where the bearer of a risk signs a contract, he has clearly *acted* to assume the risk; the non-bearer has *omitted* to assume it.

V. Collective Consent

Let's return to another one of my opening examples:

> The mayor of a small town wants to persuade a chemical plant to locate in his town. You and nearly all of the citizenry support him, although you know that there is the distinct risk of a dangerous chemical accident. The mayor campaigns on this very platform and is elected by an overwhelming majority.
>
> An accident occurs. Given your support for the mayor's platform, should you be able to complain?

There are a number of reasons why one might object to a finding of assumption of risk, most notably because of the symmetry problem. But I want to pursue a different objection here, one which lies behind much of our discomfort with finding an assumption of risk in cases like the above: how can we say that the citizens of that small town assumed the risk of a chemical accident when their actions made absolutely no difference to the outcome? That is, the risk was going to be imposed on them whether they welcomed it or not. Can we really say that you assumed a risk when you did not in fact cause it to be imposed on you?

I think we can. We are here encountering a familiar problem in a slightly unfamiliar setting. The familiar problem is what to do when a group brings about a forbidden result but every one of its members is perfectly superfluous to the outcome. Overdetermination is the hallmark of group activity, and the law of complicity recognizes this by imposing liability on all members of the group regardless of their causal relationship to the outcome. Without it, a lot of patently immoral conduct would go unpunished.[13]

[12] R. v. Speck, 2 All ER 859 (Court of Appeal, 1977).

[13] See also *Bad Acts and Guilty Minds*, ch. 5.

The law of complicity, however, harbors one serious puzzle: if we are not allowed to use causal criteria for assessing responsibility, what criteria should we use? How exactly are we to decide who is a member of the criminal group and who isn't? Surely not just anyone who hoped for and applauded the outcome qualifies, but who does? It helps to think of a specific example: consider several assassins simultaneously (and jointly) firing away at their victim. We know that all of them should be held liable, even though the efforts of any one of them are redundant. But how is each assassin different from the person who looked out her window and inwardly rejoiced while the assassination happened? One difference immediately suggests itself. We can say one thing about each assassin that we cannot say about the pleased spectator: if we subtracted every other assassin from the scene, the defendant-killer's contribution would then become indispensable. We cannot say the same thing about the rubberneck. Or can we? Certainly, if we are willing to make the process of subtraction sufficiently outlandish, we might arrive at a situation where the mere fact that someone was watching was enough to induce an assassin, who otherwise wouldn't have, to carry out his mission. So for this test of group membership to work, we will simply have to insist that the subtraction process be carried out in a non-outlandish way.

It will now become apparent what is right and what is wrong with the causal objection to finding assumptions of risk in the case of the chemical plant. It is wrong to insist that one cannot assume a risk if one did not cause it to be imposed, just as it would be wrong to insist that no member of a team of assassins is guilty if they fired simultaneously. It is right to worry about group membership. Wouldn't we have to imagine a pretty outlandish set of events for the enthusiastic support of any one citizen to make a difference to the election and the actions of the mayor? That *should* make us hesitate to find an assumption of risk.

So much for the implicit assumption of risk. I turn next to problems that plague both its explicit and its implicit versions.

VI. Victimless Injuries

Let's return to the question of whether insider trading is immoral. For the assumption of risk argument to justify insider trading, the victim of insider trading must have some interaction with the perpetrator that can be read to constitute an assumption of risk. Unfortunately, no such interaction is to be found.

How can that be? It would seem that the victim of insider trading is the person who sells his stock to the insider – it most certainly looks as though he is interacting with the insider. But is he the real victim of insider trading? The real victim of insider trading is presumably someone who would be better off if the insider didn't violate the insider trading laws. Is the person who sells his shares at the time that the insider is buying someone who would be better off if the insider didn't violate the laws? The problem that appears most immediately is that there are two alternative ways of complying with the insider trading laws: making a clean breast of what one knows *or* abstaining from trading. It is certainly true that if the insider had decided to make a clean breast of things, the sellers of the stock would have been much better off – they would have been able to sell their stock for a much higher price than they did. But if the insider had complied with the law, he presumably would not have done so by disclosing what he knew. Rather, he would have abstained from trading, in which case the sellers of the stock would still have been selling at the price at which they actually sold it, and would have been no better off.

If the sellers of the stock aren't the victims of insider trading, who is? Could it be that no one is? Not likely. After all, the insider did get richer. That money must have come out of somebody's pocket – his victim's. But whose pocket? Which victim? Well, if not the person who sold the stock, then the person who would have bought the stock if the insider had not bought it. Who would have bought it? No one knows. No one will ever know. Not even the people who would have bought it! Thus the real victims of the insider's misconduct never have had any dealings with him, and presumably never had any occasion to assume the risk of what he did to them. (Ironically, the Supreme Court has limited standing in insider trading lawsuits to purchasers and sellers of the stock.)

The problem of the elusive victim is a more general one. Often the victim isn't just inaccessible, but nonexistent – even though, quite clearly, an injury has been inflicted. How can that be? After all, if there has been an injury, then there is someone who was injured. And if someone was injured, then presumably he is the victim. Well, not quite. Clearly, not just anyone who would not have suffered an injury but for the defendant's conduct qualifies as a victim – remote victims don't count, only proximate ones do. But why is that? Why don't remote victims count? The answer to that question will make it clear how there can be injuries, but no victims.

To repeat: why do we distinguish between remote and proximate consequences – remote and proximate victims? Why doesn't every "but for" victim qualify as a plaintiff?

Imagine a town full of negligent drivers. Suppose that, in that town, 90 traffic fatalities occur each year. Suppose also that based on statistics in comparable towns with few negligent drivers, we know that without negligence the number of fatalities would only have been 70. Why would there be any fatalities at all in a town of careful drivers? Because accidents are a fact of life. Even a careful driver might suffer a sudden heart attack and kill a pedestrian. Our aim then is to hold the negligent drivers liable for the accidents which they added to the accident toll. But won't the but-for test accomplish that already? No, it won't. Almost none of the accidents would have happened if the driver had not occupied the precise spot he occupied at the precise moment that he did. And in almost none of the accidents would the driver have occupied the precise spot he occupied at the precise moment he did if he had not been negligent. The but-for test would therefore have us hold nearly all 90 drivers liable, rather than just the 20 who increased the accident toll beyond its base rate. So "but for" won't do. The proximate causation limitation is required to isolate the 20 from the 70.

The various tests we have for ferreting out proximate victims are clearly designed with this objective in mind – the objective of curing the shortcomings of the but-for test. This is most obvious in the *Palsgraf* test, which asks whether a given accident is the sort we usually associate with negligent driving; it's only slightly less obvious in the probability test (long a part of civil law and recently embraced by American legal economists), which asks whether the accident is the kind whose probability was increased by the defendant's conduct. With a little effort one can see it in the Model Penal Code's test, which asks whether the accident "is too remote and accidental to have just bearing on the defendant's responsibility" or Hart and Honoré's test, which asks whether the chain of causation included a very abnormal event: "Remote and accidental consequences," following a chain of events that includes a very "abnormal event," presumably are equally common in towns with and without negligent drivers. The accidents that remain must therefore be the accidents negligence adds to the total.[14]

Unfortunately, what these tests are designed to accomplish is often an impossible goal. They are meant to ferret out the "extra" victims added to the previous accident toll by the defendant's conduct. But those extra victims may be beyond detection. Consider the following: a corporation is looking for a site on which to build a nuclear power plant. The corporation is closely considering two sites: one is near town A, with a population of 10,000, and another is near town B, with a population of 50,000. Inevitably, the radioactive pollution near such a plant results in a .001 cancer rate of nearby populations in a twenty-year period. Let us also assume that there is no other source of cancer than radioactive fallout. Building such a plant near town A would produce 10 cases of cancer. Considering the benefits that the plant will confer on the region as a whole, let us consider that as non-negligent. Building such a plant near town B would produce 50 cancer cases. Considering that nearly the same benefit would have been achieved by building near town A and considering that now 50 people will die, let us suppose building the power plant near town B is negligent. Nevertheless, the corporation builds near town B. Who are the victims of the company's negligence? It makes no sense to ask! We know that the company's negligence increased the victim total from 10 to 50, but there is no point in looking for the "extra 40" added to that victim total by the corporation's activities. There ain't none.[15]

The nuclear plant example is one illustration of a victimless injury. Let me add another – the phenomenon of "wrongful births." Imagine an AIDS-infected man who deliberately has intercourse with a woman and fathers a child. The woman, let us assume, never actually contracts the disease, but only the infection; she lives out her entire life unperturbed. The child, however, develops the full-fledged disease. Has there been an injury? If one asks whether there has been a victim, that is, whether there is someone who would be better off had the man not acted as he did, the answer is no. The child certainly isn't a victim in that sense – but for the man's actions the child wouldn't be around at all, that is, he would not be better off (unless one views being born an AIDS victim as worse than not being born at all). Judges have dismissed wrongful birth suits on just this ground.

But does the absence of a victim mean that there really hasn't been an injury? If we say that, we would also have to say that future generations can never be injured

[14] Model Penal Code, section 2.03. H.L.A. Hart and A.M. Honoré, *Causation in the Law* (2nd ed. 1985).
[15] *Bad Acts and Guilty Minds*, ch. 4.

by past generations. If the past generation had done something very different from what it did, chances are that a very different set of couplings, a very different set of conceptions, and a very different set of births would have resulted. Thus the complainants cannot complain that *they* would be better off if the past generation had behaved differently.[16]

Even after the foregoing examples, the notion of a victimless injury may seem quite paradoxical and counterintuitive, if not downright muddle-headed. It is hard to give up the intuitive belief that where there is an injury there must be a victim, someone who can say that, but for the perpetrator's injurious conduct, he would be better off. Derek Parfit has invented a splendid example to show how this intuitive belief can have some very counterintuitive consequences.

> There are two rare conditions, J and K, which cannot be detected without special tests. If a pregnant woman has Condition J, this will cause the child she is carrying to have a certain handicap. A simple treatment would prevent this effect. If a woman has condition K when she conceives a child, this will cause this child to have the same particular handicap. Condition K cannot be treated, but always disappears within two months. Suppose next that we have planned two medical programmes, but there are funds for only one; so one must be cancelled. In the first program, millions of women would be tested during pregnancy. Those found to have Condition J would be treated. In the second programme, millions of women would be tested when they intend to try to become pregnant. Those found to have Condition K would be warned to postpone conception for at least two months, after which this incurable condition will have disappeared.[17]

Suppose further that the first program prevents 1000 handicapped children per year from being born, whereas the second prevents 2000 handicapped children from being born. Suppose also that financial constraints force us to eliminate exactly one of the two programs, and that they cost the same to maintain. Which program should be cut? If we really believed that there can be no injury unless there is a victim who can say that he would have been better off if the defendant had behaved differently, the second rather than the first program should be cut – *even though* the second program would prevent twice as many handicapped births as the first.

The point of these examples is more general. Even in contexts where we don't seem to be dealing with victimless injuries, where it seems possible to pinpoint the "extra" injury and to identify the "but for" victim, there is a deeper sense in which the actual victim is just as inaccessible and the putative victim quite undeserving of being called that. Consider this case: a company is thinking about where to build a chemical plant. There are only two practicable sites: village A and its neighbor, village B. The company chooses village A. Through no one's negligence, through sheer bad luck, an accident occurs. The company, however, has not put enough safety mechanisms in place so as to confine the factory's fumes to the immediate

[16] Derek Parfit, *Reasons and Persons* (Oxford: Oxford University Press, 1985), pt. IV.

[17] *Reasons and Persons*, p. 367.

vicinity. Had it done so, only the residents of village A would have suffered harm. As it is, the fumes spread to village B and harm its inhabitants as well. Are those who live in village B victims of the company's negligence? The company denies that they are by arguing: we would have been entitled to build our plant in village B. If we had done so, then even if we had not been negligent in the installation of safety precautions to confine the fumes, those who live in village B would have suffered more harm than they presently did. They therefore have nothing to complain about.

In other words, the defendant is arguing that inasmuch as he chose a course of action that did less harm to the residents of village B than he could *legally* have chosen, the villagers have nothing to complain about. The answer to this argument is that the defendants' negligence harmed extra people. We may not be able to say *which extra* people, but that shouldn't matter. What this illustrates is that in an important sense many, if not most, complaints are derivative – they are justified not because the plaintiff was injured, but because society was injured and the plaintiff was a convenient party to bring suit.

Although the company's argument in my hypothetical case may seem preposterous and my reply superfluous, the argument is in fact made all the time, frequently taken very seriously, and rarely rebutted. Here is just one fairly commonplace instance:

Company X is trying to acquire company Y. This would greatly concentrate the industry to which X and Y belong. Some fledgling competitors of X and Y complain, fearing they will have an even harder time competing with the newly formed giant of X&Y. Y's managers also complain, fearing for their jobs. Both groups are going to meet with the same objection: yours is not an antitrust injury. The antitrust laws are meant to reduce inefficiency – as manifested by higher consumer prices and the like – and not to save small competitors or managerial jobs.

To say this is to make the argument that, above, we found unacceptable. It amounts to saying: "It would have been all right for Y to wipe out the competition by other means: it would also have been all right for them to oust the managers from their positions by other means. So neither group is entitled to complain having done to it by these means what Y is already entitled to do by other means."

The notion of a victimless injury wreaks havoc with all sorts of doctrines that depend on the impossibility of such a thing, most notably the various doctrines of standing (e.g., mootness, ripeness, the "cases and controversies" requirement, etc.). For our purposes, what matters is what this notion does to the assumption of risk. If it is possible for injurious conduct to occur without victims, then of course there is no one whose consent would absolve the perpetrators of such conduct. Even where those who have given their consent appear to be victims, they may in reality be little more than private attorney-generals to whom we have seen fit to delegate the task of complaining. Everybody realizes that those bringing class actions function in this way and shouldn't be permitted to give away the store too easily. My aim has been to show that many others who seem to be representing only themselves in fact represent many more.

VII. Ignorance and Incommensurability

I dismissed at the outset a common objection to certain assumptions of risk: that they don't count for anything because they are uninformed. I said the notion of an uninformed assumption of risk makes no sense. The uninformed assumption of a small risk is equivalent to the well-informed assumption of a big risk – a risk which includes uncertainty about the facts about which the decision-maker was uninformed. But there lurks behind this objection a valid intuition that somehow the uninformed decision-maker's choices don't merely become riskier, but also less rational. I will try to refine that intuition into a coherent claim. Psychologists have, of course, compiled an amusingly long list of the cognitive foibles that decision-makers under risk are subject to, and I have no wish to recapitulate these. I believe that the lack of information causes irrationality in a much more fundamental way than is suggested by these experiments, and that even those who are relatively immune to the psychologists' pet howlers cannot escape this kind of irrationality. My point is best made through a seeming digression on the nature of slippery-slope arguments.

What makes us so vulnerable to slippery-slope arguments? Consider a typical instance of an argument of this type in the criminal law: someone wants to argue that what the defendant has done has not yet reached the level of a criminal attempt: it amounts to no more than preparation. His basic argumentative strategy will be simple. He will divide what the defendant has done into a million little steps. The first few steps will clearly not amount to an attempt, and every additional step will be so small that we will find it impossible to say that *that* step should make the difference between guilt and innocence. Why will we find it difficult? Because when we compare our moral aversion toward the person who has actually bought his gun to our aversion toward the person who has also bought the binoculars he will use on this venture, the two seem indistinguishable in intensity. It would therefore seem that *moral* sentiment does not furnish us with a reason for treating the two cases differently. But since the route between merely thinking about murder and actually firing one's gun can be crossed by taking a large enough number of such steps, it is easy to maneuver us into concluding that there is no moral difference between the person who has merely thought about murder and the person who fired the gun. But where did we go wrong? Which of those steps were we not entitled to take?

I claim that we made a mistake each step of the way. The mistake was in thinking that sufficiently small differences are imperceptible and therefore irrelevant. In fact, many cases deemed indistinguishable – be it along moral or any other grounds – are quite distinguishable if only one looks at them in the right way. What I have in mind is this: imagine that we had to rank by length ten thousand sticks which vary in length between one meter and two meters. The smallest of these is one meter long, the longest two meters, others evenly distributed between them. In other words, each stick differs from its neighbor by about a tenth of a millimeter. Suppose further that a tenth of a millimeter is an imperceptibly small distance – so small that when two sticks differing by that much are placed side-by-side, the human eye is incapable of determining which is longer. Suppose further that a millimeter is the smallest perceptible length-difference. Given that the differences between each stick and eighteen of its neighbors (nine on either side) will generally be imperceptible, it would seem impossible to rank these sticks by length. In fact, however, it can be done.

One simple method would work like this: take two sticks that seem indistinguishable, and see if there is a stick that is distinguishable from the one, but not the other. There will be at least one such stick – a stick that is one millimeter longer than the shorter of the two sticks will be indistinguishable from the longer and easily distinguishable from the shorter of the two. Use this trick often enough, and you will achieve a perfect ranking of all sticks.

The lesson I hope to draw from this example is merely that what is indistinguishable on direct inspection may be quite distinguishable indirectly. Thus, our moral aversion to the would-be murderer who has bought the gun and to the would-be murderer who has bought gun *and* binoculars may be indistinguishable on direct inspection, but suppose we attempt a three-way comparison. Suppose we compare (1) the gun-purchaser, (2) the gun-and-binocular purchaser, and (3) the gun-and-binocular-purchaser-who-has-also-rented-a-car-in-which-to-carry-out-his-plan. (1) and (2) seem indistinguishable, (2) and (3) seem indistinguishable. But (1) and (3), on the other hand, seem distinguishable. One could therefore conclude that there is an important perceptible difference between (1) and (2), albeit one that is only indirectly perceptible: they differ in their degree of similarity to a third case. If (1) and (2) were genuine equals on the scale of moral aversion, this could not happen. (If this particular example doesn't work for you, you should have no difficulty constructing one of your own that does work.)

Could we always use this trick when two alternatives we are considering seem too close to directly distinguish – that is, find a third alternative which is distinguishable from the one but not the other? Unfortunately, the trick won't always work. It will often lead to inconsistency. The reason is instructive, and it takes us back to the problem with which we began: the inherent irrationality of uninformed risk assumption.

Suppose someone were asked to say which of the following two bets he preferred: a 55 percent chance of winning \$1 or 50¢ straight out? He might find it hard to decide. But he would not be sure that that is because he is genuinely indifferent, or because he simply cannot distinguish his own preferences as to items that are very close together on the preference scale. He decides to use the above method. He notices that he would prefer a 60 percent chance of winning \$1 to a 55 percent chance of winning \$1, but that as between a 60 percent chance of winning \$1 and a sure 50¢ he would still be unsure. He concludes that the sure 50¢ alternative must be slightly higher on the preference scale than the 55 percent-\$1 combination (since 55 percent-\$1 is clearly inferior to 60 percent-\$1 and 50¢ is not).

But if he so concludes, he would almost certainly be wrong. For if he had paid attention, he would also have noticed that he liked a sure 58¢ better than a sure 50¢, and that he was also indifferent between a 55 percent chance of winning \$1 and a sure 58¢, which would, by his method, force him to conclude that he likes a 55 percent chance of winning \$1 better than a sure 50¢.

Why does the method that worked so well for sticks fail us for bets? The reason will become obvious if we imagine that some of those sticks had their sizes written on them, and that in discriminating between sticks we failed to pay attention whether we were doing it on the basis of coded sizes or on the basis of our perceptions. We might then conclude that a stick marked 1.0005 m was longer than an unmarked stick of length 1.0007 m because only the 1.0005 m stick is easily distinguishable from the (marked) 1.0000 m stick. That is, our method fails to work, when some sticks are more easily comparable – or, in the language of ethics, more *commensurable* – than others. It will then lead us to confuse small but clear differences with large but less clear differences. Something like this probably explains the sense behind the proverb that a little knowledge is a dangerous thing. More importantly, however, it explains our inconsistent ranking of risks. Our ability to distinguish 60 percent-$1 from 55 percent-$1 and our inability to distinguish either from 50¢ does not mean that 50¢ is closer to 60 percent-$1 than is 55 percent-$1, but only that 60 percent-$1 and 55 percent-$1 are more commensurable.[18]

What has all this to do with the assumption of risk? Suppose someone is asked to choose between two alternatives, A and B. Suppose he is indifferent between them. Suppose he is also indifferent between A + C and B, even though he clearly prefers A + C to A. Then we are dealing with an indifference by reason of incommensurability. We might then well observe someone choosing A over B, A + C over A, and B over A + C. The choice would not be a very meaningful one, not one worth a lot of respect. This happens pretty often: People may find it difficult to distinguish between a Chevrolet and an Oldsmobile, and feel equally indifferent between an Oldsmobile plus some option and a Chevrolet. The indifference is thus due to incommensurability, and the choice between them is a little suspect. But it would be a lot more suspect if this happened not just with the addition of a small option to the Chevrolet, but even after the addition of many other things.

But this is precisely what happens when people are asked to choose between very uncertain prospects – say, what's behind curtain A and what's behind curtain B – without having been told anything about what might be behind those curtains. It will then be true – and more true the more uncertain they are about what's behind each curtain – that even adding a substantial number of benefits to whatever will turn out to be behind curtain A will not make the chooser prefer A over B. With so little known about A and B the two are just too incommensurable. It is thus quite possible for someone to choose A over B, A plus those other items over A, and B over that whole package. Such a choice would not be very meaningful and not worthy of a lot of respect. We need not feel many qualms about undoing it.

[18] Although I first came by the idea of incommensurability by following up on some ideas of Nelson Goodman, *The Structure of Appearance* (Dordrecht: D. Reidel Publishing Company, 3rd ed. 1977), chapters IX and X, in fact incommensurability receives a very explicit and deep discussion in Raz, *The Morality of Freedom*, ch. 13, and James Griffin, *Well-Being: Its Meaning, Measurement, and Moral Importance* (Oxford: Clarendon Press, 1988), ch. V, albeit along somewhat different lines than I give it here.

VIII. The Assumption of Risk as a Form of Permission

What follows will explain, I think, another of the problem cases with which we began – a case in which the assumption of risk argument fails, but not for any obviously discernible reason:

> You are a retired army general. The government is about to adopt some controversial policies. To forestall criticism from certain quarters, it offers all retired officers an increase in their pension if they promise not to criticize the government in public, come what may. You accept the pension increase. When the policies are finally adopted, you are shocked. You write a book vehemently attacking them. The government threatens to sue you for going back on your promise. If they do, do you have anything to complain about?

This case epitomizes a well-known problem of constitutional law: the problem of unconstitutional conditions. The government commonly imposes special burdens, restrictions, and risks on those who receive some governmental benefit – a subsidy, a job – which the constitution would bar it from imposing on just anyone. When individuals object, they meet with the assumption of risk argument, or a variation thereof. Sometimes their objections carry the day, and the government's requirements are declared unconstitutional conditions; sometimes the assumption of risk wins out. But nobody is quite sure how or why.[19]

Let us approach this problem indirectly by examining another, seemingly unrelated, hypothetical: you drive into a garage. Before parking your car for you, the garage owner hands you a contract that conspicuously states, somewhere near the top: "CUSTOMER ASSUMES ALL RISK OF DAMAGE TO HIS CAR." The garage owner repeatedly points to that phrase, asks if you have read it, and inquires whether you understand what it means. Then, just to make sure you really understand the full scope of what you are signing, he adds that he has a lot of ex-convicts working for him, that in the past at least a few cars (but not many) have been seriously damaged while on his lot, and that he really will not be liable if any such damage should befall your car. This is a dangerous neighborhood, he says, and it's probably not a good idea to park here in the first place, but if you insist he will be glad to have your car parked in his lot. And so you leave your car with him.

"I assume all risk of damage to my car" seems to me to mean "I permit any and all damage to my car." At least it means nothing *more* generous than that; perhaps it means something *less* generous. What I aim to show is that even under this very generous interpretation of risk assumption, the customer has assumed less risk than he appears to have assumed at first glance.

Suppose any of the following were to happen:

(1) Thugs enter the garage, steal everything valuable they can find inside your car, and vandalize it in the process.

[19] The problem of unconstitutional conditions gets a detailed discussion (from a different point of view, one not incompatible with the more general points made here) in Richard A. Epstein, "Unconstitutional Conditions," *Harvard Law Review*, vol. 102, p. 5 (1989), and Kathleen Sullivan, "Unconstitutional Conditions," *Harvard Law Review*, vol. 102, p. 1415 (1989).

(2) The garage owner's own employees steal everything valuable they can find inside your car, and vandalize it in the process.

(3) The garage owner himself steals everything valuable he can find inside your car, and vandalizes it in the process.

(4) The garage owner knows that you have some valuable Persian rugs inside your tightly locked trunk. Since he is unable to open it himself, he forces you to open the trunk at gunpoint and to hand over the rugs.

Have you assumed the risk of (1) to (4)? It would seem you did. After all, you did say you would permit any and all damage to your car. But you might try to raise a variety of objections. Let's examine them one-by-one:

Objection 1: "I didn't permit any deliberate misconduct." Rejoinder: But didn't you? Not only did you fail to make an explicit exception for intentional misconduct, what's more important is that I can think of a lot of intentional misconduct that you could not possibly contend is not covered. Suppose the garage owner has parked too many cars. Someone wants his car very quickly. The owner knows that if he tries to get that person's car out quickly, he is going to end up making quite a few dents in your car, which is parked nearby. Fearing the wrath of his impatient customer, he moves that customer's car and in the process dents yours. Your permission would very much seem to cover that.

Objection 2: "I permitted damage to my car, but not theft or personal assault." Rejoinder: But is that right? There are many ways of achieving the permissible goal of vandalization. Different ways of carrying out the vandalization will entail different sets of crimes. You have permitted at least some of those crimes by permitting vandalization. Why doesn't that list include theft and assault?

Objection 3: "To permit something is not to permit any means whatsoever of bringing it about. To permit something is to allow it to be brought about by those means which entail a minimum amount of deviation from the path of lawful conduct." Rejoinder: The only way to achieve vandalization while only deviating to the minimum extent possible from lawful conduct would be to, say, scratch the windshield. But surely something more than the scratching of the windshield has been permitted?

Objection 4: "To figure out what was meant by this permission, one has to ask what the parties would have agreed to had they thought about these specific contingencies. Surely all of the above contingencies, had they been mentioned at the outset, would have been excluded from the scope of the permission." Rejoinder: Unfortunately, in most cases there exist innumerable arrangements that parties might have been arrived at. Indeed, if it were possible to figure out what a contract says without actually having the parties negotiate and write it out, what's the point of having them do so? Aside from that, the best way of figuring out what someone means when he grants a permission is not likely to be to figure out what he thought he meant when he granted the permission. To lean on an example from Michael Moore: it would hardly be proper to interpret a life insurance contract drafted fifty years ago according to the definition of death then current and therefore on the drafter's mind. By that definition, someone who is comatose but fully revivable might qualify as dead.[20]

[20] Michael Moore, "A Natural Law Theory of Interpretation," *University of Southern California Law Review*, vol. 58, pp. 279, 297 (1985).

Does it follow that you were in fact foolish, that you really did consent to everything that happened to you? I don't think so. Imagine that thugs outside the garage kidnap you and demand that you turn over papers for the car, along with papers for a few other cars you own. Surely then one couldn't say: this is just another way of bringing about damage to your car, which is what you have permitted.

The conceptual problem we face has to do with an important difference in the logic of prohibitions and commands on the one hand, and the logic of permissions on the other. It will help to put the matter somewhat formally. Before a master issues his commands and prohibitions or grants his permissions, his servant has a large number of options – sets of activities – available to him. When a command or a prohibition is issued, some of those options are foreclosed: namely, those options (that is, sets of activities) which do not include the commanded activity or those which include the prohibited activity. When a permission is granted, some of the foreclosed options are restored – namely a variety of options that include a previously prohibited and now permitted activity. But not all such options are restored. Suppose the master has previously commanded his servant to work seven days a week and prohibited him from guzzling the master's wine. He then permits the servant to take Sunday off. He has not thereby restored to him all previously foreclosed options that include the activity of being idle on Sunday. He has not restored to him the option that includes idling away Sunday by guzzling the master's wine. The puzzle is to figure out which options the permission restores and which it doesn't. I have no answer. What I say is merely meant to prove that our instinctive feeling about the wrongness of a "literal" interpretation of the assumption of risk is right. But I am fairly confident that whatever the true, non-literal interpretation of permissions turns out to be, it will not mean that you have permitted every one of the four incidents discussed above to occur.[21]

What light does all of this shed on the hypothetical case set forth at the outset of this section and the problem of unconstitutional conditions? It makes it clearer why we run into the problem of unconstitutional conditions. More concretely, it makes it clearer why the retired general does indeed have a good case against the government. The constitution *prohibits* the government from abridging anyone's freedom of speech. On the other hand, the constitution *permits* the government to hire or not hire employees, to pay them or not pay them pensions, to raise or not raise those pensions over time. The problem with this permission, as with any permission, is that while it confers upon the government options it did not previously have, such permission does not confer upon it all previously foreclosed options that happen to include the hiring and firing of employees, the paying or not paying of pensions, and the raising or not raising of those pensions. It obviously does not confer on the government the option of firing an employee by first killing

[21] My discussion here closely parallels and greatly draws on David K. Lewis, "A Problem about Permission," in *Essays in Honor of Jaakko Hintikka*, E. Saarinen, R. Hilpinen, I. Niiniluoto, and M. Provence-Hintikka, eds. (Dordrecht: Reidel, 1979), pp. 163–79. For a discussion of other, closely related problems, see also Peter Gardenfors, *Knowledge in Flux: Modeling the Dynamics of Epistemic States* (Cambridge: MIT Press, 1988), pp. 99–103.

him. Does it include the option of raising his pension by offering him a contract that abridges his freedom of speech? I don't know. All I mean to show is what there is about the logic of permissions that makes this question a hard issue.

There is another way of making this same point, and it may prove illuminating to make it in that other way. That's what the next section tries to do.

IX. The Assumption of Risk as a Conditional Promise

Every assumption of risk can be construed as a conditional promise. "I assume the risk that my open heart surgery may go awry" can be translated into "If my open heart surgery goes awry, I won't complain." (Or, more precisely, "I will be sorry, but I won't sue.") Many conditional statements – statements of the type "If A, then B" – have an odd property: they do not mean what they seem to mean. To understand them literally is to misunderstand them. What "If A, then B" seems to mean – what is means to someone who reads it literally – is: "If A happens, then, whatever else may be the case, B will happen." Therefore, when a literalist finds that A has happened, but B has not, he has to conclude that the statement is wrong. And yet that's not how things are.[22]

Consider thet statement "If George Bush had not won the election, Michael Dukakis would be President." Compare it with the statement "If George Bush had not won the election and Michael Dukakis had had a heart attack on Inauguration Day, Michael Dukakis would *not* be President – Lloyd Bentsen would." A literalist would have to say the two statements are inconsistent: the first says that if George Bush had not won the election, then, whatever else may be the case, Michael Dukakis would be President. The second says that if George Bush had not won the election, and something else were the case as well, then Michael Dukakis would *not* be President. The literalist would clearly be wrong.

The opening passage of a book of psychology aptly titled *ReFraming* neatly and revealingly exploits this feature of conditional statements:

> A very old Chinese Taoist story describes a farmer in a poor country village. He was considered very well-to-do, because he owned a horse which he used for plowing and for transportation. One day his horse ran away. All his neighbors exclaimed how terrible this was, but the farmer simply said "Maybe."
>
> A few days later the horse returned and brought two wild horses with it. The neighbors all rejoiced at his good fortune, but the farmer just said "Maybe."
>
> The next day the farmer's son tried to ride one of the wild horses; the horse threw him and broke his leg. The neighbors all offered their sympathy for his misfortune, but the farmer again said "Maybe."
>
> The next week conscription officers came to the village to take young men for the army. They rejected the farmer's son because of his broken leg. When the neighbors told him how lucky he was, the farmer replied "Maybe" . . .[23]

[22] David K. Lewis, *Counterfactuals* (Cambridge: Harvard University Press, 1973), p. 10.

[23] Richard Bandler and John Grinder, *ReFraming: Neuro-Linguistic Programming and the Transformation of Meaning* (Moab: Real People Press, 1982), p. 1.

Conditional promises are like other conditional statements. "I will do B, if A occurs" (where B might mean not complaining and A might mean the surgery going awry) is not inconsistent with every statement of the form "I will *not* do B, if A and C occur." "If you rent me this room for the king's coronation, I will pay you a thousand pounds" is not necessarily inconsistent with "If you rent me this room for the king's coronation but there is no coronation, I will *not* pay you a thousand pounds." "If you are willing to sing in my opera house next season, I will pay you a thousand pounds" is not necessarily inconsistent with "If you are willing to sing in my opera house next season, but my opera house has burned down, I will *not* pay you a thousand pounds." In other words, doctrines of impossibility or of frustration of purpose are simply rules of construction that make explicit what we implicitly understand to be the case when we interpret ordinary conditional statements. It is worth noting, moreover, that these rules of construction result in a very different interpretation of contracts than asking the ever-popular question: what would the parties have contracted to do if they had thought about this contingency – the cancellation of the coronation, the incineration of the opera house. Had they thought about it, the parties would probably have decided to split the risk rather than allocate it wholly to one side.[24]

It's worth noting, in passing, that the logic of conditional statements serves to explain a good deal of what looks like freewheeling statutory interpretation – and reveals it to be far more disciplined than first appears. Take a statute like section 16(b) of the 1934 Securities Act, which provides that directors and officers of corporations must give up all short-swing profits garnered by buying and selling their company's shares within a six-month period. Courts have held that someone whose shares are exchanged in a subsequent merger or disposed of in some other "extraordinary" transaction is not "selling" his shares for purposes of the statute. Is that inconsistent with the strict wording of the statute? Let us assume the statute reads: "If a director or officer buys and sells his company's shares within a six-month period, he must give up all his profits." The court's decision basically reads: "If a director or officer buys and sells his company's shares within a six-month period, *but the sale results from an involuntary merger*, he need not give up all his profits." These two statements – statute and court decision – are no more inconsistent with each other than the two statements about George Bush.

So far I have left a critical question untouched: some conditional statements are inconsistent with each other. We know that sometimes "If A, then B" is indeed inconsistent with "If A and C, then *not* B." But exactly what determines that? The answer is not so clear – though our judgment in many specific cases is quite clear. It depends somewhat on the kind of conditional statement involved. The rule for one species of conditional, the counterfactual, is nicely summed up in the opening statement of David Lewis's book *Counterfactuals*: "*If kangaroos had no tails they would topple over* seems to me to mean something like this: in any possible state of affairs in which kangaroos have no tails and which resembles our actual state of affairs as

[24] Michelle White, "Contract Breach and Contract Discharge Due to Impossibility: A Unified Theory," *Journal of Legal Studies*, vol. XVII, p. 353 (1988).

much as kangaroos having no tails permits it to, the kangaroos topple over." Some analogous rule holds for conditional promises.[25]

What is the moral of all this for assumptions of risk? Just this: even a very faithful reading of an assumption of risk statement demands qualifications that are not apparent on the face of it. Many cases in which we do not want to recognize the assumption of risk as being binding are really cases where we do think it binding but inapplicable. Most notably in the case of the retired general, it means that his promise not to comment on government policy – his assuming the risk that he will be shut out of a debate he then very much wants to participate in – is by its nature not absolute, but highly qualified: it is qualified in the way that all conditional statements are qualified.

X. Forced Gambles

Not all risk assumption is risk reduction. The person who buys disability insurance is in fact assuming a risk – the risk that he will never become disabled, and that his premiums will have been paid in vain. He is also, of course, getting rid of a risk: the risk that he will become disabled and have no means of support. We speak of risk reduction here because a big risk has been exchanged for a small one. When we think of troubling instances of risk assumption, we usually think of those that aren't risk-reducing. After all, to worry about someone's decision to put himself in harm's way only seems humane; to worry about his decision to take himself out of harm's way seems cruel. But in fact, without realizing it, we are quite troubled by many instances of risk-reducing risk assumption.

Here is a classic instance of it – a slightly stylized version of the typical plea-bargain, based on the movie *The Morning After.* A woman wakes up next to a dead man and a gun with her fingerprints on it. She was severely drunk the previous night and has no recollection of what happened. Given the look of things, she has every reason to think that she killed him. She is arrested and charged with the man's murder. The prosecutor is delighted: the woman has been implicated in a number of fatal "accidents" in the past, but there never was adequate proof for a conviction. At last, it seems, he will be able to take her out of circulation. But shortly before the trial, the prosecutor learns of some surprise evidence: a film of the events on the night of the murder that has, somehow or other, come to rest in a certain safe deposit box. The film will settle, once and for all, whether the defendant or someone else is to blame for the murder. The prosecutor is less than pleased – what if this evidence should exonerate the defendant whom he has for so long tried to lock up?[26]

He tells the defendant about the new evidence. He also tells her that he doesn't know yet whether it will be exculpatory or inculpatory. The defendant is as uncertain as he. Both are simultaneously hopeful and fearful. The prosecutor then suggests a plea-bargain – a significantly more lenient sentence than the one that

[25] *Counterfactuals*, p. 1.

[26] For a more general examination of the arguments for and against plea-bargaining, see Albert W. Alschuler, "The Changing Plea-Bargaining Debate," *University of California Law Review*, vol. 69, p. 652 (1981).

would result from a murder conviction, but a heavy sentence nonetheless. The defendant feels the same way and accepts his offer.

Should we permit this plea bargain to go through? It is a bargain both sides desperately want to strike: neither side wants to be exposed to the not insignificant risk that the evidence might not turn out "well." It also does not look like the usual kind of case in which we meddle with freedom of contract: there is no obvious way in which a third party is being injured by this contract. Society's interest in adequate deterrence certainly isn't affected: the probability of apprehension and conviction for criminals remains unaltered.

Nevertheless, I suspect that, in this case, even those who ordinarily have no problem with plea-bargains must have qualms: after all, whatever the evidence finally reveals, we are 100 percent certain to regret our present decision to let the plea-bargain go through. Why are we certain to regret it? Well, if the evidence proves the defendant guilty, we will have let her off too lightly; if not, we will have been too harsh. A decision we are certain to regret a moment from now should, presumably, never be rendered. What's worse, this isn't even a case where plea bargaining saves us money, since waiting for the evidence doesn't cost us anything. Nor is this a case where waiting takes an excessive emotional toll on the parties to the contract, since the evidence could be obtained almost instantly. The only reason for the plea bargain is the risk-aversion of its participants.

Now suppose the same suit were a civil one – a wrongful death action. Replace the prosecutor with a private plaintiff, who offers a settlement as soon as the existence of that tell-tale film is revealed. The plaintiff is eager to avoid the possibility of recovering nothing; the defendant is eager to avoid the possibility of horrendous liability, and they settle on an intermediate amount.[27]

Is there anything special about a wrongful death case? Would a settlement in another kind of case on the eve of the discovery of conclusive evidence be any more acceptable? I fail to see how. That is, imagine that the plaintiff is suing the defendant for selling him a painting which he warranted to be an authentic Rembrandt but which, upon closer examination, appeared to be a forgery. In the midst of this litigation, some conclusive piece of evidence turns up that will, once examined, unequivocally determine whether or not the painting is a forgery. The defendant, fearing the risk of nonrecovery, and the plaintiff, fearing the risk of ruinous liability, settle. The argument I made about the plea-bargain and the wrongful death suit can be remade yet again. It would seem that settlements in general are immoral.

But are settlements very different from other kinds of contracts? Compare the settlement of the Rembrandt lawsuit with the following contract: D owns a painting which he thinks is a Rembrandt, but he has some doubts about its authenticity. D tells his would-be purchaser P all about these doubts. P is

[27] Second thoughts about settlements (and second thoughts about second thoughts) are the subject of Jules R. Coleman and Charles Silver, "Justice in Settlements," *Social Philosophy & Policy*, vol. 4, p. 103 (1986), as well as Owen M. Fiss, "Against Settlement," *Yale Law Journal*, vol. 93, p. 1073 (1984). Frank Easterbrook takes issue with both pieces in "Justice and Contract in Consent Judgments," *University of Chicago Legal Forum*, vol. 1987, p. 19.

nonetheless eager to buy. In the midst of negotiations, some conclusive piece of evidence turns up that will, once examined, unequivocally determine whether or not the painting is a forgery. But buyer and seller, both risk-averse, are still eager to go through with the deal – the seller to insure against the possibility of its being a forgery, the buyer against the possibility of its being real. Should we let them? The same argument can be made once more. Does this mean that all contracts involving uncertainty are immoral?

That depends: could I play this sort of game with any contract? I think not: it would be hard to play it with, say, an insurance policy covering accidental death. No piece of evidence exists on the eve of contracting, that would, if the parties only waited 24 hours, tell them whether the insured was in fact going to suffer accidental death. Not every contract involving uncertainty would thus be immoral. If the uncertainty pertains to a future event – a prospect – it may be contracted around. If the uncertainty pertains to a past event – an unknown right – it may not be contracted around. The distinction may seem a bit tenuous – indeed, metaphysical. What are we to do with the person purchasing disability insurance who shows no signs of any disability when he makes the purchase but whose genes, if they could only be examined, would foretell the certain prospect of crushing disability at age 40? Is there any sense to the distinction between a past event and a future event if neither can be known about until some time in the future? Is there any sense to the distinction if both can be known about today? The distinction *must* make sense, because we make it all the time. We make it in deciding whether somebody has already realized taxable income or is still awaiting its certain arrival. We also make it in deciding whether a divorcing couple has already received and must therefore share some property, or whether the husband is still awaiting its certain arrival. (Just think of the litigation over whether a medical school diploma is shareable property or merely evidence of yet-to-be acquired, unshareable property.)

Why is it, however, that we seem to feel differently about plea-bargains, settlements, and the simple sale of a Rembrandt? I claim that all of them are immoral, but our degrees of moral aversion to the three, even after I have made my argument, differ greatly. Why? As best I can tell, the difference has to do with the extent to which the claims being bargained about are conceived of as uncertain prospects or as uncertain rights. Guilt and innocence don't look like prospects, but like attributes that one either does or does not have – acquittal, therefore, is a right the defendant either does or does not have. Civil liability or nonliability looks more like a prospect, which a future event, the successful staking of a claim (much like the filing of a patent), is required to transform into a fully vested right. The entitlement of the Rembrandt owner looks most prospect-like (and least right-like), because we no longer believe in the notion of a "just price."

I have been claiming that some assumptions of risk are immoral – namely, all those that involve bargains about uncertain rights rather than uncertain prospects. Yet such instances abound. Indeed, it would seem as though our economy might collapse if they weren't allowed. Few people would gather hard-to-find information if they couldn't expect to reap a profit from it. Am I claiming that a lot of indispensable economic activity is immoral? Yes and no. I am claiming that the individual transactions are immoral, but not that the system which encourages them is. As Derek Parfit has neatly demonstrated, it may be perfectly moral to encourage immoral conduct, just as it may be perfectly rational to encourage irrational conduct. But it would be incorrect to say that morally causing yourself to be immoral is the same thing as being moral through-and-through, or that rationally causing yourself to be irrational is the same thing as being rational through-and-through.[28]

XI. Penal Lotteries

The assumption of risk argument isn't much favored in the criminal law. One rarely hears about it at all; if one does, it is with unease. At first glance, that must seem odd. Criminal and tort law cover similar, often identical, kinds of conduct. Why, then, should one hear the argument made so often in the tort context and so rarely in the criminal one? And when it is encountered, why does it inspire such unease?

Part of the explanation is the special sense of paternalism that permeates the criminal law. Paternalism is what prompts us to say that when A intentionally kills B, he is (generally) guilty of murder even if B consented to be killed, or that when A kills B through extreme carelessness, he is guilty of manslaughter even if B expressly assumed that risk. Such paternalism would be much harder to accept if A killed B through simple negligence, but the criminal law does not in fact punish simple negligence. Nor would such paternalism be easy to accept if only harm to property is involved, but the criminal law typically only punishes intentional harm to property, and here it is more natural to speak of consent than assumption of risk.

Nevertheless, even though the assumption of risk argument isn't really a big part (some would say is no part) of the doctrines of the criminal law, it is an important part of the justifications of those doctrines. I gave some examples at the outset: it is used to justify strict liability statutes, broad definitions of complicity, the felony-murder rule, and the unequal punishment of completed crimes and failed attempts. Whatever objections are raised to these are met by saying: if those rules are established in advance, the criminal knows what he lets himself in for when he embarks on his path. He assumed the risk. Sometimes the argument is specially adapted to the setting at hand. It is said, for instance, that the different punishment of completed crimes and failed attempts – of the assassin who hits his mark and the one who misses – doesn't really amount to unequal treatment, because both kinds of criminals are given the same lottery ticket: hard punishment if you hit your mark, easy punishment if you miss.

We are rightly filled with unease by this use of the argument because it proves too much: indeed, its flaw is one we identified at the very outset. If a robber tells you he will keep your stolen car unless you pay him $1000, that doesn't mean you have validly consented to his keeping the car if you don't pay him. If the state tells you it will punish you severely for something it is immoral to punish you for, that doesn't mean you have validly consented to the punishment if you don't obey those laws.

[28] *Reasons and Persons*, pt. I.

But if we don't have the assumption of risk argument available for justifying the wealth of controversial practices cited at the outset, how can they possibly be justified? If we want to keep them, mustn't we find some way of salvaging that argument? I don't think so. Some of these practices may not be justifiable, but many others are. It is an unfortunate consequence of the easy availability of the assumption of risk argument that it tends to discourage such efforts.

Let me give one example of a practice that is often justified through the assumption of risk argument but which could, indeed, be given a better alternative justification: the unequal punishment of completed crimes and failed attempts – more concretely, the unequal punishment of the assassin who hits his mark and the assassin who misses. It has struck many as mighty peculiar that circumstances utterly external to the actor should determine how culpable we deem him and how harshly we treat him. Let me sketch out a partial explanation of why this practice doesn't strike me as peculiar at all.[29]

First, let me loosen the powerful intuitions in favor of treating completed and attempted crimes equally by mobilizing a countervailing intuition. At present, we do not punish those who attempt crimes but abandon their attempts in midstream. This is no historical accident: the abandonment defense feels morally compelled. But if we decide to treat attempts and completed crimes the same, it would seem as though we would also have to treat the successful perpetrator's remorse as equivalent to the unsuccessful perpetrator's abandonment. In other words, we would have to acquit all who are genuinely contrite – and that seems absurd.

Second, let me cast doubt on the typical kind of argument that leads people to want to treat the successful and the unsuccessful criminal alike. They mentally juxtapose the assassin who hits his mark and the one who doesn't. They note that only external circumstances differentiate the two. Then they appeal to the fundamental precept of the criminal law that we should only be punished for our actions, not for events outside our control. Punishing the one assassin more harshly than the other seems to violate that precept.

An analogy will show why this kind of argument is flawed. Using this very argument, any murderer will be able to say: "If I had killed my victim in just the manner I did, but without meaning to, I would not be guilty of murder. Therefore what distinguishes me from the accidental killer are only my thoughts. But a fundamental precept of the criminal law says that no one should be punished for his thoughts."

Third, and finally, consider the various steps the assassin has to go through to bring off his feat. He has to buy his gun, find out where his target lives, wait for his target to exit from his house, aim his gun, and fire. Only when he has taken a sufficient number of these steps will he be guilty of an attempt, rather than "mere

[29] For a sampling of some pieces having bearing on this, see David Lewis, "The Punishment That Leaves Something to Chance," *Philosophy and Public Affairs* (Winter 1989), p. 53; Stephen J. Schulhofer, "Harm and Punishment: A Critique of Emphasis on the Results of Conduct in the Criminal Law," *University of Pennsylvania Law Review*, vol. 128, p. 1497 (1974); Thomas Nagel, "Moral Luck," *Mortal Questions* (Cambridge: Cambridge University Press, 1979), pp. 24–38; Bernard Williams, "Moral Luck," *Moral Luck* (Cambridge: Cambridge University Press, 1981), pp. 204–39.

preparation." The requirement of more than mere preparation before holding someone liable has good moral (as opposed to just evidentiary) reasons, which I will not here explore. Although the line is often hard to draw, clear cases on either side of it exist aplenty. Now suppose you think the line should be drawn after the defendant has bought his gun, but before he has inquired into his target's whereabouts. (It doesn't really matter whether you would draw the line there or elsewhere. My argument works as long as you agree that *some* physical act, however minimal, is required for an attempt.) Assume assassin A has taken one step beyond that line and is therefore clearly guilty of an attempt. Assume further that assassin B thinks he has taken all the steps assassin A has, but in fact he is wrong: he thinks he has bought a gun, but in fact the package he was handed at the store is empty; he thinks he has inquired after his target's whereabouts, but his mastery of English was so poor that in fact he has merely asked for a beer. Since you just specified the minimum physical requirements for an assassination attempt, and since I arranged for B to fall short of those requirements, B cannot be guilty of an attempt. Yet what distinguishes A and B are circumstances completely beyond their control. It is therefore possible for A to be more blameworthy than B, even though circumstances beyond their control are the only ones that distinguish the character of their actions. The analogy to the case where A hits his mark and B does not is not hard to see.

As I said before, all this is only a sketch of an argument, much in need of filling out (which I intend to do elsewhere). I only offer it here to show that even in those areas of the criminal law where the assumption of risk argument crops up most frequently, it is quite superfluous and indeed misguided. Better arguments exist to do the job it sets out to do.

XII. Conclusion

Assumption of risk arguments are made all the time. Sometimes they persuade; sometimes they sound preposterous. What is odd is that when they sound preposterous, it is often very hard to say *why* they sound preposterous. This essay tried to outline some of the chief reasons beyond the two or three most familiar ones: the indeterminancy of the argument in some circumstances, the special problems posed by collective assumption of risk, the phenomenon of victimless injuries, the incommensurability of choices under extreme uncertainty, the built-in qualifications of conditional promises, the immortality of avoiding certain gambles, and the inappropriateness of the argument in the criminal law.

DEFENSIVE FORCE AS AN ACT OF RESCUE

By George P. Fletcher

Jewish law takes an approach to self-defense that differs dramatically from the conventional assumptions of Western secular legal systems. The central theme of Talmudic jurisprudence[1] is that self-defense rests on a duty not to stand idly by while one's neighbor suffers. "Do not stand on the blood of one's neighbor," as the point is cryptically put in Leviticus 19:16.[2] This way of thinking about self-defense departs in two significant ways from common Western assumptions. First, it stresses that the roots of self-defense are a duty rather than a right to act; second, it treats the case of third-party defense (defense of others) as logically prior to the first-party case of *self*-defense.

[1] A brief sketch of the literary history of Jewish law follows. For an expanded summary of this history, see Marilyn Finkelman, "Self-Defense and the Defense of Others in Jewish Law: The Rodef Defense," *Wayne Law Review*, vol. 33 (1987), pp. 1257–59, n. 2.

Jewish law (*halakhah*) embodies only a portion of the wider corpus of Jewish source material, or *Torah.* The most authoritative *halakhah* is to be found in the first five books of the Hebrew Bible [sometimes also called *Torah*]. Legal writing located outside of these five books is viewed primarily as interpretive commentary that has lesser obligatory force.

Alongside the Hebrew Bible an oral tradition developed which supplemented and interpreted the written text. The first written version of the oral tradition was assembled by Rabbi Judah the Prince (d. 219 C.E.); it was called the *Mishnah* ("study" in Hebrew). The four centuries of discussion that followed the Mishnah comprise the *Gemara* ("study" in Aramaic). Together, the Mishnah and the Gemara form the *Talmud.* Two parallel schools each produced a Talmud: one in Palestine, the other in Babylon. It is the Babylonian Talmud that has had the greater impact on the development of Jewish law.

The *Geonim*, or heads of various Babylonian academies, produced their own *responsa* (commentary on the Talmud with application to specific contemporary concerns) until the year 1000. Following them, with the shift of Jewish scholarship from Babylon to northern Africa and southern Europe, the writings of the *Rishonim* ("first ones") attempted to clarify problematic or inaccessible material. Primary within this group was Rabbi Solomon ben Isaac (1040–1105), who was known by his acronym, Rashi. Rashi's line-by-line commentary on the Talmud is printed in virtually every modern version. Rashi's studies drew the commentary of succeeding generations; their work is included as the final component of the modern versions of Talmud, and is known as the *Tosafot* ("additions").

Rabbi Moses ben Maimon (Maimonides, or Rambam as he is referred to in Jewish texts; 1135–1204) was perhaps the most prolific of the *Rishonim.* He wrote on such diverse topics as medicine, philosophy, and Jewish law. His magnum opus *Mishneh Torah* (repetition of Torah) systematically codified all of Jewish law.

One of the final works of the *Rishonim* came at the end of the fifteenth century. The *Schulchan Arukh*, written by Rabbi Joseph Caro of Spain (1488–1575) and supplemented by Rabbi Moses Isserles of Poland (a contemporary of Caro), consolidated Caro's conclusion, themselves drawn from a compendium which he produced of all the writings of the previous centuries.

Commentary on the Talmud continued over the next five centuries. Today, in the form of modern responsa, it reflects the variety of living conditions and contemporary issues related to *halakhah.*

[2] This is a literal translation of the Hebrew: *Lo taamod al dam reekha.* The Jerusalem Bible translates the passage as "Neither shalt thou stand aside as when mischief befalls they neighbour." The new French translation in *La Sainte Bible* (Paris: Editions du Cerf, 1972) is intriguingly misleading: *et tu ne mettras pas en cause le sang de ton prochain.* Luther rendered this passage as *Du sollst auch nicht auftreten gegen deines Nächsten Leben.* Perhaps the French and the German accurately capture the active force of the Hebrew injunction *lo taamod*, but they miss the sense of the passage captured in the English phrase "Do not stand idly by." The point of the passage is that one must intervene to save one's neighbor, rather than let him die.

I intend to explore the implications of these two assumptions in Jewish law which diverge from Anglo-American jurisprudence. Before turning to a deeper study of the Talmudic materials, however, I should review the interweaving strains of thought about defensive force that run though Western jurisprudence.

The Western tradition draws on three distinct sources of the contemporary right to defend oneself and to defend others. The first officially recognized form of self-defense in the common law tradition was *se defendendo*, a defense that came into judicial practice by way of the Statute of Gloucester in 1278. *Se defendendo* applied when someone's back was to the wall, when there was no choice but to kill or be killed. There was no requirement that the opponent start the fight and thereby bear the stigma of being the aggressor. The commentators sometimes referred to *se defendendo* as killing in "a chance medley," thus underscoring the point that the origin of the fight remained unclarified. The defense operated by way of confession and avoidance; asserting *se defendendo* conceded the illegality of the killing, but sought to avoid the capital penalty, routine for ordinary cases of murder. If the plea prevailed, the defendant's life was spared – but as atonement for the unlawful killing, he forfeited his property to the Crown.

The plea of *se defendendo* provides the origin of the common-law concept of excusable homicide, a category of liability that occupied the halfway station between total liability and total acquittal. The partial acquittal in cases of excusable homicide stood between two options that were more favorable to the defense. One was a total acquittal based on a finding that there was no human act entailed in the killing – that is, that natural causes accounted for the death. The assumption in these situations was that if there was no act, there was no taint on the defendant in being close in some respect to the killing. Perhaps it was simply his body that was the medium of causing death, as if someone pushed him off a cliff onto a victim standing below; or as if by virtue of an epileptic fit, he uncontrollably flailed his arms and pushed the victim onto a sharp object. In these cases of "no action," the defendant warranted a full acquittal.

The other possibility of acquittal lay in a claim of justifiable homicide. Until the Statute of Henry VIII, passed in 1532, however, there was no theory of self-defense that rendered a killing fully lawful, justifiable, and therefore free of the taint that affected excusable homicide. The only available theory of justification applied on behalf of killings in the name of the law, such as executions under a court order. Prior to 1532 a private party, killing in self-defense, could not make an analogous claim of lawful conduct.

With the introduction of justifiable self-defense in 1532, the common law endorsed a second rationale for acquitting private individuals of homicide. The statute was directed primarily against robbers and highwaymen. The sentiment must have been that the killing of an overt aggressor was simply not a criminal wrong – not a violation of principles governing civil life. Viewing this sixteenth-century development through the prism crafted by Kant and Hegel, we would be inclined to say that the aggressor violates the Right or *ius* (the law, in the sense of a just social order) and that repelling the attack restores the Right, upholds the principles of *ius*, and for that reason is *jus*tified. Thus, even before Kant addressed himself to the problem of a drowning, shipwrecked sailor seizing a life-sustaining plank from a shipmate, theories of justifiable and excusable homicide found development in seventeenth-century common law.

A third theory of self-defense emerged in Blackstone's writing about justifiable homicide. The great mid-eighteenth century synthesizer of the common law was appalled by an implication of a liberal theory of justifiable homicide. Punishment may be designed to fit the crime; the same principle of proportionality, however, does not apply as a limit to the amount of force that may be used in self-defense. Today, the death penalty may not be used in rape cases – but no one, so far as I know, seriously challenges whether women (or men) may use deadly force to thwart an otherwise unpreventable rape. Though we accept this discontinuity between the institutions of punishment and self-defense, Blackstone balked at permitting deadly force against petty criminals, like thieves, who would not be executed for their crimes. No act, he reasoned, "may be prevented by death unless the same, if committed, would also be punished by death."[3]

Though Blackstone's principle has hardly prevailed – witness the punishment/self-defense disparity in rape cases – it hints at a way of thinking about self-defense that has a strong following. In neither of the first two theories is one concerned about balancing the interests of the embattled parties. If a defender has no choice but to kill, he or she will be excused for doing so. Balancing the interests at stake is relevant only insofar as protecting a relatively minor interest might indicate that the defense was less responsive to instincts of survival. If a defender may restore the Right by killing, when necessary, an unjust aggressor, he may do so without concern for the proportionality of his response. Now comes Blackstone and teaches generations of common lawyers that if an act does not merit the death penalty *ex post*, preventing that act does not justify deadly force *ex ante*. If punishment must fit the gravity of the crime, then defensive force must also fit the threatened act.

This way of thinking about self-defense gained in the late nineteenth and twentieth centuries, when reformers began to take seriously the possibility of justifying certain crimes on the grounds of balancing the competing interests in a situation of conflict. A justification of necessity, as it eventually came to be adopted in most jurisdictions around the world, refashioned the common perception of self-defense. More and more theorists and legislators came to see self-defense as but a special instance of the general utilitarian justification of furthering the greater good in a situation of conflict. The Model Penal Code unabashedly adopted this way of enthroning a balancing of interests as the "general principle of justification" and then proceeded to treat self-defense as a special instance of this general principle.

With this review as a background for comparative analysis, I return to a consideration of the biblical and Talmudic approaches to self-defense. The Bible itself contains only a limited discussion of self-defense, and that discussion appears to be confined to the case of a homeowner's defense against a thief breaking in.[4]

[3] William Blackstone, *Commentaries on the Law of England* (1765–1769; Chicago: University of Chicago Press, 1979), vol. 4, p. 181.

[4] Exodus 22:1. For elaboration of the Talmudic discussion of this aspect of self-defense, see my paper "Punishment and Self-Defense," to be published in *Law and Philosophy*, vol. 8, (1989), pp. 201–15.

This passage in the book of Exodus and the oral law that developed around it[5] could conceivably be extended to a case of self-defense against an aggressor in public, but defending one's home – one's castle, as the English judges were wont to say – is a relatively easy case. The intruder crosses a clearly demarcated boundary. He trespasses against a zone of intimacy that is fundamental in any legal system that takes individuals and their possessions seriously. When one person breaks into another's private dwelling, there is no doubt – to borrow a phrase from a neighboring passage in Exodus – about whose ox is goring whose.

When the interaction of two people in the public sphere degenerates into a fight, one can never be entirely sure who started it. True, someone swings first, but behind the swing lies verbal and other potentially provocative behavior that makes it difficult to distinguish between a "chance medley" and an unequivocal attack. It makes sense to think about imposing a duty to retreat from these potentially ambiguous fights in the public arena, but no one has ever seriously suggested that a homeowner has a duty to retreat from his own home rather than use deadly force against an intruder. These differences explain why, in the Talmudic discussions of self-defense, one cannot find the argument that the case of the homeowner defending his private space provides a paradigm for all cases of resisting aggression.

Though the Bible remains silent about the general right to use defensive force, the oral law, as codified in the *Mishnah*, clearly recognizes the right to kill an aggressor in certain specified cases. The technical term for an aggressor is *rodef* – usually translated as a "pursuer." The text gives us three cases in which one should kill a *rodef*: to stop him from chasing another "in order to kill him," to stop him from chasing a man, and to stop him from chasing a betrothed woman. The latter two cases do not specify the purpose of the *rodef* in pursuing his intended victim. The context makes it clear, however, that illicit sex is his aim. Unfortunately, what makes the sex illicit in these two cases is not so obvious. We cannot assume the *rodef*'s intent must be to rape either the man or the betrothed woman; seeking consensual intercourse might be sufficient in both cases to justify forcible intervention by a third party.[6]

In three cases, intervention is impermissible: where the pursuer is after a beast (again, presumably for sex), where he is about to desecrate the Sabbath, and where he is about to engage in idolatrous practices. Significantly, these latter three cases constitute capital offenses, but none of them directly endangers the welfare of a human being. Apparently, individuals are barred from acting to prevent these heinous acts. Upholding God's law – even in matters as basic as sexuality, the Sabbath, and worship – is not enough; a human interest in life or sexual integrity must be at stake. If Talmudic thinking were based on a principle of protecting the legal order – analogous to the Kantian argument of defending the Right – one

[5] See the discussion of the second *Mishnah*, eighth chapter, tractate *Sandhedrin*, discussed in my "Punishment and Self-Defense."

[6] It is generally assumed that purpose must be to rape; see Finkelman, "Self-Defense." So far as I can tell, however, the sources are ambiguous on this point. It is significant that there is a right to intervene to prevent the seduction (or rape) of a betrothed woman. This implies that the violent aspect is secondary. See also Calum M. Carmichael, *Law and Narrative in the Bible* (Carlisle: Edinburgh University Press, 1985), p. 217.

would expect to find a broader right to intervene. There would be no apparent reason why individuals would not be empowered to prevent bestiality, desecration of the Sabbath, or idolatry.

The oral law clearly goes beyond the Biblical prescriptions. The term *rodef* does not even appear as a legal term in the canonical texts. Yet the right to protect life and sexual integrity so obviously warrants deadly intervention that the rabbis could articulate this principle without clear biblical warrant. As indicated at the outset, a primary source for the right of forcible intervention derives from general principle: "Do not stand on the blood of one's neighbor," or, more colloquially, "Do not stand by as your neighbor bleeds."[7] The attack by an aggressor is treated as analogous to a natural disaster that befalls the potential victim. Intervening to stop the aggressor is like inserting oneself between a falling rock and the innocent person below it.

The Talmud invokes another mode of proof to demonstrate the right of intervention. Take note of the following narrative in Deuteronomy 22:23–30:

> If a girl that is a virgin be betrothed to husband and a man find her in the city and lie with her; then you shall bring them both out to the gate of that city, and you shall stone them with stone that they die; the girl because she cried not, being in the city; and the man, because he has humbled his neighbour's wife: so thou shalt put away evil from among you.
>
> But if a man find a betrothed girl in the field, and the man force her and lie with her; then only the man that lay with her shall die: but to the girl thou shalt do nothing; there is in the girl no sin worthy of death: for as when a man rises against his neighbour and slays him, even so in this matter: *for he found her in the field and she cried out, but there was none to save her.* [my emphasis]

In the Talmudic discussion, the rabbis take the italicized passage as proof that the Bible implicitly recognized a right of forcible intervention to save the girl. What would be the point of her crying out in order to summon someone who might save her unless third parties had the right to do just that? The text here is taken as confirmation of the right of intervention, even though that right is not directly stated.

The first implication of grounding self-defense in a duty to rescue is that the third-party case (protecting a third party) seems to take logical priority over the first-party case (protecting oneself).[8] Western legal systems typically take the case of self-help to be fundamental, and the third-party case as an extension of the right to protect oneself. The extension follows with difficulty from the theory of *se defendendo* as an excuse, but it flows readily from the idea that the defender is acting to protect the lawful order.[9] If the third-party case is fundamental, however, the

[7] See the discussion in note 2.

[8] The second party in these interactions would be the aggressor.

[9] Significantly, if the rationale for the defense is the third theory, based on the balancing of competing interests, the third-party case might be easier to justify. The legal system might be properly skeptical of the individual's ability to balance competing interests where the benefits of the act accrue to himself and the costs to a stranger. See Meir Dan-Cohen, "Decision Rules and Conduct Rules: On Acoustic Separation in Criminal Law," *Harvard Law Review*, vol. 97 (1984), p. 625. If both the benefits and costs affect other persons, then the balancing is likely to be skewed by subjective, self-interested considerations.

Talmudic system confronts the problem of justifying the self-serving use of deadly force. I suppose one could say that everyone has a duty to preserve himself that is at least as strong as his duty to rescue others; everyone is his own closest "neighbor" and therefore no one should sit idly by if he himself, as well as his neighbor, is bleeding to death. This move seems a bit strained, for the biblical commandment has the clear connotation of altruistic commitment. Perhaps it is simply the case that we need to be reminded of our duty to rescue others. There is apparently no need to constrain our natural impulses with an imperative to save ourselves.

In another Talmudic passage, devoted to the implications of the homeowner's right to kill an intruder, the rabbis assert, "And the Torah holds, 'If someone comes to kill you, rise up and kill him first.'" The passage suggests that Jewish law recognizes a general right to defend oneself on the street, as well as within the confines of one's own home. But the word *Torah* is used here in a wonderfully ambiguous way. Narrowly defined, the Torah refers to the Bible; as I have suggested, however, the Bible does not explicitly recognize this general right of first-party self-defense. 'Torah' is understood here as the entire body of Jewish law, including unwritten principles as well as the explicit revelation at Sinai. Even within the framework of a religious legal system based upon a single text, the lawyers engaged in interpreting the text may properly assume that some matters – such as the right to defend oneself – are so obvious that the lawgiver need not expressly mention the right in laying down the law.

I use the notion of a right of self-defense, but we should not forget that the basic Talmudic idea is that of duty: in particular, a duty to God to fulfill the divine commandments. The notion of individual rights in the modern sense does not appear in either the Bible or the Talmud. This may explain why the focus is on the duty to rescue others; rescuing oneself, an expression of the instinct to survive, need not require the same legal recognition of a duty to act.

The duty to rescue a person in danger presumably entails a right and a justification for acting to fulfill the duty. The assumption is not only that 'ought' implies 'can', but that 'ought' implies 'may'. One might have doubts about this derivation of rights from duties if the system tolerated conflicting duties of the same rank, but potentially conflicting duties must be ordered in any consistent moral or legal system. For example, the duty to rescue might well conflict with the duty to observe the Sabbath, but saving someone's life is treated as logically prior to the sanctity of the Sabbath.

Grounding a right of self-defense in a duty to rescue implies, however, that the notions of right and duty must be coextensive. If the foundational idea is the individual's right to protect himself and vindicate his autonomy, then the system of norms might encourage a notion of right broader than the duty to act on that right. Indeed, Western legal systems typically maintain that defense is a right, not a duty. Whether one acts to protect anyone's body or property can be left to individual judgment. Rights to use force then come into focus as permissive, rather than mandatory. Extralegal considerations of compassion might lead one to desist from the use of force, even though the law would tolerate intervention. This gap between rights and possible duties to act collapses as soon as the duty to act is taken to be logically prior.

Thinking about defensive intervention as a duty-based act of rescue seems to threaten the universality of the right to defend others. After all, is one under a duty to rescue everyone? The way we think about the duty to rescue in modern, secular legal systems is that the scope of the duty is limited to family members and a special set of persons with whom one stands in a special relationship of trust and responsibility. Starting from the premise of a duty limited in this way, we could invoke the duty to rescue as the basis for a general right of defensive intervention against aggression. The biblical duty not to stand idly by while one's neighbor bleeds extends, more broadly, to all members of the community – which, in the Talmudic context, means to all Jews. Yet the Talmudic sources suggest that the scope of the duty stops short of idolaters.[10] Though modern thinking about self-defense is pitched to multiethnic, diversified societies (*Gesellschaften*), the Talmud approaches the duty to rescue and defensive intervention in the context of a closely-knit, homogeneous community (*Gemeinschaft*).

The difference strikes me as significant, for it captures the interpenetration of the notions of Right – the abstract legal order – and of civil society – a society in which its members interact in the public arena for limited purposes. The Kantian theory of self-defense, based on the vindication of Right, dovetails with a notion of civil society that rests on an abstract structure of maximum freedom to pursue private ends.

Grounding defensive force in the duty to rescue expresses the communitarian orientation of Talmudic jurisprudence. All Jews are responsible to each other for each other's sins on the Day of Atonement and for each other's welfare in daily life. Only hyperbole can capture the Jewish passion for interdependence: "If one saves the life of [a Jew], the Scriptures treat him as though he has saved an entire world."[11] This statement, found in the *Mishnah* among legalistic propositions about interrogating witnesses, follows an analogous claim about the meaning of killing a single Jew: it is as though one kills an entire world. These poetic testimonials to the value of human life derive, in part, from the view that each person carries within him not just the seed of his offspring but the seed of infinite generations yet to be born. These unborn generations are sacrificed by every act of killing or failing to rescue.

It is not surprising, then, that contemporary orthodox Jewish ethicists have considerable difficulty with the distinction between active and passive euthanasia. Contrary to the growing consensus of the medical community, they deny that there is a morally significant difference between killing and letting die, between causing death and standing idly by as one's neighbor dies of natural causes. Every case of letting someone die violates the imperative of Leviticus 19:16: that one not stand idly by as one's neighbor bleeds. Every case of letting someone die sacrifices an entire world.

[10] Babylonian Talmud, *Avodah Zarah* 26a, 26b.

[11] Babylonian Talmud, *Sanhedrin* (the last *Mishnah* in chapter 4). One basis for this view, discussed in the same *Mishnah*, is that each person carries within himself the seed of all his descendants, and thus if the descendants of each person are extrapolated into the future, there is a sense in which a "whole world" is at stake in saving the life of each human being.

These are beautiful thoughts – but, in the end, the effort to collapse killing and letting die does not carry through. The cleavage reasserts itself in the Talmud, which relates a case that rings of sensitivity to the distinction between killing and letting die. A group is lost in the desert. One member of the party has a canteen with enough water for himself alone. He can share the water with the others; if he does, though, no one will have enough water to survive. He has three options: to give all the water to another person, to share the water, or to keep it for himself. The rabbis debated the case, and only one voice came forth for sharing the water. The great Rabbi Akiba, however, held that the owner of the canteen should keep the water to himself and survive.

Rabbi Akiba's guiding principle is put simply: "Your own life comes first."[12] This is undoubtedly correct in a moral system that realistically accepts self-love and self-interest as a premise of correct action. It reminds us of Hillel's famous teaching: "If I am not for myself, who will be for me? If I am only for myself, what am I?"[13]

Yet favoring oneself in a situation of life and death would hardly be tenable if there were no clear moral difference between killing and letting die. If self-love provides for a justification that overrides the duty to rescue the other members of the party, it is hardly a justification of general application. The interests of one person in his own survival could hardly justify taking the canteen away from someone who had a prior claim to it. Even if there were a net gain in utility in taking the canteen, the cost/benefit argument would hardly justify taking the canteen and causing the owner to die of thirst.

Suppose that two thin travelers in the desert could survive on the canteen's contents, while the owner, being obese, needed the entire supply. Even if taking the canteen from one obese person saved two thin travelers, a taking that issued in death would be an unjust killing. It would be as clearly wrong as a shipwrecked sailor's action of pushing the first occupant off the only life-saving plank at sea.[14] It seems that only utilitarians would favor a general defense of lesser evils or cost/benefit analysis in homicide cases, and there is no evidence that Talmudic thinkers were inclined toward utilitarian arguments. Thus, if they thought that the self-interest of the canteen owner justified his drinking the water, the justification, by its nature, would be limited to cases of letting another die.

This discussion brings a serious problem into focus that derives from conceptualizing self-defense as an act of rescue. We are driven to invoke a justification of self-love in order to explain why the duty to rescue does not require the canteen-holder to hand it over to another person in danger. Under the conventional analysis in secular legal systems, the use of defensive force (in order to help oneself or others) is a right, but not a duty. The defender may simply decide that the situation is too dangerous for intervention. He has the right to use force or

[12] In Hebrew: *chaicha kodmim lchai chaverach.* See Babylonian Talmud, *Baba Meziah* 62a.

[13] Expressed in Hebrew, the maxim is overpowering in poetic simplicity. *Im lo ani li, mi li? Im ani raq li, mah ani?*

[14] See the treatment of this case in Immanuel Kant, *Metaphysical Elements of Justice*, tr. John Ladd, (Indianapolis: Bobbs-Merrill, 1965), pp. 41–42.

not as he sees fit; there is no legal scrutiny of his choice to stay out of the fray. If his self-interest tells him that he should not risk getting involved, no one presumes to demand a justification for his holding back.

If the use of force is considered a duty to intervene, then some check or limit must apply to cases in which the intervening party would risk great danger to itself. The standards for permissible nonintervention remain inescapably vague. Obviously, something more must be allowed than an exception for cases of catastrophic losses. Even in theory, however, it is not clear how far the legal system should go in tolerating breaches of duty to rescue for fear of danger to oneself. The German Criminal Code (§ 13) addresses the problem, but provides no more specific guidance than to require an assessment as to whether the intervention could be "fairly expected" under the circumstances (the standard of *Zumutbarkeit*).

As a general matter, the Talmudic conception of self-defense has considerable difficulty coping with the concept of *permissive* intervention. The notion of permissive action – where one has a choice whether or not to intervene – presupposes, it seems, a concept of rightful but not duty-bound action. Permissive action fills the space between the range of the individual rights and the onset of duty. Making the notion of duty primary in the Talmudic fashion squeezes out the intermediate space of permissive action.

Yet Rashi, a medieval commentator, suggests that a homeowner's killing a burglar is permissive, rather than mandatory.[15] Unfortunately, to make this point, he must treat the killing as a trivial act. How he does this requires a word of clarification.

In order to express the notion of justifiable conduct, both the Bible and the Talmud use the suggestive expression "he had no blood." This phrase is usually taken to mean that there is no bloodguilt for killing him – no bloodguilt because the killing is considered proper under the circumstances. No blood need be spilled for the slain burglar. Rashi turns this expression on its head and claims that "he has no blood" means that as a result of breaking in, the burglar must be treated as equivalent to someone without blood – that is, like someone who is already dead.

This is a version of the familiar theory of forfeiture as a grounding of self-defense. The burglar forfeits his life by breaking in. The homeowner may kill him if he wishes, for there is no legal prohibition against killing a dead person. This way of thinking about self-defense raises numerous problems – not the least of which is the explanation of why the forfeiture is revoked and the burglar's life reinstated as soon as he flees from the house. Neither the Talmud nor modern secular legal systems recognize the right of the homeowner who is the victim of a burglary to hunt down the burglar wherever he is and kill him, and yet this right would seem to follow if the burglar indeed forfeited his life.

The modern conception of self-defense as justification presupposes that killing the aggressor is at least a nominal wrong (an "infringement," as Judith Thomson dubbed it[16]). Seeing the killing as the fulfillment of a duty cuts against this

[15] For a discussion of this as well as two other cases of "permissible action" in the Talmudic framework, see Finkelman, "Self-Defense," pp. 1284–86.

[16] Judith Jarvis Thomson, "Some Ruminations on Rights," in *Rights, Restitution, and Risk*, (Cambridge: Harvard University Press, 1986), pp. 49, 51–55.

perception of nominal wrong; it thus ultimately works against appreciating the act of thwarting the aggression as an invasion of human life.

In the end, it appears that a number of significant features of self-defense are sacrificed by deriving the Right from a duty to rescue. We lose the sense that the right to rescue third parties is universally attached to everyone, regardless of whether or not the party deserves to be rescued. The notion of self-defense as permissive intervention falls victim to the primacy of a duty to intervene, as well as (most significantly) the idea that self-defense and the defense of others are acts of justification – rightful and free of reproach, but nonetheless an acknowledgment of the wrong of taking human life.

Law, Columbia University

EQUAL RESPECT AND THE ENFORCEMENT OF MORALITY*

BY GERALD DWORKIN

INTRODUCTION

In recent years, there has been renewed interest in the question of when, if ever, the state may use coercion to enforce majority views about what types of conduct are right or wrong, noble or base, decent or indecent. Such interest has been generated by both political and philosophibal pressures. In recent political history, controversies over such issues as abortion, homosexuality, pornography, textbooks in schools, new reproductive technologies such as surrogate parenting and *in vitro* fertilization, and faith healing have focused attention on the role of the state in supporting or opposing various moral views. In political philosophy, often a theoretical reflection of the political debates of the time, we have seen renewed attempts to provide a satisfactory foundation for traditional liberal (in the sense of Millian) views of the legitimate scope of state power. In particular, there has been an emphasis on the neutrality of the liberal state and the right of individuals to be treated as equals by the state.

I want in this essay to examine the arguments advanced against the enforcement of morality by Ronald Dworkin. While I do not believe his arguments succeed, they present strong and subtle points which must be addressed by those (such as myself) who are more sympathetic to the legitimacy of some forms of the enforcement of values.

I. THE RIGHT TO MORAL INDEPENDENCE

In "Is There a Right to Pornography?", Ronald Dworkin addresses the specific issue of pornography and the more general question of the enforcement of morality.[1] One of the interesting features of Dworkin's view is that in arguing against other ways of reaching his conclusion, particularly that of the Williams Report, he presents the opposing view in very strong and attractive terms.[2] He points out that any argument which proceeds from some idea of autonomy (in

* I would like to express my appreciation to All Souls College, Oxford, where the final version of this essay was written. I would also like to thank Ronald Dworkin for helpful discussions of his views. Needless to say, he does not endorse my criticisms.

[1] Ronald Dworkin, "Is There a Right to Pornography?", *Oxford Journal of Legal Studies*, vol. 1, no. 2. (Summer 1981). All quotes are from this article unless otherwise specified.

[2] *Report of the Committee on Obscenity and Film Censorship* Cmmnd 7772, HMSO, London, 1979. This committee, chaired by the philosopher Bernard Williams, examined the legal restrictions in England on written material, film, and live performance from the standpoint of their sexual content. Its general recommendations were that it is legitimate to have some restrictions on the availability of material considered obscene, but not for such material to be forbidden. An exception to the latter was the ban on live sex shows.

particular, the idea of individuals deciding for themselves what kinds of lives to lead) must reckon with the conception of politics as an appropriate way by which people determine their environment – including their views about what ideals to pursue and the conditions under which it is most propitious to pursue those ideals.[3]

For Dworkin, this means that his conclusion about pornography – namely, that although it may be regulated, it may not be prohibited in private – has a price. A community which recognizes a right to consume pornography in private limits by that recognition the ability of individuals to control the factors which influence their (and their children's) development.[4]

Dworkin is, to my knowledge, the only critic of the enforcement of morality to recognize that community autonomy and a strong right of privacy

> are in fact antagonistic ideas because the protection of a private sphere, the recognition of an individual right to privacy of that sort, in fact reduces the power of people generally to put into play their own ideas about the best circumstances for human flourishing.[5]

This recognition of loss is why Dworkin believes that only a rights-based strategy, rather than a goal-based one such as Williams presents, will support the non-enforcement of morals.[6] Or, more precisely, that any goal-based strategy will rely on the truth of contingent claims, making the argument hostage to the very uncertain truth of such claims and to the dependence of such protection on the changing nature of the social environment.

Dworkin, therefore, puts forward what he calls the right to moral independence (henceforth RMI):

> People have the right not to suffer disadvantage in the distribution of social goods and opportunities, including disadvantage in the liberties permitted to them by the criminal law, just on the ground that their officials or fellow-citizens think their opinions about the right way for them to lead their own lives are ignoble or wrong.[7]

The first thing to note is that in various versions of this argument – that is, arguments for RMI – Dworkin uses different criteria to characterize which motives are illegitimate. Let me give a complete list of the alternative formulations.[8]

[3] "It is only in politics, for example, that people can express in any effective way their sense of justice, or of conservation of the art of the past, or of the design of the space in which they will live and work, or the education their children will at least for the most part, receive." "Pornography," p. 190.

[4] "It would limit their ability to bring about a cultural structure they think best, a structure in which sexual experience generally has dignity and beauty, without which structure their own and their family's sexual experience are likely to have these qualities in less degree." *ibid.*, p. 190.

[5] *ibid.*, p. 191. For similar ideas used to support some form of the enforcement of morality, see William Powers, "Autonomy and the Legal Control of Self-Regarding Conduct," *Washington Law Review*, vol. 51:33 (1975).

[6] By a goal-based strategy, I mean an argument which assumes some desirable state of affairs, such as human well-being or autonomy, and then claims that some other state of affairs or condition is required or useful to achieve that desirable end.

[7] "Pornography," p. 194.

[8] Many of these formulations refer to the issue of sexual morality, but Dworkin intends these claims to have a wider scope.

> (1) ... on the grounds that their officials or fellow citizens *think* that their opinions about the right way for them to lead their own lives are ignoble or wrong. (italics mine)[9]
>
> (2) ... when the only apparent or plausible justification ... includes the hypothesis that the attitudes about sex ... are demeaning or bestial or otherwise unsuitable for human beings of the best sort, *even though this hypothesis may, in fact, be true.* (italics mine)[10]
>
> (3) ... justification includes the proposition that most people in the society *accept* that hypothesis [i.e., hypothesis (2)], and are therefore pained or disgusted when other members ... look at dirty pictures. (italics mine)[11]
>
> (4) ... the judgment that pornography should be treated differently from the Bible because *the people who prefer it are worse people.* (italics mine)[12]
>
> (5) ... that constraint is justified in some way that depends on the fact that others *condemn his convictions or values.* (italics mine)[13]
>
> (6) ... by assuming that some ways of living are inherently wrong or degrading, or by counting the fact that the majority thinks them so.[14]

Since I will be looking at his most recent arguments against the enforcement of morality, I include the formulations from "The Place of Liberty."

> (7) ... legal prohibition cannot be justified on the sole ground that the conduct prohibited is offensive to some dominant religion or moral orthodoxy.[15]
>
> (8) (no constraints) justified on grounds of religious or moral virtue.[16]

The problem is that these are by no means equivalent to one another, and arguments that are addressed to some of these formulations may not be applicable to others. There is an ambiguity that is crucial to understanding exactly what Dworkin's claim amounts to. There are two possible ways of understanding the claim that certain motives entitle us to disregard certain preferences. The first (what I shall call the weaker interpretation) refers simply to the fact that people *have* these preferences, based on certain motives. What RMI rules out on this interpretation is an argument to the effect that certain conduct may be constrained because the amount of utility is greater with such constraints than without – *given* that people have the preferences in question.

[9] "Pornography," p. 194.

[10] *ibid.*, p. 195.

[11] *ibid.*

[12] *ibid.*, p. 196.

[13] *ibid.*, p. 207.

[14] *ibid.*, p. 209.

[15] "The Place of Liberty," *Iowa Law Review*, vol 3, no 1 (October 1987), p. 29.

[16] *ibid.*, p. 31. In an earlier draft of this article, Dworkin uses a version closer to that we have been considering.

"The principle of independence therefore prohibits constraints whose justification, for a particular community, must appeal to the popularity of forms of life which include or involve contempt or distaste for other forms of life or a sense of superiority over other people." "What Liberty Is: Draft," October 16, 1986, p. 20.

On this interpretation, there is no direct reference to the validity, correctness, or reasonableness of the preferences. All we need to know is that enough people prefer that others not act in a certain way, and that the preferences are based on moral or religious grounds or that they reflect contempt for certain ways of life.

The second way of understanding the claim is not simply that more people have one set of preferences, but that the *content* of the motives or the *reasons* for the preferences provide the state with a justification for constraining certain behavior. Here, the numbers alone do not count. If there were far fewer women than men in the society, this would not affect the question of whether rape should be constrained.

On the weaker interpretation, nothing follows about whether the reasons given for believing that pornography is degrading (etc.) are good reasons for making it illegal. All that follows is that the mere fact that people believe it is degrading and should be suppressed should not carry any weight in the argument. The reasons for accepting the weaker interpretation are two-fold. First, it is consistent with Dworkin's general project: to *assume for the sake of argument* that preference utilitarianism – i.e., the view that the right thing to do is that which maximizes the satisfaction of people's preferences – is the background theory setting the framework of the debate. It is relative to that position that it becomes important to decide which preferences ought to be counted in the utilitarian calculus. Second, in his reply to a criticism by Hart, Dworkin seems clearly to adopt the weaker view. He says that liberals who argued for making homosexuality legal had certain political preferences but they

> did not *appeal* to the popularity of these preferences as providing an argument in itself for what they wanted, as the unrestricted utilitarian argument I oppose would have encouraged them to do.[17]

Further clarifying his view, he argues against the misunderstanding of his argument which suggests that he condemns all political processes which appeal to reasons broader than self-interest. Such a view would not support the right of citizens in a democracy to vote for social welfare programs or aid to foreign countries. What he condemns is

> a political process that assumes that the fact that people have such reasons is itself part of the case in political morality for what they favor.[18]

Note that this view, while weak, does allow balancing for certain kinds of preferences – those for security, for example. The fact that the majority of citizens prefer to be free from violent attack on the streets provides a reason why such conduct should be outlawed, even if there is a minority that would prefer to be allowed to engage in such conduct (perhaps because they are more aggressive and stronger, and believe that on balance they would gain). And this is independent of our believing that the desire for security is a worthy or legitimate desire.

[17] "Pornography," p. 208.
[18] *ibid.*, p. 209.

II. The Argument for the Right to Moral Independence

I turn now to Dworkin's defence of RMI. He considers two modes of argument. The first is that some other goal or ideal than utility is more important than utility, and pornography must be protected if that goal or ideal is to be achieved. Dworkin believes that such an argument will not work, but his strategy is to ignore such arguments in favor of another argument: assuming utilitarianism as a legitimate background assumption of political theory, a proper understanding of utilitarianism itself justifies RMI. The argument proceeds from what Dworkin believes is inherent in any utilitarian theory – a principle of equality which states that in any preferential calculus, each person's preferences are to count equally.[19]

Dworkin's claim is that RMI is required to prevent utilitarianism from degenerating into a system which gives some people's preferences less weight than others because those people are less worthy or their way of life is thought less worthy.

> ... if utilitarianism in practice is not checked by something like the right of moral independence (and by other allied rights) it will disintegrate, for all practical purposes, into exactly that version.[20]

The structure of his argument is not clear. He begins his discussion with a different kind of case: one in which he thinks utilitarian equality is directly undermined.

> Suppose a community of many people including Sarah. If the constitution sets out a version of utilitarianism which provides in terms that Sarah's preferences are to count for twice as much as those of others, then this would be the unacceptable, non-egalitarian version of utilitarianism. But now suppose that the constitutional provision is the standard form of utilitarianism, that is, that it is neutral towards all people and preferences, but that a surprising number of people love Sarah very much, and therefore strongly prefer that her preferences count for twice as much in the day to day political decisions made in the utilitarian calculus. When Sarah does not receive what she would have if her preferences counted for twice as much as those of others, then these people are unhappy, because their special Sarah-loving preferences are unfulfilled. If these special preferences are allowed to count, therefore, Sarah will receive much more in the distribution of goods and opportunities than she otherwise would. I argue that this defeats the egalitarian cast of the apparently neutral utilitarian constitution as much as if the neutral provision were replaced by the rejected version. Indeed, the apparently neutral provision is then self-undermining because it gives a critical weight, in deciding which distribution best promotes utility, to the views of those who hold the profoundly un-neutral (some would say anti-utilitarian) theory that the preferences of some should count for more than those of others.[21]

[19] "Utilitarianism claims that people are treated as equals when the preferences of each, weighted only for intensity, are balanced in the same scales, with no distinctions for persons or merit." *ibid.*, p. 202.

[20] *ibid.*, p. 202.

[21] *ibid.*

I find this argument obscure. Sarah's preferences do not count for more than anyone else's. It is simply that when Sarah's preferences are added to those of Sarah-lovers, the net result is that utility is increased more by satisfying Sarah-preferences than would be the case if there were no Sarah-lovers. But this situation is inherent in utilitarianism; nothing except an *ad hoc* restriction can avoid some similar result. Suppose parents care for the satisfaction of their children's preferences. When all citizens are considering how much money is to be appropriated for playgrounds, and parents plus children outnumber the childless, there will be more money appropriated for playgrounds than would otherwise be the case. It is not that children are more *entitled* to have their preferences satisfied. It is just that the preferential calculus works out that way. But what about, to consider an example Dworkin gives, the preferences of a Nazi that Aryans have more and Jews less of their preferences satisfied?

> A neutral utilitarian cannot say that there is no reason in political morality for rejecting or dishonoring that preference, for not dismissing it as simply wrong, for not striving to fulfill it with all the dedication that officials devote to fulfilling any other sort of preference.[22]

I do not see the distinction between this unjust political preference and other preferences the utilitarian may believe wrong – e.g., that bag ladies should have the same chance of receiving organ transplants as Nobel Prize laureates. If we were deciding on the allocation of scarce medical resources, would Dworkin say (*qua* utilitarian) that such preferences should not be counted?

We both agree that a society which honored certain preferences, such as that of the Nazi and (perhaps) that for Nobel Prize laureates, would be unjust. Our difference is that Dworkin believes that a utilitarian is committed by his own theory to ruling these preferences out, while I believe that, since he is not, this shows the inadequacy of utilitarianism. What is essential for the utilitarian is that nobody's preferences are disregarded, not counted, or counted as having less weight than other people's. But in a three-person society, if the preferences of two of the members happen to combine in such a way that the third member never has his preferences satisfied, then I do not see how on *utilitarian* grounds the third member can complain.

Of course it is true that, for the utilitarian, it would

> be contradictory to say . . . that the Nazi is as much entitled to the political system he prefers as is the utilitarian.[23]

But the Nazi does not have his political system. That system would be one in which the preferences of Jews do not count. But, in Dworkin's case, they count equally with others. It is just that they get outweighed consistently.

Suppose, however, that Dworkin is right. Suppose, further, that he is right when he claims that the right to political independence – i.e., the right that goods and

[22] *ibid.*, p. 203.
[23] *ibid.*, p. 204.

opportunities not be distributed unequally "on the grounds that others think he should have less because of who he is or is not, or that others care less for him than they do for other people"[24] – is needed to avoid disqualifying any person's preferences.

It is not clear that, as Dworkin claims, RMI can be defended "in a parallel way."[25] Here is his argument in total.

> Neutral utilitarianism rejects the idea that some ambitions that people might have for their own lives should have less command over social resources and opportunities than others, except as this is the consequence of weighing all preferences on an equal basis in the same scales. It rejects the argument, for example, that some people's conceptions of what sexual experience should be like, and of what part fantasy should play in that experience, and of what the character of that fantasy should be, are inherently degrading or unwholesome. But then it cannot (for the reasons just canvassed) count the moral preferences of those who do hold such opinions in the calculation whether individuals who form some sexual minority, including homosexuals and pornographers, should be prohibited from the sexual experience they want to have. The right of moral independence is part of the same collection of rights as the right of political independence, and is to be justified as a trump over an unrestricted utilitarian defense of prohibitory laws against pornography, in a community of those who find offense just in the idea that their neighbors are reading dirty books, in much the same way as the latter right is justified as a trump over a utilitarian justification of giving Jews less or Sarah more in a society of Nazi or Sarah lovers.[26]

Both the premise and the inference are wrong. Why is a utilitarian debarred from evaluating certain people's conceptions of sex as inherently degrading or unwholesome? It is true that, for a hedonistic utilitarian, there is nothing intrinsically bad except certain unpleasant states of consciousness. But Dworkin is certainly not working with this conception of utilitarianism. His utilitarians have views about human flourishing; nothing precludes their having views about which sexual relationships are better or worse than others. A few pages earlier Dworkin had argued that a utilitarian is not "committed to the proposition that a life of push-pin is as good as a life of poetry."[27] Similarly, a utilitarian is not committed to the proposition that a sexual life revolving around necrophilia is as good as any other mode of sexual fulfillment.

What about the inference? It is puzzling when Dworkin says that

[24] *ibid.*, p. 205. Query: Does this allow for elections in which some persons lose simply because others dislike them?

[25] *ibid.*

[26] *ibid.*

[27] *ibid.*, p. 203.

> To the extent to which ... motives ... are moral preferences about how others should behave, and these motives are counted, then the neutrality of utilitarianism is compromised.[28]

Remember, the right to political independence ruled out preferences based on *who* people were or whether others cared for them less. These are quite different from views about *how* people should behave morally, which could include believing people are acting wrongly when they mistreat animals, steal from others, mutilate themselves, or coarsen their character. In none of these is it merely a matter of who they are.

Dworkin's argument seems to be that, with respect to sexual life styles and pornography, moral condemnation of people's behavior is equivalent to treating people as other than equals. In answering one of Hart's criticisms, that despising someone's conception of a desirable form of life is not equivalent to treating them as inferior or of less worth than others, he replies

> Hart says ... that I assume that if someone's liberty is restricted this must be interpreted as a denial of his treatment as an equal. But my argument is that this is not inevitably or even usually so, but only when the constraint is justified in some way that depends on the fact that others condemn his convictions or values ... If the utilitarian justification cannot succeed without relying on the majority's moralistic preferences about how the minority should live, and the government nevertheless urges that justification, then the message is very different (from one referring to public safety) and, in my view, nastier. It is exactly that the minority must suffer because others find the lives they propose to lead disgusting, which seems no more justifiable, in a society committed to treating people as equals, than the proposition we earlier considered and rejected, as incompatible with equality, that some people must suffer disadvantage under the law because others do not like them.[29]

Now, if we accept his earlier argument that people should not suffer disadvantage because others do not like them, must we also accept the view that people should not suffer disadvantage because (many) others believe that their lives are wicked and degrading? More precisely, are we not treating people as equals if they suffer disadvantage for such a reason?

Note that Dworkin takes a different view with respect to the preferences of a majority who believe that pornography interferes with the kind of sexual experience that people want for themselves (as opposed to believing that those who consume pornography are degraded). He allows those preferences to be balanced against the desire of others to consume pornography. He gives an argument, essentially a specification of the abstract right to moral independence, that the appropriate balancing is allowing restrictions on public display.[30] The essential difference between this case and that of, say, the desire for security is that we are

[28] *ibid.*, p. 205.
[29] *ibid.*, pp. 203–4.
[30] *ibid.*, pp. 197–98.

suspicious that the motives for wishing to restrict access to pornography are mixed; they may include those of the illegitimate kind. RMI is a device for protecting, in an indirect fashion, against motives that are claimed to be inconsistent with utilitarian equality.

Let us consider four different cases. In the first (security), the majority have a preference that they not be assaulted by others. In the second (nuisance), the majority have a preference that others refrain from playing loud music late at night. In the third (structure), the majority prefer that a stadium, rather than a concert hall, be built. In the fourth (moral), the majority have a preference that others not engage in certain kinds of commercial behavior: e.g., accept money in return for bearing a child to term, or engage in polygamous marriage. Dworkin believes that (for a utilitarian) the mere fact that a majority prefer one thing rather than another provides a reason – and, given certain assumptions about the intensity of preferences, a conclusive reason – for the society to favor the majority preference in three of these cases, but not in the fourth one (the moral case). Why this distinction? Here are the reasons that he gives.

(1) In all but the moral case, the preferences are personal rather than external. In the moral case, either the preferences are external, the situation is mixed, or it is difficult to tell which is the case. But on Dworkin's own view of what a moral position is, it is not the case that the preferences associated with such a position are either personal or external.[31] Suppose, for example, one objected to the sale of bodily organs on the grounds that it is intrinsically wrong for body parts to be commodities. That judgment, and its associated preference, is not about what I desire for myself rather than for others, or even what I desire for others rather than for myself. It is about what states of affairs I find good. Of course I will prefer that others abide by the moral requirements that are linked to valuable or disvaluable states of affairs, but in the case of personal preferences (such as that I be allowed to sleep undisturbed) I will have the same desires about others' behavior.

Note that the same mistake is made in Dworkin's earlier treatment of this question when he observes that if a community passes restrictive legislation against homosexual acts or pornography based on the belief "that a community that permits rather than prohibits these acts is inherently a worse community," then this would be acting on an external preference.[32] But such beliefs about inherently good or bad states of affairs simply do not fit the model of personal vs. external preferences. Of course, Dworkin could simply stipulate that if a desire is not a desire for a good or opporunity for oneself, he will call it an external preference. In that case, however, arguments calling for a more just or equal society on the grounds that these are inherently good will also fall prey to the argument that we require a "right" to protect us against utilitarian arguments based on such "preference."[33]

[31] Compare Dworkin, "Liberty and Moralism," in *Taking Rights Seriously* (Cambridge: Harvard University Press, 1978), pp. 248–53.

[32] *Taking Rights Seriously*, p. 276.

[33] This is not quite a *reductio*. Dworkin would point out that only the argument from the *numbers* of people who believe that something is just or unjust is ruled out. It is left open that the fact that something *is* just or unjust is still relevant. But I should think that it is often legitimate to decide on the basis of counting heads that, say, a certain tax measure perceived as fair by the majority should be public policy.

(2) In the moral case, it is likely that the preferences have been shaped by attitudes that are suspect, such as those of the Nazi; thus, our only way of guarding against them is by RMI. Both parts of this claim have to be regarded as empirical, and I don't see any more reason for supposing contamination in the moral case than, for example, in the case of nuisance. The playing of loud music – for example, boom-boxes (assault by battery) – is at least as likely to be part of a judgment that is contaminated by class and racial prejudices. The very same people who would object to hearing such sounds at 9 a.m. on a Sunday morning are perfectly prepared to put up with the sounds of power mowers at the same time. But, even so, I think there is nothing wrong with the majority having the right to restrict the conduct of a minority on the grounds of nuisance. Note also that Dworkin's objection to a goal-based strategy was its reliance on contingent assumptions which could well be false. The strategy of the above argument has exactly the same character.

(3) Only in the moral case does the state fail to treat people as equals. But why must the state fail to treat people as equals when it restricts their conduct on the grounds that the ways of life they wish to engage in are inherently wrong or degrading? Consider the attitude of the Catholic Church, which condemns the sin, but not the sinner. Similarly, if one regards a life led in complete subjection to the need for drugs as degrading, one must regard such people as being misled or mistaken – but why must one regard them as less than the moral equal of other citizens in the society? And while I undoubtedly have some negative attitudes toward people who engage in the conduct I find bad, it is not that I must believe them inferior to myself or to be less than my moral equal.[34]

(4) Dworkin gives an argument to the effect that if anyone denies that banning homosexual relationships treats homosexuals as less than equals because that decision to deny is based on an unrestricted utilitarian balancing, then that person cannot have any reasons for nevertheless believing that such a decision invades the rights of homosexuals.[35] Now utilitarians have notorious difficulties with any notion of rights, but, that aside, I fail to see why any of the traditional moves invoked by utilitarians cannot be invoked in this case. Given the importance of sexuality in defining one's identity and designing one's life, and given the psychological complexities involved in our attitudes towards other people's sexual orientations, one might believe that the calculations of the majority are particularly liable to error and bias, and therefore we are all better off in providing a zone of protection around such behavior. This is basically the same argument as Dworkin's, but it is based on welfare maximization rather than equality of concern. Or one might believe, with Mill, that there are particular epistemological difficulties in assessing what is in the best moral interests of other people whose actions are self-regarding.

I do not see that a principled distinction has been drawn between the first three cases and that of the enforcement of morality.

[34] As John Ely has noted, Dworkin's scheme would forbid people forming their political preferences on utilitarian grounds (since these preferences would explicitly incorporate the preferences of others). See "Professor Dworkin's External/Personal Preference Distinction." *Duke Law Journal*, vol. 1983, pp. 959–986.

[35] "Pornography," p. 212.

III. Equality of Resources and the Right to Moral Independence

Perhaps because of the unsatisfactory nature of the utilitarian background assumption or dissatisfaction with the argument, Dworkin has recently developed a completely different line of argument for the same conclusions. It is based on the conception of equality of resources that he has been developing in a series of articles.[36] While conceding that there are arguments for the enforcement of morality that he will not consider – e.g., the view that freedom of religion should be restricted in the interests of everyone's salvation – he argues for the conclusion that the majority in a society is not entitled to the moral environment it wishes to have as a matter of distributional justice. The argument is as follows.

(1) The best conception of equality is one of equality of resources.

(2) The measure of equality of resources is that of opportunity costs: i.e., the value of any transferable resource one person has is the value others forgo by his having it.

(3) The auction which will provide a distribution that will satisfy an envy-free test – i.e., nobody prefers anybody else's set of resources – must have a satisfactory baseline of liberty/constraints.

(4) The principle of abstraction provides this baseline. The principle states that

> the true opportunity cost of any transferable resource is the price others would pay for it in an auction whose resources were offered in as abstract a form as possible, that is, in the form that permits the greatest flexibility in fine-tuning bids to plans and preferences.[37]

His conclusion is that the

> principle of abstraction ... seems to endorse the liberal thesis that legal prohibitions cannot be justified on the sole ground that the conduct prohibited is offensive to some dominant religion or moral orthodoxy.[38]

The first thing to note is that, although the conclusion is at first stated as above, it is restated after the argument has been presented as the "baseline liberty/constraint system should be innocent of any constraints justified on grounds of religious truths or moral virtue."[39] This exhibits the same ambiguity I have discussed earlier: ambiguity between conduct limited because many people are offended by its violation of moral orthodoxy and conduct limited because it is morally wrong (according to the moral views of the majority). As usual, I assume that it is the former that Dworkin is arguing for.

How does the actual argument go? It seems to work like this. Suppose that the majority restricted the actions of a minority on the grounds that the actions were offensive to the majority for moral reasons. Then the majority would be getting

[36] "What is Equality? Equality of Welfare, Part 1," *Philosophy and Public Affairs*, vol. 10, p. 185 (1981). "Equality of Resources, Part 2," *Philosophy and Public Affairs*, vol. 10, p. 283 (1981). "What is Equality? Part 3: The Place of Liberty," *Iowa Law Review*, vol. 73, no. 1 (October 1987).

[37] "The Place of Liberty," p. 26.

[38] *ibid.*, p. 29.

[39] *ibid.*, p. 31.

something – the environment they prefer – without having to pay for it. Instead of having to bid for the right to have the minority act differently – a cost that would be prohibitive, given certain assumptions about the importance to the minority of the right to lead their lives in certain ways – the majority would secure the environment for free. But this is unfair to the minority; it does not treat their plans neutrally with respect to the plans of the majority.

As stated so far, the argument makes no use of the principle of abstraction. It relies on the ideas of the auction, of opportunity costs, and of a fair baseline. However, the key idea of the abstraction principle (i.e. the idea that resources must be offered in as abstract a form as possible) appears nowhere. But Dworkin thinks that it is crucial; his account of its relevance is as follows.

> [The principle of abstraction] plays a crucial part in fixing the baseline aspect that we are studying: the liberty/constraint system that defines the place of liberty in equality of resources. Abstraction requires some legal limits on total freedom because resources cannot be fine-tuned to plans and projects unless people can count on controlling the resources they acquire. The principle of abstraction might therefore be thought to embrace what I called the principle of security . . . But legal constraints beyond those necessary for security obviously compromise abstraction: clay is not auctioned in its most abstract form if the baseline system forbids satirical sculpture, because people anxious to express themselves in that way cannot tailor their resources to their plans as effectively with that constraint as they could without it. So the principle of abstraction insists that people should in principle be left free, under the baseline system, to use the resources they acquire, including the leisure they provide and protect through their bidding program, in whatever way they wish, compatibly with the principle of security.[40]

This argument obviously begs the question (Dworkin concedes this) by assuming that the following parallel argument is not valid.

> . . . clay is not auctioned in its most abstract form if the baseline system forbids throwing it at others, because people anxious to express themselves in that way cannot tailor their resources to their plans as effectively with that constraint as they could without it.

Dworkin assumes, without argument, a principle of security meant to provide the usual protections of person and property against force and fraud.[41] Dworkin's proposal is that except for these limitations which are built into the baseline, all other limitations of liberty must be bid for by persons starting from equal resources. But this is quite a drastic provision, for it doesn't just prevent people from limiting others because they are thought to act immorally. It also prevents them from limiting others on the basis of any notion of offense. To prevent people from wandering around naked, or having sex in public, or playing music loudly at

[40] *ibid.*, p. 29.

night, or burning crosses, or eating feces in public would also be cases of a majority securing the environment it prefers without having to bid for it with valuable resources. It would also seem to preclude using public resources to preserve wilderness areas or conserve historical sites since these would seem to fall under the ban on "collective judgment about the . . . comparative worth of projects."[42] So the principle of abstraction would seem to secure too much liberty.

What is striking about this new argument is that it seems to abstract from the specific considerations that motivated the earlier arguments: namely, distinguishing views which denied the equal worth of persons from those motivated by other considerations. For the principle of abstraction is indeed abstract; it favors maximum freedom. To get some limitations, Dworkin assumes a security exception. In the absence of the argument for this exception, one can only suspect that the reasoning to allow this exception, and possibly one for nuisance and offense, but *not* legal moralism, will be similar to the line of reasoning criticized earlier.

There is one form of argument which Dworkin invokes in the auction context which might be helpful to him. A form of argument similar to his might be invoked to rule out, for example, zoning restrictions based on aesthetic criteria. Why, it might be argued, should the fact that the majority of people in a community prefer to have two-story residences rather than twenty-story parking garages entitle the majority to prevent the latter from being built? Dworkin's reply is that the imaginary auctioneer might

> decide to limit freedom of choice, in the baseline system of liberties and constraints, just for the purpose of correcting the auction in advance toward a result that better reflects opportunity costs as they would be revealed in an auction of perfect knowledge and costless organizational transactions.[43]

So, in the zoning case, the auctioneer might anticipate that the majority would outbid the garage builders for the use of the land in question if the majority were efficiently organized, perfectly knowledgeable, and so forth. Thus zoning laws might compensate for externalities in the market.

This, however, illustrates nicely the basic point that I have been making: allowing aesthetic (or anti-pollution or anti-noise or anti-assault) preferences, but not moral preferences, begs the question. For why not argue that an omniscient auctioneer, knowing the preferences of the majority of people living in San Francisco about the life styles of the gay community, could limit freedom of choice on the same ground of correcting externalities? At the very least, Dworkin would have to concede that it is an *empirical* question of whether the majority would be prepared to outbid the minority for the right to purchase land for housing, and therefore no longer a matter of principled argument.

[41] Compare *ibid.*, p. 26.

[42] *ibid.*, p. 30. To be fair, Dworkin is restricting his attention to the criminal law, so a better example would be the restrictions on the use of certain kinds of recreational vehicles (e.g., snowmobiles) to preserve wilderness areas.

[43] *ibid.*, p. 32.

The only principled argument Dworkin gives is that when we stop people from striking others with their fists, or polluting the air, or building garish structures, we are not passing any judgment about the equal worth of persons. But when we prevent them from buying babies, or defacing the flag, or selling books protraying sexual violence against women, we are viewing some people as less worthy than others. On Dworkin's own explication of this root idea, to treat the people in the latter cases differently from those in the former is to somehow fail to take their interests (equally) into account with those of other citizens.

Perhaps the idea is that in the case of crimes such as assault, the perpetrators have their own interests protected against assault, and so their interests as potential victims are counted along with their interests as potential assaulters. But the same symmetry is true for those prevented from acting on the grounds that their conduct is wrong or wicked. They are protected against living in a world in which such wickedness occurs. It will not do to say that they do not object to living in such a world, or that they do not recognize such a world to be bad; the same points could be made by a potential assaulter who believed that he would flourish in a world in which assault was allowed.

There is a gap between a premise which requires the state to show equal concern and respect for all its citizens and a conclusion which rules out as legitimate grounds for coercion the fact that a majority believes that conduct is immoral, wicked, or wrong. That gap has yet to be closed.[44]

Philosophy, University of Illinois at Chicago

[44] In some recent unpublished work – particularly an essay called "Liberal Community" – Dworkin uses a very different (and, in my view, more promising) line of argument for his anti-enforcement views. These are arguments based on the impossibility of making people's lives better by the use of force, because (roughly) nothing adds value to someone's life if he does not (genuinely) endorse it as a valuable component. This controversial conception of well-being clearly warrants separate discussion.

POSITIVE RETRIBUTIVISM

By C. L. Ten

I. Introduction

One dark and rainy night, Yuso sexually assaults and tortures Zelan. In escaping from the scene of his crime, he falls heavily and becomes an impotent paraplegic. Instead of treating his fate as divine retribution for his wicked acts, Yuso sees it as sheer bad luck. He shows no remorse for what he has done, and vainly hopes that he will recover his powers, which he now treats as involuntarily hoarded resources to be used on less rainy days. In the presence of others, he pretends that he has turned over a new leaf. He asks for religious and educational books, hoping (he tells everyone) to make up for his poor education and deprived social background. But he immediately discards them when he is alone in favor of the pornographic magazines which he has bribed a nurse to smuggle in for him. His deception and various obscene acts committed in the hospital are exposed; by the time he comes up for trial, everyone knows that he is still a lustful, sadistic, and unrepentant man.

Most retributivists have a sufficient justification for punishing Yuso independently of the social consequences of his punishment. Two features of the case might cause some difficulties. First, Yuso has already experienced considerable suffering and deprivation both before and after his crime, and retributivists might disagree about the relevance of the suffering to his punishment. Secondly, Yuso is unrepentant, and it is unlikely that punishment will change him. This might, as we shall see, create a problem for those who think that the justifying aim of punishment is the moral reform of the offender. Given certain assumptions, consequentialists would also justify Yuso's punishment. There is obviously no need to punish him in order to prevent him from committing similar acts in the future or in order to incapacitate him. His unlikely reformation will also serve no useful social purpose. His punishment, however, will satisfy grievances and quench the thirst for revenge. Most important of all, it will act as a general deterrent against potential offenders like Vassary, Wong, and Xavier, orderlies waiting in the hospital wings for those private moments in which Yuso regales them with stories about the pleasures of sadism.

The main consequentialist justification of Yuso's punishment will be rejected by retributivists (and others) on the ground that it unjustly uses him as a means to the deterrence of potential offenders. Yuso is not responsible for the acts of independent moral agents. If general deterrence is unacceptable, then the main function of punishment cannot be to prevent or to reduce crime. Have retributivists and other nonconsequentialists a convincing alternative justification for punishment? I shall argue that they do not, and I shall then consider whether it is indeed unjust to punish offenders like Yuso for the purpose of general deterrence.

It should be noted that the defense of general deterrence does not necessarily involve an appeal to an unconstrained consequentialism. Those who are to be punished for the purpose of general deterrence are convicted wrongdoers; they are not the innocent. There are also limits to the extent to which they are to be punished. These limits are set by some requirement of proportionality, that the punishment should be proportionate, not to the total harm that potential offenders would cause, but to the harm that the convicted offender has already caused. For our present purposes, it is not necessary to defend these constraints on the pursuit of consequentialist aims, because the nonconsequentialist views to be discussed reject even this constrained consequentialism.[1]

J.L. Mackie distinguishes between negative retributivism and positive retributivism. Negative retributivism maintains that those who are not guilty must not be punished, whereas positive retributivism asserts, as a principle with "immediate appeal and underived authority," that the guilty ought to be punished.[2] Negative retributivism is not at issue here. The issue is whether the guilty ought to be punished for nonconsequentialist reasons, and in particular for reasons which rule out the deterrent and incapacitative effects of punishment. The thesis of positive retributivism is, however, ambiguous as between the claim that there are sufficient nonconsequentialist reasons for punishment and the weaker claim that there are good nonconsequentialist reasons. Although my discussion here will have some bearing on the weaker claim, it is the claim that there are sufficient nonconsequentialist reasons for punishment on which I shall directly focus. I leave it open that retributive considerations might play a role in the justification of punishment when it is combined in various ways with consequentialist reasons.[3]

In *Crime, Guilt, and Punishment*, I considered at length and rejected various traditional and contemporary positive retributive theses.[4] I shall not discuss here the theories already examined in the book. Instead, I shall focus on two new and subtle attempts to provide justifications for punishment without invoking consequentialist aims such as general deterrence. If these theories fail to justify punishment, it does not, of course, follow that there might not be other, as yet unexamined accounts which will succeed. But given the range, variety, and depth of the nonconsequentialist theories which have been considered elsewhere, or will be discussed here, it seems unlikely that others will succeed where these have failed.

[1] See, in particular, R.A. Duff, *Trials and Punishments* (Cambridge: Cambridge University Press, 1986) and R.A. Duff, "Punishment and Penance – A Reply to Harrison," *The Aristotelian Society*, supplementary vol. LXII (1988), pp. 153–67. I discuss Duff's view at length in Sections III and IV.

[2] J.L. Mackie, *Persons and Values* (Oxford: Clarendon Press, 1985), pp. 207–8.

[3] See C.L. Ten, *Crime, Guilt, and Punishment* (Oxford: Oxford University Press, 1987), chs. 3–4.

[4] *ibid.*, ch. 3. The views examined in the book include the following: punishment annuls crime, punishment connects the offender with correct values, wrongdoers deserve to suffer, punishment gives satisfactions, and punishment is justified because the offender has taken an unfair advantage of law-abiding citizens. See also Ted Honderich, *Punishment: The Supposed Justifications* (Harmondsworth: Penguin Books, 1984), postscript.

II. Punishment in the Balance

George Sher's thoughtful book *Desert* is not primarily devoted to punishment, but he discusses it in the wider context of a theory of desert.[5] He develops an original version of the theory that punishment restores a fair balance of benefits and burdens which the criminal's act upsets. The most widely discussed version of this theory was presented by Herbert Morris in his paper "Persons and Punishment."[6] Morris maintains that the system of criminal law provides each person with the benefits of a protected sphere. But these benefits can only be obtained if people also accept the burdens of self-restraint by obeying the rules proscribing certain forms of behavior. Criminals enjoy the benefits of the system, but they renounce the burdens which law-abiding citizens assume. They therefore take unfair advantage of these law-abiding citizens. Punishment restores the equilibrium of benefits and burdens.

Morris's theory runs into various difficulties which Sher tries to circumvent.[7] One of these difficulties revolves around the measurement of the excess benefits of offenders against which their deserved punishment is to be equated. For example, if these benefits are identified as the lack of self-restraint, then one possible measure of the excess benefits obtained through criminal conduct is the strength of the inclination to commit forbidden acts: the stronger the inclination, the greater the resultant benefit. But this would mean that if most people have a stronger inclination to evade taxes than to murder, then tax evaders deserve a more severe punishment than murderers.[8]

Sher provides an alternative basis for measuring the relevant benefits and burdens. He maintains that our belief that the murderer should be punished more severely than the tax evader depends on the view that murder is by far the more seriously wrong act. He suggests that it is the strength of the moral prohibition violated by murderers which determines the degree of their excess benefits. Wrongdoers gain extra benefits by violating moral prohibitions, and these benefits increase with the degree of wrongness of their acts. Benefits consist in freedom from the demands of the moral prohibitions observed by others. The freedom gained by wrongdoers increases with the strength of the prohibitions violated. Sher believes that retributive desert is pre-institutional, and not necessarily dependent on violations of legal codes. His theory can account for this because even if, for example, Nazi leaders broke no laws, they have still gained an unfair advantage of

[5] George Sher, *Desert* (Princeton: Princeton University Press, 1987).

[6] Herbert Morris, "Persons and Punishment," ed. Jeffrie G. Murphy, *Punishment and Rehabilitation* (Belmont: Wadsworth, 1973), pp. 40–64.

[7] See, for example, Richard W. Burgh, "Do the Guilty Deserve Punishment?", *The Journal of Philosophy*, vol. 79 (1982), pp. 193–210; Richard A. Wasserstrom, "Capital Punishment as Punishment: Some Theoretical Issues and Objections," *Midwest Studies in Philosophy*, vol. 7 (1982), pp. 473–502; D.J. Galligan, "The Return to Retribution in Penal Theory," ed. C. Tapper, *Crime, Proof, and Punishment* (London: Butterworth, 1981), pp. 144–71; R.A. Duff, *Trials and Punishments*, ch. 8; C.L. Ten, *Crime, Guilt, and Punishment*, pp. 52–65. A spirited defense of a theory like Morris's is given by Wojciech Sadurski, *Giving Desert Its Due* (Dordrecht: D. Reidel, 1985) ch. 8. See also Michael Davies, "Harm and Retribution," *Philosophy and Public Affairs*, vol. 15 (1986), pp. 236–66.

[8] George Sher, *Desert*, p. 80. Sher is referring to an objection made by Richard W. Burgh, "Do the Guilty Deserve Punishment?"

extra freedom by their violation of the moral rules which others have observed. The theory depends on our being able to assess different acts as being wrong to different degrees. He believes that we in fact accept this when we claim that one moral obligation overrides another conflicting obligation.[9]

Sher thinks that his account of punishment is not affected by the fact that the benefits of wealth and opportunities might be very unequally and unjustly distributed in a society in which wrongdoers are said to deserve punishment. Thus, criminals who come from socially and economically deprived backgrounds have unusually heavy burdens, but their previous hardship does not justify their taking the benefits of criminal acts. This is because only punishment, and not past burdens, can offset the benefits gained through wrongdoing. The extent of the past burdens is assessed in terms of the degree of unhappiness caused, but Sher argues that the benefits which criminals accrue from their crimes is measured on a different scale. These benefits depend on the degree of freedom from moral restraint which they gain through their wrongful acts. The benefits from criminal conduct are incommensurable with the burdens suffered by offenders in the past; they cannot therefore offset those burdens. On the other hand, Sher argues that punishment removes the unfair advantage of freedom from moral restraint gained by offenders. Punishment involves treating offenders in normally impermissible ways. It removes some of the moral restraints on our behavior which have protected offenders. Both the extra benefits of crime and the removal of benefits through punishment are measured in the same way – in terms of the degree of freedom from moral restraints. However, Sher's argument raises the question of why, if one is interested in balancing benefits and burdens, one should choose Sher's measure of what count as the relevant benefits and burdens, rather than an alternative which allows commensurability. It is as if an accountant, asked to balance the books, simply ignores certain items because taking them into account would not allow the books to be balanced easily.

The notion of balancing the wrongdoer's benefits and burdens is supposed to explain why punishment is justified. But the unfair benefits simply consist in freedom from moral restraint, and the size of the benefits is measured by the degree of moral wrongness of the acts committed. In counting punishment as the removal of the wrongdoer's extra benefit, rather than as another violation of a moral prohibition on a par with the criminal's act, Sher seems to presuppose that an act which is normally wrong ceases to be so when it is done in retaliation for a past wrongful act. It is difficult to see how the notion of balancing benefits and burdens is crucial to Sher's account. The offender's wrongdoing seems to provide a sufficient basis for her punishment. Morris's account does not run into this particular difficulty because the relevant benefits and burdens are identified independently of what is right or wrong, and can therefore be used to explain how a particular act is justified if it restores the balance of benefits and burdens.

However, let us consider a case in which, if the notion of balancing is to play a crucial role, it will not require punishment even though there is wrongdoing.

[9] *ibid.*, p. 82.

Suppose that *A* assaults *B*, *B* assaults *C*, and *C* assaults *A*. In each case, an equivalent harm is inflicted on the victim. So we have three distinct acts of equal wrongdoing which proceed in a nice circle, balancing the benefits from moral restraint that each person receives. If the balancing of benefits and burdens is crucial to punishment, there should be no punishment. But if, on the other hand, the wrongdoing is crucial, then all three persons should be punished, in spite of the fact that none has gained extra benefits overall.

Sher, in fact, shows his willingness to accept some of the curious implications of the balancing view when he concedes that if *X* has previously wronged *Y*, and *Y* now harms *X*, then "*Y*'s ordinarily wrong act will merely right the balance, and so our account will indeed imply that *X* deserves no further punishment."[10] But this makes the role of the victim central to Sher's account of deserved punishment, and it is now unclear how Sher is to justify punishment by the state rather than retaliation by the victims of crime. Let us pursue this point further.

I shall now follow Sher in restricting the relevant benefits and burdens to those that he brings into the balance. The notion of restoring a fair balance of benefits and burdens through deserved punishment presupposes that the initial distribution, which the offender's wrongdoing upsets, is a fair one. So is it the case that all people, including criminals, have received their fair share of the benefits of restraint from wrongdoing? Sher acknowledges that some criminals might have been wronged by others in the past, or by unjust social arrangements. These criminals would not then have enjoyed the full protection of the moral restraints on the conduct of others.[11] So, on the balancing view, it looks as if some criminals do not deserve punishment, because the extra benefits they gain from their wrongdoing merely offset their previous extra burdens. However, Sher argues that previous wrongs done to criminals cannot be offset by wrongs committed by criminals against innocent third parties. It is at this point that he concedes that a wrong inflicted on the wrongdoer by her victim can indeed constitute the wrongdoer's deserved punishment, ruling out further punishment. But he sets aside private punishment by the victims of crime in favor of state punishment, because of the dangers alluded to by Locke of "confusion and disorder" which will result from the practice of private punishment.[12]

But how can the fair balance be restored if the victim is not allowed to punish the wrongdoer? The wrongdoer loses the extra benefit if she is punished by a third party, but it is the third party who now gains extra benefits from the removal of moral restraint on his conduct, whereas the victim is still left with the additional burden imposed by the wrongdoing. Sher first argues that if the third party performs a normally impermissible act merely to remove the wrongdoer's excess benefit, and not for pleasure or profit, then he is acting on behalf of the victim or the victim's society; he therefore gains no extra benefits for himself because the moral restraints on his behaviour have not been lifted. But, again, this seems to presuppose that it is not wrong to retaliate; it does not explain why it is not wrong.

[10] *ibid.*, p. 85.
[11] *ibid.*, p. 85.
[12] *ibid.*, p. 86.

The victim's position is left unchanged, and so the balance has not been restored. Sher's second reply is a bit more helpful:

> Second, while punishment does not restore to the victim the protection that effective moral restraints on the wrongdoer would have afforded him, its administration on the victim's behalf does represent at least a symbolic lifting of the corresponding moral restraints on *his* behaviour. Thus, it does go some distance toward restoring a benefit that he, but not the wrongdoer, has forgone. Because the resulting balance of benefits and burdens is far from perfect, this account captures the common feeling that punishment never fully sets things right. However, because the resulting balance is the fairest that remains possible after the wrong has been done, disinterested punishment is nonetheless required.[13]

But it is unclear how punishment, administered on the victim's behalf, represents "a symbolic lifting of the corresponding moral restraints on *his* behaviour," but not on the behavior of others. The state is not a privately appointed agent of the victim; its relation to the victim is the same as its relation to all other law-abiding citizens. It acts on behalf of all its citizens. Punishment does not confer any special rights on victims, nor does it remove any obligation which they have in common with others. Victims of crime are not allowed to attack offenders any more than others are. In punishing the wrongdoer, the state upholds a general prohibition applicable to all. Perhaps victims are made happier than others by the punishment, but such happiness is not the measure of whether extra benefits have been gained. Of course punishment is meted out for a wrong done to the victim, but this helps to locate the source of the extra burden imposed without, at the same time, conferring any extra benefits.

Furthermore, if (as Sher claims) state punishment only goes some distance toward restoring a benefit that victims have forgone, then it is incorrect to assert that "the resulting balance is the fairest that remains possible after the wrong has been done." In many cases, a fairer distribution – within the terms of Sher's theory – would be obtained by allowing victims to punish wrongdoers under state supervision. This does not involve the kind of private punishment that Sher deplores. The punitive activities of the victims of crime are conducted within strict constraints laid down by the state. But there will be a real lifting of moral restraints to allow victims to reverse roles with those who have wronged them, and to inflict on wrongdoers the same harms that were inflicted on them. Indeed, whenever applicable, this new version of the *lex talionis* is the form of punishment that is *required* by Sher's theory because it ensures that the fair distribution of benefits and burdens is restored by taking away from wrongdoers exactly the same extra benefits which they have illicitly gained, and by giving victims the balancing benefits of freedom from moral restraints. So in many cases, contrary to Sher's claims, state punishment would not be justified. It deviates too far from the deserved punishment, which may only be imposed by the wrongdoer's own victims

[13] *ibid.*, p. 87.

under the conditions specified. Like the traditional *lex talionis* formula, "an eye for an eye, a tooth for a tooth," Sher's account of deserved punishment seems to be committed to forms of punishment which inflict the same grave harms on wrongdoers that they have inflicted on their victims. Thus, in Yuso's case, the deserved punishment would be most closely approximated if the moral restraints on torture were lifted to allow Zelan, if he still had the strength, to torture Yuso.

III. Punishment as Penance

In *Trials and Punishments*, R.A. Duff develops a challenging view of the criminal law, the criminal trials, and the punishment of criminals. "The criminal law and the criminal trial are, like moral criticism, communicative enterprises which seek the assent and the participation of those whom they address."[14] The criminal law treats citizens as rational moral agents by providing them with relevant moral reasons to justify its demands. The purpose of the trial is to engage in rational dialogue with defendants about the wrongness of their crime, and to persuade them, if they are convicted, to accept the moral condemnation expressed in the verdicts of the courts. This is, of course, a description of an ideal situation, not a description of the actual operation of the criminal law and trial. But it provides the basis for justifying these enterprises as showing respect for the autonomy of citizens. Ideally, the purposes of punishment are continuous with those of the criminal law and the trial. Punishment expresses condemnation of the criminal's act, and seeks to persuade her to accept the condemnation as justified, repent her crime, and reform herself. Punishment is not, however, a contingently efficient means for making the criminal repent. The required repentance can only be achieved through the suffering involved in punishment.

But why should we choose punishment in the form of "hard treatment," such as imprisonment, to express our condemnation of the criminal's conduct? Condemnation can be expressed by a system of purely symbolic punishment. In any case, the verdict of the court already expresses condemnation. Hard treatment is apparently chosen because it is meant not just to express condemnation, but also to serve as penance. Ideally, penance should be self-imposed. Self-imposed punishment serves both to express one's repentance and to reinforce that repentance by focusing one's attention on one's past wrongdoing. Through penance, a person hopes to reform herself and to restore relationships severed by the condemned act. By accepting punishment, the criminal gains the moral benefit of being reconciled with the shared values of her community, and of restoring her relationships with its other members. This moral benefit is internally related to the criminal's genuine penitential remorse, and is gained even if, as a matter of fact,

[14] R.A. Duff, *Trials and Punishments*, p. 233. Duff's important book has already attracted two detailed responses: Robert Justin Lipkin, "Punishment, Penance, and Respect for Autonomy," *Social Theory and Practice*, vol. 14 (1988), pp. 87–104 and Ross Harrison, "Punishment No Crime," *The Aristotelian Society*, supplementary vol. 62 (1988), pp. 139–51. Duff replies to Harrison in the same volume: R.A. Duff, "Punishment and Penance – A Reply to Harrison." See also Jerome Bickenbach, "Critical Notice of R.A. Duff, *Trials and Punishments*," and R. Antony Duff, "A Reply to Bickenbach," *Canadian Journal of Philosophy*, vol. 18 (1988), pp. 765–86, 787–94.

members of her community are self-righteously unforgiving and continue to ostracize her.[15]

So far, Duff has shown the value of punishment as penance when it is self-imposed. But how can punishment, in the form of hard treatment, be justified when it is externally imposed by the state? Duff argues that the punishment helps repentance by making communication with the criminal more effective. Her attention is forced onto the expressed message. It is easy to ignore a mere conviction or a purely symbolic punishment, but more difficult to ignore the pain and suffering of hard treatment.[16] Through hard treatment we seek to provide criminals with an understanding of the wrongness of their crimes, and to persuade them to repent and to accept the punishment as an appropriate vehicle for repentance. Duff insists that "it is not a contingent matter that punishment – the infliction of suffering on an offender for her offense – is the appropriate way of trying to achieve the kind of penitential reform which is its justifying aim: that aim can, of its nature, be achieved only by bringing the offender to suffer for what she has done."[17]

An externally imposed punishment can, however, fail to achieve its purpose of persuading criminals to repent and to accept penance for the wrong they have done. But Duff argues that even such failures do not show that punishment is unjustified. To refuse to punish criminals because we believe that they are beyond redemption is to give up any respect or hope for them as moral agents with capacities or potentials for moral development and reform. "We owe it to every moral agent to treat him as one who can be brought to reform and redeem himself – to keep trying, however vainly, to reach the good that is in him, and to appeal to his capacity for moral understanding and concern."[18]

Duff's justification of state-imposed punishment in the form of hard treatment is not very convincing. He concedes that some of the communicative aims of punishment are already achieved by the criminal trial and the verdict. The "rational dialogue" with criminals and the expression of condemnation for the wrong done are communicative acts which do not require hard treatment. Punishment also "aims to induce repentance and self reform,"[19] but it is difficult to see why state-imposed punishment is needed here. Duff believes that criminal punishment should ideally aim to become self-punishment, and in the case of self-punishment one can indeed treat the punishment as an expression of remorse and as penance. But an externally imposed punishment will only achieve these justifying aims if it is eventually accepted by the criminal as necessary for these purposes. Whether or not it will be accepted is an empirical question, not one which depends on the internal relations between punishment, repentance, and penance. Duff makes no serious attempt to provide the evidence to back up this empirical claim. He seems to think that it is sufficient to show that, under ideal conditions,

[15] *Trials and Punishments*, pp. 256–57.
[16] *ibid.*, p. 261.
[17] *ibid.*, p. 262.
[18] *ibid.*, p. 266.
[19] *ibid.*, p. 272.

punishment *can* achieve the desired aims. But the communicative and penitential aims of punishment *can* also be achieved in other ways which involve less suffering and less social cost. Punishment may be quite unnecessary; it therefore cannot be justified even at the level of ideal theory. The choice between hard treatment and some other means of achieving the desired aims should be made by taking into account their respective effectiveness in preventing or reducing crime.

Duff asserts that "hard treatment aims to make the inattentive criminal hear the message it expresses – to force his attention onto his crime."[20] But there are other ways of engaging the attention of the criminal. One can shout, ring a bell, or ask him to stand at attention. Of course, the unpleasantness of hard treatment makes it more difficult to ignore such punishment, but this says nothing about its effectiveness as an instrument for persuading the criminal to repent and reform. After a long criminal trial, and after hearing the verdict of guilt and the subsequent denunciation by the judge, only the most obtuse criminals will be unaware of what is being communicated to them. But the regret that many of them show is only that of being caught. The message they hear is already loud and clear; they hear, but silently sneer.

Duff is right to the extent that hard treatment can indeed serve as penance if it is successful in inducing repentance: "the pain or suffering which begins as a coercive attempt to attract and direct the unrepentant criminal's attention should become the penitential pain which the repentant criminal accepts for himself."[21] But the crucial question is whether it will be successful. We are told nothing to convince us that it will.

In a revealing passage, Duff writes:

> If someone suggested, for instance, that we might hope to develop some kind of drug or psycho-surgical technique which would provide a more efficient and less painful method of securing the kind of reformative change at which punishment aims, we would not need to question the empirical plausibility of her suggestion: for the suggestion itself is incoherent. No such technique could, logically, produce the results at which punishment aims: such techniques do not address the criminal, as punishment must address her, as a responsible moral agent who can and must come to understand the moral implications of what she had done; they are not, as punishment must be, attempts to solicit and arouse her repentant understanding of her crime; and the acquisition of such an understanding must of its nature be painful to the criminal.[22]

What this shows is that certain techniques are ruled out because they do not treat the criminal as "a responsible moral agent." But it does not show that the justifying aim of punishment – penitential reform – can only be achieved through hard treatment or indeed, through any kind of externally imposed punishment. Thus moral advice and discussion, verbal reminders of the nature of the crime, and visits

[20] "Punishment and Penance – A Reply to Harrison," p. 162. See also *Trials and Punishments*, pp. 260–62.
[21] *Trials and Punishments*, p. 261.
[22] *ibid.*, p. 262.

to victims of crime are all morally acceptable, any may be just as effective (or ineffective) as means of inducing penitential reform. In his brief discussion of sentencing, Duff entertains some of these possibilities, especially the suggestion that offenders should be confronted with their victims as well as the view that purely symbolic punishment would be adequate for many offenses.[23] But he does not seriously consider the possibility that, within the framework of his own theory, there is no justification for any state-imposed punishment after the criminal trial and verdict.

Duff is, of course, right in insisting that penitential reform necessarily involves some suffering. But the suffering of being punished and the suffering that is part of what it is to repent are distinct, and the former is neither a logically nor a causally necessary condition for the latter.

It would appear that, in Duff's view, hard treatment should not be imposed on those criminals who are already fully repentant. They might, for example, plead guilty to spare their victims and others the ordeal of the trial, seek to compensate their victims in appropriate ways, and volunteer to work in arduous and menial jobs for the benefit of the community. Of course, insofar as these self-imposed tasks involve suffering, they may be regarded as penances or self-imposed punishment. But they do not include spending any time in prison; on Duff's account, there does not seem to be any justification for the state to insist on these criminals' imprisonment, even if this will better serve the purpose of general deterrence. Of course, in particular cases there may be doubts about the sincerity of a criminal's apparent remorse, and her choice of imprisonment to express her feelings may help to remove these doubts. But it would be going too far to insist that if a criminal were fully repentant for her crime, she would choose to be imprisoned. Indeed, the choice of imprisonment is in itself no guarantee of genuine repentance, as it might be made for various reasons.

Consider the case of the former South Korean president, Chun Doo-Hwan. To the dismay of his critics, he has not been brought to trial for his misdeeds as president. The allegations against him include "corruption, influence peddling and abuse of power."[24] Chun made a humiliating, nationally televised public apology. He then abandoned his luxurious lifestyle to live in self-exile with his wife in a small room in a remote Buddhist temple. He refuses to read newspapers or watch television, wakes up at 4 o'clock every morning (even in the freezing winter), and prostrates himself 108 times daily before a statue of Buddha.[25] If there were more confirmed reports of Chun's behavior along these lines – if, for example, he also gave away all his money to the poor – then there could be little doubt about his remorse. There is no need for a really contrite Chun to spend time in an ordinary jail to convince us of his sincerity. Of course, self-exile in a remote temple can be regarded as a form of self-imposed punishment. But it is clear that Chun prefers it to any ordinary jail, and it would appear that the prospect of life in the temple, austere as it is, would be a poor deterrent to others as a punishment for the abuse of

[23] *ibid.*, p. 287–88.
[24] *Far Eastern Economic Review*, July 7, 1988, p. 27.
[25] *The Australian*, January 18, 1989.

political power. But if penitential reform, not general deterrence, is what is aimed at, there is no need to imprison the remorseful Chun.

My account of Chun is meant to show the different forms in which penitential reform may express itself. However, it does not convey a full picture of Chun's behavior and attitudes. He is also reported to be drinking heavily (even though it is forbidden in the temple) and weeping frequently (perhaps out of self-pity); he has been overheard saying to himself, "Do I have to live here like this?" In the real Chun there is obviously much room for further repentance, although not necessarily through any form of state-imposed punishment.

In a later section of the book, Duff acknowledges that "one who already repents his offence, or seeks to make reparation for it, is in effect doing for himself the work which punishment would do; and in recognition of that the court may withhold any further punishment."[26] This passing remark does not, however, apply to those who have committed those more serious crimes for which even the contrite offender should receive "further punishment." Duff argues that "the task of coming to understand, to repent, and truly to disown my crime may be a long and arduous one"; although the "penitent perpetrator of a serious crime might, if left to herself, find and undertake an appropriate penance . . . the court whose proper task it is to ensure that wrongdoers undergo suitable punishments, may properly specify her penance for her."[27] Again, it remains unclear why a court-imposed punishment will be a suitable penance. With serious – as with minor – crimes, there may be ample evidence of genuine repentance on the part of offenders before they come up for sentencing. The insistence that minor offenders may be exempted from "further punishment," whereas serious offenders may not, cannot really be justified unless one appeals to considerations external to the aims of penitential reform.

If the already penitent offender is a problem for Duff's theory, so too is the hardened and unrepentant offender like Yuso. Duff believes that even if punishment fails to persuade the criminal to repent, the punishment is still justified.

> We owe it to every moral agent to treat him as one who can be brought to reform and redeem himself – to keep trying, however vainly, to reach the good that is in him, and to appeal to his capacity for moral understanding and concern.[28]

But Duff fails to explain why this appeal to the moral capacities of criminals requires punishment. If their penitential reform is what we want, we can continue to persuade them in the way that we often try to persuade others – by moral argument and discussion. If we are going to fail in our mission, then it is better to fail without causing the additional suffering that is involved in hard treatment. Thus, in Yuso's case, we can always send our best preacher or moral advisor to visit him regularly, and we can continue to shower him with the most persuasive moral

[26] *Trials and Punishments*, p. 286.
[27] *ibid.*, pp. 289–90.
[28] *ibid.*, p. 266.

and religious literature. We will, then, still be trying to reach the good (if any) in him. But we will not be punishing him any more.

IV. General Deterrence

As we have already seen, the penitential aim of punishment can often come into conflict with the consequentialist aim of using punishment as a general deterrent. One possibility is that if we abandon a system of deterrent punishment in favor of Duff's scheme, there will be a sharp increase in the crime rate. What would Duff do when such conflicts arise?

In the closing pages of his book, he discusses the application to the actual world of his account of "what punishment ought to be if it is to accord to both law-abiding and criminal citizens the respect and concern which is their due."[29] He maintains that existing penal institutions operate in societies in which, quite often, the criminal law does not serve the common good. He believes that punishment meted out under existing conditions will not satisfy communicative and penitential purposes, but will instead violate "the categorical demands of justice and autonomy."[30] But he concedes that such a system of improperly manipulative punishment helps to prevent or reduce crime, and keeps the heavens from falling. After some agonizing, Duff admits that he would act unjustly to prevent the heavens from falling. He reluctantly embraces a system of deterrent punishment, arguing that it at least constitutes "a less seriously damaging infringement of the autonomy of those subjected to it than, for instance, a system which aims at the purely preventive detention of actual or potential offenders."[31]

However, the problem is not just one of having imperfect penal institutions which fail to achieve penitential aims. It is also one of having imperfect criminals who will not be dissuaded from crime by the penance of other criminals, and who will only be dissuaded by prudential considerations introduced by a system of deterrent punishment. Even if our existing penal institutions can effectively promote penitential aims, they might do so at the cost of undermining general deterrence. Any theory which seeks to justify punishment should find a place for general deterrence and then subordinate penitential aims to it. This is not just because we will thereby prevent the heavens from falling – a laudable enough purpose – but because it would be unfair to make the innocent suffer, as victims of increased crime, in order to save the souls of criminals.

This claim throws doubt on Duff's view that a system of deterrent punishment is improperly manipulative and violates the demands of justice and autonomy. Recall that we are not referring to a system in which innocent people are punished in order to deter others from committing crimes, nor are we seeking to punish a guilty person in a manner which is disproportionate to the seriousness of her crime. Let us consider an example.

A is attacked by *B*, who intends to torture and kill him. *A* has two effective defenses, an Ali-punch and a Tyson-punch. The Ali-punch has to be repeated

29 *ibid.*, p. 291.
30 *ibid.*, p. 296.
31 *ibid.*, p. 298.

many times before it is effective: each punch causes little damage, and it is the cumulative effect of many punches which will be telling. The Tyson-punch, on the other hand, is a short, sharp shock which causes a lot of damage in one go. Each defense is sufficient not only to rebuff *B*'s current attack but also to deter *B* from further attacks. If *A* uses his Ali-punch, "floating like a butterfly and stinging like a bee," he would have to engage in a long fight with *B* which would leave him quite exhausted. On the other hand, if he uses his Tyson-punch, he would quickly subdue *B* and remain fresh but would cause him more harm, although still much less harm than *B* intends to cause him. *A* generously decides to defend himself with the Ali-punch. But just as he is about to land his first Ali-punch, he notices two cowardly and sadistic enemies of his hiding in a nearby bush, ready to torture and kill him if he should survive *B*'s attack physically weakened. If he uses his Ali-punch, he won't deter them, and would be too feeble to defend himself further. If he uses the awesome power of his Tyson-punch, he will frighten them away. *A* switches to his Tyson-punch, shouting a conditional threat to the enemies in the bush as he flattens *B*, "This is what I will do to you if you attack me." They prudently run away. *A* justifiably defends himself.

Now there is a sense in which *A* uses *B* as a means to deter others, but this does not seem to be improperly manipulative. The alternative is for the innocent *A* to be tortured and killed in order to spare the aggressive wrongdoer *B* the extra harm that the Tyson-punch would cause over the Ali-punch. But if *A* is justified in Tyson-punching *B*, then some cases of general deterrence are vindicated.

Daniel M. Farrell has persuasively argued that self-defense is a matter of distributive justice, and the principle of distributive justice invoked can be extended to cover some cases of general deterrence.[32] Farrell believes that I have a right to both direct self-defense and indirect self-defense. If someone comes at me intending to kill me, I have the right to resist. This is the right to direct self-defense which I exercise when I do what is necessary in order to prevent a current attack from an unjust aggressor. But suppose now that I have rebuffed several attacks by the same aggressor and that I can rebuff a current attack, but the attacker is going to continue these attacks unless I subject her to additional physical pain on this occasion. I know that if I do not inflict the additional pain, I will still succeed in rebuffing her current attack, but I will not be able to resist the next attack because I will then be incapacitated by a recurrent illness. If I am allowed to resist a current attack by killing her if necessary, surely I am allowed to inflict the additional physical pain to rebuff a future attack. I have the right of indirect self-defense. It is the aggressor who brings about a situation in which the intended victim has to make a choice as to who should suffer. The intended victim is entitled to choose that the aggressor is the one who suffers, rather than accept the suffering herself. The principle to be extracted here can also be applied beyond the cases of self-defense to defend other innocent people against unjust aggressors. One formulation of the relevant distributive principle which Farrell gives is: "one must suffer if

[32] Daniel M. Farrell, "The Justification of General Deterrence," *The Philosophical Review*, vol. XCIV (1985), pp. 367–94. See also Daniel M. Farrell, "Punishment without the State," *Nous*, vol. 22 (1988), pp. 437–53.

one's decision to do wrong makes it necessary that someone must suffer and that sufferer must either be the wrongdoer or some innocent victim."[33] Of course, the principle would have to be qualified by some requirement of proportionality that the suffering of the aggressor should be proportionate to the suffering which the victim would have experienced.

In the case of special or individual deterrence, punishment is used to prevent convicted criminals from repeating their crimes. According to Farrell, special deterrence can be construed as a form of indirect self-defense in which the state, acting as one's agent, exercises the right on one's behalf. But suppose now that by unjustly attacking innocent people, wrongdoers increase the vulnerability of the innocent to harm caused by others, and the wrongdoers know, or ought to know, that this is what will happen. The principle invoked to justify special deterrence will also justify imposing some penalties over and above what is required for special deterrence. For the wrongdoers have forced us to choose whether they or some innocent persons should suffer – and, as before, we are justified in choosing that they should suffer. They are both causally and morally responsible for placing us in a situation in which, if we do not harm them more than what is required to deter them from attacking the innocent again, innocent people are more likely to be attacked by other wrongdoers.

This crude summary of Farrell's argument does not take into account some of the qualifications and complications which he introduces. But it is sufficient to indicate one attractive line of argument for supporting at least some instances of general deterrence. Farrell maintains that the vindication of general deterrence is "weakly retributive" in the sense that wrongdoing makes a person a suitable object of social use.[34] This is very similar to Hart's version of constrained consequentialism, which insists that we need a "moral licence" to use offenders for the benefit of society. The conditions of the licence are that they should have the capacity and fair opportunity to conform to the law. But Hart points out that "though we must seek a moral licence for punishing a man in his voluntary conduct in breaking the law, the punishment we are then licensed to use may still be directed solely to preventing future crimes on his part or on others' and not to 'retribution'."[35]

But Duff is worried not just by the actual punishment meted out to the convicted wrongdoer for the sake of general deterrence, but also by the fact that a system of general deterrence works by threatening all those whose obedience the law tries to secure. He cites the example of a gunman robbing a bank who "threatens to shoot anyone who disobeys, and shoots a cashier who tries to raise the alarm."[36] What is the difference between the gunman's threats, which we

[33] "The Justification of General Deterrence," p. 373. I use similar considerations to justify the preventive detention of dangerous offenders; see *Crime, Guilt, and Punishment*, pp. 134–40.

[34] "The Justification of General Deterrence," pp. 368–69.

[35] H.L.A. Hart, *Punishment and Responsibility* (Oxford: Clarendon Press, 1968), p. 208; see also pp. 180–81. Farrell distinguishes his view from Hart's but gives an incomplete picture of Hart's theory in "The Justification of General Deterrence," pp. 368–69, n. 1.

[36] *Trials and Punishments*, pp. 179–80. Warren Quinn argues forcefully that it is morally legitimate to create threats of punishment "because it is morally legitimate to protect ourselves in this way against violations of our moral rights" of self-protection. He believes that "the right to establish a genuine threat is prior to the right to punish." See Warren Quinn, "The Right to Threaten and the Right to Punish," *Philosophy & Public Affairs*, vol. 14 (1985), pp. 327–73.

all acknowledge to be unjustified, and the government's use of the threat of punishment to obtain compliance with the law? He argues that the crucial difference cannot simply depend on the legitimacy of the law's demands as opposed to those of the gunman, for we are not entitled to use unacceptable methods for the promotion of desirable ends. For example, you are not justified in using the threat of violence to make me repay the money that I owe you.

Duff's analogy is weak. First, the use of violence may be disproportionate to the desired end. Secondly, we do not wish people to take the law into their own hands. In the context of an operative legal system, creditors should go through impartial public procedures for settling disputes. The resort to private procedures will have undesirable consequences of prolonging and intensifying disputes. On the other hand, the government's pursuit of its legitimate goals by the use of threats does not have the undesirable effects of the private enforcement of legitimate claims. So the difference between the government's purposes and those of the gunman is relevant in determining the means that they may adopt. No doubt threats – from whatever source they come – close people's options, but the government's threats only close those options which are not morally permissible in the first place: namely, harming the innocent. On the other hand, the gunman restricts options which should be freely available. In the case of governmental threats, there is also no mutually exclusive division between those who are being threatened and those for whose benefits the threats are issued. If, for example, general deterrence works, then threatening to punish anyone who harms the innocent, as well as punishing offenders, reduces the risks of innocent people being harmed.

The claim that the pursuit of general deterrence involves the improper use of persons, therefore, does not carry much weight. The rules prohibiting certain forms of conduct are intended to benefit all, and they apply equally to all. Violations of these rules are reduced by the threats of punishment, and by the actual punishment of malefactors. The conditions under which punishment is to be meted out are reasonably avoidable. On the other hand, potential victims of crime cannot reasonably avoid being harmed by increased criminal activities brought about by the failure to operate a system of general deterrence.

If we now take the discussion back to Yuso's case, we can see that it is fair to use him to deter others from criminal acts. This does not mean that he consented to being punished. He did not, but his consent is not necessary in order to justify his punishment. It also is not necessary that Yuso should be related to potential offenders in the way that he is related to the hospital orderlies who avidly listen to his tales of sadism. The relevant consideration is that they are potential offenders who would have committed acts similar to Yuso's if he were not punished, and he ought to be aware of this fact. They need not be identifiable individuals. So in this respect, what holds true for Xavier, Wong, and Vassary applies equally to Tom, Dick, and Harry.

Philosophy, Monash University

GETTING EVEN: THE ROLE OF THE VICTIM

By Jeffrie G. Murphy

Not if his gifts outnumbered the sea sands
or all the dust grains in the world could Agamemnon
ever appease me – not till he pays me back
full measure, pain for pain, dishonor for dishonor.

Iliad (IX.383–386)

I. Introduction[1]

Achilles is vindictive; he wants to get even with Agamemnon. Being so disposed, he sounds rather like many current crime victims who angrily complain that the American system of criminal justice will not allow them the satisfactions they rightfully seek. These victims often feel that their particular injuries are ignored while the system addresses itself to some abstract injury to the state or to the rule of law itself – a focus that appears to result in wrongdoers being treated with much greater solicitation and respect than their victims receive. If the actual victims are noticed at all (other than to alert the state to a violation of *its* interests), they will likely be told that there is another branch of law – tort law – that has the job of dealing with private injuries and grievances and that, if they pursue this route at their own expense, they might ultimately get some financial compensation for the wrongs done to them. However, just as Achilles felt that mere compensation was inadequate to the kind of injury done to him by Agamemnon, many of these victims will often claim that the injuries they have suffered (brutal rape, perhaps) do not admit of financial compensation. How, they might ask, can a dollar value be set on the humiliation and degradation they have experienced? They might also note that those who injure them tend, unlike Agamemnon, to be judgment-proof – so lacking in resources as to be unable to make any meaningful contribution to any compensation package that the victim may win. From such a perspective and from such feelings has the "victims' rights movement" in part been born.[2]

[1] The present essay builds on some ideas initially developed in ch.3 ("Hatred: A Qualified Defense") of *Forgiveness and Mercy,* by Jeffrie G. Murphy (Chapters 1, 3 and 5) and Jean Hampton (Chapters 2 and 4), (Cambridge: Cambridge University Press, 1988).

[2] The phrase "victims' rights movement" refers to those who advocate changes in criminal law and procedure that will (at least in their view) make crime victims more satisfied with the system. Rules of evidence that make it harder for defense attorneys to probe a claimed rape victim's sexual past, finding ways to allow claimed victims of child abuse to testify with less embarrassment or fear (e.g., on video or behind a screen), and allowing crime victims to influence criminal sentencing (e.g., by presenting victim impact statements to the sentencing judge) are examples of developments that may be viewed as victories for the victims' rights movement. The 1987 United States Supreme Court case of *Booth v. Maryland,* where victim impact statements were ruled unconstitutional in capital cases, may be viewed as a setback for the victims' rights movement. (This case will be discussed below.) It should be noted that the phrase "victims' rights" is

In this essay I will address simply *one* of the many issues raised by this movement – namely, the issue of the legitimacy of hatred and desires for revenge as operative values in a system of criminal law. It is widely assumed – as a part of liberal culture, particularly Christian liberal culture – that such psychological states are either unambiguously evil or unambiguously sick and that, in either case, they deserve no place in the moral and legal outlook of civilized people. Thus opponents of the victims' rights movement will often characterize it as simply the institutionalization of vindictiveness – where such a characterization is supposed to serve as a *reductio ad absurdum* of the movement. Proponents of the movement will then generally take great pains attempting to show that the movement is *not* based on these admittedly evil feelings but on something else – social utility or justice, perhaps. Thus, both sides seem to agree that if the movement is indeed based on these feelings and the desire to institutionalize them, then the movement is a mistake.

Since I am skeptical that this agreement is justified, I will in this essay attempt to do two things: (1) I will suggest that the burden of proof should be placed on those who in principle *oppose* hatred, vindictiveness and revenge – that someone other than the champions of these responses should be put on the defensive for a change; and (2) I will suggest that this burden might not be as easy to bear as some might initially think. My purpose is neither to celebrate hatred and its close cousins nor to argue positively that this feeling and its associated practices should be built into the criminal law. I rather seek to expose some bad arguments against it and its institutionalization (but also to highlight some important arguments against it) in the hope that its possible role – and indeed the whole victims' rights movement – can be seen in a clearer and fairer light.

II. Who Has the Burden of Proof?

As a starting point in inquiry, I am inclined to accept what might be called a bias or presumption in favor of common sense – namely, that absent some good argument to make us withdraw our common-sense beliefs and attitudes, we should regard them as reasonable. We should not always feel obligated to defend our ordinary views, but should rather impose the burden of challenge on others – being honestly willing, of course, to abandon the comfort of the received wisdom if we are indeed provided with good arguments for so doing. The underlying assumption behind this bias or presumption can, I think, partly be understood in (loosely) evolutionary terms. Our ordinary views and attitudes must, at least at one time, have had *something* going for them – some useful and adaptive contact with our social world or with the world of nature. Otherwise, it would be hard to see why

importantly misleading as a characterization of some of the practices noted above. Since the use of a victim impact statement occurs after a criminal conviction (though prior to sentencing), the word "victim" here is appropriate. Prior to a conviction, however, we do not know for sure that we actually have a victim; all we know for sure is that we have an *accuser*. Thus it would be better if those who favor such things as shield laws to prevent unnecessary probing of an alleged rape victim's sexual past would refer to these practices as a matter of "accusers' rights." Also, is it correct to refer to these practices as *rights* at all, or should they simply be characterized (by those who favor them) as good policy?

these beliefs and attitudes would survive and be so deeply entrenched in our psyches. Of course, some beliefs and attitudes that might have been adaptive at some distant time in our evolutionary history (e.g., racist beliefs and attitudes, perhaps) can properly be seen in present circumstances as maladaptive, irrational, and evil. But we come to see this, I assume, not because this was always obviously so (it clearly was *not*), but because we have listened to and been persuaded by overwhelming practical and moral arguments for a change in these beliefs and attitudes. Such an example, however, does not demonstrate the unreasonableness of a presumption in favor of common sense any more than the confident conviction of some guilty people demonstrates the unreasonableness of the presumption of innocence in criminal procedure.

In my role as armchair, anecdotal social scientist, I have come to the conclusion that most of us *do* accept, as a matter of common sense, the appropriateness of hatred and revenge in some circumstances – specifically, when these responses are exhibited by victims of serious wrongdoing and are directed against those who have wronged them. (In *Forgiveness and Mercy,* I call this "retributive hatred."[3]) Although most people pay a kind of general Sunday school lip service to the idea that even these hatreds are evil, their more casual conversations and practices will often fly in the face of these pious clichés. Give them the right criminal (e.g., John Mitchell for Watergate era liberals) and they will warm to shared fantasies of giving that criminal his "pain for pain, dishonor for dishonor." This also comes out rather clearly in people's entertainment preferences. For example, I recently resaw (with some equally civilized and equally liberal friends) the movie *Silverado.* In this classy Western, we are presented with four honest and decent men (and their friends and families) being subjected to unspeakable injuries by thugs of unspeakable evil. When, in the closing moments of the movie, these men take – and, indeed, *gleefully* take – their violent revenge on those who have wronged them, all who watched cheered them on and found this outcome not only aesthetically pleasing but morally satisfying. And I think that the vast majority of other normal people would have experienced a comparable reaction – otherwise, how could we explain the great popularity of revenge entertainment? We like to see the portrayal of evil people getting their painful but just deserts, and we particularly enjoy it when these deserts are administered by their victims. Portrayals are, of course, fiction and fantasy – and many of those who approve of the fictional portrayal of revenge might still have deep and even final objections to having it occur in the real world. (Perhaps, for example, they believe that we are never actually able to know that we confront the kind of genuine evil that is simply a given in the world of fiction – that, unlike The Shadow, we are unable to know what evil lurks in the hearts of men.) But this is a practical objection; it makes no contribution to establishing that all feelings of hatred and revenge are intrinsically, or inherently, or in principle irrational or immoral. Feelings that we genuinely regard as inherently depraved (e.g., racial hatred) we would not even welcome as fantasy or fiction; thus, I think,

[3] Although I tend to support the legitimacy of what I call retributive hatred, I am inclined to agree with Willard Gaylin's claim that much anger and hatred in contemporary culture is – though understandable – irrational and maladaptive. See his *The Rage Within: Anger in Modern Life* (New York: Penguin Books, 1989).

we would have great doubts about a person who applauded the fictionally portrayed successes of a Nazi deathcamp commandant – even if he followed up his entertainment by saying "But, of course, I would hate to see this happen in the real world." Thus I think that most typical, decent, mentally healthy people have a kind of commonsense approval of some righteous hatred and revenge (but not of simply unprovoked malicious hatred or racial hatred) and are in some sense willing publicly to admit this, at least symbolically – e.g., they will stand without shame in line to see such revenge movies as *Silverado*, but not to see a film that glorifies racial hatred.

So perhaps we can grant that those who are willing to take the trouble to present a case in favor of some hatreds and acts of revenge are really seeking not to challenge but simply to reinforce common sense – that most people, even if unwilling to provide verbal endorsement of such a view, do in fact find it acceptable in principle for victims to resent and hate those who wrong them and to seek revenge against those who victimize them.[4] (Perhaps Christianity's victory over pagan common sense here is largely verbal.) But, if this is so, then it looks as though we have the beginnings of an argument for the institutionalization of these feelings – an argument from *democracy*. For what is a democracy except a form of government in which the majority gets to have its dominant preferences enacted into law – even if those preferences are condemned by a refined and condescending elite? Thus, if most people want to create a system of criminal law that institutionalizes and expresses the hatreds and desires for revenge that crime victims feel toward those who have wronged them, what principle would allow anyone to say nay to the will of the people thus expressed?

This principle, perhaps: that the fundamental rights of citizens may not be abridged even when the majority so desires. Such a principle defines a *constitutionally constrained* democracy (as opposed to a pure democracy) and characterizes the kind of democracy at least theoretically present in the United States. Thus, since one of the presupposed principles of this society is that the government may not treat people (even criminals) in brutally inhuman ways, the United States Constitution imposes (in the Eighth Amendment) an absolute ban on

[4] Those who have come out in support of some instances of hatred and revenge include God ("Vengeance is mine ... etc."), Aristotle (*Nicomachean Ethics*, 1125b ff.), Adam Smith (*The Theory of Moral Sentiments*, Indianapolis: Liberty Press, 1982, p. 38), James Fitzjames Stephen (*A History of the Criminal Law of England*, London, 1883, Vol. II, pp. 81ff.), Ernest van den Haag ("In Defense of the Death Penalty," *Criminal Law Bulletin*, Vol. 14, No. 1, Jan.–Feb. 1978), Walter Berns (*For Capital Punishment*, New York: Basic Books, 1979), and Robert Axelrod (indirectly – as an endorsement of the strategy of "tit for tat" in iterated prisoner's dilemmas – in his *The Evolution of Cooperation*, New York: Basic Books, 1984). I also present a supportive case for these responses in *Forgiveness and Mercy*. In this book I suggest that, in addition to the social usefulness of these responses in some contexts, some considerations of *vice* and *virtue* also offer relevant support – namely, that a person's failure to resent wrongs done to him and to manifest retributive hatred toward the wrongdoer may be a sign that he has the vice of *servility* (a lack of proper self-respect and a lack of proper tendencies for self-defense). I would hate to have readers unfamiliar with the book conclude from the present paper that I see no moral and social problems with retributive hatred, however, so let me note that the book contains numerous qualifications and cautions with respect to my defense of this emotion – qualifications and cautions that considerably constrain the domain of its legitimacy. No doubt the reader will want to check this out, and I recommend that he do so by purchasing – preferably in the hardcover edition – a copy of the book.

such "cruel and unusual" punishments as torture.[5] This ban is not to be seen as an expression of the will of the people; it is rather a principled check, an absolute side-constraint, on what the people will be *allowed* to will.

I think that this constitutional excursion dramatically reinforces the point I want to make about burden of proof here. We may, I think, regard American society as one in which the majority may do whatever it jolly well feels like *unless* one can demonstrate that what it feels like doing is *fundamentally wrong in principle.* (I take it that the Bill of Rights seeks to provide an initial – but not a final – analysis of what it means to say that a governmental act is fundamentally wrong in principle.) To use my earlier language: the presumption is that the will of the majority should determine policy, and thus the burden of proof lies upon those who – for any majoritarian outcome – would seek to prevent it. My question, then, is this: can it be shown to be fundamentally wrong in principle for the suffering that criminals receive from the state to be contingent to any degree on hatreds and desires for revenge felt by their victims? Do criminals have a fundamental right to be shielded from the consequences of such feelings? Since I think I have shown that it is not obvious that they do (and that, in fact, people, tend to believe quite the contrary), those who would argue for the irrelevance or injustice of those feelings and their institutionalization should do just that – namely, *argue.* They have the burden of proof. I will thus now begin to explore what these arguments might be and the degree to which, if at all, they are successful.

III. Making the Case Against Hatred and Revenge

Those who condemn hatred and revenge can avail themselves of two different strategies of argument. They can argue (1) that the emotions involved in these responses are inherently irrational (like phobias) or inherently evil (like sadism or unprovoked malice). Or they can argue (2) that, whatever the merits of the emotions themselves (even assuming they are intrinsically splendid), it would either be unwise or wrong in principle for these emotions to have any effect on the administration of criminal punishment. (Some – e.g., Kant – have reasoned this way about compassion and mercy – suggesting that compassion, though a splendid and admirable emotion in itself and often productive of wonderful results in other contexts, may produce excessive acts of mercy – and thus undermine justice – if too influential on judges or those with the power of pardon.[6]) While (2) is my primary interest in this paper, it is so frequently tied in with (1) that I think it will be worthwhile to discuss and evaluate them both in the present context.

[5] Amendment VIII of the United States Constitution reads as follows: "Excessive bail shall not be required, nor excessive fines imposed, nor cruel and unusual punishments inflicted." This has been interpreted by the United States Supreme Court to rule out such inherently barbaric punishments as torture, punishments that are radically disproportionate to the gravity of the offense, and the punishment of death when administered in an arbitrary and capricious fashion.

[6] Might not hatred and compassion stand or fall together with respect to criminal punishment? If it is wrong to increase a criminal sentence out of hatred, will it not also be wrong to decrease a criminal sentence out of compassion? Can one consistently be meticulous and strict about justice only in one direction? Perhaps we tend to be more lax about mercy because we think that the compassion on which it is based is, unlike hatred, an acceptable or even admirable emotion. But this, of course, needs to be shown. For Kant's discussion, see his *The Metaphysical Elements of Justice* (Indianapolis: Bobbs-Merrill, 1965), p. 107.

IV. The Rational Case Against Hatred

Surely hatred cannot be regarded as irrational simply because it is an emotion. Emotions (e.g., guilt, shame, fear, envy, jealousy, hatred, love, and compassion) are not like mere sensations (e.g., headaches): one sign of this is that we can speak sensibly of irrational emotions but not of irrational headaches or other sensations. (What is a phobia except an irrational fear? And what would it mean to call some fears irrational unless it makes sense to refer to others as rational?) Of course we sometimes speak of people themselves as being irrational if they allow emotions to dominate their personalities to an excessive degree – e.g. Spinoza's point about a rational person being one who is not *led* by a fear of death.[7] But is there any good reason to assume that hatred and desires for revenge are uniquely able to dominate or lead in a way that other emotions are not? Consider the character of Michael Kohlhaas in von Kleist's famous story.[8] Why will so many people say of a character such as Kohlhaas that he was overcome, or dominated by, or in the thrall of vindictiveness – but would not tend to describe (for example) Mother Teresa as overcome, or dominated by, or in the thrall of compassion? (Is this anything more than a misleading way of noting that one likes compassion and does not like vindictiveness? Is a moral point masquerading as a psychological point and a question thereby being begged?) The literature of hatred and revenge does, of course, tend to portray these responses carried to a pathological extreme, but this may tell us more about what makes literature interesting than anything basic about human psychology. (What a boring story it would have been had Kohlhaas simply beaten up a couple of people and taken his horses back.) Surely *any* emotion can be carried to a pathological extreme; does not the fact that we can identify pathological extensions of retributive hatred (e.g., Michael Kohlaas's) suggest that there must be non-pathological instances of this emotion? And must this emotion have an inevitable tendency to provoke excessive behavior – as it did for Kohlhaas? What if the person is provoked by this emotion to seek only a level of revenge that we, on other grounds (utility or justice), would find acceptable? Are there no such people? Are all people who seek revenge really after consequences so extreme and socially disruptive that we must regard them as crazed? (It is, of course, question-begging to say that these feelings are irrational simply because they often prompt people such as Kohlhaas to act outside the law. For perhaps these feelings prompt people to illegality only because we, not learning the lesson of Athena and the Furies, have refused to make a proper home for them and institutionalize them into the legal system.) And consider Nietzche's famous argument against *ressentiment* (a kind of hatred) – namely, that it tends to poison a person from within.[9] But why, according to Nietzsche, does it so poison? It is because it is *repressed*; thus, Nietzsche's point argues equally for getting rid of the emotion *or for expressing it* – e.g., through getting even.

[7] *Ethics*, Four, LXVII.

[8] Heinrich von Kleist's 1810 story *Michael Kohlhaas* portrays a man who, when he fails to receive legal justice over a comparatively small injury done to him (theft and abuse of his horses), takes matters into his own hands. In his pursuit of revenge, he forms an army, kills large numbers of people, and nearly topples the government under which he lives. This story was retold by E. L. Doctorow in his 1975 novel *Ragtime* – wherein Michael Kohlhaas becomes Coalhouse Walker.

[9] *On the Genealogy of Morals*, Essay I, Section 10.

We might, of course, regard an emotion as irrational if it lacks any point or purpose that we can understand or with which we can sympathize. John Rawls argues in this way, for example, about the emotion of (malicious) envy. For what is the point, Rawls asks, of simply desiring that another lose some benefit when that benefit was not wrongfully acquired and when the benefit, when lost, will not transfer to the malicious envier?[10] Although I think that Rawls's position is not without problems, I will for present purposes grant it. Analogous arguments will not obviously condemn retributive hatred as irrational, however, since this emotion (with which, I have already argued, most of us sympathize) often has as its point the desire to annul (perceived) wrongful gains and to give people their (perceived) just deserts – in short, to "get even" through revenge. That, and not something further, is its point. Unless the desire to bring about these states of affairs is itself always wrong or irrational, then surely the emotion of retributive hatred – as a desire to bring them about – cannot be condemned as pointless and thus as irrational. (One would surely not want to give as one's argument against retributive hatred an appeal to some notion of pointlessness that would, if accepted, refute all deontological considerations in ethics.) But is revenge acceptable? I will explore this question in the final section of the paper, but it would, of course, beg the question simply to assume at this point that it is not.

The above considerations suggest to me that it is going to be very difficult to make a case that hatred (as a desire for revenge) is inherently irrational – the moral equivalent of a phobia. Though obviously (because by definition) pathological extensions of this emotion will not be present in a rational person, a lesser degree might well play some roles in the psyches of rational and healthy people – e.g., prompting them to seek restitution for injuries, liberating them from the bondage of resentment (through getting even), maintaining their self-respect, and even (by making themselves known as disposed to revenge) warding off some aggressors who might otherwise challenge their security and invade their "moral space." Thus if a case is to be made against the emotion of retributive hatred itself, the case will have to be *moral* – a case that the emotion, however rational it may be in some prudential or therapeutic sense for the person who experiences it, is still evil and would not be present in a truly virtuous person. It is to this moral case that I will now turn.

V. The Moral Case Against Hatred

The idea that hatred and desires for revenge are evil dispositions of character is linked, in our Christian culture, to the idea that these dispositions are *sinful.* God, through Jesus Christ, commands that we love and forgive our enemies rather than seek from them the "eye for an eye" that was characteristic of the older law.[11] If

[10] *A Theory of Justice* (Cambridge: Harvard University Press, 1971, secs. 80 and 81).

[11] Matthew 5:38–48. The older law is well represented in Psalms 58:10–11: "The righteous shall rejoice when he seeth the vengeance: he shall wash his feet in the blood of the wicked. So that a man shall say, Verily there is a reward for the righteous." In Aeschylus's *Oresteia,* the Furies represent sentiments of this kind. Athena refuses to banish them, however, because she respects the impulses they represent and believes that, by institutionalizing them under due process of law, she can make them such valuable forces in support of community morality that they will become known as "the kindly ones."

somebody embraces the Christian religion (so interpreted), then such a person does have – in my view – a sufficient moral reason to regard hatred as a vice and all acts based upon it as evils. All argument on the issue could thus stop here, as arguments have a way of doing when they collide with total faith.

My present inquiry, however, is this: does the moral case against retributive hatred essentially depend upon such faith or can a case that does not depend upon religious belief – a purely secular case – be made? I think that such a case may be possible and, indeed, that it might be possible even to draw a large part of the case from a secular interpretation of some Christian parables. This should not be surprising, since many Christians wish to regard their God as a supremely rational being. If so, He presumably did not command love and forgiveness of enemies capriciously (e.g., He did not flip a coin to get this command) but rather knew that such dispositions were of some benefit to us, His creatures. But if God had good reasons for issuing these commands, it is not impossible that we – with our reason – could discover at least part of the case that prompted Him and see its good moral sense for ourselves.

Consider, with this in mind, the story of Jesus at the stoning of the adulteress (there cautioning the crowd to "Let him who is without sin cast the first stone").[12] Think of this story in conjunction with the famous passage, "Vengeance is mine; I will repay, saith the Lord."[13] Consider also the parable of the unforgiving servant.[14]

The fact that God reserves vengeance for Himself suggests that, in His view, the desire for vengeance is not an inherently irrational (or even inherently evil) disposition of character. (Otherwise, God would be condemning Himself.) It is rather that He has reasons for claiming that the disposition to vengeance is a uniquely divine prerogative. What might these reasons be? Presumably they are that only God *knows enough* and only God is *good enough* to seek vengeance reliably and without hypocrisy. His creatures lack these epistemological and moral qualifications; they must therefore wait and depend upon God to get the job done.[15] Thus these scriptural passages can be interpreted to mean that human beings, given their radical limitations, always manifest vices – specifically, the vices of *presumption* and *hypocrisy* – if they have and indulge feelings of retributive hatred.

[12] John 8:7.

[13] Romans 12:19.

[14] Matthew 18:21–35.

[15] God seems to promise that the job of vengeance will get done. Is this to reassure His creatures that their hated enemies may not go eternally unpunished? But why should He pander to His creatures' desires for vengeance, unless these desires are in some sense both rationally and morally legitimate on their part? May these creatures not even look forward with delight to the coming divine retribution on their enemies? May they not even have pleasing fantasies of it? When it happens, may they not look down from heaven with delight at the torments of their enemies below? Is God here in some sense promising (like Athena) to "institutionalize" (in His divine law) these legitimate feelings and thereby make their personal expression unnecessary? I raise these questions not to be impious, but simply to make the point that the "Vengeance is mine" passage can be read simply as a command that humans not *act* on retributive hatred – leaving open the possibility that *feeling* retributive hatred is neither an evil nor a vice. I do not believe that the simple command to love and forgive one's enemies is comparably ambiguous, however, for here feelings themselves are clearly the object of the command.

Is this claim plausible? Are we too ignorant to be reliable retributive haters? Are we ourselves too morally flawed to hate, without hypocrisy, those who wrong us? Let us consider each of these questions separately.

What is it that we are unable to know about wrongdoers that poses no problem for God? We surely know what *acts* are unacceptable, and thus perhaps the problem is supposed to lie in some lack of ability we have in knowing the *mental states* and *dispositions of the will* present in wrongdoers. Kant, for example, claims that only God can "know the heart"; given his view that moral condemnation is addressed to the inner disposition of will, he argues (in his *Religion*, but not elsewhere) that human ignorance of such matters precludes the acceptability of the kind of harsh condemnation of others that legitimately hating them would involve.[16]

I think that this argument is important – one that should make us (as I stress in great detail in the book) *very cautious* of what we do in this area – but I am not convinced that it makes a fatal case against the moral legitimacy of all retributive hatred. For Kant is well known as being (to put it mildly) in favor of punishment; given his commitments to justice, he would want to condemn strenuously a system of punishment that employed only strict liability. This means, of course, that he would (like us) want a system of criminal liability that involves *mens rea*, excuse, and justification. But such a system can be administered only if, *in some sense*, we *can* "read the heart." Thus those who would make flip arguments against retributive hatred based upon some supposed inability to determine the appropriate inner dispositions should note the massive (and certainly unwelcome) reforms in the criminal law – and perhaps in our whole moral conception of personal responsibility – that would flow from the literal acceptance of such a slogan.

So too, I think, for those who would make an overly ambitious use of the important insight that each one of us is morally flawed ("Let him who is without sin...") and often stands in need of some gentle response, such as forgiveness from others (a point of the parable of the unforgiving servant). For such things are in fact, of course, matters of degree. That I have certain vices (a certain lack of generosity, perhaps) does not mean that I ever have or ever would even contemplate treating another human being in the way that Michael Kohlhaas was treated by those who wronged him, or in the way that some rape victims are brutalized by their attackers. Thus it seems that although I may not be utterly without sin, I may well be without sin *in the relevant sense* in some cases. And why may I not, without hypocrisy, indulge retributive hatred in these cases? John Rawls has taught us the useful device in ethics of imagining ourselves in all possible roles that will be affected by the moral rules we adopt. As one who may sometimes need the love and forgiveness of others, I will of course want a world where retributive hatred does not reign unchecked. But as someone who may sometimes want to get even for terrible wrongs done to me, I might not want to create a social world

[16] For a discussion of those aspects of Kant's moral philosophy that appear to be in tension with his commitments to retributivism, see my "Does Kant Have a Theory of Punishment?" in *Columbia Law Review*, Volume 87, No.3 (April 1987).

wherein desires for revenge are utterly condemned – regarded as, in themselves, signs of irrationality or vice.

Finally, there is the argument from moral equality. According to this argument (often appealed to by Christians), all human beings are of equal moral worth – perhaps even absolute moral worth – and are to be equally loved, because it is both irrational and immoral for any one of these creatures to rule any of his equals outside the domain of benevolent concern – as hatred certainly does. (In religious terms, this Kantian point might be made by saying that we are all children of God and equally beloved in His sight; that God's perspective should then be adopted in our own dealings with our fellow humans.) To this argument I have the following response: that all human beings (no matter how morally vile) are to be loved strikes me as a claim whose *intrinsic implausibility* is staggering. Thus, I can imagine no reason for taking such a claim seriously unless one views it as a command of God – i.e., one therefore has an *extrinsic* reason for taking it seriously. Here, then, we perhaps have a good example of an ethical issue where a secular world view leads us in one direction and the Christian world view leads us in quite another – perhaps dashing any hasty optimism (present, I think, in some strands of liberal Christianity) about the ultimate compatibility or reconciliation of the two.[17]

I conclude from the above that the case against the rationality and morality of the emotion I have labeled retributive hatred has not been made. Thus, I think that we may properly retain our common-sense belief that this feeling is sometimes acceptable – and sometimes even laudable. Those of us who want to retain the concept of genuine evil – in discussing the Holocaust perhaps – the perpetrators of which merit hatred are not yet defeated. As noted earlier, however, this does not establish that it is ever permissible for us to *act* on such feelings or that the law should ever assist us in so acting. Desires for revenge are one thing; acts of revenge are quite another. Thus I shall now move to a consideration of the permissibility of revenge itself.

VI. The General Case against Revenge and Its Role in Criminal Law (Especially Sentencing)

By "revenge," I will mean any injury inflicted on a wrongdoer that satisfies the retretributive hatred felt by that wrongdoer's victim and that is justified because of that satisfaction.[18] I here assume again (for the reasons earlier noted) that the

[17] Suppose I am willing to grant that hatred would properly be addressed toward me if I performed (with full responsibility) certain evil acts. Perhaps I would even resent it and regard it as an insult (because it would challenge my status as a responsible moral agent) if such hatred was *not* directed toward me in these circumstances. If I then address such hatred to others when they (with full responsibility) perform such acts, it is not clear that I violate any important equality demand. Saint Augustine tells us that we should "hate the sin but not the sinner." But if it is permissible to hate the act because it is bad, why is it wrong to hate the actor because he is bad? Of course, if the wrongdoer sincerely *repents,* this may block the legitimacy of hating or even resenting him – a theme I pursue in Ch.1 of *Forgiveness and Mercy.*

[18] Revenge is not to be identified with vigilante activity, and indeed I will assume for purposes of this paper that anyone who seeks revenge in ways that are illegal acts wrongly (not to mention uncreatively). The issue that I mainly want to explore, of course, is if the law itself should find a way of institutionalizing some of this revenge and thereby perhaps eliminate some temptations to self-help. I will also be assuming throughout that we are dealing with cases where the victims are not fantasizing the wrongdoing but have accurate beliefs that

burden of argument lies on those who would oppose the legitimacy of revenge, and I assume that the arguments given will (like all arguments in ethics) be either consequentialist arguments or arguments of principle.[19] I also believe that the really impressive and important arguments will be those of the latter sort.

Why might revenge be disutilitarian – wrong on consequentialist grounds? The most common thing said against it is that it is socially disruptive – it is likely to provoke an unpredictable and destabilizing level of conflict. But this argument, of course, seems most impressive as an argument against *private* revenge – vigilante activity – and, if this is the only argument, really supports rather than undermines the claim that revenge ought to be institutionalized by the state: that is, that the state, taking on the personae of crime victims, should elevate (at least some of) the private grievances of individuals to the status of public grievances. If revenge is not intrinsically evil or wrong in principle, why should its public expression not be justified by these two consequences: (1) the satisfaction given to victims and (2) the resulting tendency to defuse the potentiality for private revenge and its resulting social turmoil?[20] (This does not mean that the state should take on all desires for revenge – some are excessive – but it does suggest reasons why the state might take on some of them.) And consider the standard utilitarian value of deterrence: might not potential criminals be given an extra incentive to remain law-abiding if they know that they live in a system where victim outrage (or, in murder cases, survivor outrage) might have a bearing on their level of punishment?[21]

The above considerations suggest that the purely utilitarian or consequentialist case against the institutionalization of revenge is going to be fragile. Some utilitarian arguments will tell against the practice, and others will tell in its favor;

---

they have been wronged, accurate beliefs about the nature and degree of the wrong done to them, and accurate beliefs that the wrongdoer is as fully responsible for that wrongdoing as any human being ever is for any wrongdoing.

[19] Some people might also suggest virtue arguments, but I am suspicious of their use in this context. For example: it is often suggested, as an argument against capital punishment, that it is wrong because of what it does to the characters of those who favor and inflict it – namely, it degrades and debases and dehumanizes them. But this is by no means obvious. In my view, a person is debased by the doing of X only if X is wrong (unjust, say), and thus – absent an independent showing that X is wrong – the character debasement argument will not get off the ground. Similarly, engaging in revenge will debase people only if it can be shown, on independent grounds, that revenge is wrong. So too for the common "two wrongs do not make a right" cliché that is often trotted out here. Obviously, those who regard revenge as justified will not see it as a wrong; they will thus quite properly fail to see the relevance of the cliché to their claim.

[20] This, I take it, is the point of James Fitzjames Stephen's famous analogy between the criminal law and the law of marriage (see note 4). He argued that we deal in each case with a passion that is legitimate (the desire for revenge in the one case and sexual desire in the other), but we have also learned that the passion in question has high potential to provoke disruptive behavior. Thus, the way to honor the passion without risking serious social disruption is for the law to regulate that passion – to provide it with a proper channel for expression. Taking victim hatred seriously in this way (by building it into legal practice) may thus benefit both the community and the victims themselves, for the practice recognizes the validity of the hatred while placing important constraints on its excess. Such institutionalization might even help to educate persons on the legitimate bounds of hatred.

[21] One might, of course, argue that such a deterrent system is unpredictable – an acceptable consequence from the point of view of deterrence, perhaps, but a disutilitarian consequence from many other points of view (e.g., liberty). I think that this is an important argument. However, since I think that unpredictability is an evil essentially because of its *unfairness* rather than because of its potentially disruptive social consequences, I will treat this as an objection of principle in the next section.

an impartial observer might well conclude that the latter arguments, on balance, win the day. This is, of course, often the case with utilitarian arguments on complex issues; we often, after all, lack the kind of hard empirical evidence that would be needed really to establish the probability of the claimed consequences. We thus often run the risk of lapsing into anecdotes and hunches that are often tailored to the outcome we want to justify. For this reason, those who want a *fatal* argument to block the institutionalization of revenge had better attempt an argument from principle, for one great virtue of such arguments is that they are invulnerable to the shifting winds of empirical guesswork.

Are there good arguments that institutionalized revenge is wrong in principle? I think that there are two that must be taken very seriously:

(*1*) *The Argument from Retributive Justice.* "All criminals have a fundamental right not to be punished in excess of their just deserts. A person is punished in excess of his just deserts if he is punished with greater severity than the blameworthy character of his conduct would justify. A person cannot coherently be held blameworthy for the degree to which he is hated by those he wrongs (very blameworthy for injuring thin-skinned victims and minimally blameworthy for injuring stoic victims?), and thus any criminal sentencing that takes account of victim hatred (as any revenge system would have to do) violates a fundamental right, is unjust, and is thus wrong in principle."

(*2*) *The Argument from Equal Protection and Due Process.* "All criminals have a fundamental right to be protected against sentencing procedures that are inherently arbitrary and capricious. Sentencing systems based on victim hatred will inevitably have this feature and are thus wrong in principle."

These are very important arguments. (They were also the essential arguments at issue in the 1987 United States Supreme Court case of *Booth v. Maryland* – a case, regarded by many as a major setback to the victims' rights movement, holding that victim impact statements may not influence sentencing in capital cases.[22]) I take these arguments seriously, and I would like to consider them with some care. I will consider them in reverse order.

VII. The Argument from Equal Protection and Due Process

The best argument that revenge systems are inherently arbitrary and capricious lies in the fact that retributive hatred – the basis for such systems – is essentially a *subjective* response to being wronged; as such, it can vary enormously from one victim to the next. Thus, the very same injury that will be brushed off as trivial by those with a stoic disposition will generate anguish and deep hatred in the highly sensitive. Also, the level of hatred involved might well be a function of factors about the criminal that any reasonable person would regard as clearly irrelevant to culpability – e.g., the white rape victim who feels more deeply wronged if raped by a black person than if raped by a white person. If fairness requires that potential

[22] 482 U.S. 496 (1987). A victim impact statement is a statement from the crime victim or some representative of the victim that seeks to influence sentencing by stressing the impact of the crime on the victim and the victim's desires (or perhaps the survivor's desires in a murder case) with respect to the sentence.

criminals receive accurate notice of the exact nature of the proscribed conduct and its attached penalties, it is hard to see how such notice could be given in a system where sentencing might actually depend upon factors that admit of such wide and subjective variation.[23] And if criminals have a right to be protected against mere prejudice (e.g., racial hatred), it might seem difficult if not impossible to give them this protection in a hate-based system, since hatreds often are a function of prejudices. I am by no means sure that it would not be possible to design procedures that would keep arbitrary and capricious sentencing at an acceptable level – i.e., at a level no greater than that already present and accepted at other points in the system – but we have at last found a principled objection to revenge that cannot simply be summarily dismissed. Those who look fondly upon revenge have an obligation to take this objection very seriously – i.e., seriously enough to recognize that the burden of argument may now have been properly shifted back to them and to take on the burden of formulating procedures to control these potential abuses. Of course, if it can be shown that criminals have a fundamental right to be sentenced in proportion to personal blameworthiness and that revenge is inconsistent with such a right, then we have the basis for an absolute ban on revenge (an absolute ban on its institutionalization) regardless of procedure. The procedural argument is thus secondary to what I have called "the argument from retributive justice," and it is to this most important argument that I shall now turn.[24]

VIII. The Argument from Retributive Justice

In *Booth v. Maryland* Justice Powell, writing for the majority, held that victim impact statements (VISs) are constitutionally impermissible in capital sentencing. Such statements – or actual testimony by victims if they are allowed to attend and speak at sentencing hearings – are very likely, according to Powell, to influence judges (or juries in states where juries have a sentencing role) to inflict cruel and unusual punishments. Their use and influence thus violates the Eighth Amendment.[25]

[23] Expressions of hatred might, of course, be *evidence* that something of assumed relevance to criminal liability – e.g., the existence of a certain level of *harm* – is present. I will explore this idea a bit later in the paper. As Ellen Paul has pointed out to me, one could argue that if criminals knew that they would face varying degrees of punishment based on the degree of hatred felt by their victims, they would factor this into their calculations of advantage/disadvantage before committing the crime. A rational criminal might then presume that his victim might be one with great capacity for hatred, and this might augment the deterrent value of the law. The criminal, by committing an illegal act, puts himself willingly and knowingly (but within limits, of course) in a kind of punishment lottery with respect to the harm that actually results from what he does. So why not a comparable lottery (again within limits) with respect to hatred and desires for revenge that might be felt by his victim?

[24] Had the United States Supreme Court held that capital punishment is, like torture, inherently cruel and unusual punishment, consideration of the procedural problems surrounding the administration of that punishment would never have achieved their current prominence. The reason why *Furman v. Georgia* (408 U.S. 238 (1972)) and most later death penalty cases have dealt primarily with procedural matters – the desire to avoid arbitrary and capricious capital sentences – is that the Court has held that the penalty of death is *not* inherently cruel and unusual – at least with respect to some crimes of murder. Thus, it is not surprising that, in America, most principled legal objections to the death penalty now take a procedural form.

[25] The Court did not clearly indicate what it will rule on VISs in non-capital cases. In capital cases, of course, the VISs are not primary victim impact statements (the primary victim being dead) but rather statements from concerned survivors – e.g., family members considered as secondary victims.

Powell essentially gives two arguments to support this view. One argument (a procedural one of the kind explored above) is that emotional appeals from attractive and articulate victims are likely to focus the judge's attention away from the legally relevant issues and produce arbitrary and capricious sentencing.[26] More fundamental than this procedural argument, however, is Powell's articulation of the principle that, in his view, defines what *is* legally relevant. Speaking essentially as a retributivist, Powell claims that criminal defendants in capital cases have a right that their sentence be solely a function of their personal *blameworthiness* – i.e., factors solely based on "the character of the individual and the circumstances of the crime" or on the defendant's "personal responsibility and moral guilt." Since VIS information may be, according to Powell, wholly unrelated to the blameworthiness of a particular defendant, and may cause the sentencing decision to turn on irrelevant factors such as the degree to which the victim's family is able to articulate grief and defend the victim's worth, such evidence will inevitably and improperly shift the focus away from the defendant and what he deserves. The essence of the argument, then, is this: sentencing should be based on what is morally blameworthy about the defendant; one is blameworthy only for that which is one's fault or which one brings about under one's own control; the degree to which a victim will be upset or outraged by what is done to him or will be able to articulate feelings is subjective and variable; it is thus not within the defendant's control; therefore, it would be wrong in principle to let sentencing depend to any degree on such matters.

Given the wide variety of penal purposes that are often articulated by judges in sentencing (see, for example, Judge Frankel's well-known sentencing opinion in *U.S. v. Bergman*[27]), it is odd that Powell should only emphasize the one retributive purpose of making suffering proportional to blameworthiness. (I will, for present purposes, ignore the special problems posed by the fact that *Booth* is a capital case, since I am interested in victim revenge and VISs in general.) We know that judges – both in sentencing and in approving plea-bargain agreements – typically weigh such factors as jail crowding, likelihood of recidivism, impact on the defendant's family, the defendant's age and health, possible service the defendant might perform for the community, the need for special and general deterrence, the need for incapacitation, and the possibility of reform; none of these having any obvious connection with moral blameworthiness or any other valid retributive purpose. It is hard to see, if this long laundry list of (perhaps laudable) social and personal goals properly gets to play a role in sentencing, why it would be wrong in principle to find room for VISs as well.

[26] It is not made clear why this poses any greater problem than that posed when the same victim appears as a witness during trial. Freedom from cross-examination, perhaps? Might it not be possible to allow such cross-examination at a sentencing hearing?

[27] *United States v. Bergman*, United States District Court, S.D.N.Y., 416 F. Supp. 496 (1976). Rabbi Bergman, owner of several nursing homes, had been part of a scheme to defraud the United States government with respect to Medicaid payments. In his sentencing opinion, Judge Frankel explores a variety of punitive purposes that he believes must be weighed: retribution, community outrage, community support for the Rabbi because of his many philanthropic ventures, special and general deterrence, etc.

Consider also the major (and, no doubt, quite unwelcome) reforms in the criminal law that a literal application of the moral blameworthiness principle would entail. As Justices Scalia and White noted in their dissents in *Booth*, we currently feel comfortable with making the penalty for successful murder more severe than that for an attempted murder that fails through a fortuity; yet it is obvious that the moral blameworthiness in the two cases is identical. We also punish reckless driving that kills much more severely than reckless driving *simpliciter*; yet, as Thomas Nagel would say, it is surely differences in "moral luck" rather than any differences in moral blameworthiness that distinguish the two cases.[28] Thus a decision to endorse some strong blameworthiness principle will not be cost-free; for it will force us to ignore other important factors – e.g., *harm* caused – that have typically been thought to be central to criminal liability. And with respect to the other factors, it is by no means obvious that VISs will be utterly irrelevant to them. For example: can the victim's personal response to the person who violated him tell us *nothing* about the degree of harm suffered? Is the revenge interest present in the victim worthy of no attention in a world where (for example) the community's supposed interest in service that the defendant might perform is regarded as relevant? All of this needs to be thought about much more deeply.[29]

But perhaps blameworthiness should be viewed simply as a *negative* retributive constraint on permissible punishment – a factor that sets an upper bound on the degree to which the state may legitimately pursue its other interests in punishing (e.g., crime deterrence). This might solve, for example, the puzzle about attempts. For even if attempters and succeeders have the same degree of blameworthiness, the state might have good reasons for punishing attempters less severely; no wrong will be done in such a system so long as the succeeders are not punished in excess of their just deserts understood as a function of their moral blameworthiness.

If we accept this weakened notion of retributivism, however, it is hard to see how this will form a principled objection to the institutionalization of victim revenge and the use of VISs. For, on this view, why not simply allow these factors to have influence – perhaps to counter sentimental tendencies to show mercy or make plans for community service – so long as their influence is capped off at the point when maximum just deserts for the offense is reached? This would, of course, simply be to restate Stephen's point: respect victim hatred and revenge, but institutionalize them so that their excesses can be constrained by other values equally worthy of respect in a system of criminal law.

IX. Conclusion

Let me close these ruminations on hatred and revenge by considering one final challenge to them. I can imagine a critic now arguing as follows: your case for

[28] Thomas Nagel, "Moral Luck," in his *Mortal Questions* (Cambridge: Cambridge University Press, 1979).

[29] The problem being noted here is that of the inconsistency of insisting on a blameworthiness basis for punishment in a system that gives the same weight to harm that most systems of criminal law currently do. This does not entail abandonment of a blameworthiness basis, of course, for one might instead avoid the inconsistency by arguing on retributivist grounds for the abandonment (or considerable qualification) of the relevance of harm. For an exploration of this issue, see Stephen J. Schulhofer, "Harm and Punishment: A Critique of Emphasis on the Results of Conduct in the Criminal Law," 122 *University of Pennsylvania Law Review* 1497 (1974).

hatred and revenge within the limits set by blameworthiness and desert has saved hatred and revenge at a very high price – namely, you have made them *redundant*. If these responses must operate within a context defined by retributive just deserts, then how does the account of punishment you call hatred-based revenge differ from what Kant, and Herbert Morris, your own previous self, and others have simply called retributivism?

My short response to this is the following: I have elsewhere argued that, given a traditional liberal-libertarian conception of the state (as modelled in social contract terms), it is hard to see why there is any important state interest served in securing retributive values – in seeing that wrongdoers get their just deserts – for the sake of these values themselves.[30] If rational contractors were forming a state, it is easy to see why they might give up some liberty and resources to protect themselves against assault (a basic human desire) by adopting a deterrence scheme of criminal law. It is very hard, however, to see why they would do this simply to achieve a state of affairs that seems of merely abstract worth – namely, one where wrongdoers get their just deserts. In short: given the rarity of an intense sense of abstract justice, classical retributivism seems unmotivated within liberal theory.

If desires for revenge are basic and important to many people, however, this would provide some motivational grounds – in victim hatred – for those schemes of criminal justice we tend to call retributive; securing the revenge interests involved might, even in traditional liberal terms, prompt social contractors to be willing to make the sacrifices necessary to maintain a (constrained) system of revenge. Abstract concern for justice might explain the blameworthiness cap on punishment, but garden variety desires for revenge may generate – and quite properly generate – some of the values that drive the system up to that point.[31]

I will not, however, press this argument. If a consequence of my view is that it will ultimately be impossible to draw a sharp distinction between the desire for retributive justice and the desire for revenge, then this in itself will put revenge in better philosophical company than it normally enjoys. Perhaps it will achieve the kind of impartial re-hearing for hatred and revenge that it has been the primary purpose of this essay to provoke.[32]

[30] See my "Retributivism, Moral Education, and the Liberal State" in *Criminal Justice Ethics*, Vol. 4, no. 1 (Winter/Spring, 1985). For a skeptical attack on the common idea that there is a sharp distinction in principle between criminal law (with the state as injured party) and tort law (with individual victims as injured parties), see my "Why Have the Criminal Law at All?" in ch. 3 of *The Philosophy of Law: An Introduction to Jurisprudence*, by Jeffrie G. Murphy (Chapters 1, 2 and 3) and Jules L. Coleman (Chapters 4 and 5) (Totowa: Rowman and Allanheld, 1984). (A revised edition of this book will appear from Westview Press in late 1989.)

[31] Even Herbert Morris's very abstract notion of criminal punishment as annulment of wrongful gains or unfair advantages (in his "Persons and Punishment," *The Monist*, Volume 52, Number 4, October 1968) may ultimately depend not upon some abstract sense of justice (the desire to see justice done for its own sake) but on something very like victim revenge. What, on Morris's theory, motivates me to want the criminal (as free-rider) punished? That he has taken an unfair advantage of those who have been law-abiding. But that means, given that *I* am one of those who has been law-abiding, he has taken unfair advantage of *me* – he has derived a wrongful gain at *my* expense. If this is what is most vivid in my mind (as it surely will be), then in what sense is my desire to see him punished impersonal and not a kind of victim revenge?

[32] Most philosophical defenses of retributivism (including some of my own previous essays) take great pains to distinguish retribution (which is taken to be just) from vengeance (which is taken to be unjust or evil in some other way). Perhaps such attempts at drawing a sharp distinction have been misdirected.

Let me now close by summarizing the main thrust of my argument. Crime victims often want to influence sentencing, and their motives for this are often vindictive. Perhaps such motives are dishonorable; perhaps giving a legal role to victims so motivated would indeed produce deep harm to our system of criminal justice. I have attempted to show that this has simply been assumed and not demonstrated, however, and that – in fairness to those victims – it should be demonstrated before the state simply dismisses as irrational or evil the passionate claims of those whom it has failed to protect from criminal violence.

Law and Philosophy, Arizona State University

ON THE COMMON SAYING THAT IT IS BETTER THAT TEN GUILTY PERSONS ESCAPE THAN THAT ONE INNOCENT SUFFER: *PRO* AND *CON*

By Jeffrey Reiman and Ernest van den Haag

Introduction: The Punishment Constraint

Truism and Core

In *Zadig*, published in 1748, Voltaire wrote of "the great principle that it is better to run the risk of sparing the guilty than to condemn the innocent."[1] At about the same time, Blackstone noted approvingly that "the law holds that it is better that ten guilty persons escape, than that one innocent suffer."[2] In 1824, Thomas Fielding cited the principle as an Italian proverb and a maxim of English law.[3] John Stuart Mill endorsed it in an address to Parliament in 1868.[4] General acceptance of this maxim continues into our own period,[5] yet it is difficult (and for us so far, impossible) to find systematic attempts to defend the maxim. It is treated as a truism in no need of defense. But the principle within it is not at all obvious; and since it undergirds many of our criminal justice policies, we should be sure that it is justifiable. First, however, we must clarify what the principle means.

Since the principle is intended to constrain our punishment policies, we will, for simplicity's sake, refer to it as "the punishment constraint." If the task were to

The following debate originated when the authors found that they had inconsistent intuitions about Blackstone's famous saying, but no serious arguments. A search of the literature produced none; so we set to work. Our Introduction offers an analysis of Blackstone's phrase and of some arguments; it is by both authors. Accordingly, it is written in the first person plural. The "Pro" section offers the views of Jeffrey Reiman and is written by him; the "Con" section expresses the views of, and is written by, Ernest van den Haag. All the sections have been revised in light of the comments of both authors, but each is wholly responsible for the section he wrote. To Professor van den Haag goes the credit for suggesting the subject and the idea for the debate. Peter Darvas assisted in the literature search.

[1] Jean Francois Marie Arouet de Voltaire, *Zadig, or Fate*, in *Candide and Other Stories* London: Dent & Sons, 1962), p. 20.

[2] William Blackstone, *Commentaries on the Laws of England*, 21st ed. (1765; London: Sweet, Maxwell, Stevens & Norton, 1844), bk. IV, ch. 27, p. 358. In his *History of the Pleas of the Crown* (1694), Sir Matthew Hale put the ratio at 5:1; George Fletcher (*Yale Law Journal* 78 [1968], p. 881) uses 20:1. There has been some inflation since Sir Matthew.

[3] "Thomas Fielding, *Proverbs of All Nations*, p. 59 (1824). Citing an Italian proverb, which is also a maxim of English law, Fielding says it originated in Italy, and that Dr. Paley was against it, while Blackstone and Romilly approved of it" (*The Macmillan Book of Proverbs, Maxims, and Famous Phrases*, ed. B. Stevenson [New York: Macmillan, 1948], p. 1249).

[4] Hansard, "Parliamentary Debate on Capital Punishment Within Prisons Bill," April 21, 1868.

[5] For example, in the widely-read essay "Persons and Punishment," Herbert Morris describes an ideal criminal justice system (not far from an idealized version of our own) as one in which it is thought "a greater evil for society to interfere unjustifiably with an individual by depriving him of some good than for the society to fail to punish those that have unjustifiably interfered" (Morris, "Persons and Punishment," *The Monist* 52, no. 4 [October 1968], p. 479).

prove the literal truth of the claim that it is more than ten times worse to punish an innocent person than to acquit a guilty one, it could not be accomplished. We possess neither moral intuitions nor moral theories which could establish such a specific ratio. However, we can separate the core content of the constraint from the specific ratio proposed. After all, the truism is not a carefully quantified principle, but a slogan meant to convey a message quickly and memorably.

Shorn of rhetoric, the punishment constraint asserts that *it is morally worse to punish innocent people than to acquit guilty ones.* This is the part of the constraint that most matters, since, if we came to believe that punishing the innocent was no worse than acquitting the guilty, our criminal justice policies should change in important ways. For example, we might lower the standard of proof of guilt in criminal cases.

If this seems to make the constraint vaguer than the truism, other considerations make it more specific. The constraint has at least the following two renderings: (1) it is morally worse *to punish the innocent intentionally* than it is *to acquit the guilty intentionally*, and (2) it is morally worse that *unintentional punishment of the innocent occurs* than that *unintentional acquittal of the guilty occurs.*

The first of these formulations will be the natural starting point of those whose moral views are deontological – particularly Kantians – since they are concerned primarily with what people do intentionally. The second formulation will be the natural starting point of those whose moral views are consequentialist – particularly utilitarians – since they are concerned primarily with the consequences of actions, intended or not. We shall consider both deontological and consequentialist arguments for the punishment constraint. Therefore, it will be useful to have a single formulation that can be evaluated from both moral perspectives. Toward this end, we get some help from the fact that no moral principle can guide our behavior unless it can translate into differences in how we are to act intentionally. Form (1) gives this directly, but form (2) does not. For (2) to guide behavior – even for consequentialists – it must be translated into something like: (3) it is morally worse *to risk punishment of the innocent intentionally than to risk acquittal of the guilty intentionally.*

This rendering covers intentional acts of punishing the innocent or acquitting the guilty, treated as cases of intentionally risking high likelihoods of these occurrences. And it also applies to the acts of those who make criminal justice policies which determine the risk of these occurrences. But, most important, (3) is a formulation upon which both consequentialists and deontologists can converge from their divergent starting points. Consequentialists can think of (3) as a translation of the ranking stated in (2) into possible courses of action among which they can choose. Deontologists, on the other hand, can think of (3) as an extension of what one may rightly do intentionally as stated in (1). Of course, those who emphasize intentions are not indifferent to consequences, nor are those who emphasize consequences indifferent to intentions. The Kantian, for example, considers the moral worth of consequences by asking for the moral worth of intending them. And the utilitarian considers the moral worth of intentions by asking for the moral worth of the consequences they intend. Nonetheless, this difference in emphasis and direction is important. We shall accommodate it by considering justifications of the constraint in the form of (3), and allowing that such justifications may follow a path that starts at (1) or (2).

This is possible because judgments of comparative worth, like ratios, remain constant across changes in the values of their components as long as all components change in the same way. Hence, whatever difference is made by the change from doing or occurring to risking, since the difference will apply equally to all the components of our judgments, the judgments of comparative worth should hold across that difference. Thus, all other things being equal, if it is worse to do X intentionally than it is to do Y intentionally, then it is worse to risk a probability p of X intentionally than a probability p of Y. (If it is worse intentionally to kill than to injure someone, then it is worse to risk a given likelihood of killing than to risk the same likelihood of injuring someone.) And, likewise, all other things being equal, if the occurrence of X is worse than the occurrence of Y, it is worse to risk a likelihood p of X intentionally than it is to risk a likelihood p of Y intentionally. Thus, while it is the constraint in form (3) rather than (1) or (2) that must be defended, we can assume that, all other things being equal, arguments for (or against) propositions (1) or (2) are arguments for (or against) proposition (3).

Some Bad Arguments for the Punishment Constraint

A number of ways which might seem to prove the correctness of the constraint do not, on close inspection, work. Some may think that since God will punish the wicked in the hereafter, not punishing them on earth does not mean that they won't get what they deserve, whereas punishing the innocent inflicts something that they do not deserve. Even if God compensates them in the hereafter, they did suffer undeservedly. Thus we do injustice in punishing the innocent, but only delay justice in not punishing the guilty. Therefore, it is worse to punish the innocent than to acquit the guilty. However, this argument rests on a religious belief as contestable as the truth of the constraint. Thus, the former cannot provide firm support for the latter. Principles of justice must rest on purely secular criteria.

Others may think that they can prove the constraint by showing that it conforms to people's intuitions. They might set up examples of the following sort: "One of two identical twins is witnessed committing cold-blooded murder. It is impossible for anyone but the twins to tell themselves apart and each claims that he was elsewhere when the murder was committed. You must choose between executing both or acquitting both." Since you would choose the latter (wouldn't you?), you regard it as *worse* to punish an innocent person than to let a guilty one escape punishment. The example-giver might then increase the size of the suspect family. "Two of three indentical triplets are witnessed committing cold-blooded murder (etc). You must choose between executing all three or acquitting all three." Since you would still choose the latter (wouldn't you?), this implies even more strongly that you regard it as worse to punish an innocent person than to let a guilty one escape punishment. Such exercises in intuition-testing are revealing. But they cannot give us what we need, because intuitions are creatures of our upbringing and character, and susceptible to the same errors to which our rearers and teachers are susceptible. Moreover, the wide acceptance of the punishment constraint already shows that it conforms to people's intuitions. It is these very intuitions that must be tested once we question the constraint; thus, they cannot (without vicious circularity) be marshaled to justify it.

A third strategy might resort to the moral distinction between acts and omissions. Just about everyone thinks that it is worse to put a bullet in a person's head than to fail to send food to someone starving in Bangladesh, though the result in both cases is the death of an innocent person. Presumably, even where the results are morally comparable, it is worse to bring them about by action than by omission. Therefore, even if the results (considered in isolation) were morally comparable, it would be worse to punish an innocent person than to fail to punish a guilty one, since the first is an act and the second an omission. But this won't do, because the acts-omissions distinction is not merely a matter of whether or not energy is exerted toward some end. Much depends on whether there are preexisting obligations. For instance, where a person has a preexisting obligation to try to save another's life (the kind of obligation that physicians have toward their patients), then intentionally refusing to try to prevent a threat to their lives from succeeding is morally indistinguishable from intentionally causing that threat to succeed. If one is responsible for feeding a starving person (e.g., one's child), then intentionally refusing to do so is morally no better than actively taking food from that person. Now, the proper subjects of the punishment constraint are those who are entrusted with responsibility for meting out punishments in our society. These people have preexisting obligations both to punish the guilty and not to punish the innocent. Their failure to punish the guilty cannot get an automatic moral discount because it is an omission. If their obligation to punish the guilty is as strong as their obligation not to punish the innocent, then failure at the first obligation is as bad as failure at the second. This leaves us with the task of determining the relative strength of these obligations, which is where we were before taking up the acts-omissions distinction.

Another strategy that may appeal to some is linguistic. It is contended that the problem is logically impossible because punishment means a harm imposed on someone because he is guilty; thus it is not possible to "punish" the innocent. But punishment of the innocent can no more be eliminated by reference to the meaning of words than punishment of the guilty was eliminated by calling it "corrections." The issue here is not words, but actions. It has to do with doing to innocent people what, when done to the guilty, we call "punishment," whether or not it is linguistically proper to continue to so call it. Thus we can understand the punishment constraint as including under the term "punishment" the things that, when done to those we think are guilty, we call punishment. And then it is obvious that we cannot get rid of the problem by waving our dictionaries at it.

Having cleared the field of some appealing but ultimately disappointing proposed solutions, we are now ready to consider more serious arguments for and against the punishment constraint.

I. Pro: Three Arguments for the Punishment Constraint (Jeffrey Reiman)

The Argument from Retributivism

Retributivism is the view that punishment is justified because criminals deserve it, rather than because of any benefits that punishment produces. Accordingly, retributivists are hostile to punishment of the innocent, and thus it would seem that there would be ample support for the punishment constraint from this quarter. However, the constraint is not a matter of the absolute wrongness of punishing the innocent, but of the relative wrongness of this, compared to that of not punishing the guilty. And retributivists are very insistent that the guilty be punished. Indeed, some are as insistent on this as they are hostile to the punishment of the innocent. Retributivism, then, while holding that we have a duty not to punish the innocent, might hold as well as that we have an equally strong duty to punish the guilty. And that would deny the truth of the punishment constraint.

To consider this possibility, I shall formulate retributivism in terms that lead to the strongest denial of the punishment constraint. I call this formulation "strong retributivism." It holds, first, that the *lex talionis* is the proper measure of punishment, that is, that criminals ought to be punished (as nearly as is feasible) with harm equivalent to that which they intentionally caused their victims; and, second, that intentionally failing to so punish criminals is as bad as intentionally committing their crimes. In addition, I shall assume (for like crimes and punishments, à la *lex talionis*) that committing a crime against an innocent person is as bad as punishing an innocent person. This assumption is, I think, highly questionable, since (as I suggest later) there is a special awfulness in being punished undeservedly. Nonetheless, this questionable assumption serves to strengthen the retributivist case against the punishment constraint and since I aim to test the strongest retributivist case, I adopt the assumption *per argumentum*. With it, strong retributivism implies denial of the punishment constraint because, if failure to punish the guilty is as bad as committing a crime against an innocent victim, then it is as bad as punishing an innocent person.

Strong retributivism draws its inspiration from views held by Kant and Hegel. Kant held that it is our duty to punish the guilty with harm equivalent to that which they have intentionally caused their victims, and that failure to fulfill this duty places the guilt of the offender upon us.[6] Hegel held that punishment annuls crime, and that failure to punish is tantamount to allowing the crime to continue to exist.[7] Whether either Kant or Hegel would have endorsed the whole of the doctrine that I call "strong retributivism" is not important for our purposes. What is important here is that this doctrine provides the strongest retributivist claim that could be made for the badness of not punishing criminals, and thus the strongest retributivist argument against the punishment constraint. If the punishment constraint can be defended against this argument, then it can be defended *a fortiori* against milder retributivist views on this issue.

[6] Immanuel Kant, *The Metaphysical Elements of Justice, Part I of the Metaphysics of Morals*, tr. J. Ladd 1797; (Indianapolis: Bobbs-Merrill, 1965), p. 102.

[7] G.W.F. Hegel, *The Philosophy of Right*, tr. T.M. Knox (1821; Oxford: Clarendon Press, 1962), p. 69.

I contend that the strong retributivist denial of the punishment constraint cannot be maintained. The argument that I shall make has two features that may strike the reader as odd, because retributivism is a doctrine that is generally inhospitable to questions of the sort posed here. Thus we shall have to bully retributivism just a bit to get it to give us answers to those questions. I claim, nonetheless, that these strongarm tactics do not disfigure retributivism and that the answers we get are true.

The first unusual feature of the argument is that we shall have to get retributivism to yield measures of the relative badness of not punishing guilty people compared to that of punishing or criminally victimizing the innocent. This will seem odd since retributivists normally speak of evil acts as simply evil, without reference to their degree of badness. Indeed, it may even sound like attributing relative (negative) utility functions to these acts, and thus like mistranslating retributivism into utilitarianism. However, such relative measures are not incompatible with retributivism. Even retributivists need to measure the relative badness of wrong acts so that they may determine their appropriate degree of retribution. Retributivists must also compare the relative size of evils when they must choose between them. The general disbelief with which philosophers greet Kantian insistence that it is wrong to lie even to prevent murder suggests that retributivism goes awry when it refuses to allow such relative measures.

To measure the relative badness of wrong acts, we must rank – according to their gravity – the injuries to which those acts give rise. Some may suspect that this imports a forbidden reference to consequences into retributivism, which is a deontological and thus not a consequentialist doctrine. But this suspicion rests on a straw-man conception of deontological ethical views. Deontological ethical doctrines are ones that do not determine what is right by what maximizes some kind of consequence – such as satisfaction – which is counted good. This does not imply that consequences play no legitimate role whatsoever in deontological theories. Quite the contrary, no deontological theory could get off the ground if it did not consider at least the immediate consequences of the acts it condemns.[8] There is no way, for example, to distinguish surgical cutting from murderous stabbing except by reference to the different consequences the two actions have or are intended to have. And there could be no reason for calling one right and the other wrong without referring to those consequences.[9] A deontological condemnation of murderous action, then, would not be one that condemned the action wholly irrespective of its consequences, but one which condemned that action-with-its-intended-consequence-of-death irrespective of its further consequences, such as its contribution to aggregate satisfaction.

[8] "It should be noted that deontological theories are defined as non-teleological ones, not as views that characterize the rightness of institutions and acts independently from their consequences. All ethical doctrines worth our attention take consequences into account in judging rightness. One which did not would simply be irrational, crazy" (John Rawls, *A Theory of Justice* [Cambridge: Harvard University Press, 1971], p. 30).

[9] One exception to this might be a theological deontological ethics that took its duties strictly from God's commands. We can exclude this possibility since, for reasons mentioned in the previous section, we are limited to secular considerations.

Once consideration of the direct negative impact of wrongful behavior is seen to have its rightful place in deontological ethical theories, then it is permissible to take the next step and rank wrongful behaviors by the relative gravity of their negative impacts.[10] In what follows, I shall try to rank the wrongful behaviors of punishing the innocent and not punishing the guilty by the relative gravity of their direct negative impacts. And I shall do that by identifying the parties to whom the duties of not punishing the innocent and of punishing the guilty are owed, and then comparing the losses to those parties of failures in those duties.[11] Bear in mind that I am not claiming that deontological duties are required *because* they are owed to these parties or *because* of the harm that failure in the duties causes these parties. I claim only that we can use those harms to measure the relative badness of failures in the different duties. Since I shall ignore any further losses (or gains) likely to result from these failures, we shall not cross the boundary that distinguishes retributivism from consequentialist doctrines such as utilitarianism. There will be none of utilitarianism's concern with aggregate satisfaction, and, of course, no consideration of the deterrent effects of punishing.

The second unusual feature of the argument that follows is this. Since retributivism generally resists the sort of relative judgment that we need to get from it, we shall find it hard to show that failure to acknowledge the relative judgment contained in the punishment constraint leads to the forms of doctrinal perdition (such as absurdity or self-contradiction) into which philosophers normally try to force their quarry. We can, however, show that failure to acknowledge the relative judgment contained in the constraint leads to conclusions which render retributivism implausible. Although it is not *logically* impossible for a retributivist to deny the punishment constraint, I shall argue that such a denial cuts from under retributivism the beliefs that lend it support, and therefore makes it harder for anyone but extreme diehards to endorse it.

To show this, I shall make use of the assumption that (for crimes and their punishments of comparable harm à la *lex talionis*) punishment of the innocent and crime against the innocent are equally bad. If this is so, then, it follows that to deny the punishment constraint, retributivism must insist that nonpunishment of the guilty is as bad as crime against the innocent. But, once we consider the losses that the various failures of duty impose on those to whom they are owed, we shall see that the claim that nonpunishment of the guilty is as bad as crime against the

[10] It is because Kant did not take this step that his theory is pilloried for not accounting for the permissibility of lying to prevent murder. But there is nothing in Kant's theory that rules this step out. Kant's test of universalization of maxims can be applied to maxims that state priority relations between actions just as easily as it can be applied to maxims that refer directly to specific actions. That I cannot universalize the maxim that one may lie when it is convenient does not imply that I cannot universalize the maxim that one may lie when (and only when) necessary to prevent some other immoral (i.e., nonuniversalizable) action, such as murder.

[11] Though I do not want to assert generally that deontological theories view duties as owed to specific persons, there is nothing non-deontological about treating duties this way. For example, retributivists often hold that the victim of an offense has the right to pardon his offender and thus spare him from the punishment he deserves. (See, for example, Kant, *Metaphysical Elements of Justice*, pp. 107–8.) This makes sense on the assumption that the duty to punish offenders is owed to victims. This is Hegel's view, too. See *Philosophy of Rights*, tr. T. Knox (London: Oxford University Press, 1969), sec. 100.

innocent is implausible. To be plausible, then, retributivism must accept that crime against the innocent is substantially worse than nonpunishment of the guilty. But, since punishment of the innocent is as bad as crime against the innocent, it follows that, to be plausible, retributivism must grant that punishment of the innocent is substantially worse than nonpunishment of the guilty.

Granting, then, that we have a duty to punish the guilty and a duty not to punish the innocent, to whom are these duties owed? In the case of the latter duty, the answer is not far to find. The duty not to punish the innocent is owed to the innocent. Things are not as open-and-shut with the other duty, however. The duty to punish the guilty may be thought to be owed either to the guilty criminal or to his innocent victim or to all the law-abiding citizens in the society. The first of these may seem implausible, but, since some philosophers have gone so far as to speak of an offender's "right to punishment,"[12] it must be thought of as at least a possible candidate. In any event, rather than trying to adjudicate among these three possibilities, I shall consider them all. We can then compare the loss that undeserved punishment (or comparable crime) imposes on the innocent with the loss to the criminal, to the victim, and to law-abiding citizens generally, imposed by failure to punish the guilty. Bear in mind that, for reasons already mentioned, whatever the losses to the law-abiding are from not punishing the guilty, lack of deterrence cannot be reckoned among them.

Suppose first that punishment of the guilty is a duty owed to the guilty. If it is, and even if – as implausible as this is – the failure in this duty imposed a loss on the guilty comparable in gravity to that imposed on the innocent by punishing (or committing crime against) the innocent, it still seems undeniable that it is worse to impose a loss on an innocent person than on a guilty one. If retributivism were to deny this, it would undermine the importance of the distinction between guilt and innocence as decisive in determining the treatment to which people are rightly entitled. And since this distinction is the very spine of retributivism, undermining it would lead the doctrine to implausibility.

The case where we take punishment of the guilty criminal as owed to his innocent victim is a harder one. Remember here that strong retributivism embraces the *lex talionis,* such that a crime of harm X is to be dealt a punishment of harm X. We must ask, then, whether – for a given crime and its appropriate punishment – failing to punish the guilty criminal imposes a loss on his victim that is as bad as the loss that punishing the innocent imposes on the innocent. Since crimes and punishments are to be equivalent in harm, we can think of punishing an innocent person for the crime of X as equivalent to committing that very crime on him. Then we can translate our question into the following: for a given crime and its appropriate punishment, does failing to punish the guilty criminal impose a loss on his victim that is as bad as the loss that the crime imposed on the victim? It seems clear that however greatly the victim of a crime wants his victimizer to be punished, a person undergoes a greater loss in being the victim of a crime than in having his victimizer go unpunished. A crime causes its victim more palpable

[12] For example, see Morris, "Persons and Punishment," pp. 475–76.

harm, subtracts more from his ability to pursue his own purposes, than the failure to punish another person. And since punishment of the innocent is as bad as crime against the innocent, punishment of the innocent must be worse than acquitting the guilty. Denying this undermines the importance of the badness of crime against the innocent which, for retributivism, bears the weight of justifying punishment in the first place. Thus it, too, would drive retributivism toward implausibility.

When we turn to the third case, where the duty to punish the guilty is taken as owed to law-abiding citizens generally, we find that most of our work is already done. To preserve the nonutilitarian nature of retributivism, we exclude consideration of all losses that failure in the duties to punish the guilty and not punish the innocent would lead to beyond the immediate losses to those to whom the duties are owed. If we consider the duties owed to the law-abiding generally, then we must consider the losses to them without considering the further consequences of failure in the duties, such as increases or decreases in the likelihood of the law-abiding being victims of crime or of undeserved punishment. With such further consequences eliminated, the question reduces to that of whether any given law-abiding person would suffer more from being a victim of undeserved punishment (or of the comparable crime) than from having the criminal who victimized him go unpunished. And that is the same question as the one posed previously to the actual victim of crime, and receives the same answer.

The crux of the matter is that any plausible retributivist theory must recognize the fact that, however strong the duty to punish the guilty criminal is, failure to do so cannot be as bad as his committing his crime was. And since punishing the innocent is (at least) as bad as committing a crime against the innocent, any plausible retributivist theory must acknowledge that it is substantially morally worse to punish the innocent than to acquit the guilty. This conclusion is directed to *intentionally* punishing and acquitting. It also implies that it is substantially morally worse *to risk the occurrence* of punishment of the innocent *intentionally* than *to risk the same likelihood of the occurrence* of acquittal of the guilty *intentionally*. Thus, to be plausible, retributivism must agree with the punishment constraint. Bear in mind here that I have not proven that it is always wrong on retributivist grounds to increase the likelihood of punishment of the innocent. I have argued only that, to be plausible, retributivism must regard it as substantially worse to do that than to cause a similar increase in the likelihood of acquitting the guilty.

The Argument from Utility

Utilitarianism ranks all possible alternative policies according to their expected contribution to aggregate net satisfaction (that is, the sum of all the resultant satisfactions minus all the resultant dissatisfactions of all the people affected by the policies under consideration). A policy's utility is its contribution to increasing this sum; its disutility is its contribution to decreasing it. That policy is right which has the highest net expected utility. If we compare punishment of an innocent person with nonpunishment of a guilty one, *without reference to their wider consequences,* it is obvious that punishing an innocent person produces considerable disutility, while not punishing a guilty person produces little if any disutility at all. Even if we count the frustrations such nonpunishment will produce for the victim and his friends, this will surely be small compared to the dissatisfaction that the innocent one would have experienced in being punished. Thus, considered in isolation, not punishing the guilty will produce little if any disutility, and surely less disutility than punishing the innocent.

But this is not the whole story. The utilitarian cannot consider either punishing or not punishing the guilty or the innocent in isolation from their wider consequences. Though punishing some number of guilty persons causes suffering and thus subtracts from aggregate utility, it is thought to deter some number of potential criminals from committing crimes against the innocent. And this is thought to have a multiplier effect such that for each guilty criminal punished, several potential criminals are deterred. If this is so, then (for crimes and punishments comparable in the suffering they produce) punishing the guilty will decrease expected suffering overall and add to expected aggregate utility. Moreover, if the deterrence of this number of potential criminals is caused by punishing some number of guilty persons, then *not* punishing these guilty people will leave this number of potential criminals undeterred. Since the number of those undeterred (due to nonpunishment) exceeds the number unpunished in the same amount as the number deterred (by punishment) exceeds the number punished, it follows that (for comparable crimes and punishments) not punishing the guilty will increase expected suffering overall and subtract from expected aggregate utility *by the same amount* as punishing the guilty decreased expected suffering and added to expected aggregate utility.

In the previous section, I assumed that punishing an innocent person was comparable (not identical, of course) to committing a crime against an innocent victim. It is arguable, however, that for crimes and punishments which are similar in intended harm (such as murder and execution), punishing an innocent person is considerably worse than committing a crime against an innocent victim. The victim of a crime is generally surprised by his victimizer and is thus spared the terrible contemplation of his impending fate. The innocent victim of wrongful punishment, by contrast, has plenty of time to contemplate his fate, and to experience not only the painful knowledge of his punishment but also the knowledge of how undeserved it is. However, even if the suffering or disutility that results from punishing the innocent is greater than what results from criminally victimizing the innocent, it is not infinitely greater. It follows that if punishment of the guilty deters enough criminals, it will result in more utility than punishment of the innocent results in disutility.

Suppose that punishment of each guilty person deters n potential criminals, while punishment of one innocent person produces t times as much suffering as a comparable crime committed against an innocent victim. Then, as long as $n > t$, punishment of a guilty person will produce more utility than punishment of an innocent person will produce disutility. Since deterrence can affect thousands, maybe millions, of people simply by their knowledge that criminals are punished, it seems reasonable to grant that in general $n > t$. Then, since not punishing a guilty person will produce disutility equal in quantity to the utility produced by punishing a guilty person, it follows that not punishing a guilty person will produce more disutility than punishing an innocent person will. And then, on utilitarian grounds, it will be false that it is morally worse that punishment of an innocent person occurs than that nonpunishment of a guilty person occurs. And this implies that the punishment constraint rendered as (2) is false.

How does the falsity of (2) affect the truth or falsity of the punishment constraint understood as (3)? It has already been suggested that, all other things being equal, an argument against (2) is an argument against (3). And this is true, as long as all other things are equal. I grant that, on strict utilitarian grounds, it cannot be maintained generally that it is always morally worse that punishment of an innocent person be risked than that an equal likelihood of acquittal of a guilty one be risked. Indeed, if the innocent is punished while generally believed guilty, this may increase the deterrent effect, and if the guilty one is acquitted while generally believed innocent, this may not lessen the deterrent effect.

But this last point suggests something sticky about utilitarian moral arguments: namely, that they are dependent on what people can actually be expected to come to believe. It is not, after all, that the guilty get punished that deters others from committing crimes – it is that the others come to believe that the guilty get punished that deters. Utilitarianism justifies punishment of the guilty on the assumption that this is the most effective way of making it widely believed that the guilty are punished. This is, to be sure, a plausible assumption. But note that it is necessary to appeal to such plausible assumptions about what people will come to believe in order to get from utilitarianism to punishment. After all, if it could be assumed that there are equally effective ways of getting people to believe that the guilty are punished without punishing them, then utilitarianism would have to opt for these over punishments, since these produce all the utility of deterrence without the disutility of actually punishing.

If utilitarianism must appeal to plausible assumptions about what people will come to believe about existing punishment policies, then all candidate punishment policies must be considered in light of similar plausible assumptions, such as the following: if a criminal justice system (in a society such as our own) were to adopt the policy of intentionally punishing the innocent for deterrent purposes, the news would leak out. Further, if such a system were to tolerate a large risk of punishing the innocent, the news would get out. And if such a system were to reverse the punishment constraint and be willing to tolerate as large a risk of punishing the innocent as of acquitting the guilty, that news would get out. And it seems to me that any of this news would be deeply troubling to the citizenry, enough to change profoundly their understanding of their relationship to their government. This in turn might have the effect of shifting the utility to be expected from any such policy. In short, I grant that if a society abandoned the punishment constraint and *this fact was generally unknown*, utility might increase as a result. However, in light of utilitarianism's general dependence on plausible assumptions about people's beliefs, and of the plausibility of thinking that people will find out what the criminal justice system's actual policies are, we are entitled to consider the utility of adopting or abandoning the punishment constraint on the assumption that people will find out what's actually going on either way. And in that case, if a society abandoned the punishment constraint, utility might decline as a result.

Here we must be more than normally speculative, because our own system is one in which the punishment constraint is widely and deeply honored – so much so as to go generally unnoticed. What deterrence our system accomplishes currently is not easily disentangled from this fact. This means that we cannot take the current level of deterrence as a baseline and assume that increases in deterrence due to increased tolerance of punishment of the innocent are increases from that baseline. Moreover, it also means that it is not easy to imagine what the effect would be of shifting away from the punishment constraint in a way that everyone was aware of. But consider that if you come to believe that your government is not very concerned about preventing punishment of the innocent, this will do more than just increase your risk of being punished undeservedly. It may transform entirely the way in which you view your government, changing it in your eyes from an ally into something else: a violent gang that happens to be statistically less dangerous than the other violent gangs. I think it is hard to overestimate the way in which a willingness on the part of government to tolerate a large risk of punishing the innocent will dramatically increase anxiety, suspicion, anger, and alienation, and (of course) decrease the willingness of citizens to respect, pay for, and cooperate with government voluntarily – which, in turn, may reduce the criminal justice system's capacity to deter crime. And all of these effects will tend to reduce aggregate utility.

I don't know how to calculate the magnitude or probability of these effects, but they seem large enough and likely enough to stop any utilitarian in his tracks who wants to up-end the punishment constraint. Against this, it might be objected that we do not need the punishment constraint to prevent these untoward consequences. All we need is for the government to display a real commitment to taking precautions against punishing the innocent. And it might display such a commitment even if it were willing to risk punishment of the innocent in the same degree as acquittal of the guilty. After all, the punishment constraint is a comparative principle – it does not say anything about how much risk of punishing the innocent is tolerable, only that it be less than the risk of acquitting the guilty. But the magnitudes of these risks only have meaning taken together. The only reasonable justification for tolerating a risk of punishing the innocent is the need – within the limits of existing resources – to reduce the risk of letting the guilty go unpunished. Thus the only way the government can expect its citizens to believe in its commitment to minimize punishing the innocent is by actually treating the risk of punishing the innocent as worse than the risk of not punishing the guilty. And if that is so, then utilitarianism supports the notion that it is morally worse (for governments) to risk a given likelihood of punishing the innocent than to risk the same likelihood of acquitting the guilty.

The Argument from the Social Contract

Although it comes in many forms, the basic strategy of social-contractarian moral reasoning is to imagine people in circumstances in which they must agree on some set of rules, not knowing how they in particular will fare under the rules. Lacking knowledge of their particular fates, they cannot tailor rules to their own advantage; they thus must agree to rules that are reasonable from everyone's point of view. Such rules are arguably fair to all, since they are what all would agree to, subject only to those limitations necessary to keep anyone from taking advantage of anyone else. We can pose our question, then, by imagining people suitably ignorant of whether they will be innocent citizens or guilty criminals, and asking whether it would be more reasonable for all to agree to the punishment constraint to guide criminal justice policies than to agree to some alternative principle.

If punishment is an effective means to deter crime, then, in light of everyone's interest in being secure from crime (an interest shared even by criminals), everyone will have an interest in the existence of some punishment system. People may also have an interest in the satisfaction of seeing wrongdoers suffer, which will add further to their interest in having some punishment system. On the other hand, where a punishment system exists, everyone (even the innocent person) runs some risk of being punished (deservedly or undeservedly), and everyone has an interest in minimizing this risk. This latter interest isn't large enough to outweigh people's interest in the existence of a punishment system entirely, but it does suffice to make it reasonable for all to insist on fairly strict limits on the application of punishment. And it would seem reasonable for all to agree to the punishment constraint as one of these limits for at least two reasons. First of all, even more powerful than everyone's interest in avoiding punishment is everyone's interest in avoiding punishment when they are innocent. I take it that even those who think that punishment of the innocent is no worse than crime against the innocent will grant that undeserved punishment produces more suffering than deserved punishment. (The guilty offender has at least the consolation of having taken the illegal advantage for which he is now paying.) The second reason is that establishing a strong tie between guilt and punishment gives people effective control over whether they get punished. If I can be certain that my government will take every precaution against punishing me when I am innocent, then I have a dependable way of avoiding being punished: avoiding crime. Thus there is at least a *prima facie* case for believing that appeal to the social contract will support the punishment constraint.

But trouble arises for this *prima facie* case in the following way. Suppose that we treat the risk of being undeservedly punished and the risk of being criminally victimized as components of a single risk of undeserved harm that can be measured along a single dimension. Then different trade-offs between the probability of acquitting the guilty (and thereby weakening the deterrent effect) and the probability of punishing the innocent (and thereby substituting state-imposed harm for criminal harm) can be ranked by the overall risk that they pose to the citizen of being undeservedly harmed from any source (straight or crooked). These risks will be weighted in terms of the harms involved; if there is more harm from being punished undeservedly than there is from a comparable criminal injury, this will be factored in (that is, risk of harm will be a product of the magnitude of the harm and the likelihood of its occurrence). It would seem that if we can rank all the possible trade-offs in this way, then the rational thing for all to agree to is the lowest possible risk of undeserved harm from all sources. It is then an open question whether the punishment constraint would provide this lowest overall risk, since it is possible that an even greater deterrence effect may be obtained as a result of relaxing the precautions against mistakenly punishing the innocent. If this were the case, then the argument from the social contract would support some alternative to the punishment constraint.

This conclusion would be valid if the most rational way to deal with risk were to make no discriminations between its various sources and to aim simply at reducing its overall level. But this is not the case. Consider the way in which people's worlds are normally organized with regard to security against risk. At the core, there are some zones which are likely to be very secure (our homes, for example), and then there is a rather sharp drop in security (going from our homes to our neighborhoods, or from our neighborhoods to our cities), and then an additional sharp drop (going from our cities to unfamiliar parts of our nation, or from our nation to foreign nations), and so on. In actual practice, we seem to arrange things in a sharply articulated pattern such that a line describing our security against risk would look like a descending staircase.

Suppose that we could choose between a world with this articulated pattern of security levels and a world in which the level of security was the same everywhere, and that that level was slightly higher than the overall average level available to us in the articulated pattern. Security against risk in this alternative world would be represented by a horizontal line that started out lower than the highest step in the descending staircase and ended higher than the lowest step. And, representing the fact that this alternative world has a higher level of security overall, the area under the horizontal line would be somewhat larger than the area that subtends the descending staircase. Would it be rational for us to select the world characterized by the horizontal line over the world represented by the staircase? Would it be rational for us to opt for an indiscriminate level of risk over an articulated pattern simply because the overall risk in the former was lower than that in the latter?

In response to this, I think it must be granted that if the horizontal line represents a very large increase in security over the average level provided by the staircase, it would be rational to prefer the former. But, realistically, the overall levels of risk that might actually be offered by these alternatives are not likely to differ enormously. (Few experts believe that changes in criminal justice policies can produce more than small changes in crime rates.) Therefore, if the surplus of security in the indiscriminate world over that in the articulated world is small (though not insignificant), it seems clearly rational to prefer the articulated world. In it, the environment is a kind of visible security map, in which we know where we are safe and where we are not, where we can turn to avoid risk or to escape it, where we can go to chance risk or even invite it, and so on. It gives us safe houses and hiding places, secure niches to rest in and open spaces to venture in, so that we can adjust our behavior to the level of risk and security we desire or that our activity requires. Compare this to a world in which both bedroom and city street are equally moderately risky. The very flatness of the risk line in such a world undermines the possibility of choosing appropriate sites for different activities; it robs us of the possibility of repairing to low-risk niches in which we can conduct those activities most in need of security, and in which we can let our guard down and gather strength for the next foray into higher-risk zones. To object that the preference for this more articulated world is irrational unless it results (beknownst or unbeknownst to us) in the lowest possible average risk is simply to restate the alternative preference for indiscriminate treatment of risk as if it were the only way of being rational.

I contend, then , that – as long as the differences in overall security are within the range it is realistic to expect – it is rational for people to prefer a world with some very secure zones even at the expense of the lowest possible overall risk. But then it seems to me that it is rational to want one's government to be one of these very secure zones. Given that the government is established (authorized, funded, and armed) to protect us, it is rational to want to be able to depend on it, to turn to it without fear that it is also a source of risk. Here, too, it is rational to prefer a staircase-like security line, in which the government is one of the very high steps. It is rational, then, to want the government to be very, very unlikely to cause us undeserved harm, even if this reduces its capacity to protect us against the harm from criminals and thus increases our overall level of risk. Then it would be reasonable for the parties to a social contract to insist on the punishment constraint – even at some cost in deterrence – in order to establish the dependability of the government that is empowered to protect them. And this, in conjunction with the *prima facie* case presented at the outset of this section, implies that the social contract supports the punishment constraint.

II. Con: The Paramount Importance of Punishing the Guilty (Ernest van den Haag)

A perfect system of penal justice would succeed in punishing all the guilty and none of the innocent.[13] But in an imperfect world, we must be content with punishing as many of the guilty as we can and as few of the innocent. In trying to convict the guilty, we face alternative risks: 1) high standards of proof make sure that fewer innocents are convicted, but also that fewer criminals are, and 2) low standards of proof make sure that more criminals are convicted, but also more innocents. The "punishment constraint" tells us to prefer the first risk, by requiring the highest standard of proof – proof beyond a reasonable doubt – because it is morally worse to punish an innocent person than not to punish a guilty one. Is it? Always?

The Sine Qua Non *of Penal Justice*

Punishing the guilty surely is the purpose of penal justice, just as finding gold is the purpose of digging for it. Separating the gold from the surrounding earth is the purpose of sifting, just as separating the guilty from the innocent is the purpose of the courts. The courts cannot succeed completely, because evidence is sometimes insufficient or even misleading. The conviction of some innocents is an

[13] The legal action normally taken against a convicted defendent will be called punishment, regardless of whether he actually is guilty or not.

unintended, yet unavoidable, byproduct of bringing the guilty to justice. We are prepared to risk punishing some innocents for the sake of punishing the guilty, because punishment of the guilty is more important than the nonpunishment of any innocents. If it were not, we could not have any system of criminal justice.[14] What ratio of convicted guilty to convicted innocents – what standard of proof – is acceptable? That is the question.

Reiman's Defense of the Punishment Constraint

Jeffrey Reiman believes that the acquittal of the innocent is always more important than the conviction of the guilty. He does not defend Blackstone's ratio of ten to one, or propose a ratio of his own. Since he knows the ideal 0 (innocents) : 1 (guilty) ratio to be unattainable, yet thinks the acquittal of innocents not *as* but *more* important than the conviction of the guilty, his ratio must be above 0 : 1 and below 1 : 1. (Although these ratios may seem abstract, they merely project the effects of lower – more convictions of criminals and innocents – versus higher – fewer convictions – standards of proof.) For even if they are not designed to produce them, standards of proof codetermine conviction rates.[15] In contrast to Reiman, I favor lower standards of proof (at least sometimes) over the conviction of a smaller proportion of criminals for the sake of sparing more innocents. The punishment of criminals would become less important than the nonpunishment of innocents, however, when the number of innocents being convicted so nearly approaches the number of criminals that punishment would no longer be perceived to be directed at them. Further, unlike Reiman, I do not believe that the acquittal of the innocent has the same importance and the same moral priority over the conviction of the guilty at all times and in all circumstances. On the contrary: a high crime rate would lead me to stress the punishment of more of the guilty, although it would mean the conviction of more innocents as well. A low crime rate would lead me to stress acquitting the innocent by means of higher standards of proof.

Let me concentrate now on the principle, regardless of context: the moral weight given to not punishing innocents – versus punishing the guilty – first by deontological (retributivist) theory and second by consequentialist (utilitarian and deterrence) theory.

Retributivism and the Punishment Constraint

Unless they accept the punishment constraint, Reiman argues, retributivists are in an unacceptably implausible position. To them, retribution is a duty owed to criminals, their victims, or the law-abiding, all of whom, Reiman calculates, would

[14] Although conceding that conviction of the guilty is socially more important, one may hold that acquittal of the innocent remains morally more important. Some philosophies find a difference between what is morally right and what is socially important. However, for a policymaker, this may be a distinction without a difference.

[15] So does what is admissible as proof and what is not, although the criterion of admissibility is not designed for the quantitative result. (Standards of admissibility are ignored here, for most of the effects do not differ from those of standards of proof.)

regard the nonpunishment of the guilty as less of a loss than the punishment of the innocent. Is the duty of retribution really owed to any of these groups?[16]

Retributivists regard punishment of the guilty as a moral good and inflicting it as a moral obligation. However, the obligation does not become obligatory because it is owed to the guilty, their victims, or the law-abiding. The obligation to punish is owed only secondarily to beneficiaries. Their alleged lower valuation of the duty to punish criminals, compared to the duty not to punish innocents, is therefore far from decisive. Indeed, it is irrelevant. The duty of doing right is an end in itself, not a means to anyone's satisfaction. The two duties, to punish the guilty and not to punish innocents, are ends in themselves, independent of the losses or gains of beneficiaries. The duties are categorical, to be carried out unconditionally. If one prefers a less abstract form of deontological retributivism, one may hold that moral duties are owed to the perpetual community of which both the guilty and the innocent are members. This gives a somewhat more instrumental air to moral duties. Still, a deontological moral duty must be carried out *qua* moral duty, regardless of benefits and beneficiaries, even at the expense of the contemporary community.

Reiman may have been misled by an analogy. When I promise you X, I obligate myself to deliver X to you. You can release me from my promise, or exact damages for non-performance. But the retributivist obligation to punish is not analogous. It is not primarily a promise to any beneficiary. It is a duty. The offender must be punished because he deserves to be, regardless of any benefit or harm. Even his victim, however forgiving, is not entitled to relieve society of its duty. Retribution, after all, is not (at least not primarily) the revenge of the victim (which, indeed, he may renounce), but the vindication and defense of the legal order of society offended by the crime. Revenge may be an individual motive, but the moral function of retribution is independent of any motive; it is rather to do justice, and to express the morality of the community.

How, then, do retributivists determine which has priority: the obligation to punish the guilty, or the obligation not to punish the innocent? They don't. The retributivist theory of punishment tells us that punishment must be deserved, but cannot tell us how much punishment crime A deserves, or how much more punishment it deserves than crime B.[17] Just so, retributivism tells us that we have an obligation to punish the guilty and not to punish innocents. We are not told which duty has priority. Should we try to convict fewer innocents and risk letting more of the guilty escape, or try to convict more of the guilty, and, unavoidably, more of the innocent? Retributivism (although not necessarily retributivists) is

[16] Although Reiman explicitly disavows "claiming that deontological duties are required *because* owed to these parties," unless the duties are indeed owed to these groups, there would be no point in "comparing the losses to those parties of failures in those duties" and inferring, as Reiman does, that if failure in the duty not to convict innocents causes a greater loss to them than failure to convict the guilty does, it is morally worse to punish innocents than not to punish the guilty.

[17] Jeffrey Reiman and I made our disagreement on this point explicit in "Justice, Civilization, and the Death Penalty: Answering van den Haag," and "Refuting Reiman and Nathanson," *Philosophy & Public Affairs* 14, no. 2 (Spring 1985), pp. 115–48 and 165–76.

mute on how high standards of proof ought to be; it can neither impose nor oppose the punishment constraint.[18]

Indeed, Reiman admits that, to get retributivism to endorse the punishment constraint, he had to "bully it just a bit." As is often the case, the subject of the bullying gave the desired answer, but not the true one. To get the answer he wants, Reiman adds a teleological element to retributivism, arguing that "no deontological theory would get off the ground if it did not consider the immediate consequences of the action it condemns ... there is no way to distinguish surgical cutting from murderous stabbing except by reference to the different consequences." Why? Reference to the different intentions of the surgeon and the murderer would be sufficient (the consequences may not differ at all).[19] Note also that the surgeon is entitled to his action, but the murderer is not – he violates the law and the rights of the victim. I agree with Reiman that intentions include intended consequences (what is intended if not consequences?). But I do not think the retributivist principle authorizes those who might be harmed or benefited by the consequences of carrying out a duty, such as retribution, to decide whether it should be carried out. Note, moreover, that if the victimized or the law-abiding were to decide on retribution and were retributivists, their decision would have to depend on the retributive principle (fittingness or desert), not on comparative or aggregate harms to the guilty or to the innocent, contrary to what Reiman supposes.[20] Retribution could be "owed" to the community, including these groups, only by virtue of being a moral duty imposed by the principle of retribution.

The consequentialist calculus which Reiman adds to the duties retributivism postulates makes retributivism plausible, as promised – by replacing it with something else.[21] Retribution is an expressive good, not an instrumental one. It does not depend on being "plausible" in the sense of being useful or advantageous to anyone. The very idea that moral duties primarily are means to satisfy people,

[18] Historically, retributivism (despite Blackstone) has stressed punishing the guilty more than acquitting innocents.

[19] Reiman's distinction between "immediate" and other consequences is too inchoate. Is the distinction temporal? Spatial? Does it depend on the density of relationships? The vagueness of the distinction would make it hard to distinguish retributivism from utilitarianism (which considers non-immediate consequences as well). Fortunately, that distinction does not actually depend on distinguishing immediate consequences from other ones. Suppose by executing Roger we save a hundred other innocents. Utilitarians certainly would. Deontologists would not, but not because the death of Roger is more immediate than the death of the hundred. They would oppose the swap because of the categorical nature of the prohibition against intentionally killing innocents, and because of their refusal to aggregate or offset. Although deontologists recognize more or less important duties (and, thereby, priorities), they do not justify failure to carry out a duty for the sake of some beneficial effect. Kant did not believe that the prevention of a murder could justify lying. Reiman may be right: Kant's view is implausible, an unintentional *reductio ad absurdum*. Yet, however good an argument against retributivism, its implausibility does not justify Reiman's addition of utilitarian reasoning while keeping the label of retributivism.

[20] I agree with Reiman that the guilty will favor the punishment constraint. The reduction of the probability of punishment would not disturb them, even though it should, according to Kant and Hegel. If the obligation to punish is to them, they would release us from it. The beneficiary can release the makers from a promise – although not from a threat. If punishment were owed to criminals, it would be a promise, not a threat. But, to reiterate, for retributionists punishment is primarily neither a promise, nor a threat, but an obligation to do justice – *pereat mundus*.

[21] For discussion of that ingenious calculus, see "Utilitarianism and the Punishment Constraint," below.

rather than ends in themselves, strikes me as non-deontological. So does the idea that the relative importance of moral duties depends on the size of the benefits (or harms) to those to whom they are allegedly owed.

Reiman also believes that retributivists are bound by the *lex talionis* not to harm the criminal more than he harmed his victim. I do not. There is a historical association between the *lex talionis* and retributivism, but no logical relationship.

Anyway, the *lex talionis,* only concerns the victim's right to revenge or compensation for the harm suffered. But the harm retribution is concerned with is to the legal, social, and moral order, not to the victim. Retribution is not a tort action. Punishment may be imposed independently of the suffering of any specific victim, or even when no one individual was harmed by the crime. Further, skyjacking, kidnapping, treason, or rape may justify punishments inflicting suffering greater or lesser than the suffering of the crime victims (if those sufferings could be measured and compared – which is doubtful). Retribution (justice) only depends on the moral importance of the criminal law violated. (Incidentally, doesn't any crime victimize and impose costs on society quite apart from the direct victim?)

Although it cannot be squared with retributivism, Reiman's argument (at least his conclusion) seems intuitively persuasive. But intuitions are not probative. I ascribe the intuitive persuasiveness of Reiman's conclusion to the strong motivation innocents – most people – have to prefer the nonpunishment of innocents (themselves) to the punishment of the guilty, which, as Reiman notes, yields no direct and immediate benefit to them individually, even though it benefits the community. The resulting preference, however, is not a moral argument for retributivists. It is not even a moral argument for utilitarians, as will be seen now.

Utilitarianism and the Punishment Constraint

Now consider the punishment constraint in the light of consequentialist-utilitarian theories.

Punishment in such theories is an evil, as is any suffering imposed on the guilty or the innocent. Imposing it on the guilty serves a beneficial purpose – the control of crime – which may offset the evil. The utilitarian branch of consequentialism further implies that if innocent persons are punished when they are believed to be guilty, the deterrent (crime-reducing) effect could more than offset the evil of their punishment, just as it would for actually guilty persons. Deontologists have always thought it a decisive objection to utilitarianism that a net gain in total happiness, which justifies any act to utilitarians, can be produced by punishing persons known by the authorities to be innocent but depicted as guilty as well as by punishing actually guilty persons.[22] I see no utilitarian reason to believe that the punishment of the innocent is a greater evil than that of the guilty.[23] Provided it deters crime no less than the punishment of the guilty, the punishment of innocents would have the

[22] This objection is far more limited (to unqualified utilitarianism rather than general consequentialism) than is usually realized. See my "Punishment as a Device for Controlling the Crime Rate," 33 *Rutgers Law Review* 3 (Spring 1981).

[23] I deal below with Reiman's belief that innocents, *qua* innocents, suffer more when punished.

same beneficial net effect on aggregate happiness. Thus, utilitarians would have no reason to accept the punishment constraint.

Jeremy Bentham pointed out, however, that the deterrent effect of punishment, which offsets the suffering it causes, would be nullified if and when it became known that the persons punished were innocent. He surmised that their innocence would unavoidably become known. Once known, the punishment of innocents as a social policy would make it pointless (or at least less rewarding) to avoid crime, since doing so would not avoid punishment. Therefore, punishing innocents would defeat the deterrent purpose of punishment. Hence Bentham opposed punishing innocents. So does Reiman.[24]

Bentham's argument addresses the question: why must we punish the guilty rather than innocents? Why is punishing the guilty useful, and punishing innocents not? However, the dilemma before us does not concern choosing between punishing guilty persons or innocents, but choosing between punishing more guilty (*and* innocent) or fewer guilty (*and* innocent) persons by means of lower or higher standards of proof. Bentham's hypothetical deceptive substitution of innocent for guilty persons is not involved. Any increase of the number of innocents punished would be an unavoidable, undesired, and nondeceptive byproduct of an increase of the number of guilty persons punished.

Attention should be drawn here to the distinction between intention and awareness, which we did not make explicit in our Introduction. Awareness is simply the knowledge that something will happen regardless of (or against) intention. An airline does not intend accidents to happen, but it is aware that, contrary to intention, over a period some will. Precautions to minimize accidents are needed, but must be consistent with the purpose of the airline; they must not prevent flying or make it impractical. Similarly, precautions against miscarriages of justice must be consistent with the purpose of the courts. They must not make justice impractical. Bentham's argument against convicting innocents concerns courts that intend to convict them, pretending that they are guilty although knowing that they are not. However, the argument against the punishment constraint does not rest on a deception or favor an intention to convict innocents. Reiman infers intention when, although we are aware of the risk, less than all possible precautions are taken to prevent the conviction of innocents. His argument appears to conflate awareness with intention. For to take all possible precautions would mean to give up punishment altogether. Even short of that, Reiman's precautions – a very high standard of proof – may not be consistent with the purpose of criminal justice: to punish the guilty.

Indeed, Reiman's utilitarian argument does not show that the acquittal of more innocent and more guilty persons increases aggregate happiness more than their conviction. He does not fully address the question: shall we convict more guilty persons if *thereby* we convict more innocents, or shall we convict fewer guilty and thereby fewer innocent persons? Yet the punishment constraint concerns that

[24] The effects of indiscriminate political terrorism in discouraging opposition, defined as crime, are beyond the scope of this discussion (and of Bentham's).

question. It is not answered by pointing out that excessively low standards of proof, once known, would undermine confidence in the courts. So would excessively high standards, which would leave many guilty persons unpunished.

Since we cannot punish the guilty without convicting innocents, utilitarians have to decide whether it is better to punish few innocents and few criminals, or more innocents and more criminals. If the punishment of additional criminals increases deterrence, while the unintentional but unavoidable punishment of additional innocents mistakenly believed to be guilty diminishes deterrence by less, lower standards of proof may produce a net increase of deterrence. They will, provided that many of the convicted persons are actually guilty and that standards of proof are not irrational.[25] (Those found guilty by rational standards would be unlikely to be shown innocent later on, even if they actually were innocent. But my argument does not depend on this contingency.) Additional convictions would increase deterrence and thus reduce the suffering caused by crime more than they would increase the suffering of criminals and innocents; this would produce a net gain in happiness.

To avoid this conclusion, Reiman speculates that "the news will get out" about the conviction of additional innocents; it will ultimately "reduce the criminal justice system's capacity to deter crime." This speculation seems implausible unless Reiman has Bentham's intentional conviction of known innocents in mind, and not simply a higher risk of miscarriages of justice associated with higher conviction rates.[26] There is no basis for the belief that the "system's capacity to deter" depends on requiring proof "beyond a reasonable doubt" for a conviction, and would be diminished by a lower standard leading to more convictions.[27] (We do not lack confidence in non-penal justice, which requires only a preponderance of evidence.)

Reiman's fear that the willingness of the courts to assume a larger risk of punishing the innocent may, in the eyes of the citizens, change the government from an ally to an enemy, a "violent gang," is unfounded. Frontier justice did not have this effect, despite very low standards of proof. Not even Stalin's justice did. Why should a reduction of standards of proof, leading to the conviction of more guilty persons (and, unavoidably, more innocents) cause us to perceive the government as a "violent gang," if, as intended, there also would be fewer crime victims because of more deterrence? Unless the increase of convicted innocents more than offsets the decrease of crime victims (which would require irrationally low standards of proof), a reduction of net aggregate suffering (of crime victims and of guilty and innocent convicts) would occur.

Reiman also speculates that an innocent person suffers more than a guilty person on whom the same punishment is imposed, wherefore punishing innocents

[25] Low standards need not, but standards of proof perceived to be irrational will erode the necessary belief that the guilty are sought out.

[26] Bentham's idea that innocence unavoidably will become known applies to innocents deliberately convicted, when their innocence was known to the authorities. It does not apply to innocents convicted in good faith by clear and convincing evidence. Indeed, their conviction may well add to deterrence.

[27] Similarly, "capacity to deter" does not depend on jury unanimity, or on the number of jurors, or finally on constitutional or common law exclusionary rules, some of which are quite irrational.

diminishes total happiness more than punishing the guilty, and not punishing the guilty diminishes total happiness less than punishing innocents. Why do innocents, when punished, suffer more than the guilty? According to Reiman, their innocence, their knowledge of the injustice of their punishment, produces extraordinary suffering. He seems to believe that, since justice is morally desirable, it causes less suffering to the punished than injustice, which is not. This idea confuses the moral and the psychological. Actually, innocents may be comforted by their innocence, or, as Socrates was, by suffering for the sake of the law, however misapplied. The guilty person is unlikely to be comforted by his guilt, and may be racked by it, if he has a conscience;[28] if not, he may be pained by his knowledge that he made mistakes in committing the crime which led to his conviction.[29] I am not arguing that my speculations are better than Reiman's, but only that his are no better than mine. Perhaps the suffering inflicted by punishment depends less on innocence or guilt than on the character and circumstances of the convict.

Reiman finally speculates that a crime victim suffers less from victimization than an innocent does from punishment, wherefore acquitting innocents is more important than punishing criminals: even if it increases crime, the acquittal of criminals would cause less suffering than the conviction of innocents. I can see no basis for comparing the suffering of the victims of a miscarriage of justice to that of the victims of crime. The degree of suffering will depend mostly on the harm done by the crime versus the harm done by the unjust punishment; these depend largely on vulnerability, on the kind of person who suffers either. How can the suffering of a victim of assault and of a victim of a miscarriage of justice be compared? Is four years of prison suffered by an innocent really worse than, say, lifelong paralysis suffered by a crime victim?

Contractarianism

Reiman suggests that we can best protect ourselves from the risk of crime in certain security zones (e.g., our homes) and least in other zones (e.g., on the streets). These differences in protection from crime appear preferable to an equal risk everywhere. Reiman adds that "it is rational to want one's government to be one of those very secure zones" by honoring the punishment constraint. This view is imputed to contractarianism. It appears to mean that we would not want the risk of innocents to be punished by the government to be high – a matter already discussed. But the risk of punishment is the same at home and in the street and, although the risk of crime differs according to where one is, that difference is not affected by standards of proof for conviction, i.e., by the punishment constraint. By

[28] The *malum poenae,* St. Thomas thought, would, through suffering, induce repentance and thus ultimately annul the *malum culpae* (sin). He believed that guilt adds to the suffering imposed by punishment. Surely the point of the penitentiary, as it used to be called not so long ago, was to redeem the guilty by their psychological suffering – from which the innocent being imprisoned would be exempt, even though they suffered the same material deprivations.

[29] Even though they are found guilty beyond a reasonable doubt, most imprisoned convicts persuade themselves that they are blameless. They are outraged by their punishment and full of rage against "the system" that inflicted it. It seems that blameworthy people are rarely able to accept blame, whereas there are many people outside prisons willing to accept blame for almost anything, including the punishment of convicts – which may upset some non-convicts more than the crimes the convicts were found guilty of.

metaphorically depicting the courts as a "very secure zone," Reiman conflates the risk of crime and the risk of miscarriages of justice to argue for minimizing the latter. But standards of proof are not a zone, and nothing is added to the arguments for the punishment constraint that has not already been discussed.

Conclusion

I believe I have shown that neither retributivist, utilitarian, nor contractarian theory justifies the punishment constraint. Innocents are more protected without the punishment constraint than with it – less protected from punishment, but much more protected from crime. A net gain in protection is likely if standards of proof are lowered somewhat but remain reasonable. Since the punishment constraint is unjustifiable, so is the current requirement of proof of guilt "beyond a reasonable doubt."

What standards of proof should be adopted then? "Clear and convincing evidence" should suffice for a guilty verdict, which should require only a two-thirds majority of jurors. A "preponderance of evidence" (more evidence for guilt than for innocence – the current standard for civil matters) seems insufficient for criminal conviction of first offenders. However, a preponderance of evidence should suffice to convict defendants with relevant prior convictions.[30] If the law permits a death sentence or a sentence in excess of ten (actual) years of prison, a jury which does not want to exclude such a sentence should be required to find guilt "beyond a reasonable doubt."[31] The imposition of very severe punishments should be based on more conclusive proof than is needed for lesser punishments.[32]

Philosophy, American University
Law, Fordham University

[30] The Bayesian probability of guilt is no less than it is with a more restrictive standard for defendants without relevant prior convictions.

[31] The primary purpose of trials should be, once more, to determine guilt or innocence. Secondary purposes, such as disciplining the police, however important, should not be allowed to interfere. Hence, all relevant evidence should always be admitted. (Further discussion of the curious trial rules which have accumulated is beyond my present scope.)

[32] The converse conclusion might appear as logical: these are the crimes we want to deter most and should most readily punish. However, they also are exceptional enough to enable us to take special precautions to avoid convicting innocents without much fear of reducing deterrence.